THE BRITISH ISLES
A Regional Geography

THE BRITISH ISLES

A Regional Geography

HENRY REES, M.Sc.(Econ.), Ph.D.
Principal Lecturer in Geography
St Paul's College of Education, Rugby

SECOND EDITION
Revised and Metricated

HARRAP LONDON

First published in Great Britain 1966
by GEORGE G. HARRAP & CO. LTD
182–184 High Holborn, London WC1V 7AX

Reprinted 1968

Second edition, revised, 1972
© *Henry Rees* 1966, 1972

ISBN 0 245 50745 0

*Composed in Monophoto Times type. Printed by
Redwood Press Ltd, of Trowbridge, Wiltshire*

Made in Great Britain

PREFACE

THIS BOOK is addressed to sixth formers and to students in Colleges of Education and in the early stages of university courses; it is hoped that it will also interest the general reader who wants a concise geographical account of Britain.

I have tried to produce a text which is both accurate and readable: one which not only provides information, but also stimulates the reader to delve more deeply into the subject.

The raw material for this study lies in the publications of the Ordnance and Geological Surveys and in the first and second Land Utilisation Surveys, in the files of periodicals, and on the ground itself. The accounts of specimen farms in Somerset, north Wales, county Kerry, and Warwickshire are from personal observation, and are introduced by courtesy of the farmers; the others are included by kind permission of the Association of Agriculture.

Fig. 10, illustrating some characteristic British grasses, has been very kindly contributed by my colleague, Mrs P. Wendy Darby. The maps on pp. 232, 288, 300, 327, 341, and 345 are based on Geological Survey maps with the permission of H.M. Stationery Office, Crown Copyright reserved.

HENRY REES

COVENTRY
July 1966

PREFACE TO THE SECOND EDITION

IN THIS second edition, at the request of the publishers, I have converted all Imperial measurements into their metric equivalents. For those readers who may find this conversion disconcerting, the following observations are offered.

The basic metric unit of length is the metre, which is a little longer than a yard; thus three metres are nearly equal to ten feet (more accurately, 9·84 ft). In the text all heights have been converted into metres. Where necessary, as in the heights of individual summits, these have been given to the nearest metre; more usually the conversion is approximate, though certain key heights change conveniently into metric equivalents.

The three Thames terraces, at 50 feet, 100 feet, and 150 feet, become 15, 30, and 45 metres high, respectively. The mountain areas, above 1000 feet, are above 300 metres; and the summits, at about 3000 feet, are at 900 metres. For an approximate conversion of feet to metres multiply by 3 and divide by 10; to convert back, multiply by 10 and divide by 3.

All map scales have been amended; but the maps themselves will retain their contours and spot heights in feet until those on which they are based are converted to the metric system. This will take many years to complete.

Conversion of miles into kilometres presents no special difficulties: five miles equals approximately eight kilometres. The metric ton (tonne), 1000 kilograms, is so close to the ton avoirdupois that conversion is needed only when accurate trade returns are quoted. The English ton equals 1·016 tonnes; 1 tonne equals 0·984 English tons. The petroleum industry, it may be noticed, has for long used the metric ton.

Rainfall in the metric system is measured in millimetres. An inch contains approximately $2\frac{1}{2}$ centimetres or 25·0 millimetres (more accurately, 25·4 mm). If we adopt 25·0 as an approximate equivalent, then the 30-inch isohyet, which traditionally divides Britain into a drier and a wetter side, becomes 750 mm. The rainiest place in Britain—probably Snowdon summit—with 200 inches, receives 5000 mm. For an approximate conversion of inches into millimetres multiply by 100 and divide by 4; to convert back divide by 100 and multiply by 4.

The unit of area is the hectare (abbreviated to ha), a square of side 100 metres. It is approximately $2\frac{1}{2}$ times as large as an acre (more accurately, 2·47 times as large). A moderately large farm of the English lowlands, of 250 acres, contains 100 hectares, while the very small holdings of western Ireland, of $12\frac{1}{2}$ acres, comprise 5 hectares. To convert acres to hectares multiply by 4 and divide by 10; to convert back, multiply by 10 and divide by 4.

In addition I have brought the entire text up to date. This has meant in particular virtually rewriting the sections on Milford Haven and the Port of London, on petroleum, nuclear power, and motorways. I have redrawn Figs. 37 (Milford Haven), 61 (Tyneside), 107 (Oil and Natural Gas), and 109 (Motorways), and in Fig. 106 I have substituted a section through a North Sea gas structure for that through the now exhausted Eakring oilfield. Population figures are taken from the 1971 Census (Preliminary Reports).

HENRY REES

COVENTRY, *January* 1972

CONTENTS

PART 3: ECONOMIC GEOGRAPHY

ILLUSTRATIONS

PLATES

MAPS AND DIAGRAMS

ix

PART 1
The Physical and Human Background

CHAPTER ONE

THE PHYSIOGRAPHIC
EVOLUTION OF THE BRITISH ISLES

T HE BRITISH ISLES as we now see them represent the latest
chapter in a long story of change. In order to see these events
in their true perspective we must first acquaint ourselves
with the scale of geological time. It is to be counted not in centuries
(as we reckon human history), nor yet in thousands or hundreds of
thousands of years, but in tens of millions.

Fig. 1 shows the relative time which is believed to have elapsed
during the formation of the various systems of rocks, and is drawn
to scale. The figures on which it is based are those deduced by
Professor C. Schuchert, accepted by our own Geological Survey,
and displayed on the geological column in the Geological Museum
in South Kensington, London.

The earliest rocks of this country – the Pre-Cambrian – are also
among the oldest in the world. These, such as the white quartzites
found in the cliffs at South Stack, off Holyhead Island, are at least
500 million years old, and perhaps as much as 2000 million years
old.

Near the middle of the time scale are the Carboniferous rocks,
which occupy much of northern England, central Scotland, and
central Ireland. We may think of these and all the preceding
formations as the older rocks of Britain. They are found almost
everywhere north and west of a line which runs from the mouth
of the Tees, skirting the Pennines, to the mouth of the Exe. Here
are the hardest rocks, the chief mountains and plateaux, and the
major dislocations – the folds, faults, and thrusts.

To the south and east of the Tees–Exe line are the newer rocks,
and they become progressively younger as we move from (say)
Birmingham to London. The rocks are softer, the relief is more
subdued, and there are few important folds or faults. The Trias
whose red sandstones and clays underlie most of the English
Midlands is about 155 million years old; the Chalk about 100
million years old, and the London Clay about 60 million years old.

Still younger are the clays, sands, and gravels left behind by glaciers during the Great Ice Age: they are a mere 30,000 years old; and the Quaternary era itself is so short (about one million years) that it can be represented only by the top boundary line of the table. Youngest of all are the alluvial clays and silts which are deposited every time a river overflows its banks.

As we thread our way through the last 500 million years or so of the story of the British Isles we meet three important landmarks – or rather, 'time marks'. These are the major periods of mountain-building. There were, indeed, earlier movements in Pre-Cambrian times, but they are imperfectly charted, and have had little real effect in the present-day landscape.

The landmarks are separated by 100 to 200 million years. The first of them, named the Caledonian from the clear effects in Scotland, overlapped the end of Silurian and the beginning of Devonian times (about 325 million years ago): and therefore bears the convenient alternative name of the Siluro–Devonian movements. The second landmark is that of the Hercynian or Armorican movements – the terms derive from areas of the ♦Roman Empire in which the geological effects are well displayed: Hercynia included the Harz Mountains of western Germany, and Armorica coincided with Brittany. These movements occurred about 210 million years ago, in late Carboniferous and early Permian times, and are therefore conveniently remembered as the Carbo–Permian. In the British Isles their effects are seen in the Pennines and Mendips of England, in the downfolds of south Wales, and in the south of Ireland. Third and last are the Alpine movements, which took place about 25 million years ago. They raised the Alps, the Himalayas, the Andes, and the Rockies; but in the British Isles they are represented only by the outpourings of lava in Antrim and the Hebrides, and by the gentle warpings of southern England.

There seems, then, to have been a regular pulsation throughout geological time, and this, of course, is a world-wide phenomenon – it is not confined to the British Isles. We cannot allow ourselves to be sidetracked into this fascinating avenue except to notice that Professor Joly has evolved a cyclical theory to account for this rhythmic pulsation. He links each period of mountain-building with a rise in the general level of the continents, which he asserts is followed by an ice age. That may be so in other parts of the world; but in the British Isles there is clear evidence of only one ice age – that which followed the Alpine earth movements, and which has left its imprint so extensively on our landscapes.

With these signposts as guides we may look a little more closely into some aspects of the evolution of the British Isles.

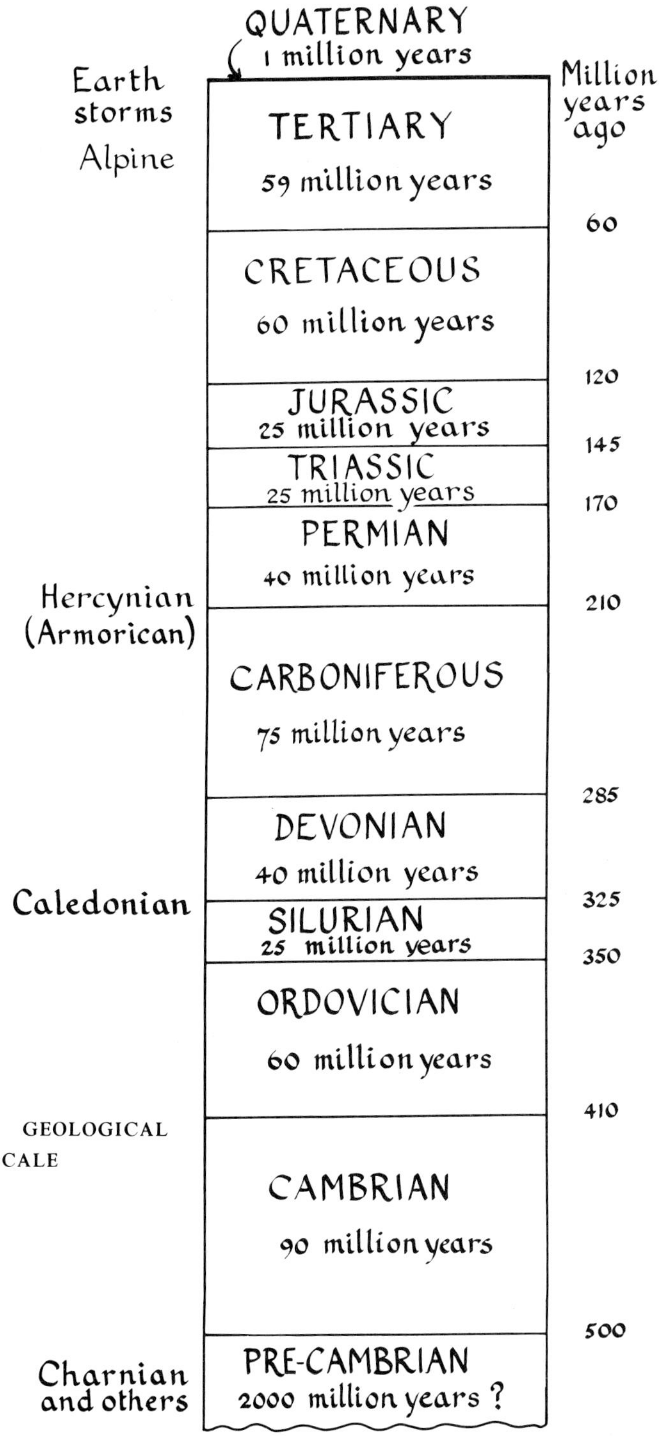

QUATERNARY
1 million years
Earth storms
Million years ago
Alpine
TERTIARY
59 million years
60
CRETACEOUS
60 million years
120
JURASSIC
25 million years
145
TRIASSIC
25 million years
170
PERMIAN
40 million years
Hercynian (Armorican)
210
CARBONIFEROUS
75 million years
285
DEVONIAN
40 million years
Caledonian
325
SILURIAN
25 million years
350
ORDOVICIAN
60 million years
410
CAMBRIAN
90 million years
500
Charnian and others
PRE-CAMBRIAN
2000 million years ?

Fig. 1. GEOLOGICAL TIME SCALE

The Cambrian, Ordovician, and Silurian periods we may consider together. Throughout this long age (175 million years) most of the British Isles formed part of a geosyncline – a major downfold in the earth's surface – into which were poured the sediments of shallow seas. By the end of Silurian times about 10,000 metres of strata had accumulated, which necessarily implies that as fast as the sediments were forming the sea-bed was sinking. For the most part these were periods of quiet deposition; but in Ordovician times this calm was broken by the violent outbursts of volcanoes, whose remnants survive in Snowdon and the Lake District.

The seas swarmed with varied creatures: it is a remarkable fact that while there are few signs of life in the Pre-Cambrian rocks, the Cambrian seas from the beginning show a rich fauna. There were no vertebrates, land animals, or plants; but there were sponges and worms, bivalves and gastropods, graptolites and trilobites, whose remains can still be seen in the Wenlock Limestone of Dudley, looking as fresh today as when they sank to the bottom of the Silurian sea.

It is for the Ordovician period that the palæogeographers draw their first tentative maps. They show a continent, 'North Atlantis', which extends from the north Atlantic to include the Scottish Highlands and the north-western fringe of Ireland (in Donegal and north-west Mayo). There was land from the Midlands to the Bristol Channel, and perhaps also in the Lake District. Everywhere else was sea.

Towards the close of Silurian times there began the Caledonian earth movements. These had profound effects on the structure of Britain. They buckled the accumulated sediments into folds ranging north-east and south-west; the folds were broken by thrusts, and masses of strata were transported bodily. In Scotland the rocks gave way from coast to coast, and the fractures which limit the Scottish Lowlands can also be traced throughout Ireland, from Down to Galway and from Londonderry to Mayo. The rocks were arched or domed in the Lake District, the Isle of Man, and in south-east Ireland, and the main trend lines of north and central Wales were established.

With the end of the Caledonian earth movements a new phase began in the physical development of the British Isles. In Devonian times there were mountain ranges in the Scottish Highlands and Southern Uplands, in the Lake District and north Wales, extending into Ireland; and for the first time there was land in the greater part of the area now covered by the British Isles.

The hollows which separated these highlands were occupied by gulfs or enclosed seas – in the Scottish Lowlands and the Moray Firth area, in central Ireland and in south and central Wales. Into these depressions swiftly flowing rivers poured their sediments, stained red from mineral compounds in the surrounding rocks, gradually eroding the mountains and filling the basins. From time to time changes in temperature and salinity of the land-locked seas resulted in the wholesale slaughter of the primitive armoured fishes, whose fossils, crowded together, have been preserved for us.

The resulting strata comprise the Old Red Sandstone system: they consist of reddish-coloured sandstones, shales, and conglomerates which appear to have accumulated in desert conditions. Farther south, however, there was open sea, and here the deposits are finer in texture and include limestones and clays (the latter now converted to slate): these are distinguished by the term Devonian, and are well displayed in Exmoor.

By the beginning of Carboniferous times the Devonian mountain ranges were worn down to mere stumps. The sea encroached farther and farther on to the land, creeping round the bases of the hills. It was not the deep sea of an ocean basin but the shallow water of a continental shelf, and its beach deposits are seen in the conglomerate which forms the lowest member of the Carboniferous Limestone series. At first sandy and muddy (forming the Lower Limestone Shales), it later became more tranquil and clearer. In the cliffs of Brean Down, in Somerset, can be seen the casts of corals and the stems of sea-lilies: these and many bivalves flourished in the warm Carboniferous seas, and their remains have built up the great thicknesses of limestone which, together with bands of sandstone and shale, reach in places some 2500 metres. Such accumulations could occur in shallow water only if the sea-floor were continuously subsiding.

Once again the greater part of the British Isles was covered by sea. But towards the south there was dry land, known as St George's Land. It extended from Wexford and Wicklow, in southeast Ireland, across St George's Channel, across central Wales, and into the south Midlands. St George's Land received no Carboniferous deposits. Though it changed its shape, it was not submerged until the end of the period. Volcanoes erupted in the Scottish Lowlands, in Derbyshire and Somerset; but elsewhere these were times of quiet sedimentation.

Towards the middle of the period a large river from the northeast began to build up a delta, filling up gradually the shallow sea between Atlantis and St George's Land. This deltaic material now forms the Millstone Grit – a gritty sandstone interleaved with shales, which builds most of the southern Pennines, and is of exceptional significance in the past and present life of the region (pp. 228, 240). At its maximum near Burnley the Millstone Grit attains a thickness of 1800 metres.

A wide stretch of low-lying land had now been formed, and slight changes in sea-level were sufficient to convert these deltaic flats into swamps and lagoons. In this manner a favourable environment was provided for the growth of the luxuriant forests of Coal Measure times.

The coal forests (whose fossil resources were destined to provide the motive power for the Industrial Revolution) included tall trees and many types of ferns and fern-like plants, but no flowering species. Giant club-mosses flourished, together with the ancestor of the modern horsetail, whose fossil stem can be recognized by its parallel longitudinal grooves and its regular constrictions. Other well-known Coal Measure trees are Sigillaria and Lepidodendron, in both of which one can see clearly the regular patterns of the leaf scars on the fossil branches. The first insects, like giant dragonflies, flitted through the forests, and there were salamanders and reptiles, but as yet no birds or mammals.

The land was in general sinking; but this was a spasmodic and not a gradual process. A sudden submergence would overwhelm thousands of square kilometres of forest and bury it below marine sediments. Today a regular sequence is discernible in the Coal Measures, and is repeated again and again.

Below the coal seam is a layer of fireclay which contains fossil roots, and evidently represents the soil in which the forest grew. The coal seam itself, which may range in thickness from a mere film to 6 metres or so, represents the compressed remains of the forest; but the original peaty layer was perhaps twelve times as thick as the present seam of coal. Above the coal are barren strata which may reach a hundred metres in thickness: they contain thin marine bands with fish remains, shells of the mussel type, and the remains of sea urchins and sea lilies, and they clearly record long periods of oscillation. First come shales, a sign of the onset of lagoon conditions; then coarse sandstones, indicating the spread of deltas once more. Resting upon these is a layer of fireclay, and above it is the next coal seam; and so the cycle continues. The details of the succession will clearly influence the layout and methods of working of individual coal-mines.

Towards the end of Carboniferous times much of the British Isles had become dry land. To the north remained Atlantis, containing the denuded stumps of the Caledonian mountain ranges;

to the south was St George's Land; and between the two was a wide belt, sometimes shallow sea, at other times low-lying land. There now occurred the second important series of mountain-building movements – the Armorican or Hercynian movements. Their effects were not confined to Britain, for they reared great mountain ranges in continental Europe, northern Asia, and the eastern United States.

In the British Isles there was renewed folding along the Caledonian trend, and further movement took place on the old fault lines: as a result the whole of central Scotland sank to form the Lowlands. Farther south there was folding in two main directions. With crumpling and fracturing along a north and south axis the Pennines and Malverns were raised; at the same time the strata were arched to form the Mendip Hills, and other ridges and furrows ranging east and west can be traced in south Wales and south-west Ireland. These pressures evidently originated to the south, for the steepest dips are seen in the northern limbs of the upfolds.

In addition, masses of magma forced their way into the sedimentary rocks of Devon and Cornwall to form the granite hills which now extend in a row from Dartmoor westward to Land's End. So by the end of Permian times much of the essential framework of the British Isles was already in existence. The Coal Measures, together with their underlying strata, had been ridged and furrowed, and soon were to be stripped from the crests of the upfolds and preserved only in the floors of the downfolds.

The Permian and Triassic rocks have much in common, and are conveniently examined together. The British Isles, together with much of Europe, were now mainly dry land, for the sea had retreated well to the south. This more extensive ancestor of the present Mediterranean has been named the Tethys. There were mountain ranges to the south of Britain; these protected it from moisture-laden winds from the Tethys so that a dry, continental climate prevailed. The newly formed mountains overlooked desert lowlands in Ulster, Devon, and the English Midlands (Fig. 2), and these were gradually filled by screes and the deposits of temporary rivers. So were formed the coarse breccias now seen in much of the Permian system.

A salty sea spread from Germany into northern England, and on evaporating formed the Magnesian Limestone of Durham and Yorkshire. Easterly winds piled up the desert sands into dunes which are now represented by the Lower Mottled Sandstone of the Bunter series in the Midlands. Temporary lakes were clogged by spreading deltas, and these deposits, now hardened into the Keuper Sandstone, have provided dry and elevated sites for several English towns (Warwick, Liverpool, and Birmingham). A salt lake occupied much of Cheshire, and on evaporating left the salt which now forms the basis of the flourishing chemical industry of Merseyside (p. 241). Driving winds helped to reduce the mountains and spread their waste over the desert lowlands, so producing the Keuper Marl, which now underlies most of the Midlands.

In the British Isles few fossils survive to indicate the life of the period; but evidence from other regions shows that the reptiles evolved rapidly. A dinosaur which stalked along in the Connecticut valley of the eastern United States has left his footprints, 46 cm long; and among these monsters the first tiny mammals crept on to the scene.

The continental conditions came to an end at last, and in Jurassic times the sea spread into the British Isles once more. Atlantis remained dry land, however, and included most of Ireland, together with north Wales and Cornwall. For most of the period there was an island extending over Scotland and the Pennines, with another from East Anglia to Belgium; but elsewhere the Jurassic seas deposited their varied sediments. The blue clays of the Lias accumulated in deep water; the oolitic and coral limestones of the Inferior Oolite were formed in shallow water, while the so-called Estuarine Series are in reality deltaic deposits. Near the end of the period the seas became deeper and received the Oxford Clay, which now forms the persistent lowland extending in a narrow belt from Dorset to the Wash.

Reptiles became the masters of the land, the sea, and the air. Some of the pterosaurs (flying reptiles) had wing-spans of 7 to 8 m; others were the size of sparrows. Among the swimming reptiles were the ichthyosaurs, typical of the Lias, with heads up to 1·5 m long, eyes 30 cm in diameter, and 200 sharp teeth. Diplodocus was one of the largest animals ever to appear on the earth: he was up to 30 m long and may have weighed as much as 40 tonnes.[1]

Near the end of Jurassic times the land rose and the British seas dwindled so that the Portland Limestone was deposited in a gulf which covered little more than the Weald and the Hampshire Basin; and in early Cretaceous times even this gulf was clogged by the delta of a large river, which formed the Wealden beds.

For the last time the land sank, and once more almost the whole of Britain was covered by sea. While the Chalk was being deposited

---

[1] Even Diplodocus cannot match the contemporary blue whale – these are up to 30 m long, and one specimen weighed 122 tonnes.

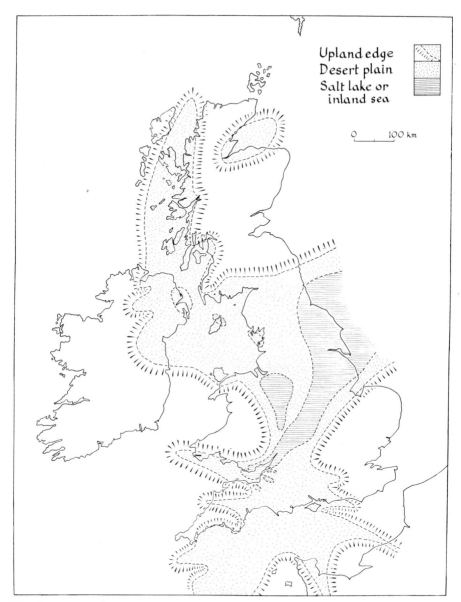

Upland edge
Desert plain
Salt lake or
inland sea

0   100 km

Fig. 2.   THE BRITISH ISLES IN TRIASSIC TIMES

A desert climate prevailed, and the evaporation of inland seas or lakes left behind deposits of salt and gypsum. Such a lake occupied what is now the Cheshire saltfield. *After L. J. Wills.*

perhaps only the highest parts of Scotland, Wales, and Ireland stood above the water.

Chalk is a remarkably pure limestone, and it must have accumulated in a sea free from sediments derived from the land. Palæogeographers accordingly presume that the lands which bordered the Chalk sea were low-lying, and experienced a desert climate. The precise origin of the Chalk, however, is still obscure; but the soft lime has consolidated into more than 300 metres of strata, forming the rolling, often wooded and sometimes cultivated, wolds and downs, and yielding the raw material for cement-making.

The end of Cretaceous time marks an important stage in the evolution of the British Isles. The primitive ferns and conifers were replaced by grasses and flowering plants; the huge reptiles perished and mammals took their place; the land rose, and the stiff and bluish London Clay was deposited in a sea which was confined to southern and eastern England. At the same time volcanoes were erupting in the Hebrides and in Antrim. These, together with others in the Faeroes, in Iceland, and in Greenland, built up a vast lava plateau which covered more than a million square kilometres.

Today we see only fragments of these lava fields. Sheet after sheet piled up, one above the other: in the Isle of Mull they reach a total thickness of 1800 metres. In Antrim the lava charred the trees and baked the surface of the Chalk before it cooled and became solid, contracting in places into remarkable hexagonal columns such as are seen in the Giant's Causeway.

Late in the Tertiary era, in Miocene times, came the third and last of the great mountain-building periods – the Alpine. During the course of the upheavals the Alps and Apennines, the Carpathians, the Himalayas, the Rockies and Andes – all were reared up until the frameworks of the continents came to approximate to those of today.

The British Isles were only on the fringe of this disturbance, and its effects were felt in the form of a relatively gentle warping and tilting of the strata in southern and eastern England. In general the rocks were raised to the north-west and lowered to the south-east, so that erosion has revealed their edges in the form of a series of parallel scarps running north-east and south-west. A down-warp formed the London Basin, and another gave rise to the Hampshire Basin; here the folding was more severe, so that at the Needles, off the Isle of Wight, the Chalk and the Tertiary beds are standing almost on edge. To the east an elongated dome was raised: today, with its crest removed by erosion, it forms the Weald of Kent, Surrey, and Sussex.

Elsewhere in the British Isles there were renewed movements along the lines established in earlier periods of disturbance. The basalt plateau of the Hebrides and Antrim was broken by faults, and the sea was admitted to form the North Channel; and in northern England the Alpine movements may have completed the uplift of the north Pennines.

The last million years or so of the geological history of the earth comprise the Quaternary era; and the events which concern us particularly are linked with the advance and ultimate disappearance of the glaciers during the Great Ice Age.

There were glaciers in North America and Asia as well as in Europe; but they did not form a solid and continuous mass of ice. For the most part the glaciers which scoured the highlands of Britain and redeposited the loose material in the lowlands were composed of 'native' ice, generated in the Scottish Highlands and Southern Uplands, in the Pennines and the Lake District, in north and central Wales, and in the hilly parts of Ireland. Only in parts of East Anglia and Lincolnshire is there evidence of the spread of Scandinavian ice into this country – and that was limited to one stage of the Ice Age.

In the Alps four distinct advances of the ice have been recognized, separated by relatively mild 'interglacial' periods. It is possible that somewhat similar conditions were experienced in the British Isles. The story, however, is complex, and deposits in different regions of Britain have not yet been correlated: the difficulties will be appreciated from the fact that in parts of East Anglia there are 12 different glacial deposits resting one upon the other.

Some facts, however, are clear (Fig. 3). The southern limit of glaciation in the British Isles is a line which passes from the neighbourhood of the Essex shore of the Thames estuary through the southern Midlands, to the southern shore of the Bristol Channel. Within these limits we can distinguish at least four separate bodies of ice, whose spheres of influence waxed and waned: the Great Eastern ice sheet, the Welsh and Irish ice sheets, and the Irish Sea ice sheet.

Of these, the Irish Sea ice, reinforced from Scotland and the Lake District, seems to have been particularly active. It forced back the glaciers of north Wales and left the shells it had dredged from the sea bed high on the slopes of Tryfan and on the hills near Harlech, and as far east as Oswestry.

When the ice fronts had retreated from the Midlands a lake (Lake Harrison) was formed, for the meltwaters were ponded back by the Jurassic scarps. Lake Harrison extended from Rugby and

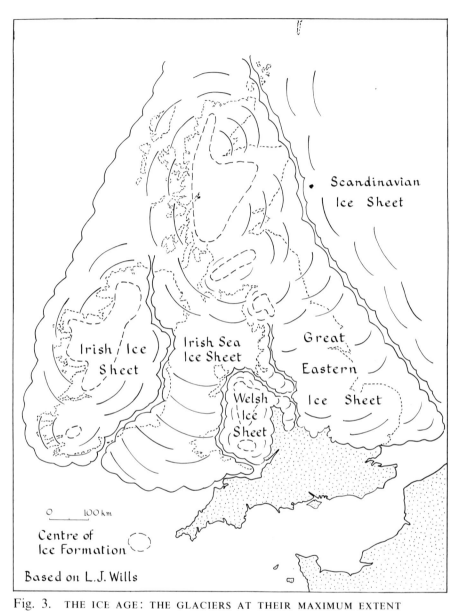

Scandinavian Ice Sheet

Irish Ice Sheet

Irish Sea Ice Sheet

Great Eastern Ice Sheet

Welsh Ice Sheet

0   100 km

Centre of Ice Formation

Based on L.J. Wills

Fig. 3.   THE ICE AGE: THE GLACIERS AT THEIR MAXIMUM EXTENT

Ice was generated in the highlands and descended into the lowlands in four major sheets. The curving lines suggest the direction of flow, and are at right angles to the paths of ice advance. Stippled areas are ice-free. The coastline is that of the present day.

Fig. 4. THE ICE AGE: A LATE STAGE IN THE GLACIATION OF BRITAIN
Terminal moraines are accumulating, and lakes have been impounded at the margins of the ice sheets.

Leicester in the east to beyond Birmingham and Stratford in the west. Its deposits, though classified on the official geological maps as boulder clays, are (as Professor F. W. Shotton has shown) in places laminated, and clearly of lacustrine origin. At a later stage the ice sheets 'withdrew' to Norfolk, where the Cromer moraine accumulated on their margin. The ice edge stood east of the Lincoln and York Wolds, skirting the Cleveland Hills, and ice occupied part of the Vale of York, where its debris collected to form the York and Escrick moraines. Once more lakes were impounded: Lake Pickering overflowed into Lake Humber, and Lake Humber overflowed into Lake Fenland (Fig. 4). The old lake floors are now cultivated, and the spillways which connect them are followed by roads and railways.

In the final stage the ice 'retreated' to the Scottish Highlands, where it all but melted away. It is perhaps of more than academic interest that in one sheltered spot near Ben Nevis a patch of ice remains throughout the year. A fall of only a few degrees in the average temperature – it seems – would suffice to send out the glaciers creeping once more into the lowlands.

FOR FURTHER READING

JOLY, J.: *Surface History of the Earth* (Oxford University Press, 1930).
RAYNER, D. M.: *The Stratigraphy of the British Isles* (Cambridge University Press, 1967).
SHERLOCK, R. L.: *A Guide to the Geological Column*, 1957.
WELLS, A. K.: *Outline of Historical Geology* (Allen and Unwin, 1959).
WILLS, L. J.: *Palaeogeographical Atlas* (Blackie, 1952).

For regional detail see the various volumes of British Regional Geology, prepared by the Geological Survey.

Note: A sound appreciation of the physical background is essential in the study of the geography of the British Isles. The most valuable general map of the geology of Great Britain is the 1:625,000 map published by the Ordnance Survey, in two sheets. A cheaper alternative, less detailed but still very useful, is the 25 miles to the inch map, which covers the whole of the British Isles.

CHAPTER TWO

CLIMATE AND WEATHER

THE BRITISH ISLES are of comparatively small extent; yet they enjoy (or suffer) a surprising variety of climate from place to place, and an equally remarkable variety of weather all the time. Our climate exerts its influence upon human activities in many ways. It sets limits to the types of farming possible or profitable: wheat, for example, does not grow well in the wetter west, where the rainfall is greater than 750 mm per annum; nor does it thrive in the cooler hills where the land rises above 180 m. Beyond these limits pastoral farming may predominate; but even this is of little consequence in the high moorlands, where, under the influence of a heavy rainfall, high winds, and low temperatures, pasture degenerates into heath or peat bog.

Climate has a direct importance to man in several ways. Textile and paper manufacture both require large and constant flows of water, and their location on the flanks of the south Pennines is to be related partly to the heavy rainfall experienced there. Nuclear power-stations demand vast quantities of cooling water, and it is significant that the only inland station – at Trawsfynydd, near Harlech – has been placed in an area of heavy rainfall. The production of hydro-electric power is dependent (among other factors) on a reliable and high rainfall, and the concentration of hydro-electric stations in Scotland, Wales, and western Ireland reflects that fact. The incidence of frost is of vital importance to the fruit-grower; many a seaside resort boasts of its sunshine records or its mild winters; and our foreign trade would be hampered severely were our ports closed by ice in winter, as are certain of their counterparts elsewhere. Not least in importance are the ever-increasing water needs of our growing towns.

Temperatures

We grumble at times about our climate: it is only when we compare it with that of other regions in similar latitudes that we see it in proper perspective. Westward across the Atlantic the harbours of

17

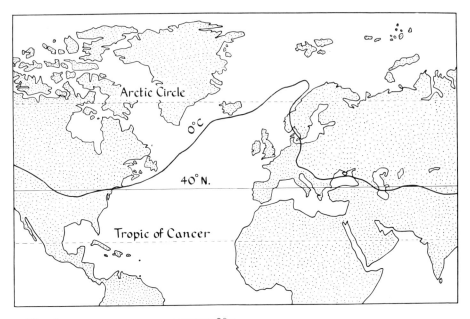

Fig. 5.   THE COURSE OF ISOTHERM 0°C.

The 'gulf of winter warmth' as outlined by sea-level isotherm 0°C.'

Newfoundland and Nova Scotia are icebound in winter, while ice floats about in New York harbour, which is in the same latitude as Rome. The average minimum temperature for January in London is about 1½°C (35°F). At Brussels it is −1°C (30°F); at Berlin, −3½°C (26°F); at Warsaw, −6°C (21°F); and at shivering Moscow, −15°C (5°F). The British Isles in general are about 11°C (20°F) warmer than the average for their latitude: they lie in what has been called a 'gulf of winter warmth', and this can be demonstrated by plotting the average January isotherms. The sea-level isotherm of 0°C (32°F), for example, crosses the eastern U.S.A. near latitude 40°N., sweeps north-eastward across the Atlantic from New York to the southern shore of Iceland, continues north-eastward beyond the Arctic Circle, and only then turns southward to regain parallel 40°, and so to continue eastward (Fig. 5).

How is this remarkable phenomenon to be explained? It is commonly attributed to the Gulf Stream, which, we are told, bathes our shores with warm water. This concept, however, needs to be examined more closely.

Surface water near the equator is urged westward by the trade winds. Some of this warm tropical water enters the Gulf of Mexico and overflows through the Florida Strait as a strong stream running at an average of 5·6 kilometres per hour, and sometimes as fast as 9·3 kilometres per hour. It flows parallel to the coast of the United States as far as Cape Hatteras; there it comes under the influence of the westerly winds, which impel it across the Atlantic towards the British Isles.

The actual temperature of the water is probably lower than one might imagine: at a depth of about 180 metres it is not more than 4°C (7°F) higher than the average for its latitude. Moreover, it is rapidly cooling, and in mid-Atlantic it is 10°C (18°F) cooler than it was south of Nova Scotia. This heat, however, is not lost to us, for even a slight cooling of the sea causes a great quantity of heat to be released into the air above. It has been calculated that 450 square miles of ocean 100 fathoms deep would in cooling one degree release sufficient heat to raise the temperature of the atmosphere by 10°F over the whole of Europe, to a height of two miles.[1] It is perhaps in this way that the warm current chiefly affects us.

During its passage across the Atlantic the warm current – now more correctly known as the North Atlantic Drift – broadens to about 210 km in width, and increases in volume, but decreases in speed. The surface layers are the warmest, and it is these which enter our bays and estuaries, for the shallowness of the Continental Shelf effectively protects us from the influence of the colder, deeper waters. No part of the British Isles is more than 160 km from the sea, and most parts are much nearer, so that the warming influence of the current is felt over the whole of Britain.

A branch of the North Atlantic Drift enters the English Channel, and another flows around Ireland and the north of Scotland, and so into the North Sea; but the main current passes along the coast of Norway, and its benefit is reflected in a row of ice-free ports as far north as Murmansk, well beyond the Arctic Circle.

The effects of the Gulf Stream, however, should not be over-estimated. The British Isles would enjoy a warming influence in winter even without the warm current. The sea changes its temperature more slowly than the land: it takes longer to warm up in summer, but during the winter it retains its heat longer than the adjacent land, and acts as a reservoir of warmth.

The westerly winds too play a fundamental part, for they carry the warmth far inland, not only across the British Isles, but also into western and central Europe. It is when the westerly air streams

---

[1] G. Kimble and R. Bush, *The Weather* (Penguin, 1943), p. 143.

are temporarily interrupted that the British Isles experience some of their coldest spells.

The three elements – Atlantic Ocean, warm current, and westerly winds – are present throughout the year; but their combined effects are felt most strongly in winter. As a result, the sea-level temperatures in general rise as one moves farther westward. John o' Groats, in the far north of Scotland, is no colder in winter than Brighton, on the south coast, and the Outer Hebrides are milder than either. Falmouth then has higher temperatures than Marseilles (though it has less sunshine). The mildest place on the mainland is Penzance, with a mean January temperature of 7°C (45°F); and the mildest part of the British Isles are the Isles of Scilly, with a mean January temperature of $8\frac{1}{2}$°C (47°F).

But in summer the land is warmer than the sea in any case, so that the warm North Atlantic Drift has no noticeable effect. The westerly winds then exert a cooling effect on the British Isles, so that our range of temperature is small compared with the average for our latitude. In short, our climate is oceanic.

The distribution of summer temperatures reflects two main tendencies. First is the influence of latitude, in accordance with which the temperature increases as one moves southward; second is the influence of the ocean, so that temperature increases as one moves farther inland, and more particularly, farther from the Atlantic. Superimposed upon these two tendencies is the effect of altitude: normally the temperature falls about 1°C for each 160 metres of ascent, though, as we see below, in certain conditions the reverse occurs. The warmest spot in the country in summer is London: it is far from the Atlantic, well to the south, and low-lying. Its high temperature, however, may be due in part to the energy released by so vast a body of people. The average July temperature in London is 18°C (64°F).

Rainfall

Several of the regions of the world which lie within the zones of the westerly winds have high mountains close to their western coasts: these include British Columbia, Scandinavia, the South Island of New Zealand, southern Chile – and the British Isles. In common with the others, Britain exhibits a remarkable range of mean annual rainfall – from 5000 mm on Snowdon summit down to less than 500 mm on the Thames estuary.

The greatest annual totals are found where high mountains face the Atlantic Ocean. Here the moisture-laden winds are forced to rise: under reduced conditions of pressure the air expands, becomes cooler, and releases its moisture in the form of heavy rain. The little corrie lake of Glaslyn, about 500 metres below the summit of Snowdon, is known to experience 5030 mm of rainfall per annum, so that it is virtually certain that Snowdon summit itself receives a higher total. This is among the world's highest rainfalls, and is of monsoon proportions, though it differs from monsoonal rain in that it is relatively well distributed throughout the year, while the monsoonal rainfall is concentrated into the summer months.

Eastward, in the lee of the mountains, the air descends, becomes compressed and warmer, and accordingly holds its moisture. The rainfall diminishes rapidly, and even at Pen-y-Gwryd hotel, barely 5 km east of Snowdon summit, the annual total is reduced to 3200–3300 mm; nevertheless, this district is the wettest to be permanently inhabited in Wales, and Pen-y-Gwryd vies in the British Isles with Seathwaite Farm, in the Lake District, and Kinlochquoich Lodge, in Inverness-shire – dwellings in the wettest inhabited areas of England and Scotland respectively.

Eastern England generally is in a 'rain shadow', though it still receives a 'basic' rainfall associated with the passage of depressions. A westerly situation alone, however, does not necessarily result in a high rainfall: the Scilly Isles receive only 810 mm (no more than the English Midlands), and Manchester, in spite of its reputation, has only 860 mm. The smallest totals are found where the land is not only sheltered by the hills but is in itself low-lying, so that there the descending air reaches a slightly higher temperature than elsewhere. The record is held by the little village of Great Wakering, near Shoeburyness, in Essex: here the computed annual average is only 467 mm. In warmer climates this would approach steppe conditions; and, indeed, given sandy soils, as in the East Anglian Breckland, dust storms occasionally make their appearance in Britain.

It is interesting to note that in the dry Thames estuary there is evidence that Iron Age man evaporated sea-water to recover its salt. This process was no doubt favoured by three factors: high summer temperatures, a low rainfall, and a gently shelving coast.

In the British Isles the distribution of the rainfall is comparatively even throughout the year. Spring and early summer (April to June) tend to receive less than the winter months, and August and September too are usually on the low side. This distribution is of distinct advantage to the farmer, for it assists haymaking and aids the corn harvest. Variations from year to year are comparatively slight, and even in the abnormally dry year of 1921 the rainfall was only 30 per cent. below normal.

Quite small variations, however, are reflected in crop yields: broadly speaking, in a dry year there is a rich corn harvest but a poor hay harvest, and vice versa (see the following table, and Fig. 6).

Annual Rainfall, England and Wales, and its relation to Crop Yields

% of average	Year	Wheat yield in 100 kg per ha	Hay yield in 100 kg per ha
117	1930	20·0	27·8
113	1935	23·0	26·2
113	1939	23·2	24·7
110	1937	20·3	26·5
109	1931	20·2	28·0
109	1936	20·3	25·5
103	1932	21·6	25·8
100	1929	24·0	19·2
99	1938	25·5	18·6
95	1934	25·0	21·6
81	1933	23·9	22·6
70	1921	24·9	19·8

Note: The average annual rainfall for England and Wales is computed at 950 mm. In this table the years 1929 to 1939 are arranged in order of decreasing rainfall, together with the corresponding yields of wheat and hay. For comparison the exceptionally dry year of 1921 is added at the foot of the table: it was the driest year on record (since 1863). In general in the dry years the yield of corn is high but that of hay is low, and vice versa. The relationship is perhaps made clearer by the graph, Fig. 6, drawn from the above data. Modified after L. D. Stamp, *The Land of Britain, its Use and Misuse* (Longmans, 1948).

Wind

We speak loosely of the prevailing south-westerly winds of the British Isles, but we should remember that winds do blow over these islands from all points of the compass. The south-west wind is the most frequent at Leith, at Greenwich, at Holyhead, and at Blacksod Point in county Mayo; but it is not dominant everywhere: at Gorleston (near Yarmouth) and at Castle Bay, in Barra (Outer Hebrides), its place is taken by the west wind; at Portland Bill and Aberdeen it is the south wind which prevails. In some cases it is no doubt the local configuration of the land which decides the dominance of a particular wind: the Firth of Forth, for example, extends east and west, so that north and south winds are rarely experienced there. More usually the wind-direction is related to the paths taken by depressions during their passage across the British Isles, for while the general drift of the atmosphere may be from the south-west, the direction of the wind itself is related to the

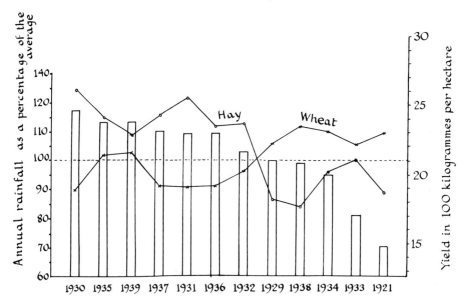

Fig. 6.   THE RELATIONSHIP BETWEEN RAINFALL AND CROP YIELDS
With a rainfall below average the yield of wheat is high, but that of hay is low, and vice versa.

position of the centre of the depression in relation to the weather station. Thus if the centre of the depression is north of the station the wind is likely to blow from the 'normal' south-west; but if the centre is west of the station a south-easterly wind is likely.

The strength of the wind tends to be greatest on exposed western coasts, where the wind may have blown across some thousands of kilometres of the open Atlantic Ocean. Lerwick, in the Shetlands, and the Butt of Lewis, in the Outer Hebrides, Holyhead, and Scilly are all very windy places. The winter months are the windiest, and at the Butt of Lewis in January strong or gale-force winds are blowing on the average for almost the whole of each day. By contrast, Kew in London experiences winds stronger than 40 km/h for less than 0·5 per cent. of the average year. Gusts of more than 160 km/h are extremely rare in Britain; but all records were shattered on February 16th, 1962, when at Shetland a gust of 285 km/h was experienced.

Wind can be of considerable importance in man's activities. Along the east coast of Scotland cold east winds penetrate far inland and slow down the growth of crops and grass. Blowing sand is a menace at times along the coast of north Somerset, in parts of the Vale of York, and in Breckland. It is wind which prevents the growth of trees on the moorlands of Devon and Cornwall; and the Forestry Commission, when seeking new plantation sites in Scotland and Wales, considers carefully the possible effects of wind. In the Fens and in the Chiltern Hills wind breaks, in the form of long and narrow plantations, are characteristic features of the landscape; and in Kent high nets screen the hop gardens from the wind.

Sunshine

The total possible period of sunshine, when averaged out through the year, amounts to 12 hours per day. As one moves from the south coast of England towards Scotland two things happen: the summer day becomes longer; but the warming effect of the summer sun is diminished by the progressive lessening of the angle at which the sun's rays strike the earth. Even in London at noon in mid-winter the sun is only 15° above the horizon: in the Shetlands the corresponding figure is $6\frac{1}{2}°$. The aspect of a slope is therefore important to the farmer everywhere in Britain, and especially so in the northerly districts, where the north-facing slope may be in the shade for most of the day in winter. On the sunny slope the pasture is likely to mature several weeks earlier than on the shady slope. In the Barnesmore Gap, in county Donegal, improved pasture land reaches 60 metres higher on the sunny side; in the valleys of Snowdonia the farms cling to the south-facing slopes.

Generally speaking, the duration of sunshine increases southward and downhill. The highest totals are recorded in the Channel Isles, where Guernsey enjoys an average of 5·16 sunny hours each day; the highest on the mainland are along a narrow strip of the south coast, where Eastbourne and Worthing tie with 5·02 hours of sunshine, while the lowest known appears to be Manchester, with only 2·65.

From the farmer's viewpoint, however, cloudy weather is not necessarily a defect. A cloud cover at night retains the warmth of the day and reduces the risk of frost; and cloud on a hot summer day prevents the rays of the sun from scorching the grass. Potatoes actually grow best in cloudy conditions.

Frost

The incidence of frost is important in several ways – for instance, the motorist is concerned with anti-freeze and slippery roads, while to the fruit-grower a late frost may spell disaster. At a station with an average of about 100 frosty days during the year January is usually the month in which frost is most frequent, with frost every other night; but all five months from November to March have high incidences of frost, and April is little better.

The average number of frosty days during the year ranges from less than 30 in the Channel Isles to more than 150 in eastern Scotland (Aberdeen has 151). Altitude in itself does not seem to be the decisive factor: Sheffield at 130 metres has only 69 frosty days, while Cambridge, at only 12·5 metres, has 111 days of frost.

More important is the local configuration of the ground. Frosty nights are particularly likely when an anticyclone is stationary over the British Isles. Winds are then light or absent, and the clear skies allow the daytime warmth to radiate quickly after sunset. A layer of cold, heavy air forms above the soil and creeps downhill, following the valleys, accumulating in the hollows, and 'flooding' the lowlands to a depth of 2 or 3 metres. During a frosty night in early May, 1938, in orchard country at Blackmoor, in Hampshire, the minimum temperature on the hillside at 158 metres was $-1·6°C$, and the fruit-trees here escaped damage; yet in the valley floor at 90 metres it was $-8·3°C$, and all the setting fruit was destroyed.

This phenomenon (known as temperature inversion) will be familiar to anyone who has cycled on a still autumn evening down' into a narrow valley and up the other side. But it is found on a smaller scale wherever the topography allows cold air to collect in a hollow whose exit is blocked. Occasionally the farmer can save his fruit crop by removing a hedge or a haystack; but sometimes there is no easy way out. Near Stretton-under-Fosse, in Warwickshire, a railway embankment spans the valley of the Smite Brook; this acts as a dam, which keeps in a reservoir of cold air. In the late spring of 1961 the level of this cold air rose so high that the Home Farm lost its apple crop completely.

Disturbances

A characteristic feature of the climate of the British Isles is its variety from day to day, and to this aspect we now turn.

Owing to the rotation of the earth, air streams in the northern hemisphere are deflected to the right. Air moving away from the north pole therefore becomes a north-east wind, and air moving away from the Tropic of Cancer towards the north pole becomes a south-west wind. These two masses of air – the one polar, the other tropical – possess and preserve their own individuality: the polar air is dry, and brings 'bracing' weather, while the tropical air is warm and moist, bringing 'relaxing' weather. The two types co-exist, but do not mix, and often preserve their character over

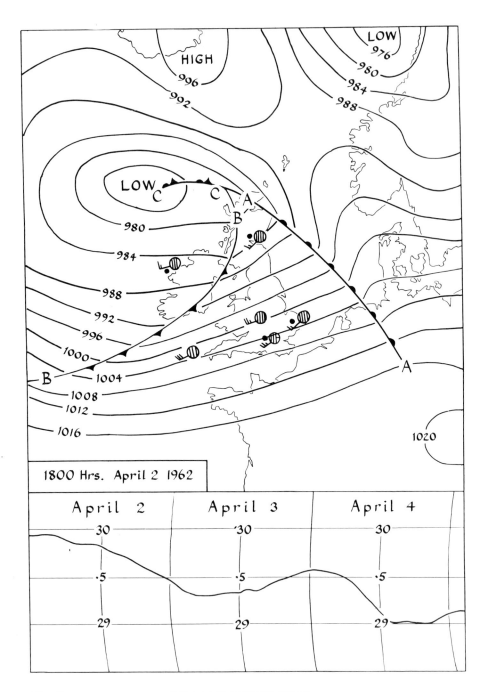

Fig. 7. A DEPRESSION OVER THE BRITISH ISLES

England and Wales lie within its warm sector; most of Ireland is in the cold sector. The weather is indicated at a few representative stations. Below the map the barograph trace indicates the rapid changes which were taking place in the pressure at a station near Coventry.

hundreds of kilometres. The plane which separates these two streams of air is termed the polar front, and it is presumed to lie across the north Atlantic Ocean.

Between the two opposing air streams there is friction. Eddies are set up; they increase in size, and move off to the north-east. These are the cyclones or depressions, which cross the British Isles in a more or less constant stream. A single depression may be 1600 kilometres in diameter, and may cover the whole of Britain: under its influence air may be drawn into the British Isles from north Africa, from the Canary Islands, or from Siberia, bringing with it the characteristics of its land of origin.

Such a disturbance is illustrated in Fig. 7. It contains, in the usual manner, a large cold sector containing heavy polar air, and a smaller warm sector, containing tropical air. AA is the warm front (the front of the warm sector) and BB is the cold front (the front of the cold sector). The warm air is continually rising, so that the warm sector gradually disappears from the surface; the cold front accordingly overtakes the warm front and gradually merges with it to form an occluded ('closed') front, CC, which is gradually growing in length. As the tropical air of the warm sector rises it cools, and its moisture condenses to form rain.

How does the depression make itself felt in our weather? At almost every station in the warm sector the sky is completely overcast and the chart carries the black spot signifying rain. In this instance the pressure gradient is steep, falling from 1008 mb in south-east England to 980 mb in north-west Scotland; consequently the winds are strong, reaching force 8 at Holyhead and force 9 in the Atlantic. The direction of these winds is controlled by the low pressure north of Ireland (air tends to move towards low pressure); but the rotation of the earth deflects the air to the right, so that it appears as a south-east wind over northern Scotland, but a south-west wind everywhere else in the British Isles. The Atlantic warmth thus penetrates into Britain, and temperatures in the warm sector are unusually high for the time of year – up to 10°C (50°F).

The cold front crossed the shores of southern Ireland and western Scotland at 6.0 P.M. on April 2nd, 1962; 12 hours later it had reached a line joining Torquay and the Tees – about 320 km to the east. Its speed was thus about 27 km/h, which is fairly typical for depressions in this country.

At other times the British Isles fall within the influence of a high-pressure system, such as that shown in Fig. 8. It relates to midnight of March 17–18th, 1962, a fortnight before the arrival of

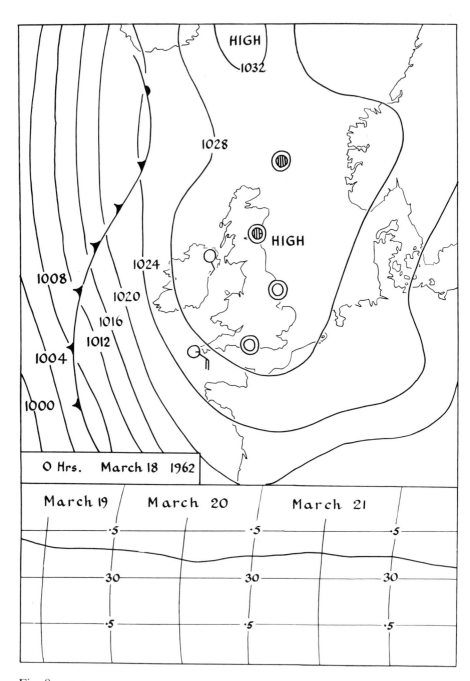

HIGH
1032

1028

1024

1020

1016

1012

1008

1004

1000

HIGH

O Hrs.   March 18 1962

March 19   March 20   March 21

·5   ·5   ·5

30   30   30

·5   ·5   ·5

Fig. 8.   HIGH PRESSURE OVER THE BRITISH ISLES

Calms and clear skies are characteristic features. The barograph trace indicates little change.

the depression of Fig. 7. Virtually the whole of Britain has atmospheric pressures of more than 1028 mb. The air, pressing down, is being reinforced from above. As it descends it becomes warmer and gains the power to hold water. Precipitation is therefore absent; the skies tend to be cloudless, and since the pressure gradient is extremely small, the winds are light (force 1–3) or there is complete calm. The double rings at several of the stations indicate calms. As we have seen, these are the conditions in which frost is likely. Temperatures are lowest where the skies are clearest, and on the south coast of England fell to −5°C (23°F).

These two types of disturbance move at different rates: the depression moves along rapidly; but the anticyclone may remain in place for days or even weeks. There are, indeed, other systems such as troughs, ridges, secondaries, and cols; but their characteristics may be resolved broadly into the two basic types we have examined.

The vagaries of the English climate have been investigated carefully by Dr C. E. P. Brooks. He sees June, for example, as having first a week of unsettled weather, then a week of fine anticyclonic weather, followed by ten days of southerly winds, with sultry heat and thunderstorms, and finally, another week of unsettled weather. There is perhaps some truth in the suggestion that 'the British Isles have no climate – only weather'.

FOR FURTHER READING

Books
BILHAM, E. G.: *The Climate of the British Isles* (Macmillan, 1938).
BROOKS, C. E. P.: *The English Climate* (English Universities Press, 1954).

Article
BUSH, RAYMOND: 'Frost and the Fruit Grower', in *Geography* (September 1945).

Maps
Climatological Atlas of the British Isles (Meteorological Office, 1952).
Weather Map (Meteorological Office, 1956).

CHAPTER THREE

SOILS AND VEGETATION

W E HAVE examined the geological structure of the British Isles and have studied the character of its rocks. We now look at the thin skin which covers those rocks – the soil. It is of fundamental importance to man. Plants cannot grow on solid rock, nor can the vast majority of species flourish in pure sand or clay; and for nearly all our food we depend upon the uppermost foot or two of the earth's mantle.

SOILS

What is soil, and how are soils formed? Broadly speaking, two components may be distinguished – the mineral particles and the organic matter. If a small quantity of garden soil is shaken vigorously in water the plant remains can be tipped away with the water, so that the mineral particles remain. When dry, these can be sorted by size with the aid of sieves of differing meshes. Much of the character of a soil stems from the dominant size of its particles and the proportions in which the several sizes are combined.

By international convention the following sizes have been adopted to define the mineral particles of soil:

clay	below 0·002 mm in diameter
silt	0·002–0·02 mm
fine sand	0·02–0·2 mm
coarse sand	0·2–2 mm
gravel	above 2 mm

A soil can thus be named according to the size of its dominant particles. Where there is an intimate mixture it is termed a loam; and intermediate stages are recognized, such as 'clay loam' or 'silty loam'.

But soil is something more than mere fragmented rock: it has a particular structure which enables it to retain water, and it possesses a stratification which can be studied in section.

The structure of soil is largely due to the existence of partly decayed vegetable matter, known as humus. When a plant dies its tissues are attacked by bacteria, earthworms, and other inhabitants of the soil, and these eventually reduce it to the mineral and other elements which are essential to the growth of new plants. Humus binds the mineral fragments together, giving the soil 'body' or 'crumb structure', and at the same time arrests the flow of percolating water, making it available for plant use. The rate at which decay proceeds varies in different soils: it is rapid in loamy soils which are well aerated and are rich in soil animals, and it is slow in cold conditions, and where saturation by water results in a restricted animal population.

In addition to the soils which can be graded by the size of their insoluble mineral constituents are the limy soils. They tend to be thin and dry, but can be quite fertile; and they support a specialized vegetation. They are not found everywhere on the chalk and limestone, for even a thin cover of superficial material will modify profoundly the character of a soil.

If a soil is examined in section its character will be seen to vary with depth from the surface – it is stratified, and this view of the soil is termed its profile. Most soil profiles consist of three main layers, which are named (from the surface downward), the A, B, and C horizons.

In oceanic climates such as our own the composition of these layers is related to the downward movement of percolating rainwater, which dissolves out much of the mineral matter together with some of the humus, and carries down with it some of the finer clay particles. The A horizon is the layer which has lost these elements; and the downward-washing process is known as leaching. In exceptionally porous soils (usually coarse sands) this results in the bleaching of the A horizon to an ashy-grey colour, and such soils are 'podzols' (so called from the Russian word *zol*, meaning 'ash'). The top few centimetres, however, remain dark in colour from the decomposing leaf mould and plant remains.

The B horizon is the layer in which the soluble constituents are deposited. In severely leached soils the minerals may be cemented together to form a hard stratum known as hardpan or ironpan; this may obstruct ploughing, or may form an impermeable layer, so that the surface may be waterlogged where one might expect dry, porous soils. The C horizon includes the zone in which the parent rock material is in process of being broken down as a prelude to incorporation in the soil.

The nature of the soil profile depends on several conditions – of climate, underlying rocks, and site. On the world scale it is climate which regulates the distribution of the major soil types. High temperatures coupled with moisture speed up the production of humus, and the balance between precipitation and evaporation determines whether the movement of soil moisture will be upward or downward. The British Isles share in only two of the major divisions – the brown earths and the podzols.

The brown earths are the soils of the deciduous forest regions: they occur especially where the parent material is a clay or a clay loam, but are found also on sandy loams provided that the water does not percolate too freely. Earthworms mix the leaf litter thoroughly with the mineral particles, and humus is produced actively. There is little leaching of the A horizon, and only slight deposition in the B horizon. To the farmer the brown earths are distinctly productive soils.

Podzols are typical of the coniferous forests and heaths; they reach their highest development in cool, humid climates, and where the parent material is sandy. The top layer tends to be peaty, for there are no earthworms to mix the organic matter with the mineral; but the remainder of the A horizon is bleached and loose in structure. Podzols are acidic, for they lack the lime which might otherwise neutralize the acids which are liberated by decomposing plants. In their natural state they form unpromising material to the farmer. Broadly speaking, the podzols are characteristic of the north and west of Britain, while the brown earths are found in the Midlands, south, and east.

There are, however, in the British Isles two other soil groups which are unrelated to climate – limestone soils and gley soils. Limestone soils are distinguished by their shallowness (they are rarely more than 30 to 40 cm deep) and by their exceptionally free drainage. The surface rooting layer is dark – almost black. Water drains away so freely that there is no deposition, and hence no B horizon. Instead fragments of the parent rock, such as oolite or chalk, occur immediately below the layer of humus, and increase in size until the solid rock is reached.

Gley soils are characteristic of areas of impeded drainage: as the water table rises and falls a zone in the soil profile is subjected alternately to drying and wetting. The chemical effects consequent on this are alternate oxidation and reduction, and they result in a mottled colouring of pale blue, yellow, and green usually below the B horizon. Gley soils tend to be covered with damp grassland, often infested with rushes; they can be grazed only in spring and summer. The pastures can sometimes be improved, however, by drainage, liming, and re-seeding.

There is a gradual transition from gley soils to peaty soils, which are found in completely waterlogged conditions. Two distinct forms are found. Fen peat occurs in waterlogged lowlands where the rivers have introduced alkaline salts such as those of calcium, perhaps derived from distant hills. These neutralize the acids which are formed by decomposing plants, and such soils when drained (as in the Fens) can be exceedingly productive. Moorland peat, on the other hand, is formed on plateaux which receive heavy rain, such as the Millstone Grit moors of the south Pennines. Here there is no alkaline material to neutralize the acids, and such soils are useless to the farmer.

In a sense peat is an example of an immature soil – a soil in a state of arrested development – for the decay of plant material ceases in the absence of air, and peat will accumulate so long as waterlogging continues. Several other examples of immature soils can be seen in the British Isles. They include the alluvial soils of coastal marshes and river flood-plains, which are constantly receiving new surface dressings; conversely, on steep mountain slopes and in areas of blowing sand the surface material is continually being removed, and the soil is equally immature.

Nor can a soil reach maturity where there is human interference. Ploughing destroys the soil profile down to 30 cm or so, and the application of fertilizers changes the character of the soil. Drainage, grazing, and planting and felling the woodlands modify the soils, so that over much of the British Isles the soils are largely 'man-made'.

Soil Surveys
In the British Isles soil surveying has taken place in several comparatively small districts, and it will be many years before a complete survey is published. The purpose of the surveyor is to distinguish between different soil profiles and to map the area over which each is constant. As an example we illustrate part of the soil survey of north Wales (Fig. 9). Each profile is named from its type area; it is examined in pits dug for the purpose, and its distribution is confirmed by auger borings. The chief single element in determining soil characteristics is found to be the physical character of the parent rock. In many areas this involves the recognition of the varied superficial deposits resulting from glaciation; and often these are not recorded on any published map.

But a soil map is more complex than a drift geology map, for many elements apart from the parent rock enter into the differentiation of soils: they include slope, drainage, and the presence of downwash material. Long-continued cultivation or grazing can also modify the soil profile more or less permanently, and such changes are recognized by the soil surveyor.

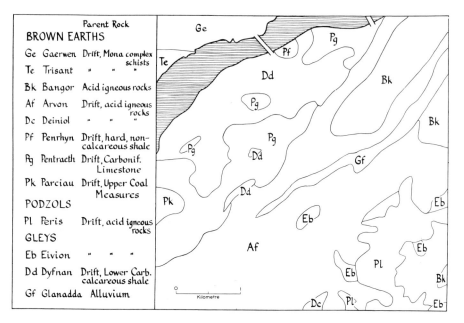

Fig. 9. A PORTION OF THE SOIL SURVEY OF NORTH WALES

The area shown appears on the Anglesey sheet of the 'Soil Survey of England and Wales'. It comprises part of Caernarvonshire bordering the Menai Strait. The whole of this surface lies below 120 m, and much of it is assigned by geomorphologists to the 80-metre platform (p. 106). The parent rocks are listed in the key, but in some cases the same parent gives rise to more than one soil. Most of the soils are described as loams or sandy loams. No key is provided for the two areas in the south-east.

Thus in Kent no fewer than 11 soils are distinguished on the Hythe Beds of the Lower Greensand east of the Medway, their different characteristics depending largely on their sites. Scarp foot, scarp face, plateau top, valley side and valley bottom – all yield different soils. As many as 7 soils are recognized in Romney Marsh in the same county. Clearly we cannot attempt to describe the innumerable soils of the surveyors: all that we can hope to do in our regional accounts is to summarize the character of some typical soils whose distributions are known to correspond with particular geological exposures.

VEGETATION

Practically nothing of the 'natural' vegetation of the British Isles remains to be seen today: almost everywhere the existing plant cover shows the effect of man's activities. Sometimes this is obvious and deliberate, such as the ploughing of the soil and planting of cereal or root crops. It is equally deliberate and almost as clear in the meadows and pastures, which are carefully managed according to established principles – grazed and mown, fertilized and re-seeded. The hill pastures of the north and west, apparently more natural, are nevertheless modified by the grazing of sheep. Woodland, even where not obviously plantation, is managed for timber or preserved for grouse or as fox coverts; in the latter cases the rodent population has enormously increased, to the detriment of the woodland (as we see below). Only, perhaps, in remote mountain crevices and in the peat bogs of Ireland and western Scotland do remnants of the natural vegetation survive, unmodified by man. It is clear, however, that before man made his presence felt the greater part of Britain was clothed in forest; and if for any reason a tract of grassland is neglected today it tends to revert first to heath and eventually to forest.

We are concerned here not with long lists of species, nor with the descriptions of plant communities for their own sakes, but rather with the ways in which man has used or is able to use the semi-natural vegetation of Britain. Cultivated crops are considered in the various regional chapters; but grassland and 'cultivated' woodland are more conveniently described in this section.

Woodland

Little more than 5 per cent. of the area of Britain is now covered with woodland – a smaller proportion than any other country in Europe. This is a result of the progressive destruction of the forests, which began in Neolithic times, and has continued almost till the present day, and often at accelerating rates.

While the Romans were the first to establish farms and towns in the lowlands, it was the Saxons who made the first serious inroads in the forests, particularly in the later phase of secondary settlement. From Norman times until the nineteenth century, oak was the favoured timber for shipbuilding and for the frameworks of buildings, while its bark was the staple raw material for tanning. The oak woods, which formerly covered the greater part of Britain, were traditionally managed by the method of 'coppice with standards', which has continued till today. It involves the thinning of the oaks so as to allow about 30 to mature to the hectare (an oak takes 80 to 120 years to mature). These are the 'standards': they have plenty of light, and room to spread their branches without interfering with their neighbours, and they can produce not only good straight planks, but also the curved timber which in earlier days was required both for the dockyard and for the building of timber-framed mansions whose ornamental woodwork we can still admire. The light then penetrates easily to the floor of the woods and encourages the growth of shrubs and smaller trees such as hazel: these are cut back ('coppiced') every ten years or so, and yield a useful supply of timber for fences and hurdles, for hop poles, pea and bean sticks, and firewood.

In this way the dense oak woods were thinned; but at the same time there was continued clearing in order to increase the available agricultural land, and in specific areas (Derbyshire, the Mendips, the Weald, and the Forest of Dean), to provide charcoal for the smelting of metallic ores. By the sixteenth century Sherwood Forest and the Forest of Dean were becoming noticeably depleted, and the Wealden iron-workers were using timber brought from Essex. A century later even firewood was scarce, 'sea coal' was burnt for fuel, and England was dependent on imported timber.

Oak is still the dominant tree over the greater part of the British Isles. The two native species are very similar in their requirements. They flourish best on the clay soils of the Midlands and East Anglia, but they also grow well in the valleys and plains of the north and west – on the Palæozoic rocks of Devon and Cornwall and the metamorphic rocks of county Galway; on the Old Red Sandstone soils of both Somerset and Kerry; and on the ancient rocks of the glens of the Scottish Highlands.

The oak woods which remain represent a mere fragment of the former cover. They have lost their real purpose, and are preserved chiefly for fox-hunting and pheasant-shooting. But such 'preservation' is liable to defeat its own purpose, for the gamekeeper destroys the larger animals which prey on pheasants – stoats, weasels, badgers, hedgehogs, hawks, owls, and crows. As a result the smaller herbivorous animals – voles, mice, squirrels, and rabbits – lose their natural enemies and multiply to such an extent that they destroy the seeds and seedlings in the wood and render it incapable of natural regeneration.

While the oak is dominant on the moderately heavy soils, it does not flourish on the shallow soils of the limestones; here it is replaced by beech in the Cotswolds, Chilterns, and North and South Downs, and by ash on the older limestones of the north and west.

Beech is a very successful colonizer of scrub, especially on shallow soils, and its virtual confinement to southern and eastern England can only be satisfactorily explained by its late arrival and its slow advance. Beech has apparently not had sufficient time to spread to Ireland. Since its seeds fall vertically it can advance only slowly: one estimate places its spread at about 30 metres a century!

Beech flourishes on the scarps and steep slopes of the Chalk and Jurassic Limestone, where the soil is only 30 to 40 centimetres deep, for its roots spread laterally rather than vertically; it thrives also on the plateaux of the Chilterns and North Downs, where the loamy soils are derived from Clay-with-flints. It withstands strong winds; it grows to 30 metres – taller than any accompanying oak or ash; and it casts a dense shade which in time destroys its competitors. The finest extent of beechwood forest in the British Isles is on the Chiltern plateau, where it provides raw material for the furniture industry of High Wycombe.

Beech woods are found on sandy soils too, such as those derived from glacial gravels (Epping Forest, in south-west Essex) and from the Reading Beds (Burnham Beeches, north of Slough), and they have been planted widely as wind breaks on the Old Red Sandstone soils of north-east Scotland. But on these sandy soils the tree does not grow so high; its leaves form a bulky litter which in acid soils (where earthworms are rare or absent) do not readily become assimilated: the seeds fall on inhospitable ground, and natural regeneration of the wood is checked.

These three types of woodland, in which the dominant trees are oak, ash, and beech, may together be regarded as the most westerly extension of the great European belt of deciduous forest. To the north of it lies the coniferous forest belt: in Scandinavia this consists largely of spruce, but this tree has not penetrated to the British Isles, and its place is taken by pine and birch.

Pine and birch grow well on sandy soils in southern England, and in particular are quick to colonize heathland, since they seed freely and grow rapidly. Of the two, pine forms the more valuable timber (it attains about 25 m in height), and so is cut more freely than birch. Both will grow in rigorous climates: they form the most northerly and the highest woodlands in the British Isles. They are well seen in the Scottish Highlands in the tributary glens of Glenmore, such as Glens Loy, Maillie, and Affric, though much of this land has been planted by the Forestry Commission. In Rothiemurchus Forest, in the Cairngorms, pines are growing above 600 metres, and here form what is perhaps the highest woodland in Britain. The Scottish woodland, however, has many enemies: in places a strong growth of heather prevents regeneration; sheep and rabbits nibble the young seedlings and saplings, and deer grub them up with their antlers. The so-called Scottish deer forests are really moorland areas whose lower slopes are fringed with woodland. The deer descend into the woods for food and shelter, and there is a danger that the forests will be destroyed through the killing of young saplings.

The Forestry Commission
The public body responsible for afforestation and forest research in Great Britain is the Forestry Commission. The scale of its operations is not always realized: the Commission employs over 10,000 forest workers, and administers 1·2 million hectares of land, of which ·8 million hectares are forest land. Half the forest land is in Scotland, where there are 427 thousand hectares; England follows, with 253 thousand hectares, and Wales has 135 thousand hectares. The estates of the Commission comprise no fewer than 341 distinct properties. While many of the forests in these properties are small (below 200 hectares), there are 20 of more than 4000 hectares. The largest is Affric, Inverness, and Ross (27,358 hectares) in Scotland. There follow the New Forest (27,051 hectares) and Thetford Chase in Breckland (20,806 hectares).

New planting is taking place at the rate of about 20 to 25 thousand hectares a year. The bulk of this consists of conifers, and Sitka spruce represents about one-third of the total, grown from seed collected in British Columbia. Scots pine and lodgepole pine together form another third, and there follow in descending order Norway spruce (grown for Christmas trees), Corsican pine, and Douglas fir.

These species take 80 to 120 years to reach their maximum growth; and since the Forestry Commission was constituted in 1919, it follows that its timber production so far has been only from thinnings. From the financial viewpoint, the Commission represents a long-term investment. Its dividends, though small, are increasing: receipts from sales and rents, etc., rose from £1·5 million in 1950 to £7·6 million in 1969 (the latest comparable accounting period), and during this period the quantity of timber sold more than trebled (from ·4 million cubic metres in 1951 to 1·4 million in 1969–70). The greater part of the output is used in paper and board mills, but Scotland is now self-sufficient in pit props.

The benefits of the Forestry Commission, however, are not to be reckoned only in economic terms. Land is being utilized which in many cases would otherwise be agriculturally unproductive; soil erosion is being checked; research is being pursued, the results of which are available to the whole world; and the Commission are providing useful employment for local people in the Scottish Highlands and the Welsh hills – two regions of declining opportunity.

Grassland
Permanent grassland is both the chief form of land use by area in

the British Isles and the most productive by value. It may be divided into three classes, using as a basis the chemical reaction of the underlying soil. There are thus the basic grasslands of the chalk and limestone subsoils, the neutral grasslands of the clay vales, and the acid grasslands of the siliceous rocks of the north and west and the sandy heaths of the south and east.

Basic Grassland
The chalk and limestone areas of southern and eastern England have been utilized in various ways. Before man appeared they seem to have been wooded; but in Neolithic times (about 2000 B.C.) the climate was becoming drier and the trees were thinning out. Neolithic man with his grazing animals probably cleared some of the woodland; and in Iron Age times much of the chalk and limestone land was under the plough, for the remains of Celtic fields are widespread in the South Downs, in Salisbury Plain, and in the Mendips. Since that time sheep have grazed the chalk and limestone pastures, and these together with rabbits effectively keep down the shrubby plants. If for any reason grazing ceases, however, the pastures are soon invaded by shrubs and trees.

On the shallow chalk and limestone soils a short, smooth turf develops, largely dominated by two of the fescues (*Festuca ovina* and *F. rubra*) and by meadow oat-grass (*Avena pratensis*). It is the resilience of the fescues which imparts to limestone pastures their pleasant springy character, and helps to explain the value of the chalklands for horse-breeding and the siting of racecourses (for example, at Brighton, Lewes, and Epsom). Much of the herbage is necessarily shallow-rooting; but there are also many species whose roots descend 9 or even 12 metres into the fissures of the solid rock. It is not easy to see how the sward can be supplied with moisture on porous chalk or limestone, but there is some evidence that water rises by capillary action.

A very similar turf is found on the older limestones and on the basic igneous and metamorphic rocks, such as basalt and schists, particularly on the better-drained slopes. But typically these rocks are in areas of high rainfall, and there is a tendency for the soils here to become leached and acid: heather then invades the grasses and the pastures become impoverished by the appearance of bent-grass (*Agrostis tenuis*).

Neutral Grassland
Most of the neutral grasslands are enclosed, and are managed either for pasture, for hay, or for both. Typically they occur on the

loams and clays of the Midlands and south of England, but they are found also in the alluvial valleys of the north and west and in the less moist parts of Ireland. They range widely in value. The best fattening pastures, such as those of Leicestershire for cattle and those of Romney Marsh for sheep, have as co-dominants perennial rye-grass (*Lolium perenne*) and wild white clover (*Trifolium repens*). The former is perhaps the most valuable pasture grass in Britain: it gives a rich yield of palatable and nutritious fodder over a long period; it is sown extensively for the formation of new pastures, and has been cultivated in England for three centuries. The latter, in addition to its value as fodder, possesses the property of converting atmospheric nitrogen into nitrate, and so enriches the soil in which it grows. Together these two species comprise up to 75 per cent. of the sward in the best Leicestershire pastures, and up to 90 per cent. of the best Romney Marsh pastures.

In the dairy pastures, such as those of Somerset, Cheshire, and the Irish vales, rye-grass and clover are joined by the bent-grasses (Agrostis sp.), which are strong-growing and long-lived native grasses and among the commonest in Britain: they are not sown, but quickly establish themselves, and, given time, dominate the more desirable species. Crested dog's-tail (*Cynosurus cristatus*) is also prominent; it thrives on a wide range of soils and altitude, and though its yield is rather low it remains green throughout the winter.

Less valuable pastures may be termed 'general-purpose' grasslands; they occupy very wide areas, and include all the above and many other grasses – in all 40 to 50 different species. Of least value are the untended pastures, which are often dominated by the common bent-grass (*Agrostis tenuis*). This flourishes on poor soils on mountainsides up to 900 metres, where other species cannot survive. A shallow-rooting grass, its shoots dry up in summer and offer little feed, so that its grazing value is rather low; but it will produce a smooth turf, and is often in demand for bowling and putting greens.

Acid Grasslands

The acid grasslands are characteristic of the hillside soils developed on the siliceous rocks of north and west Britain – on the granites of Bodmin Moor, the grits of the Pennines, the slates of north Wales and the Lake District – and on many other rocks. They are also found on sandy soils in southern England. They comprise a varied group. The rough pastures which extend up to the 'mountain wall' (that is, the highest field boundary) in north Wales often contain much bent-grass and fescue. They tend to be invaded by heather and bracken, while similar pastures in the sandy lowlands are clogged by gorse. Heather or ling (*Calluna vulgaris*) is grazed by sheep; but the bracken fern (*Pteridium aquilinum*) is unpalatable, and is exceedingly difficult to control. Indeed, bracken-infested land has often to be abandoned as pasture. Gorse is more easily eradicated: cattle will graze its young shoots, and the ground can be cleared by burning.

Two other types of acid grassland are those dominated by the purple moor grass (*Molinia caerulea*) and by mat grass (*Nardus stricta*). Molinia grows on wet, peaty moorlands where water is abundant but not stagnant: it is typical, for example, of the level plateau surfaces of south Wales. Cattle and sheep will graze it only when the leaves are young, so that its agricultural value is limited. The tough and wiry mat grass forms tussocks in which new plants pile up on the remains of old, dead plants; it flourishes in the drier moorlands of the south Pennines, Wales, and Scotland. Of all the plants of the grasslands it has the least value; but Professor Stapledon has demonstrated that it can be improved by the use of drastic methods (disk-ploughing, re-seeding, fertilizing and rolling).

There are in addition two grasses of more local occurrence but of unusual interest since they flourish in exceptional environments: marram, in sand-dunes; and rice-grass, in tidal mud-flats.

Marram grass (*Ammophila arenaria* or *arundinacea*) is the only grass which will grow freely in pure, loose sand to such an extent that it will stabilize whole dunes. A coarse, tall grass, it grows upward to keep pace with the accumulating sand, sending out new roots all the time in the moist layer which underlies the surface of the sand. It is seen growing wild in clumps almost everywhere in the dune areas around our coasts. Its value to man is immense: without its influence blowing sand would be a menace; coastal erosion would be intensified, and, in north Somerset, for instance, miles of additional expensive sea walls would be required to protect the thousands of acres of rich pasture land which lie below the level of high tides. In the shelter of the pioneer grass mosses and lichens gradually colonize the surface of the sand; then the marram thins out, wilts, ceases to flower, and finally dies.

Rice-grass (*Spartina townsendii*) is nature's most powerful agent in reclaiming land from the sea: it is the only plant which can establish itself on deep, mobile mud which is covered at high tide. Its main stem is supported by radiating stolons (horizontal creeping stems) and by anchoring roots; the mud is stabilized, silt is trapped, tidal currents are arrested, and the surface is raised so that reclamation for farming is made possible. Spartina was first noticed in 1870, in Southampton Water: it has since extended to and is flourishing in the Severn estuary. Both marram and rice-grass spread rapidly in suitable conditions; for example, near Blakeney Point in Norfolk many hectares of dunes were stabilized during the decade 1927–37 as a result of the spread of marram; and during the thirteen years 1911 to 1924 Spartina changed a large area in Holes bay (Dorset) from mudflats into grassland. These, together with other grasses mentioned in this section, are illustrated in Fig. 10.

Heath and Bog

The dominant species of our heathlands, as its name implies, is common heather or ling (*Calluna vulgaris*), which flourishes best on acid, sandy soils, though in regions of heavy rainfall it establishes itself even on limestone soils. Most lowland heaths represent a stage intermediate between grassland and forest: if grazing is introduced or increased (either by sheep or rabbits), the heath will be converted into grassland; if grazing ceases and there is protection from fire the heath will usually revert to forest.

On the hills which overlook or are near to our western shores, however, strong winds prevent the establishment of trees, and here too there is often heath from sea-level up to about 600 metres. On excessively wet soils heather is absent; but it flourishes on the drier eastern slopes of the Pennines, on the North York Moors, and in the eastern half of the Grampians. Heather is largely absent from the north-west Highlands and from the wetter parts of the Grampians: indeed, only about a third of the Scottish moors are heather moors. While they offer a limited amount of grazing for sheep, most heather moors are managed for grouse-shooting. For this purpose they are fired systematically every 4 to 10 years: such treatment rejuvenates the heather, and at the same time prevents the invasion of the moor by birch and rowan.

Fig. 10. SIX CHARACTERISTIC BRITISH GRASSES

All the specimens illustrated were collected in North Wales with the exception of No. 4, which is from Warwickshire, but they can be found in many parts of Britain. Each forms an essential element in the particular landscape of which it is a part. The key to the numbering is as follows:

1. Mat grass (*Nardus stricta*), Cwm Idwal.
2. Marram grass (*Ammophila arenaria*), Newborough Warren.
3. Rice-grass (*Spartina townsendii*), Foryd Bay.
4. Common Bent grass (*Agrostis tenuis*), upper Avon valley, Warwickshire.
5. Sheep's fescue (*Festuca ovina*), Cwm Idwal.
6. Purple moor grass (*Molinia caerulea*), Capel Curig.

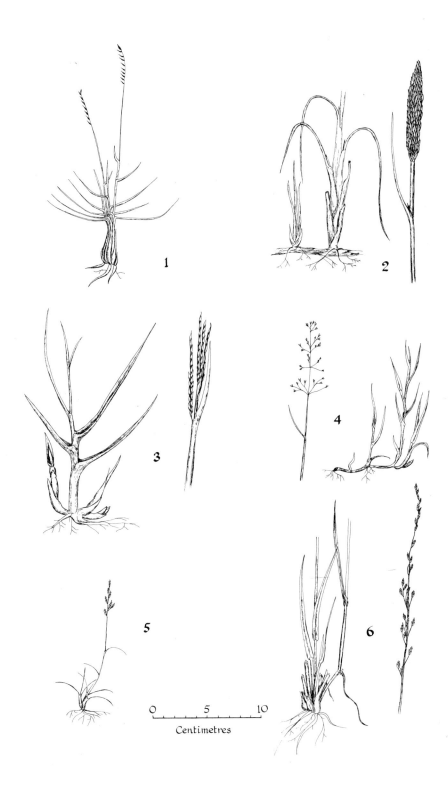

1

2

3

4

5

6

0   5   10

Centimetres

Where the soils are permanently wet heath merges into moss or bog. The Pennine bogs (locally known as 'mosses') occur on level or gently sloping plateaux: they are dominated by cotton grass (Eriophorum sp.), which forms a deep peat, sometimes reaching a thickness of 9 metres. Peat bogs are characteristic of much of the Hebrides and the Irish lowlands, but here the dominant vegetation consists of mosses of the genus Sphagnum. Their specialized structure allows them to carry water upward in their tissues as they grow. The lower layers, deprived of light and air, die, and, in the absence of soil bacteria, are compressed into peat. These bogs occupy the permanently wet hollows in the drift-covered Carboniferous Limestone. In the far west, however, in western Galway and Mayo, the rainfall is high, and the atmosphere is so damp that bog is the normal vegetation in all level country.

Bogs are estimated to cover at least a fifth of the surface of Ireland, and form a major natural handicap for both its political divisions. Even the bogs have their limited uses, however: sheep

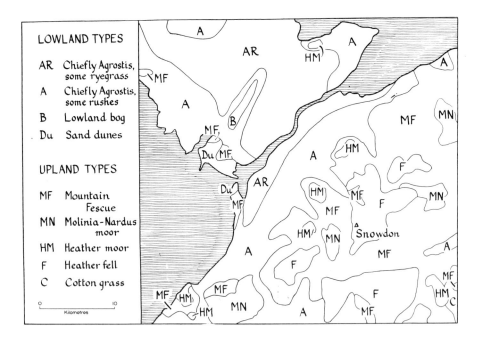

Fig. 11.   THE VEGETATION OF SNOWDONIA AND PART OF ANGLESEY

This represents a portion of the vegetation map of England and Wales compiled in 1940 by the Welsh Plant Breeding Station. *After the O.S. 1:625,000 map, Vegetation (Grasslands). Crown copyright reserved.*

and cattle find rough pasturage there, and more than 4 million tonnes of peat are cut annually for fuel. Occasionally the clearing of bog reveals land on which oats and potatoes can be grown; more usually it is a wet and stiff clay, useless to the farmer.

The distribution of a number of these vegetation types over a relatively small region is illustrated in Fig. 11, which covers Snowdonia and part of Anglesey. On the mainland the vegetation zones appear to be guided by the relief; but the influence of this factor is probably indirect, through its effect on rainfall.

FOR FURTHER READING

Books

Annual Reports of the Forestry Commissioners (H.M.S.O.).

Hubbard, C. E.: *Grasses* (Penguin, 1954).

Stamp, L. D.: *The Land of Britain, Its Use and Misuse* (Longmans, 1948).

Tansley, Sir A. G.: *The British Islands and their Vegetation* (Cambridge University Press, 1950).

There are useful sections on soils in many of the county reports of the Land Utilisation Survey, for example:

Part 40 (Cardiganshire), E. J. Howell, p. 570 ff.

Part 56 (Oxfordshire), M. Marshall, pp. 202–203.

Part 57 (Leicestershire), R. M. Auty, p. 253 ff.

Part 58 (Northamptonshire), S. H. Beaver, p. 339 ff.

Part 60 (Nottinghamshire), K. C. Edwards, p. 449 ff.

Article

Taylor, J. A.: 'Methods of Soil Study', in *Geography* (January–April 1960).

Maps

The sheets of the Soil Survey of Great Britain correspond in area and numbering with the one-inch geological maps (New Series). Attention has so far been concentrated on eastern Scotland and north Wales, together with scattered areas in England and reconnaissance work in Ireland. The memoirs which accompany the published maps are very valuable.

O.S. 1 : 625,000 map: Vegetation (Grasslands).

CHAPTER FOUR

THE SEA-COASTS OF BRITAIN

THE SEA has impressed itself on almost every facet of the geography of the British Isles. Here we examine briefly two of its aspects: its influence on the shape of our coasts and its effects on our ports.

Perhaps the most powerful influence on the shape of the coasts of the British Isles has been the changes in the relative levels of land and sea. In recent geological time there have been two opposing forces at work: on the one hand the release of vast quantities of water by the melting ice sheets has tended to produce a rise in sea-level; on the other hand the removal of the enormous load of ice from the land has allowed it to rise, so that there has been a tendency for sea-level to fall.

The effect of the additional meltwater must have been immediate and universal, for all the oceans in the world are interlinked. It has been calculated that if the present polar ice caps were to melt the existing coasts would be flooded to a depth of 45 metres; and the Quaternary ice sheets were of far greater extent than the present-day remnants. The effect of the released load, however, seems to have been delayed and localized: the rise appears to have been greatest in Scotland, where the ice was thickest, and least in southern England, which was never completely covered. In Ireland emergence of the land was confined largely to the north-eastern region.

Although the precise explanations of the changes in sea-level are not clear, the order in which they occurred has been deciphered (Fig. 12). In pre-glacial times the land stood much higher than it does today, to the extent of 90 to 120 metres. The evidence of this lies in the great thicknesses of older alluvium which are known to underlie some of our major rivers: in the Firths of Forth and Clyde borings reveal bedrock at about 90 metres below sea-level. Clearly the rivers could excavate at this level only if the land were at least 90 metres above its present height.

The weight of the advancing ice depressed the land surface, so that towards the end of the Ice Age the sea had crept up to about 30 metres above its level today. At this height the waves cut a plat-

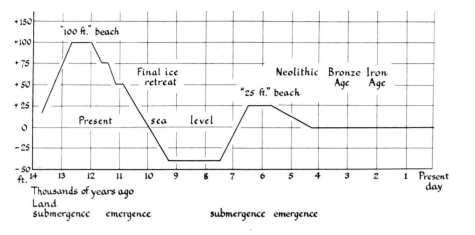

Fig. 12. CHANGES IN SEA-LEVEL SINCE THE CLOSE OF THE ICE AGE

The initial rise in sea level (= land submergence) is interpreted as being due to the weight of the ice. With the release of this load the land emerged, but this general trend was interrupted by a submergence 7–8000 years ago. This drowned the forests, whose remains are visible at widely scattered places around our shores. *After British Regional Geology, The Midland Valley of Scotland.*

form and deposited beach material, except where the ice sheet obscured the coast. This 30-metre platform has been recognized clearly at various points around the coasts of Scotland – on the north shore of the Beauly Firth (west of Inverness); at Brora and Helmsdale (on the east coast of Sutherland); and in the far south-west of Scotland near Wigtown and along the shores of Luce Bay and Loch Ryan; it is known in central Scotland around the shores of the Firths of Clyde, Forth, and Tay, and inland as far as Stirling. The date of this beach is placed at approximately 10,000 B.C.

There followed a period during which the land rose higher and higher: it halted sufficiently long when the sea stood at about 15 metres above its present level for the formation of another beach; then the emergence continued until the coastline had retreated to a new position 9 to 12 metres below that which exists today. On the freshly exposed surfaces woods of oak, ash, alder, and willow became established, and in them man may have hunted wild game.

With the melting of the ice sheets came a rise in sea-level. The forests were overwhelmed, and their remains are to be seen at many points around our coasts when the tide is low. They are known in the far north-east of Scotland at Wick and Golspie; in north-east England at Amble and West Hartlepool; in the Humber at North Ferriby; in East Anglia at Brancaster; along the south coast at

Dover, Hastings, and Bexhill and at Southampton and Bournemouth; in Somerset at Stolford, in Bridgwater bay; in Wales off
Swansea, in Carmarthen and St Bride's bays, at Borth, Barmouth,
and Rhyl; and in Ireland in Dublin bay and in Belfast and Strangford loughs.

These submerged forests provide the clearest possible evidence
of a widespread and considerable rise in sea-level, which is held to
have occurred in early Neolithic times, about 6000 B.C. Its effects
have been more profound than the mere drowning of forests.

In the Scottish Highlands the sea submerged the mouths of the
glaciated valleys, converting them into fiords; in the lowlands it
advanced into the valleys of the Forth, Tay, and Clyde to form the
three firths; in Ireland the rising sea flooded the shores of Kerry,
turning the limestone-floored valleys into long inlets and the
intervening ridges of Old Red Sandstone into bold peninsulas,
while in Mayo it converted a drumlin-strewn lowland into the
island-studded Clew bay. It entered the lower reaches of the Devon
and Cornwall rivers, giving them intricate outlines which resemble
the contour-lines that one sees on a map of a dissected plateau.
The sea flooded Carmarthen bay and advanced many miles into
Pembrokeshire to form Milford Haven, one of the finest natural
harbours in Europe. It drowned the lower courses of the Severn,
Thames, and Mersey, the Humber, Solent, and Southampton
Water, so bringing the sea into the heart of England; and it flooded
a narrow strip of low-lying land to form the Strait of Dover, so
that England was now separated from the Continent.

At the height of its advance the sea cut another platform, at
what is now about 7·5 metres O.D. Its remains are more widespread
than the earlier beaches, and man has made considerable use of it.
The raised beach is a terrace of marine alluvium, and like others it is
often covered by friable soils. Close to the sea, yet beyond the
reach of the highest tides, it offers useful sites for fishing-villages.

In Scotland much of Edinburgh and Glasgow are built upon the
old beach; so are Dundee, Greenock, Ayr, and Ardrossan, while
farther inland it accounts for the fertile carse lands west of Perth
and Stirling. In Ireland it is seen at many points along the coastline
of Down, Donegal, and Antrim. Dundalk is built on it, together
with Newry, Warrenpoint, and Dundrum; and for many miles it
supports the coastal road in Antrim. At Portrush and Cushendun
the old cliff line can be seen, with caves which are now well beyond
the reach of the sea; and the wave-cut platform appears as a rocky
bench cut into the basalts of the Giant's Causeway. In Somerset
the raised beach is clearly seen north of Weston-super-Mare, where

many 'desirable residences' have been built upon it. It is also known in Cumberland along the Solway Firth, in the Isle of Man, in the Gower Peninsula, and at various places along the south coast (Portslade, Worthing, Littlehampton, and Portsmouth).

The latest change has been the fall in the level of the sea which has left the beach stranded at a height of about 7·5 m; this is held to have taken place during later Neolithic times, about 3000 B.C.; but the extent of the emergence has been too slight to destroy the effects of submergence along the greater part of our coastline.

From Flamborough Head southward along the shores of east Yorkshire, Lincolnshire, and East Anglia, and from Selsey Bill eastward along the shores of Sussex and Kent, the coastline is rather different from that of the rest of the British Isles. Here the submergence has been slight or absent; the rocks are for the most part soft and easily eroded, and there is a strong development of longshore drift, with the active formation of sandspits. Here we find the most rapid changes in our coastline: within the historical period sandspits have lengthened, river channels have silted, and towns have been washed away.

The direction of longshore drift is eastward along the south coast and southward along the east coast: this is a direct result of the relative lengths of the fetches of those coasts (the fetch in any direction is the distance to the nearest land in that direction).

Along the east coast the greatest fetch is in a northerly direction; other things being equal, north winds will produce the largest waves, so that beach material is carried southward. Accordingly we observe sandspits at Spurn Head, Yarmouth, and Harwich, and the remarkable 18 km deflection of the Alde southward by Orford Ness. It is along this coast, particularly in Holderness, that erosion is proceeding most rapidly in Britain: the waves undercut the soft boulder clay, the cliff collapses, and the loose material is carried away southward, to expose a fresh layer to the attack of the waves. Erosion here averages 2 to 2·5 m a year, and in places has been as high as 4·5 m annually. If the rate has been constant the coast will since Roman times have retreated 4 km. Erosion is serious also along parts of the Norfolk and Suffolk coasts, at Hunstanton, Cromer, and Lowestoft. The problems caused by the destruction of fertile land in a well-peopled district can be imagined.

Along the south coast the greatest fetch is in a south-westerly direction, and as a result the drift is eastward. The mouths of all the rivers are deflected in that direction, and there is a remarkable sandspit at Shoreham. Destruction of a headland exposes the beaches to the east of it, and Old Winchelsea was overwhelmed in the thirteenth century when the continued erosion of the cliffs at Fairlight robbed it of protection. On balance, along this coast the land has probably gained at the expense of the sea. Thanet is no longer an island: the Wantsum has silted, and cattle graze where ships sailed in the time of the Venerable Bede. Romney Marsh, a shallow bay in pre-Roman times, is now valuable sheep pasture.

Tides

Tides are no mere academic matter: they are of profound importance both to shipping and to harbour authorities. A few British ports – among them Southampton, Blyth, Weymouth, Dundee, Aberdeen, and Belfast – have low tidal ranges, of about 3 metres or less, and here enclosed basins are either completely unnecessary or at least are of little modern significance. At other ports such as London, Liverpool, Hull, and Avonmouth the tidal range is so great that large vessels can approach only at or near high tide; large basins fitted with locks are essential, and they are difficult and expensive both to construct and to maintain. How do the tides vary around our coasts, and what is the cause of that variation?

Less than a generation ago it was confidently asserted that a 'tidal wave' entered the Atlantic Ocean from the south and penetrated into the English Channel from the west and into the North Sea from the north. This view offered no convincing explanation of the differences in tidal range which are found along the coast except to suggest that the ranges were greatest near the heads of funnel-shaped estuaries.

According to the current view – which is accepted by the Admiralty and illustrated on its charts – the narrow seas are divided into separate stretches, each with its own tidal phenomena (Fig. 13). Associated with each stretch there is a point (the amphidromic point) where no tide is experienced. Around this point the water has both a rocking and a spinning motion: the spinning is a result of the earth's rotation; the rocking is set in motion by tidal oscillations in the Atlantic. We are not concerned with the mechanics of the tides (which are exceedingly complex), but we may observe that at any point along our coast the time of high tide will depend on its radial position in relation to the nearest amphidromic point, while the height of its tide will depend on its relative distance from this point. Three such points are charted in the North Sea and one in the North Channel; but in the English Channel and Irish Sea the known phenomena can be explained only by assuming the existence of amphidromic points 'projected' on to the neighbouring land.

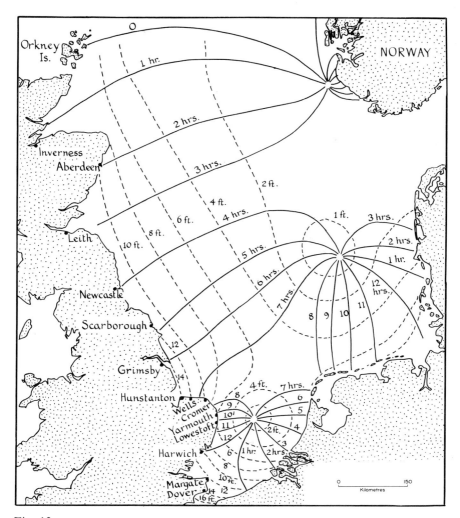

Fig. 13. TIDES IN THE NORTH SEA

Three amphidromic points are indicated: round these the tidal surge is considered to rotate anti-clockwise once every 12 hours. The broken lines are co-range lines, and they show that the height of the tide increases with the distance from the amphidromic points. The continuous lines are co-tidal lines and join all places having high tide at the same time. If we assume that it is high tide at midnight (or midday) in the Orkneys, then the co-tidal lines indicate the times of high tide at other points along the shores of the North Sea (and in the sea itself). *Based on Admiralty Chart No. 5058, 1937.*

We may illustrate the tides in the British seas by a few examples. Along the east coast the time of high tide becomes progressively later as one moves south. If we assume that high tide occurs at midnight at Orkney, then at Inverness it will take place at about 1 A.M., at Aberdeen, 2 A.M., at Leith, 3, at the Tyne, 4, at Scarborough, 5, at Grimsby, 6 A.M., and so on (all these times are approximate).

Turning now to average tidal ranges, we observe small ranges – of only 1·8 m – at Yarmouth and Lowestoft, which are close to the amphidromic point between East Anglia and the Netherlands. Northward and southward the range increases: it amounts to about 3 m at Harwich and at Cromer, 3·7 m at Margate and off Wells, Norfolk, and 4·3 m at Dover and Hunstanton. Beyond Dungeness the tidal ranges are related to a projected amphidromic point north-west of Southampton. Weymouth and Southampton have ranges comparable with those of Yarmouth, and the height of the tide increases both eastward and westward, reaching 3 m at Portsmouth and Brixham, 3·7 m at Littlehampton, and 5·5 m near Rye.

Around the Irish Sea there are striking contrasts in tidal phenomena, for here we find both the highest and the lowest ranges in the British Isles. An astonishingly low range of only ·6 m occurs on the Kintyre coast near Machrihanish (though there is no port there to make use of it); it is associated with an amphidromic point between Kintyre and Islay. The lowest range of any port in Britain is about 1·2 m, and three towns share this distinction: Portrush, on the Derry–Antrim border, is close to the same amphidromic point; and Arklow and Wexford are near a projected amphidromic point south of Dublin. The port authority at Arklow tells us, 'the tide flows very little on this coast', while Wexford proclaims itself 'a natural harbour: there are neither piers nor docks'.

As we move from these places the range increases; it is 2 m at Belfast, 2·7 m at Dublin, 3·4 m at Holyhead, 5·5 m at Colwyn Bay, and about 8·2 m at Liverpool.

In the funnel-shaped Bristol Channel even greater heights are reached. The average tidal range is about 5·5 m in Barnstaple bay and 6 m at Swansea, 8 to 9 m at Cardiff, and about 11 m at Avonmouth, rising to the astonishing figure of 14 m at equinoctial spring tides. These are the second highest tides in the world, surpassed only in the Bay of Fundy, Nova Scotia. Massive walls and expensive lock gates are essential to retain the vast volumes of water needed in the docks at Avonmouth and Liverpool, and on a lesser scale at ports where the range is still appreciable. Unless the approach channels are exceptionally deep, large vessels must wait for the tide – an expensive process. In such ways are port and shipping finances linked with the tides.

FOR FURTHER READING

STEERS, J. A.: *The Coastline of England and Wales* (Cambridge University Press," 1946).
—— *The Sea Coast* (Collins, 1953).
WILLIAMS, W. W.: *Coastal Changes* (Routledge, 1960).
The various volumes of British Regional Geology (H.M.S.O.) include details of raised beaches and submerged forests.
For tides, see P. LAKE, *Physical Geography* (fourth edition, 1958), Part II, Chap. III, and *Admiralty Manual of Tides* (H.M.S.O.).

CHAPTER FIVE

THE PEOPLING OF THE BRITISH ISLES

TO ATTEMPT to describe in one short chapter the motives, characteristics, and distribution of the immigrants into Britain from Palæolithic times onward is to invite disaster. Yet the present is to be understood only by reference to the past, and the attempt must be made, even at the risk of the sweeping statement and the broad generalization.

Palæolithic Man

During Palæolithic times Britain was joined to the Continent, so that the earliest immigrants into what are now the British Isles did not need to take to the sea. The period coincides with the Quaternary Ice Age, and Palæolithic man was confined to southern England, since only there was the land free from the ice sheets. The total population is believed to have been very small, amounting, perhaps, to only a few hundreds.

As the temperature fluctuated, so the glaciers waxed and waned: in common with the Alpine ice sheets, four main advances are recognized, separated by three 'interglacials', and to some extent man's culture stages can be correlated with the movements of the ice. The beginning of the first advance of the ice into our lowlands is dated at about 600,000 B.C., and it is believed that the earliest inhabitants of Britain were then already laboriously chipping their stone tools. What are perhaps the first tools – 'eoliths' – are so similar to the natural flint that their human origin is debated: they are found in the gravels of north Kent and below the boulder clay of Ipswich. Certainly human, however, are the large hand-axes, choppers, and scrapers found in the Cromer area and in the gravels south-west of Bedford. They were the possessions of Chellean man, who is believed to have lived through the period of the first advance of the ice sheets and the following interglacial.

More widespread are the tools of Acheulian man, who hunted reindeer and mammoth during the second interglacial, about

300,000 years ago. They are found in the gravels of the Yare, the Ouse, the Gipping, and the Cam, and in Kent's Cavern, near Torquay. At Clacton, in Essex, a distinctive method of preparing flint tools was practised: Clactonian man struck flakes off all sides of his flint, then selected suitable flakes and trimmed their edges for use as knives or scrapers. In 1935 the Barnfield pit at Swanscombe in north Kent yielded up one of its secrets in the form of part of an Acheulian skull: the earliest known human bone in the British Isles. Yet its shape suggests that its owner's head would be almost indistinguishable from that of modern man.

Later representatives of the Old Stone Age left their implements of flint, bone, and ivory in East Anglia, south-east England, Devon, the Vale of Clwyd (in north-east Wales), and in the caves of Somerset; but the magnificent cave art of France and Spain is absent from Britain.

Mesolithic Man

The Mesolithic phase lasted from about 10,000 to 3000 B.C. It was a period of rapid climatic change and of land subsidence. As the glaciers finally receded the Arctic period merged into the Boreal, with a warm, dry climate, and this in turn gave way to the Atlantic period, with a warm, moist climate. The tundra was gradually replaced by forest; reindeer, mammoth, and woolly rhinoceros yielded to horse, ox, red deer, and wild boar. The land sank, the lowlands were submerged, and about 6000 B.C. Britain became separated from the Continent.

New settlers entered the British Isles from three directions, each group bringing its distinct culture. From the east came the Maglemosians, forest-dwellers who knew how to fell trees and hollow out canoes; they left behind them in the Tay alluvium at Perth what is claimed to be Europe's oldest boat. From the south came the Tardenoisians, unfamiliar with the heavy axe, but skilled in the production of tiny flints (microliths), designed for hafting in the now abundant wood. At Marsden, in south-west Yorkshire, a row of 35 microliths was found, apparently teeth from a 2-metre two-handled saw. The Tardenoisians tended to settle in lightly wooded areas such as the outcrops of Lower Greensand in south-east England. From the south-west came the Azilians: since they settled along the coast many of their sites must have been subsequently submerged. Fisher-folk, their characteristic weapon was the antler harpoon, and they left behind them piles of shellfish remains. Their settlements are known in caves near Oban, in the Isle of Oronsay, and in Holderness.

Mesolithic man lived in many parts of Britain. His implements are known along the coasts of Down and Antrim, where flints from the chalk have been strewn by the ice sheets; in the Isle of Man and at Aberystwyth; in the Mendips and in north Cornwall; on the moors of the south Pennines and in Northumberland and Durham. At Farnham (Surrey) are perhaps the oldest known dwellings in Britain: clustered around a spring were several irregularly shaped pits. Boughs were probably thrown across for roofs, for there were no signs of post-holes.

Neolithic Man

What has been called the Neolithic Revolution took place in the Middle East: there, while Britain remained in the Mesolithic stage, a whole series of advances were made towards civilization. The cultivation of wheat, oats, and barley began, and the new cooking demanded heatproof and watertight containers: to supply this need the art of pottery was developed. Cattle and sheep were domesticated for the first time, and the arts of spinning and weaving were learnt to use the supplies of wool.

About 3000 B.C. immigrants bringing the new culture began to land on the shores of southern and eastern England and on the borders of the Irish Sea. With the aid of hoes they cultivated the thin soils of the chalk and limestone; and they constructed the so-called causewayed camps: in these the ditches are crossed at intervals by causeways which allow access to the centre. The ditches were used for pit dwellings, while the animals were confined in the central area. Such are the camps at Windmill Hill (near Avebury), Whitehawk (near Brighton), and the Trundle (near Chichester); they must have formed only temporary shelters, for primitive cultivation necessitates a semi-nomadic existence.

Neolithic man searched carefully for the raw material for his implements. He mined flint in the South Downs, in Wessex, and at Grimes' Graves, near Thetford in Norfolk. Innumerable shafts were sunk and linked by underground galleries; the miners used antler picks to lever out the flints and ox shoulder-blades to shovel them up. The tools were manufactured in workshops above the mines.

The processes of grinding and polishing brought the production of the axe-head to its highest development, and suitable stone was highly prized. It was found in several places, at Penwith, in the tip of Cornwall; at Tievebulliagh Hill, in Antrim; at Great Langdale, in Westmorland; and at Graig Lwyd, on the slope of Penmaenmawr Mountain, in Caernarvonshire. These implements circulated widely in England and central and south Scotland, and give some indication of the trade routes of the time. Neolithic axes were surprisingly efficient: in an experiment in Denmark three men managed to clear 500 square metres of birch forest in four hours using a Neolithic blade: more than 100 trees were felled with the same axe, which had not been sharpened for about 4000 years.

The dead were buried in chambered tombs, designed as communal graves – perhaps as family vaults. Some are covered by earthen mounds (long barrows), and it is believed that originally they all were. These megalithic (large stone) monuments are largely concentrated in Atlantic Britain. Wessex (*i.e.,* Hampshire, Wiltshire, Dorset, and Somerset) boasts 150 long barrows; Wiltshire alone has 80. In Anglesey there are records of 40 chambered tombs; in the Scilly Isles there are 43. They are common in Caithness, in the Shetlands, and around the Irish Sea. They are to be seen in the Pennines, and on the chalk hills of Yorkshire and Lincolnshire, while an isolated group stands in the Medway valley. In Ireland they are widespread. Not all megalithic monuments, however, are of this period: the stone circles in particular date from the early Bronze Age.

The Bronze Age

The Bronze Age lasted from about 2000 to 450 B.C. It was heralded by the arrival from across the North Sea of the Beaker Folk. They have been given this name from their characteristic handleless and spoutless pottery drinking-vessels; they also brought with them small copper and bronze knives – the first metal objects to reach Britain.

Bronze had long been valued in the Middle East: unlike stone, it did not readily split, and bronze tools could be easily resharpened; but its spread to Britain was gradual, and for a long time bronze circulated side by side with flint. The British metal industry became firmly established in southern Ireland, which developed into one of the greatest producers in western Europe. Gold was collected from the streams of the Wicklow Hills; copper was extracted from the lodes of Waterford and western Cork; and the small proportion of tin required for bronze production was imported from Cornwall. Irish craftsmen manufactured gold brooches, torques, and lunulae (crescent-shaped neck ornaments), and bronze axes and daggers, swords and sickles, cauldrons, buckets, and even razors. These were traded in Britain and on the Continent. Itinerant bronze-founders collected outworn implements for recasting: eleven of their hoards have been discovered on the Sussex downs alone.

Whitby jet and amber from the Baltic were also prized, and were fashioned into beads for personal ornament.

Several Bronze Age villages are known. Some, like Skara Brae in the Orkneys, were primitive: here a pastoral and fishing community lived in massive stone huts with walls 1·5 to 2·5 m thick, furnished, however, with stone bed-frames and built-in cupboards, and supplied with efficient sewers. Others, like the village on Plumpton Plain, near Brighton, were more complex: here a group of round timber-framed wattle-and-daub huts was protected by earthen banks; close by were the cattle pens, and round about were the small, squarish cornfields, cultivated by means of the newly introduced two-ox plough.

Specific trade routes came into existence in the Bronze Age, some of them inherited from Neolithic times: they include the Icknield and Pilgrims' Ways, and a routeway from Ireland to Denmark and north Germany by way of the Aire gap and the York Wolds. Maps of the finds and sites of the Bronze Age indicate that virtually every part of Britain was penetrated.

Much energy, however, was devoted to ceremonial ends. The magnificent monuments of Avebury and Stonehenge were planned and constructed, together with many stone circles in Atlantic Britain and round barrows in the chalk and limestone districts. To see the Priddy Nine Barrows silhouetted on the Mendip skyline is an experience not easily forgotten.

The Iron Age

Between 700 and 500 B.C. Celtic-speaking tribes venturing along the western sea route reached Ireland and Wales and introduced their languages there. Though they may have used iron, their culture was essentially that of the Bronze Age; and later immigrants from the Continent hardly affected Ireland and Wales.

In England and Scotland the Iron Age is deemed to have lasted from about 500 B.C. until the Roman invasion of A.D. 43. A series of cold, wet summers seems to have ruined the harvests of northern Europe and to have sent the Celtic peoples across the Channel in search of new lands. With them they brought a knowledge of iron-smelting, and new implements quickly replaced those of bronze. With iron spades and sickles and iron-shod ploughs the newcomers cultivated the chalk and limestone soils extensively, drying grain in clay ovens and storing it in pits dug into the solid rock (Fig. 14).

Associated with these 'Celtic fields' are the hill forts which were characteristic of Iron Age society. The sites were carefully chosen, partly with a view to natural defence, but always in commanding

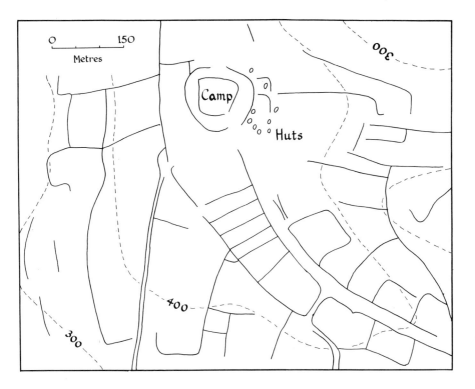

Fig. 14. THE LANDSCAPE OF THE IRON AGE

This is a camp and field system on Thundersbarrow Hill in the South Downs, near Shoreham. It lies in an area particularly rich in remains of the Iron Age – in the stretch of the downlands between the rivers Ouse and Adur there are 32 settlement sites, and field systems cover 18 per cent of the area. The Mendip Hills too are rich in Iron Age relics. Heights are in feet. *After E. C. Curwen.*

positions. The hill forts appear to have been temporary refuges rather than permanent habitations. Water-supply, now lacking, may have been easier in a climate damper than the present. At first protected by simple earthworks, they were later defended by exceedingly complex multiple banks and ditches, adapted to the use of hand catapults. Maiden Castle, in Dorset, the finest of them all, has 8 km of earthwork, enclosing 44 ha. The imagination reels at the labour involved in raising such fortifications. At Worlebury, north of Weston-super-Mare, the ramparts were formed of massive limestone blocks, and the eastern entrance was protected by six parallel ditches and banks. Here about 100 grain-storage pits can be seen within the camp.

Near Glastonbury and Meare, in Somerset, excavations have

revealed two Iron Age lake villages. An enormous amount of tree-felling must have preceded the construction of the 'rafts' of logs on which they were built. In the Glastonbury village there were about 60 round huts, supplied with a landing-stage and protected by a stockade. For the first time lead is seen in Britain; the inhabitants used it to sink their fishing-nets and to weight their looms, and they must have mined it in the Mendips. They were skilled carpenters, using the lathe to turn the spokes of wheels and the rungs of ladders. Innumerable objects of iron and bronze, pottery, lead and glass, bone, and even wood were preserved in the peat, and can be seen in the museums at Taunton and Glastonbury; and in the elegant scrolls on their pottery we see a reflection of the artistic genius of the Celts, with such masterpieces of metalwork and enamelling as the Witham sword and the Battersea shield.

In the latest phase of the Iron Age, new waves of Celtic invaders began from about 75 B.C. to overrun southern and eastern England. They brought a heavier, wheeled plough, drawn by 4 oxen, and fitted with a mouldboard to turn the sod. Here for the first time was the equipment necessary to cultivate the clay soils of the lowlands; and in the headquarters of these tribes we see the beginnings of our first towns. The Iceni settled in •Norfolk, the Brigantes in west Yorkshire, and the Atrebates in Berkshire. In Hertfordshire were the Catuvellauni, whose later capital was at St Albans; in Essex were the Trinovantes, based upon Colchester. These newcomers turned their pottery on the wheel; they used the horse-drawn chariot in warfare, and they minted the first coins in Britain. These people met the first impact of the Roman conquest.

The Roman Period

The Roman armies landed in Kent in A.D. 43 and swept across southern England. It took them only four years to reach central England, and across it they constructed as a temporary frontier the 320-km-long Fosse Way. By A.D. 49 the Romans were producing pigs of lead in the Mendip Hills.

Their leaders had a remarkable grasp of the physical geography of Britain. The Fosse Way was planned so as to utilize both the natural ramparts of the Jurassic scarps and the 'ditches' of the Severn, Avon, and Trent. South and east of it was the civil zone, with the majority of the villas and the chief towns; north and west of it was potentially hostile country, dominated by camps and forts and threaded by military roads. The Romans did not attempt to conquer Ireland; nor was their hold on Scotland, Wales, and Cornwall very secure. But to lowland Britain they brought the highest civilization it had hitherto known: suites of baths, spacious towns, monumental architecture, and mosaic pavements on the one hand; wine flagons, window glass, locks and keys, pumps, and plumbing on the other.

This civilization was imposed on the countryside: it could be supported only with the aid of tribute and slavery, and most of it perished at the end of Roman rule. Yet something survived – the lines of the roads and the sites of the towns. The Romans planned and built about 8000 km of roads in Britain, with the trunk routes radiating from London. With a width of 6 to 7 metres, soundly constructed on raised causeways, cambered and well drained, these highways formed the first road system of England and Wales, and its main lines are still in use. They include Watling Street, from Canterbury to London and on to Chester; Ermine Street, from London to Lincoln; the London to Colchester road; much of the Fosse Way, from Exeter to Lincoln; and the trunk road of south Wales.

Perhaps the greatest contribution of the Romans to posterity, however, lay in their choice of town sites. They realized the significance of the head of an estuary, and many towns of Roman foundation are so situated: among them are Gloucester, Exeter, Chester, Southampton, Carlisle, Rochester, and most important of all, London. The Romans perceived the strategic importance of Lincoln, York, and Newcastle-on-Tyne, and noted the valley focus of Manchester. They laid the foundation of the port of Dover, building a lighthouse on each side of the gash in the chalk cliffs which marked the mouth of the little river Dour.

But contemporary with the Roman towns and villas (farming estates) the native Briton carried on his traditional way of life, dating from the Iron Age or earlier (Fig. 15); some, perhaps most, of the Welsh hill forts were actually built during the Roman period. Rooted more firmly in the soil, the native culture outlasted that of the Romans.

Saxons and Danes

Sporadic raids by the Saxons were a danger during the third and fourth centuries A.D., and the Romans organized the Forts of the Saxon Shore to combat them. The Saxon homeland in north-west Germany was overcrowded; a rising sea-level was reducing the available land; the Goths were pressing from the east. Soon after the withdrawal of the Roman forces the Saxons arrived in earnest, not now as raiders but as invaders and settlers. Their spread can be deduced from the distribution of early (pagan) cemeteries, from

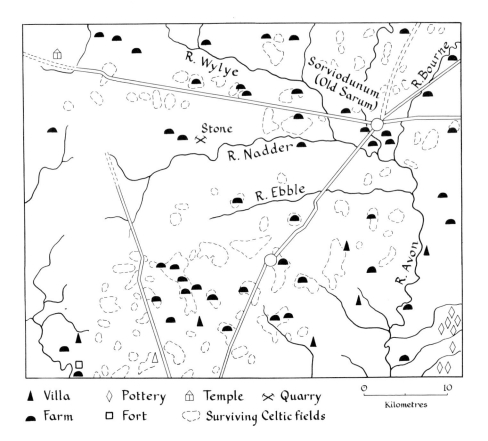

Fig. 15. THE LANDSCAPE OF ROMAN TIMES

The more sophisticated Romano-Britons lived in the towns or in villas near the valley floors, while on the hills contemporary native life continued with little change. This area in Hampshire is extraordinarily rich in Roman remains. But few of the road lines are still in use, and Old Sarum was abandoned in the Middle Ages. *After the O.S. Map of Roman Britain, 1956, text. Crown copyright reserved.*

early place-names, and from literary sources such as the *Anglo-Saxon Chronicle* and the writings of Bede.

The first landings took place about A.D. 450, in Kent. Thanet was occupied, and settlers spread westward in a zone following the line of Watling Street. Bede describes these people as Jutes, and their wheel-turned pottery and luxurious jewellery with its accomplished enamelwork certainly distinguishes them from the rest of the Anglo-Saxon invaders. The people later known as the South Saxons traditionally landed near Selsey Bill in A.D. 477, and within twenty years had occupied a broad coastal belt extending as far east as Pevensey: this formed the core of the later Sussex. Surrey ('the southern district') was peopled by way of the Thames and Wandle, and its heart consisted of the light soils on both flanks of the North Downs. The nucleus of Wessex was a group of settlements on the Thames gravels in the Dorchester–Wallingford district; though how the Saxons reached the area is not clear.

Saxon boats glided up the smooth, broad rivers of the Fens; the settlers entered west Suffolk by the valley of the Lark and Cambridgeshire by the Cam; they penetrated Bedfordshire by the upper Ouse, and Northamptonshire by the Nene, crossing the watershed to reach the Avon valley of Warwickshire. They reached Rutland and Leicestershire by the Welland, and south Lincolnshire by the Witham and the Slea. In all these districts Anglo-Saxon graves have yielded pottery and brooches datable to A.D. 500 or earlier.

Merging with the Avon valley settlers were other groups who had entered by the Humber and followed the Trent upstream, to reach the Midlands by the valley of the Soar: so was formed the nucleus of Mercia. The Yorkshire Wolds were settled early, and from there pioneers moved north into the Vale of Pickering, east into Holderness, and west into the Vale of York: the combined group formed Bernicia, which appears to have sent offshoots along the coast northward to colonize Northumberland and Durham.

Most of the present-day villages of the English lowlands originated from settlements of our Anglo-Saxon forefathers in the so-called Dark Ages. Possessing a heavy plough, the Saxons were able to cultivate clay soils, and they made determined attacks on the forests to clear the way for crops. They were not at first attracted to the remains of the Roman towns, and they avoided settling along the Roman roads. Instead they built their villages on the river terraces, or (as in the east Midlands) on patches of glacial gravel, offering dry sites and drinking-water from shallow wells. They occupied the sheltered belts at the foot of the chalk and limestone ridges, and whole strings of villages were built along lines of springs (Fig. 16). Round them the land was farmed in great open fields, cultivated in bundles of narrow strips.

The Saxons did not occupy Ireland or Atlantic Britain, where the inhabitants maintained their pre-Roman cultures largely intact. At the battle of Mount Badon, about A.D. 500, the Saxons suffered a crushing defeat at the hands of the British chieftain, Arthur: unfortunately, its site is unknown, though it may have been in Wessex. Elsewhere the British seem to have been assimilated into Saxon England. Yet some elements survived: the Roman towns, though they were abandoned, were not sacked; and many exquisite

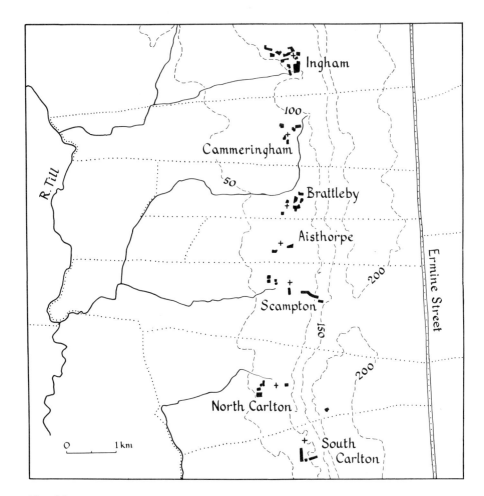

Fig. 16. THE LANDSCAPE OF SAXON TIMES

This area lies about 8 km north of Lincoln. Of the seven villages, five have Saxon and two Danish names. The settlers avoided the Roman road on the summit of the ridge. They built their huts on the level bench of Lower Lias at the foot of the scarp above the reach of flood, where springs from the base of the limestone offered a reliable supply of clean water. Each village group claimed a narrow strip of land running across the structure so that it shared in land of all types. It is tempting to see in these straight parish boundaries (shown by dotted lines) the relics of Roman administration. The line of villages can be traced through the whole length of Lincolnshire and into Northamptonshire. Heights are in feet.

bronze hanging bowls, clearly of Celtic manufacture, have been found in Saxon graves.

The Saxons had enjoyed three centuries of peaceful agriculture when the first three longships of the Danes arrived: this momentous event is described in the *Anglo-Saxon Chronicle* under the year 787.

This year King Bertric took Edburga the daughter of Offa to wife. And in his days came first three ships of the Northmen from the land of robbers. The reve then rode thereto, and would drive them to the king's town; for he knew not what they were; and there was he slain. These were the first ships of the Danish men who sought the land of the English nation.

From sporadic raids the Danes turned to invasion and settlement; but we cannot here trace the details of the Danish conquests and reverses. By a treaty with Alfred about 886 they were confined to East Anglia (north of the Thames and east of the Lea), the Fens and their borders (as far west as Bedford and the Ouse), and the land north and east of Watling Street.

In its later phase the struggle between Saxon and Dane virtually became a civil war, in which the Danes were firmly settled in eastern England. Unlike the Saxons, they made good use of the Roman roads, and they settled in the remains of the Roman towns and built others for themselves. Among the towns which owe much of their early development to Danish influence are Norwich, York, and Thetford, and the 'Five Boroughs' (each the centre of a Danish army) of Lincoln, Nottingham, Derby, Leicester, and Stamford.

The evidence of place-names suggests that in eastern England the Danes settled among the Anglo-Saxons, filling in the gaps and occupying the difficult areas; farther north the Danes were more numerous, and perhaps dominant. In the Lake District and north Lancashire Scandinavian place-names are common, but here the colonization seems to have been later, and to have been conducted not by Danes but by Norwegians, some of whom may have come from bases on the east coast of Ireland.

Many later immigrants have entered Britain, but their numbers have been small in relation to the total population: Normans, Flemings, Dutch, and Jews have all left their imprints on Britain. It is clear that the people of Britain are racially extremely mixed. They do not all speak the same language; and many of those who do speak English betray by their accents something of their origin.

In spite of the long time which has elapsed since the initial settlement, recognizable physical differences still exist in the population today. The findings of earlier anthropologists have been confirmed by recent studies of the distribution of the main blood groups.

In northern England a remarkably sharp line separates high frequencies of blood group 'O' from high frequencies of blood group 'A'. The line encircles the higher parts of the Lake District and passes eastward, north of Penrith and south of Consett, towards the coast south of Sunderland. In England south of this line and in south Wales the population with blood group 'A' is physically similar to that over most of Europe, and presumably derives from the Anglo-Saxon settlers.

But in what we may call the highland zone or Atlantic Britain, north and west of the line, is a population (with blood group 'O') of different physical character, whose origins apparently are to be sought in prehistoric migrations. The region includes Scotland, northern England, north Wales, and Ireland.

Along the western coasts of Ireland are tall, heavy folk with dark hair and eyes, broad heads, and wide faces, whose counterparts are to be seen in western Normandy, in Sardinia, among the Basques, and in Iceland. These people have affinities with what is known of the Mesolithic body frame. In the rest of the highland zone are shorter people with lighter hair and eyes, who appear to retain the characteristics of Neolithic and Iron Age folk. There are a few remote moorland areas in Wales – in the Plynlimon plateau and in the Black Mountain of Carmarthenshire – where an earlier type seems to survive. This is short, with a long head, dark hair, and prominent brows. There are high frequencies here of blood group 'B', which are unique in western Europe, though they are common in eastern Europe; and it has been suggested that in these isolated districts there remain some representatives of the inhabitants of Palæolithic times.

FOR FURTHER READING

Books

The Anglo-Saxon Chronicle (Dent, Everyman Library, 1953).

THE VENERABLE BEDE, *Ecclesiastical History of the English Nation* (Dent, Everyman Library, 1935).

COLE, SONIA: *The Neolithic Revolution* (British Museum, 1961).

COLLINGWOOD, R. G. and MYRES, J. N. L.: *Roman Britain and the English Settlements* (Oxford University Press, 1937).

FLEURE, H. J.: *A Natural History of Man in Britain* (Collins, 1951).

FOX, SIR C.: *The Personality of Britain* (National Museum of Wales, fourth edition, 1952).

HAWKES, J. and C.: *Prehistoric Britain* (Penguin, 1944; Chatto and Windus, 1947).

MITCHELL, J. B.: *Historical Geography* (English Universities Press, 1954).

OAKLEY, K. P.: *Man, the Tool-maker* (British Museum, 1961).

RIVET, A. L. F.: *Town and Country in Roman Britain* (Hutchinson, 1958).

WINBOLT, S. E.: *Britain B.C.* (Penguin, 1943).

Article

SUNDERLAND, E.: 'Anthropological Distributions in the British Isles', in *Geography* (Jan. 1961).

Maps

O.S. Map of Roman Britain, third edition, 1956.

O.S. Map of Southern Britain in the Iron Age, 1962.

PART 2
Regional Geography
Section A: The Celtic Lands

CHAPTER SIX

NORTHERN IRELAND

OUR STUDY of the regional geography of the British Isles begins with the Celtic lands – Scotland, Wales, and Ireland – where the Celtic speech persisted longest, and in some measure still survives. Cornwall, though it retains some Celtic traits, we exclude on account of its close links with Devon, and we treat these two counties as the 'province' of south-west England.

The Celtic lands border – and are united by – the Irish Sea, which throughout prehistory and history has formed a highway of culture and commerce. They share a humid and equable climate, with unusually mild winters and delayed autumns, though this is essentially a coastal phenomenon, which does not extend into central or eastern Scotland or into the heart of Wales. The Irish Sea, indeed, has been christened the 'British Mediterranean'; while this may be a fair description of its position, however, we should think of its vegetation in terms of the fuchsia and the hydrangea rather than the olive and the vine.

Geologically the Celtic lands are composed largely of Archæan and Palæozoic rocks, which range from the Pre-Cambrian of Anglesey and the north-west fringe of Scotland, through the Cambrian and Ordovician rocks of north Wales and the Silurian of southern Scotland and north-eastern Ireland, to the Old Red Sandstone of the Moray Firth, central Wales, and south-western Ireland, and the Carboniferous rocks of central Scotland and Ireland. Any later rocks are quite local in their occurrence.

Structurally we can recognize the effects of two series of earth movements. In Scotland and in most of Ireland the outcrops run generally north-east and south-west, reflecting the ridges, furrows, and faults which originated in Siluro–Devonian times: this is the Caledonian trend. In south Wales and south-western Ireland, however, the trend is more nearly east and west: this is the Armorican (Hercynian) trend, which was initiated later, in Carbo–Permian times.

In addition to their physical unity the Celtic lands exhibit a considerable uniformity of culture. The Romans did not penetrate

Ireland, and their hold on Wales and Scotland was more nominal than real; nor were these regions settled by the Saxons. Consequently, in many parts the pattern of rural settlement is descended directly from the Iron Age or even earlier cultures. Dispersed farmsteads are typical of many areas, and where the population is grouped together in hamlets the families of the different farmsteads are often related by kinship: the hamlet forms a larger family.

Northern Ireland

Northern Ireland is a self-governing state – the only one – within the United Kingdom. Since its establishment in 1921 it has possessed its own Parliament in Belfast, which legislates on all domestic matters. In addition Northern Ireland is represented by 12 Members in the Parliament at Westminster. The name of the Province is somewhat misleading, since the most northerly part of the whole island – the Malin Head peninsula – falls within 'southern' Ireland. 'North-east Ireland' would undoubtedly be a more accurate description of the country, whose boundaries run from Lough Foyle in the north almost to Donegal Bay in the west, and to Carlingford Lough in the east. Culturally and socially, Northern Ireland has close contacts with Great Britain. English and Scottish settlers were 'planted' there in the early seventeenth century, and in many parts the compact farm and the planned market town have superseded the native pattern of small, scattered plots of land.

Northern Ireland contains six of the nine counties of the historic province of Ulster, and 'Ulster' is still inaccurately used as an alternative name. These counties comprise Down, Antrim, Londonderry, Tyrone, Armagh, and Fermanagh. The boundaries of four of these counties meet in Lough Neagh (the largest lake in the United Kingdom), and that of a fifth narrowly misses it. The Lough Neagh lowlands, indeed, together with their hilly borders, form the core of Northern Ireland, beyond which lie only Fermanagh (mainly the basin of the Erne) and western Tyrone (essentially that of the upper Foyle).

From the point of view of structure and geology, Northern Ireland forms part of a larger province which extends north-eastwards into Scotland and south-westward into Eire. The same powerful faults which bound the Scottish Lowlands can be recognized in Northern Ireland: to the north the Highland Boundary fault of Scotland extends beyond the Irish Sea for 8 km from Cushendun and for a further 35 km between Omagh and Lough Erne. North of it are metamorphic rocks similar to those of the Scottish Highlands; south of it is the Old Red Sandstone corresponding to outcrops of similar material in the Scottish Low-lands; and near Cushendall, where it reaches the sea, is the appropriately named Red Bay.

The southern boundary fault passes south-west in a direct line for more than 160 km from the neighbourhood of Belfast to Cloone, in south-east Leitrim (Eire): for most of its course this forms a physical boundary, separating a lowland to the north-west, floored by Triassic and Carboniferous rocks, from a plateau to the south-east, composed of resistant Silurian and Ordovician strata.

In contrast to the Scottish Lowlands, however, much of the land between the two faults has been flooded by the great outpourings of lava of Tertiary times, which have also overflowed northward on to the metamorphic rocks. This basaltic plateau of Antrim extends northward and eastward of Lough Neagh as far as the sea. The lake itself has resulted, perhaps, from the sagging of the strata following the emission of so much material from below: it may be compared with lakes Taupo (New Zealand) and Victoria (central Africa), both of which occur in similar volcanic country.

Rural Settlement

There are two types of settlement in Ulster: native and plantation. The native pattern, of which relics still remain, consisted of open clusters of farm buildings known as clachans. The members of each clachan were related and the family name was sometimes applied to the whole hamlet: thus in the south-east of county Down 2 km or so north of Ardglass are Kearneystown, Connors-town, and Blaneystown. In 1890 three of the five dwellings in the last hamlet were still occupied by Blaneys.

Unlike the English village, the buildings were arranged to facili-tate a corporate life. In Blaneystown (Fig. 17) the barns occupied the eastern side of an open court with the stables opposite. The dwellings were on the other two sides, and centrally placed was the well. Around the settlement were large open fields, cultivated in narrow strips; and, as in the English manor, each man's strips were scattered so as to allow him a share in all the different qualities of land: these strips were re-allocated annually. Beyond the arable fields were the hill pastures, and here several individuals held grazing rights over the same tract of land.

The clachans are fast disappearing, and the strip system ('run-dale') formally ceased in the nineteenth century, but it has left behind a legacy of small farms: nearly 60 per cent. of all the farms in Northern Ireland are of less than 30 acres – and that figure includes rough grazing land. The fields themselves are tiny, and in

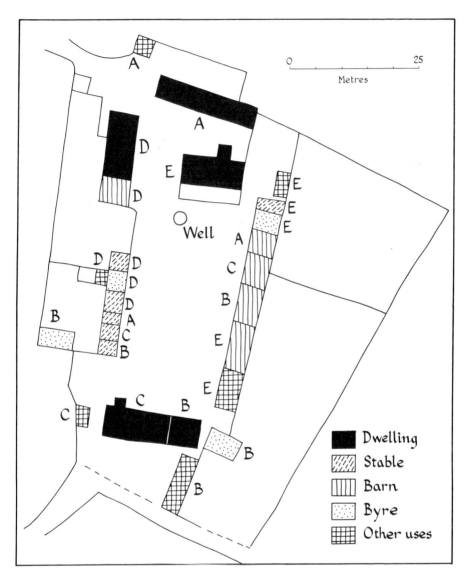

Fig. 17. A CLACHAN: BLANEYSTOWN IN 1890

The inhabitants were related to one another (there were three Blaneys), and the buildings were arranged to facilitate a corporate life. Today in the townland of which this forms part the number of farms has declined from 19 to 7, and the population has shrunk by 60 per cent. The owners of the buildings in 1890 were as follows: (A) B. Blaney; (B) J. Blaney; (C) T. Blaney; (D) W. Casselie; (E) R. Ward. The average size of holding was about 6 hectares. Blaneystown is near Ardglass in county Down.

many instances those belonging to an individual farmer are still scattered. In Corick townland[1] (in south-east Londonderry) one farmer has to manage a dozen detached plots of land; his neighbour farms 20 plots which are spread over 2·6 square km of country.[2] Rough grazing land is still often held in common: in parts of the Sperrin Mountains (on the Londonderry–Tyrone border) 30 to 55 farmers share grazing rights over the same stretch of hillside. Theoretically these rights are specified in terms of the number of stock allowed; but in the absence of supervision overgrazing can and does occur. These legacies of the past represent a real burden on Irish farming, and only slowly are they being overcome. Nevertheless, farming in Northern Ireland is gradually becoming mechanized, and scientific methods are gaining ground.

Where the farm holdings have been consolidated agricultural advance is easier. New farmsteads have been built in the middle of compact plots, and the clachan has often become deserted. In a narrow valley the new farm frequently takes the form of a long rectangle running from the valley floor to the hilltop, and in this way the farmer retains his share of each quality of land. In drumlin country such as the district west of Lough Neagh the farmstead has been built at or near the summit of the drumlin (at about 38 metres), and the hill has been divided into fields. The surrounding lowland is at about 20 metres, and consists partly of grass, partly of bog. In the boggy areas we see the clearest examples of compact farms whose layouts have been determined by the physical environment (Fig. 18).

THE REGIONS OF NORTHERN IRELAND

The Antrim Plateau

Employing as a basis structure and land use, we may distinguish 9 regions in Northern Ireland (Fig. 19). We begin our description with the Antrim plateau. Lava underlies almost the whole of county Antrim, and extends westward well into Londonderry; but the lowland areas of the Bann corridor and the fringe of Lough Neagh are distinct in character and form a separate region.

The basalt plateau presents a steep scarp to the south-east which backs the north-west shore of Belfast Lough. From 100 metres at base it rises to plateau levels of about 300 metres, and summits of over 370 metres. The original thickness of the lava flows may have

[1] In Ireland the smallest administrative unit is known as the townland – *cf.* the English parish.
[2] Jean M. Graham, *Settlement and Population, in Belfast and its Regional Setting* (British Association, 1952).

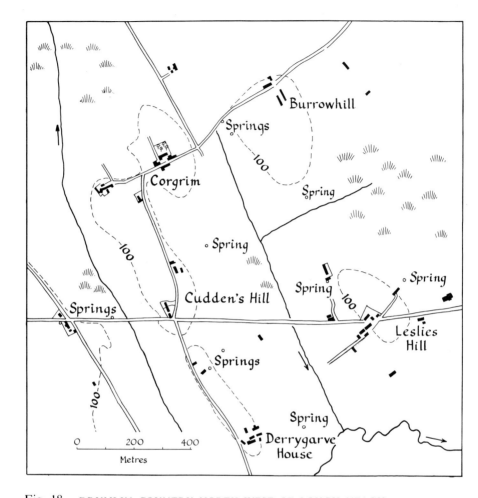

Fig. 18. DRUMLIN COUNTRY NORTH-WEST OF LOUGH NEAGH

The pattern of drainage and marsh, the location of farms, and the alignment of roads all reflect the distribution of drumlins. Heights are in feet.

been much greater: in their most complete form they now reach about 440 metres in thickness. Peaty moorland, with hardly a patch of improved land, covers a great tract of country stretching from Fair Head in the north almost to Belfast in the south and as far as the coastal headlands in the east.

Along the coast, however, the monotony is broken by a series of narrow glens which offer possibilities for stock-rearing. Their steep sides are being planted with trees, their floors are under grass, which in accordance with Irish practice is ploughed up after a run

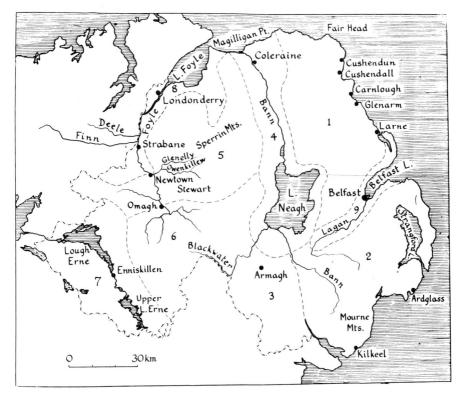

Fig. 19.   THE REGIONS OF NORTHERN IRELAND

Key to numbering: 1. Antrim Plateau; 2. County Down; 3. County Armagh; 4. Lough Neagh lowlands and lower Bann Valley; 5. Londonderry and north Tyrone uplands; 6. South Tyrone; 7. Erne basin; 8. Lower Foyle basin; 9. Belfast Corridor.

of years. The roads are lined with plots of potatoes and oats. The markets for this produce are the small centres of Cushendun, Cushendall, Carnlough, and Glenarm.

The only town of any size is Larne. A market town, industrial centre, and port, Larne has doubled its size in two generations to reach a population of 18,242. Its position on the opposite coast from Stranraer, and at a distance of only 56 km, has allowed the development of traffic on a short sea route; to this in recent years has been added the lorry-ferry link with Preston. Prominent among its industries are textiles and electrical engineering; but the port is too small to cope with the vast turbo-generators which are being manufactured there, and these are shipped from Belfast.

County Down

In county Down the Silurian rocks have been reduced to a pene-plain comparable to that of the Southern Uplands of Scotland. Its surface is strewn with glacial material which is heaped up to form innumerable drumlins. This material is quite local in origin, and can usually be traced back to the solid rocks a few km away to the north-west. Some of the drumlins can be seen on the western side of Strangford Lough, where they stand out to form islands.

Most of the surface of county Down has been cleared of bog and forms productive farm-land. Near Belfast the farmers specialize in milk production and market gardening; farther south poultry becomes more important. The Ards peninsula, east of Strangford Lough, is relatively sunny and dry, and here barley is grown, for animal food. In the hills to the south young cattle and sheep are reared, to be fattened in the lowlands: they are handled at the stock markets of Ballynahinch and Downpatrick.

In the south of Down are the granite mountains of Mourne: they rise steeply from the Irish Sea to rounded summits at more than 600 metres O.D. Above 200 metres there is hardly a farm; but the land serves as rough grazing for sheep, and as a gathering ground for the water-supply of Belfast, while its slopes have been planted with trees. In striking contrast is the lowland triangle by Kilkeel,· where farmers are busy cultivating the fertile glacial soils, for potatoes and oats in tiny holdings.

The regional capital for southern Down is Newry – a small port which retains its eighteenth-century flavour. It shares in the inshore fisheries, is a tourist centre for the mountains of Mourne, and has light industries, such as the recently (1962) established manufacture of zip-fasteners. Ardglass, south of Strangford Lough, is an important fishing-port: it lands both herring and white fish, possesses kippering kilns and a canning factory and a newly established fish-meal plant.

County Armagh

Armagh and Down are separated by a deep and narrow trench, a spillway through which the water from an enlarged Lough Neagh once reached the sea towards the close of the Ice Age. Extending from Portadown to Carlingford Lough, it is now followed by roads, railway, and canal. While the solid geology of both counties is similar, in Armagh the granites and Silurian rocks are largely masked by thick deposits of glacial material, heaped into drumlins, and for the most part intensively farmed.

There are bogs immediately south of Lough Neagh, but beyond is the most clearly defined fruit district of Ulster. Rhubarb is grown on reclaimed fens, with apples on the slopes of the drumlins. Strawberries and raspberries are characteristic small fruits, and there are jam factories at Portadown. This is a sheltered lowland floored by young (Tertiary) clays – the only deposits of their type in Ireland; and the lake may have a beneficial effect on the local climate. Equally important, perhaps, is the strength of English farming traditions in the district. Farther south the landscape is more typically Irish: the farmer grows oats and potatoes, and he rears sheep, cattle, poultry, and pigs.

Armagh, centrally placed in its county, is the most famous cathedral city in Ireland. It grew around the hill-top site chosen by St Patrick for his church in the fifth century: he in his turn may have been influenced by the proximity of Navan Fort, traditionally an even earlier capital of Ireland.

The Lough Neagh Lowlands and the Lower Bann Valley
The Lough Neagh fringe and the lowland corridor to the north geologically form part of the Tertiary basalts of Antrim; but here the surface has collapsed to form a shallow trough whose deepest part is occupied by the lake, the remainder being drained northward by the river Bann. The soils, glacial in origin, are of great diversity, and range from lake silts to outwash gravels; over wide areas there are large numbers of drumlins. The underlying lava may have enriched the soils, for they are highly productive: this is one of the most intensively cultivated districts of Northern Ireland, and in spite of a number of lowland bogs it contains a dense and well-distributed population, which reaches nearly 60 to the square km. The staple crops are oats, potatoes, and grass for seed, and, when the price warrants it, flax. Traditionally this district has been the chief flax-growing area of Northern Ireland.

The river Bann is noted for its eel fisheries, and it is from here that the London market is supplied. Coleraine is the regional centre; formerly a textile town, it now manufactures shirts. In addition it is a small port, with connections to Liverpool, Glasgow, Whitehaven, and Maryport. The bogs of the Bann corridor are cut for peat on a small scale, but they are not sufficiently large or deep for commercial mechanical methods of working.

The Uplands of Londonderry and North Tyrone
From Magilligan Point, in north Londonderry, to the far west of Tyrone there extends a great crescent of moorland. It is not uniform in geology: in central Londonderry the hills constitute the raised western edge of the basalt plateau; farther west and in north Tyrone the Sperrins are formed of metamorphic rocks similar to those of the Scottish Highlands. Everywhere, however, the effect is the same: the moors are devoid of habitation, and are used as open sheep

runs – in some cases, as we have seen, shared by many farmers. Only in a few areas is the land being put to the alternative use of afforestation.

Improved land is confined to the few valleys, such as those of the Owenkillew and Glenelly rivers. These converge near Newtown Stewart, and here is the only real gap in the moorland crescent: cut by the Strule (the name given to part of the upper Foyle), it is followed by roads and the railway from Omagh to Londonderry.

It is in remote parts such as these that remnants of the clachan and rundale survive. But not all holdings are small. Mr Sweeney farms 103 ha which stretch from the Owenkillew on to the slopes of Mullaghbolig to the south (444 m). His chief concern is his animals, and foremost among them is his flock of sheep, which comprises 5 rams, 260 ewes, and 70 ewe lambs. He runs a small herd of beef cattle, including an Aberdeen Angus bull, 10 cows, and 15 young cattle. In addition there are two sows and about 150 poultry. Only 12 of the 103 ha are arable, and half of these are usually laid down to grass. Oats is the chief cereal – it tolerates the acid soils here, derived from gneiss and schist, and there are one or two acres of barley, potatoes, and root vegetables. All these are fed to animals.

South Tyrone
In Tyrone south of the moorland crescent there are two lowlands which trend north-east and south-west, separated by a narrow tract of hill country. All three elements reflect the Caledonian earth movements, and in structure correspond to the Central Lowlands of Scotland. The larger, more northerly lowland, together with the hilly tract bordering it to the south, is developed on Old Red Sandstone; it is drained northward by a series of streams which focus on Omagh. The smaller, more southerly basin is floored with Carboniferous rocks and drained eastward by the Blackwater. Both lowlands contain extensive bogs, but otherwise the land is well-farmed and closely settled, with a density of population which reaches up to 45 per square km of improved land. These are damp areas, and as in the previous region, the emphasis is on pastoral farming. The many settlements are villages rather than towns. Fintona and Newtown Stewart each muster about 1000 people; Fivemiletown, Augher, and Balleygawley all have less than 500. Omagh (11,953) is the only town. At its sheep-fair lambs reared on the surrounding hills are sold for finishing elsewhere; its milk factory (Nestlé's) draws on farms within a radius of 25 to 30 km, and employs about 800 people.

County Fermanagh – the Erne Basin

Fermanagh thrusts south-westward into the Irish Republic, but here geography aids politics, for eastward communications are easier than westward links.

Essentially this is the basin of the Erne. Geologically the county forms the north-eastern margin of a large Carboniferous basin whose centre is floored by masses of Millstone Grit. The larger of these fall within the Republic, but the border passes through the summits of two of the smaller grit areas – Cuilcagh (669 m) and Slieve Rushen (388 m); here, as in the south Pennines, there are steep-sided plateaux whose surfaces stream with water. The limestone, which forms the solid base of the rest of Fermanagh, is largely masked with glacial drift. The exceedingly complex shorelines of the two loughs Erne reflect the countless drumlins which are present.

Near the loughs there is much lowland bog. The border runs in such a way that the two loughs Erne are in Northern Ireland, while both the headstreams and the mouth of the Erne are in Eire. Happily, the two Governments are agreed on the need for improving the drainage of the district: the Northern Ireland authorities have widened and deepened the channels between the two loughs and have improved eight tributaries which feed them; the Republican authorities have deepened the outlet channel of the lower lough, and are controlling its level from their new generating station at Cliff. It is hoped that by these means nearly 12,000 ha of potentially high-class meadow-land can be reclaimed.

There is moorland south-west of the lower lough; apart from this and the bog-land, pastoral farming is the rule (Plate 1). The only town of the region is Enniskillen, which commands the river crossing between the two lakes. Its market serves a very wide area, and some of its inhabitants engage in hand embroidery.

The Lower Foyle Basin

We have seen that at Omagh several streams combine: their water flows northward through the metamorphic rocks, first as the Strule, then as the Mourne, and beyond Strabane as the Foyle. This important north-and-south routeway is fed from the Republic by the valleys of the Finn, Deele, and Swilly, and by fertile lowlands to the south of Lough Foyle: here the Roe basin and the lakeside lowland are etched from younger rocks of Carboniferous and Triassic age, sandwiched between the metamorphic rocks to the west and the basalts to the east.

The soils of the region are based on glacial drift, and there is

Plate 1. ON DEVENISH ISLAND, LOUGH ERNE

The round tower, built as a refuge, dates from the period of the Danish raids, and stamps this scene as typically Irish. The intricate shoreline and many islands of Lough Erne reflect the drumlin topography of the district: the rounded hills in the background are drumlins. This is in a region of pastoral farming.

A. & C. Photography, Belfast

fortunately little bog here. The farmers rear and fatten cattle, both for beef and for milk. Pasture and hay are dominant everywhere, but oats and potatoes become increasingly significant as one approaches the market of Londonderry (pop. 51,850).

This city was founded in the seventeenth century by the City Companies of London (hence the name), partly as a means of easing the congestion in London. The site chosen was a hill overlooking the Foyle, and the plan included 200 houses to be arranged along a rectangular grid of streets, with a central square and cathedral, the whole enclosed by a wall. Modern Londonderry is a port, and the regional capital not only for most of Londonderry and Tyrone, but also for parts of Donegal. It is an important centre for shirt-making; but the closure of its shipyard in 1924 left a legacy of unemployment from which the town has not yet fully recovered.

Belfast and the Belfast Corridor

The Belfast corridor is a trough floored with Triassic material covered in its turn by glacial drift and in places by recent alluvium: its lowest portion has been invaded by the sea to form Belfast Lough. We have already noticed the steep scarp of basalt which bounds it to the north-west; to the south-east the boundary is equally clear, but the Ordovician and Silurian strata do not reach the height of the basalt (Braniel Hill, 179 m). This small region is the most densely peopled portion of Northern Ireland: it contains its major industries and its metropolis.

Communications are easy south-westward to the Lough Neagh basin; the Dundonald gap provides an easy passage for road and rail eastward to the farmlands of eastern Down. To the north-west the gradients are sharper, but even here roads and railways cross the hills by means of a saddle whose summit is below 120 metres. In the Belfast region Lancashire and Ayrshire coal is easily accessible, and political and cultural links are at their strongest.

Beal feirste – 'the ford of the sandbank' – originated in 1177, when John de Courcy built a castle close to the lowest fording point of the Lagan. While the modern city has many industries, there is space here to comment on only the two most characteristic activities – textiles and shipbuilding.

Domestic spinning and weaving based on locally grown flax existed before 1700. The bleaching process, which required water-power, became a specialized activity which in the Belfast district focused on the swiftly flowing Glen and Forth rivers. Side by side with the early linen industry went the manufacture of cotton; but the coal had to be imported, as well as the raw cotton, and Belfast proved unable to compete with south Lancashire. About 1850 the Belfast cotton-spinners were turning to flax, just as at the present time they are beginning to turn from flax to rayon. The large linen-mills still cling to the banks of the rivers which originally supplied the power.

The cultivation of flax has been drastically curtailed in Northern Ireland in recent years, and the industry relies almost completely on fibre imported from the Low Countries. Northern Ireland's major manufacture, the linen industry, employs about 55,000 people. Nearly three-quarters of the output is exported, the chief market being the United States.

Shipbuilding developed in Belfast in spite of a difficult river, and in the absence of a steel industry. Yet here has been built up the largest shipyard in the United Kingdom. It spreads over 120 hectares, has 18 building berths, and employs 10,000 men. In 1970 Messrs Harland and Wolff completed the world's largest ship-building dock – the only one capable of taking a million-ton vessel if and when one is built. In 1971 the yard received an order for 4 Shell tankers, each of 310,000 tons. These are the largest vessels ever to be ordered in Britain.

Belfast handles almost the whole of the coal entering Northern Ireland, which amounts to about $1\frac{1}{2}$ million tonnes a year. Other major imports include grain and feeding-stuffs and crude petroleum. The last item is a recent development and results from the establishment in 1964, in Belfast harbour, of the first oil refinery in Northern Ireland. The chief outward cargoes, in order of importance, are potatoes, iron and steel manufactures, livestock, textiles, and bacon, ham, and pork.

The port of Belfast is quite artificial. Deep and wide channels have been carved from the mudbanks of Belfast Lough, and the excavated material has been deposited in prearranged areas to build up new land for warehouses and industry. In such a manner was constructed the fine straight approach to the port, the Victoria Channel, while Queen's Island (which accommodates the aircraft plant and part of the shipyard) was formed from the debris. A low tidal range (only 3 metres at spring tides) allows the port to dispense with enclosed basins.

Belfast, indeed, with a population of 360,150, is a monument to human energy and enterprise.

FOR FURTHER READING

Books

'Belfast in its Regional Setting' (British Association, 1952).

CHARLESWORTH, J. K.: *The Geology of Ireland* (Oliver and Boyd, 1953).

—— *Historical Geology of Ireland* (Oliver and Boyd, 1963).

FREEMAN, T. W.: *Ireland,* second edition (Methuen, 1960).

ORME, A. R.: *Ireland,* The World's Landscapes (Longman, 1970).

SYMONS, L. (Ed): *Land Use in Northern Ireland* (University of London Press, 1963).

Articles

BUCHANAN, R. H.: 'Rural Change in an Irish Townland', 1890–1955, in *Advancement of Science* (March 1958).

HILL, D.: 'Land Utilisation in the Belfast Area', in *Geography* (March 1947).

JOHNSON, J. H.: 'The Commercial Use of Peat in Northern Ireland', in *Geographical Journal* (Sept.–Dec. 1959).

STEPHENS, N. and SYMONS, L. J.: 'The Lough Erne Drainage Scheme', in *Geography* (April 1956).

SYMONS, L.: 'Hill Reclamation in Northern Ireland', in *Geography* (July 1957).

—— 'Agricultural Progress in Ulster', in *Geography* (July 1959).

Maps

The Ordnance Survey Office, Dublin, publishes an excellent geological map of the whole of Ireland on the scale of 1:750,000.

A convenient topographic map is published by J. Bartholomew and Son on the scale of $\frac{1}{4}$ inch to one mile: the whole of Ireland is covered in five sheets.

The complete set of the one-inch Land Utilisation Survey maps of Northern Ireland (13 sheets) is still obtainable, published by the Government of Northern Ireland.

CHAPTER SEVEN

THE IRISH REPUBLIC

IT IS little short of impertinent to attempt to describe in a few pages the geography of the Republic of Ireland – the largest and one of the most complex of the major units that comprise the British Isles. The attempt, nevertheless, must be made, and the reader who requires a fuller treatment is referred to the excellent general work by Mr T. W. Freeman (to which the present account is greatly in debt), and to the many detailed studies, some of which are listed at the end of this chapter.

We distinguish here six major regions; our description begins with the central plain; it continues with the outlying portions of the Republic, and it concludes with the capital city, Dublin.

As the geological map (Fig. 20) shows, the underlying 'solid' formation over the greater part of central Ireland is the Carboniferous Limestone. The outlying areas almost everywhere are composed of older material: in the west and north-west they consist of ancient metamorphic rocks together with granite intrusions, and correspond with similar material in the Scottish Highlands; in the south and south-west they are formed of Old Red Sandstone, similar to central and south-east Wales; and in the south-east are Cambrian and Ordovician strata together with granite, forming a structure similar to that of north Wales. While the hilly areas of older rocks are in many places free from drift, the Carboniferous rocks of the central lowlands are largely masked by glacial material, which locally reaches a thickness of about 60 metres. In the northern part of the plain the glacial drift is heaped into drumlins; farther south it largely takes the form of eskers. There is little doubt that without the glacial material Ireland would be immeasurably poorer; it has been called her most valuable natural resource.

THE REGIONS OF THE IRISH REPUBLIC

The Drumlin Belt
The drumlin belt extends almost without a break right across the country from the neighbourhood of Dundalk to Donegal bay and to Clew bay, and there is an isolated area of drumlins in county

84

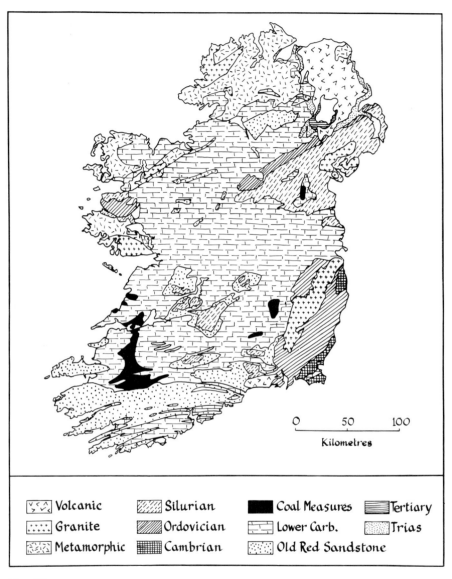

Fig. 20. A GEOLOGICAL MAP OF IRELAND

Legend:

- Volcanic
- Granite
- Metamorphic
- Silurian
- Ordovician
- Cambrian
- Coal Measures
- Lower Carb.
- Old Red Sandstone
- Tertiary
- Trias

Clare (Fig. 21). Ireland is the classic home of the phenomenon, and the Irish name (which simply means 'hill') is applied wherever it occurs, whether in the Carlisle lowlands or in New York State. A drumlin is an oval mound, usually 500 to 900 metres long, and about 15 metres high. Drumlins are composed of boulder clay, and they occur in groups or 'swarms' with their longer axes parallel and arranged in the direction of ice movement (Fig. 18, p. 74). They have been described as 'sand-banks in a sea of ice', but their precise origin is in some doubt. Their human importance, however, is clear: they form well-drained, cultivable tracts which rise from the surrounding damp pasture or bog; sometimes they form islands in a lake, such as Lough Oughter, or in the sea – for example, in Clew bay.

There is a decided contrast between the eastern and western portions of the drumlin belt, and the transition zone may be placed at the Shannon. To the east the drift is derived largely from the underlying Ordovician rocks; the climate is less moist, and there is easy communication with oversea markets through the port of Dundalk. The average farmer works 12 to 16 ha: his speciality is the production of milk, but he also rears young cattle for fattening on the rich pastures of counties Meath and Westmeath; he grows a substantial quantity of oats and potatoes, together with a little barley and flax.

To the west the drift is derived from limestone; there is a greater humidity, and the Ox mountains are almost completely covered with bog; the farms are smaller and there is little arable cultivation. This is traditionally a region of emigration, and the decline continues: county Leitrim lost as much as 10 per cent. of its population between 1951 and 1956. The contrast between east and west is well illustrated by the two regional capitals: Dundalk, in the east, is a thriving commercial centre and port with a population of 20,000; Sligo, with only 13,400 inhabitants (1966), remains essentially a market town.

The Esker Belt

South of the drumlins is the belt of eskers, whose freshness and profusion is equalled only in Finland. Eskers are long, sinuous ridges of sand and gravel which extend (often for many kilometres), across the countryside, running in a general way parallel with the major rivers. They are held to have originated either as the courses of streams below the ice sheet, or as deltas at its margin, gradually lengthening with the 'retreat' of the ice. The eskers are rarely of much agricultural value, though the drift from which they rise

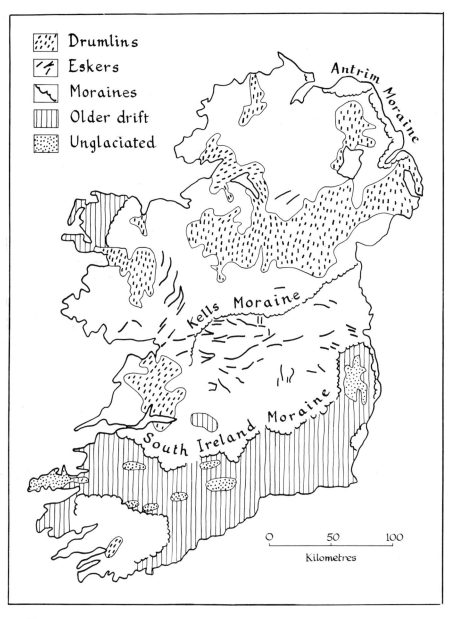

Legend:
- Drumlins
- Eskers
- Moraines
- Older drift
- Unglaciated

Antrim Moraine

Kells Moraine

South Ireland Moraine

0   50   100
Kilometres

21. SOME EFFECTS OF THE QUATERNARY ICE AGE IN IRELAND
Based on maps by F. M. Synge.

may form useful farm-land: their significance lies in the long, dry routeways which they offer, and very often the road network is a reflection of the esker systems. The Shannon crossings at Athlone, Shannonbridge, and Banagher are related to eskers, and the trunk highway between Dublin and Galway makes good use of them.

The eastern part of the esker belt comprises some of the richest grasslands of Ireland – the cattle-fattening pastures of Meath, with their extensions into Westmeath and Kildare: the market for the district is Drogheda. Farther west the proportion of bog increases and the population is more unevenly distributed; but the bogs have their value: they are exploited for fuel, they provide limited grazing, they are planted in places with conifers, and even when cut over they may reveal a clay soil on which potatoes can be raised successfully.

In east Connacht (east of Lough Corrib) the drift is largely absent, and here there is much bare limestone, with characteristic karst features, including limestone pavements, caves, and solution hollows occupied by temporary lakes. Elsewhere there are excellent limestone pastures for sheep, and this is the only part of lowland Ireland where sheep outnumber cattle. The farms, however, are small, often only 8 ha in extent; and like the corresponding section of the drumlin belt, this is a region of emigration. The regional centre for the east is Dublin, which we examine later; for the west the corresponding centre is Galway.

Commercial and fishing-port, market centre and university town, Galway is the regional capital of the north-west, and the largest town of the Irish-speaking area. Its position as a market is related to its site at the junction between two contrasting regions: to the east are lowland pastures with soils based on limestone or limestone drift; to the west are hill lands with bog and rough grazing, formed on ancient metamorphic rocks. In addition Galway commands one of the few easy routes across the barrier set by Lough Corrib and the river Corrib. Compared to English towns, Galway, with a population of 24,597 (1966), is quite small; but its service area has a radius of 80 km. There is daily bus connection with Dublin along the trunk road (T4). The port is used by vessels of up to 3000 gross tons, and it maintains regular services with the Aran Islands, where nearly 1700 people support themselves on only 47 square kilometres in virtual self-sufficiency.

Donegal and West Connacht

In spite of their physical separation, Donegal and west Connacht are sufficiently similar to be grouped together. Metamorphic rocks form the framework of each, together with granite intrusions, and the structure is similar to that of the Scottish Highlands, though the Caledonian trend (south-west and north-east) is more evident in Donegal than in west Connacht. The remarkably straight trough in Donegal between Glen Lough and the Gweebarra estuary is aligned almost exactly with Glenmore, in Scotland, and may represent a continuation of the same faults. The granites weather slowly into rounded moors, while the quartzite yields sharper, conical forms, as in the 'Twelve Bens' of Connemara.

The two sub-regions share in the heavy rainfall, the strong winds, and the high humidity of the Atlantic fringe; and over most of the area the natural vegetation is bog. There are 1000 square km of uninterrupted and uninhabited bog in north-west Mayo, and a further 750 square km west of Lough Corrib.

The population is almost entirely coastal. The farmer can make his thin soil productive only by the laborious application of sea-weed and sand. The farms are the smallest in Ireland, for by this method a single family cannot cultivate more than a hectare or so of arable land. In north-west Donegal the average holding is only 3 ha; there is thus an extraordinarily high density of population, which in places reaches 150 per square km of improved land: the cottages are so close together that the road resembles the main street of a continuous village. In these circumstances the family cannot support itself from the land alone. The farmer is also a part-time fisherman; he does his share of road-repairing in the service of the county; his children emigrate, seasonally or per-manently, and their remittances help to keep the home together. Since 1851 the population of Donegal has declined by more than 50 per cent.

The farmer grows oats and potatoes, and he keeps a few sheep and cattle on the hillside, for fattening in the richer pastures of the east. Home spinning and weaving and knitting were traditional occupations in the past, and to a limited extent they survive. Rough tweeds and 'Connemara socks' are still made at home in Galway; in Donegal there are factory industries, such as the manufacture of knitted carpets at Killybegs, of tweeds at Convoy and Donegal town, and of embroidery at Mountcharles.

Limerick and Clare

The counties of Limerick and Clare present a varied landscape of Carboniferous and Devonian strata. In the west are low plateaux of newer Carboniferous rocks in which flagstones are prominent: these form a steep east-facing scarp which overlooks Newcastle in the south and Ennis in the north. Farther east the underlying limestones reach the surface; here in north Clare is an area of karst country which continues that of east Connacht, and in particular, north of Ennis, is a district characterized by turloughs (*tuar loch* = dry lake). These are hollows in the limestone, resulting from solution, and subject to periodic flooding. They have no surface outlets, and the level of the water fluctuates with the height of the water table. Still farther east are plateaux of Devonian rocks separated by drift-covered Carboniferous lowlands.

The wealth of the region lies in its flocks and herds. On the limestone pastures sheep are reared; and on the flagstones and Devonian soils store cattle are raised, some of them for fattening on the rich pastures near Limerick city. In the drift-covered lowlands the farmer concentrates on dairy cattle, and this was the original home of the co-operative creamery which, introduced in the 1880's, has spread widely throughout the Republic. Essentially the creamery is a butter-producer; but a few have developed into large trading establishments, while many have organized mobile separating stations to serve remote areas.

Limerick city is the largest town on the Atlantic coast, and with a population of 55,912 (1966) is the third city of the Republic. Situated at the lowest Shannon bridge, it is at once a port, route centre, cathedral city, industrial town, and regional capital. It imports grain, coal, and oil, and exports dairy produce; its industries are largely based on farming, and include bacon-curing, milk-processing, butter-making, milling, and tanning. At Shannon airport it handles the transatlantic air passenger traffic.

The Armorican Ridges and Valleys

South of the latitude of Clonmel and Tralee the structural frame consists of a series of anticlinal ridges of Old Red Sandstone separated by synclinal valleys floored by lower Carboniferous strata, largely shales and sandstones (Fig. 22). The Armorican trend of the region – almost east and west – is probably related to that of south Wales and the English West Country, where it is seen in the south Wales coalfield, Exmoor, and the Mendip Hills. Submergence has resulted in the drowning of the valley mouths, producing in the east Cork and Dungarvan harbours and Youghal bay, and in the west the magnificent rias of Kerry and west Cork.

The region includes the most westerly portion of Europe, where Atlantic influences are at their most powerful. The average winter temperatures at 7°C (44°F) equal those of Marseilles, but it rains on three days out of four; in these conditions the natural vegetation

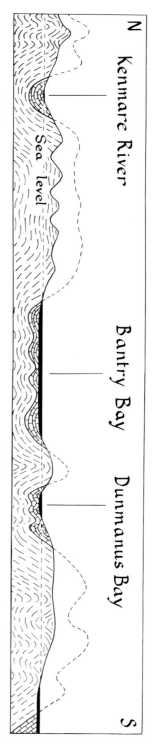

N

Kenmare River

Bantry Bay

Dunmanus Bay

S

Sea level

Carboniferous Limestone

Old Red Sandstone

Fig. 22. SECTION ACROSS THE ARMORICAN RIDGES OF KERRY AND CORK

Anticlinal ridges of Old Red Sandstone are separated by synclinal valleys floored by Carboniferous Limestone. The structure is closely related to that of south Wales and the Mendips (cf. Figs. 32, p. 120, and 50, p. 181).

Partly owing to its exceptionally deep water, of over 27 metres, Bantry Bay has been chosen by the Gulf Oil Corporation as the site for a vast oil terminal, designed to handle huge tankers of 300,000 tons d.w.

The distance represented in the section is about 56 kilometres. After J. K. Charlesworth.

over most of the surface – valley and hill – is bog. The most westerly land in Europe is the Blasket Islands, where the Devonian rocks north of Dingle bay rear above the sea in tremendous cliffs 275 metres high: they are now uninhabited. The most westerly town in Europe is Dingle, with 1450 inhabitants. It is a stock market with a creamery, and the centre of a fishing district, in a setting of fuchsia hedges.

Inland are some of the finest mountains of Ireland: the highest point of Macgillycuddy's Reeks (Carrantuohill) attains 1041 metres (only 44 m short of Snowdon), and in the same chain are 20 summits of over 600 m. Near by is the tourist resort of Killarney, where about 200 jaunting cars (open, two-wheeled horse-drawn carriages) are at the visitor's command.

In the far west there has been a long tradition of emigration, and ruined cottages are a constant reminder of this; but pressure on the land is now less severe than in Donegal or west Connacht. The farmers are essentially stock-rearers, and raise poultry and pigs as

Plate 2.   FISHERMEN AT CROMANE LOWER, COUNTY KERRY

The three cottages in the background front the single long street which forms the village. They are the modern representatives of the old stone and thatch dwellings, and are supplied with mains electricity. The wife tends the three or four cows, while the husband shares in salmon-fishing. The children have usually emigrated to England or the United States. Here the boat's crew has finished for the day and is spreading out the net on the shingle.   Photo H. Rees

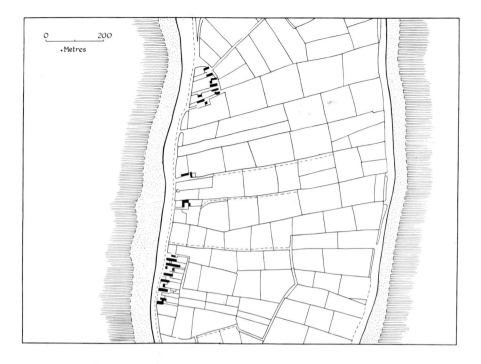

Fig. 23. CROMANE LOWER: A FARMER-FISHER SETTLEMENT

An example of rural settlement on the Kerry coast. There are 14 cottages in the area shown; each farm holding amounts to about 5 to 6 hectares. The men fish for salmon and mussels to supplement the income from the land. *Based on the O.S. 6-inch map.*

well as cattle and sheep: where possible they combine farming with fishing.

As an example of such a farmer-fishing community we may instance Cromane Lower, in Kerry (Fig. 23 and Plate 2). The 'village' occupies a 3-kilometre-long peninsula of shingle and drift which points north into the inner part of Dingle bay, and its 37 dwellings front the single long street following the line of the beach.

The family holding of a representative farmer-fisher consists of 5 hectares, which form a strip two fields deep across the width of the peninsula. He cultivates about ·4 hectare of oats (mainly for sale) and ·2 hectare of potatoes (for food), and cuts about ·4 hectare of hay. The rest is permanent pasture, which is grazed by 4 cows and their 4 calves. In addition he and his wife keep 20 hens and 20 turkeys, and a pony which hauls the churns of milk each morning to the collecting point, about a mile away, for the creamery.

For most of the year he fishes for salmon: he is a member of the dozen or so boats' crews in Cromane Lower. A crew consists of 4 men, who share equally both the expenses and the proceeds. When a salmon is seen to leap two men quickly row the small, open boat along a circular course, while a third man pays out the net from the boat: the fourth man remains on the beach holding a rope attached to one end of the net.

The net is a long, narrow strip, 219 metres in length and 6 metres wide: the object is to form it into a loop, and so enclose the salmon. The boat is then beached and the four men haul in the net from the shore. In a good catch there may be 15 gleaming salmon trapped. Weighing 3 to $3\frac{1}{2}$ kg apiece, and selling retail at about 40p per kg, this is clearly a valuable haul, though the fishermen receive considerably less than the retail price.

The salmon season lasts from mid-January until the end of July. Then the men have two months in which to gather in the oats and attend to other tasks on the farm; afterwards they engage in the dredging of mussels until the salmon season opens again. The work is hard, the hours are long, and the rewards are small; few of the younger men are entering the industry, and members of almost every family have emigrated to England or the United States. Yet social conditions have improved greatly during the last decade or two: with the help of Government grants and loans the old stone and thatch cottages have been replaced by modern bungalows, and all are supplied with electricity.

Farther east, in Cork, the rainfall is less heavy, drainage is better, and there are rich dairy pastures; while the lowland around Cork city is the most famous producer of butter in the Republic.

With a population of 122,146 (1966), Cork is second only to Dublin. It has grown at the lowest crossing and head of navigation of the Lee, and is at once a cathedral and university town, port and industrial centre. Its harbour receives vessels of up to 9 metres draught, but the transatlantic liners call at its outport, Cobh. In addition to industries which serve agriculture, Cork engages in important manufactures. It produces cars and tyres, and possesses the only oil refinery in the Republic (opened in 1959) and the only steel-works. The latter, on Haulbowline Island, is fired by oil, fed by scrap, and satisfies the whole of the home demand for steel sections.

The Leinster Chain and its Borders

For the 100 km between Dublin and New Ross there extends the largest continuous mountain area in Ireland – the Wicklow mountains, whose highest point in Lugnaquillia reaches 926 metres. Their raised core consists of granite, and their flanks are composed of Cambrian and Ordovician strata, stiffened by igneous intrusions. The hills are largely heather-covered moors or expanses of gorse and bracken; but the valleys and the surrounding lowlands, plastered with glacial drift, form productive farm-land.

The farmer concentrates on his cattle: in the north he supplies fresh milk to Dublin; elsewhere it is churned into butter at the creameries. But this is the drier side of Ireland, and substantial quantities of oats, barley, wheat, and sugar beet are grown.

The region is of interest on account of its minerals. On its western flank, centring on Castlecomer, is the Leinster coalfield, with a history of three centuries of mining. It is structurally a basin, though topographically a plateau, and mining takes place by adit from the periphery. The present annual output is of the order of 100,000 tonnes, and approximately equal to the tonnage of native petroleum produced in Great Britain.

About 65 km to the east, in the basin of the Avoca river, is one of the chief metal-mining centres of Ireland. There are gold-bearing gravels here, which were worked in prehistoric times: ornaments fashioned from Wicklow gold in Bronze and Iron Age times had a wide circulation in Britain. In 1795 a 22-ounce nugget was discovered in the district. The ores contain copper, lead, iron, and zinc; but until 1958 they had been neglected for 70 years. Then the mining of copper was resumed, and record quantities are now being produced.

On the southern border of the Leinster chain is a triangular lowland stretching from Wicklow in the north to beyond Wexford in the south. It is one of the driest portions of the Republic; the soils, mixed and of glacial origin, are fertile; and there is a relatively high proportion of arable land. The farms average about 28 ha apiece, and are larger than in most parts of the country; there is a close network of roads, and the market towns number their populations in thousands rather than hundreds. Here then is one of the more prosperous areas of the Republic. The farmers cultivate oats, barley, and turnips, and they rear store cattle for export.

Dublin

Like London, Dublin is both a river crossing and a port. Each is supreme in its own country, and each contains about one-fifth of the total population. The name *Dubhlinn* signifies the black pool and describes the early Norse harbour. The Gaelic name *Baile atha cliath* means the town at the ford bridged by hurdles.

The first town on the site of Dublin was built by the Norsemen, who occupied a dry spur to the south of the river Liffey, 15 metres high above its flood-plain. For many centuries the river wandered at will among the mudbanks at low tide, and could not receive in safety vessels of even 100 tons d.w. In the eighteenth century long training walls were built to increase the tidal scour, the river mouth was straightened, and one of the longest moles in Europe was extended into Dublin bay. The port is thus quite artificial: a vast amount of debris has been scooped out of the Liffey, and used to reclaim the mudflats; and on the new land are oil tanks, flour mills, timber yards, and shipbuilding yards.

A few cargoes provide the bulk of the traffic in the port. Coal and oil dominate the imports (about 20 colliers arrive each week, from Liverpool, Garston, Partington, Workington, and White-haven). The chief exports are livestock and beer. Live cattle, at the rate of 350 to 400 thousand annually, are shipped to Birkenhead, Holyhead, and Glasgow, mainly in specialist vessels. Dublin is the home of the world's largest brewery (that of Messrs Guinness), which spreads over 24 hectares and possesses a river frontage.Three beer tankers export the product to Liverpool, Manchester, Bristol, and Glasgow.

The Irish sea traffic accounts for most of the trade of the port, but there are in addition regular connections with many Continental ports; and while the port has been the life-blood of Dublin for 1000 years, it need hardly be emphasized that the city is the centre of education, commerce, and government for the whole Republic, and contains its major airport. Its population (1966) is 568,772.

Fuel and Power

Ireland is poor in coal, and her water-power resources are small. She possesses, however, large quantities of peat, and it is in this direction that great advances have been made.

About 250,000 tonnes of coal are mined annually, but the electricity produced from this source accounts for less than 5 per cent. of the country's total. Local coal is supplemented by imports from Great Britain, brought by a continuous stream of colliers across the Irish Sea: they amount to about 1·7 million tonnes annually, and provide about one-fifth of the electrical energy of the nation.

At present, however, water-power is the greatest contributor to Irish energy supplies: in 1961 its share of the total amounted to 43 per cent. The Shannon scheme is by far the largest: here a head of 30 metres is utilized in the 25 km of the river between Lough Derg and Limerick. A large canal concentrates the fall at the

Ardnacrusha power-station, and barges can bypass the dam by means of two locks.

The production of electricity in peat-fired power-stations is a post-war development, and one in which considerable expansion is taking place. One-fifth of the entire area of the Republic consists of bog; but for large-scale mechanical cutting the peat must be at least 3 metres deep, and must extend over areas of at least 180 ha (Plate 3). The most useful bogs from this point of view lie in the centre of the country, and the greatest producers at present are the counties of Offaly, Laoighis, Kildare, and Westmeath. Other suitable bogs extend north-westward into Longford, Roscommon, and Leitrim. Cutting is restricted to the five summer months in order to allow the peat to dry in the open. In 1961 the peat-fired power-stations produced almost one-third of the total electrical energy in the Republic. Briquettes are processed for domestic use.

This is an appropriate point to refer to the far-sighted development in Bantry Bay, south-west Cork. It may be viewed in relation to the earlier projects to provide deep-water oil terminals at Finnart, in the Scottish Highlands (p. 372) and Milford Haven in south-west Wales (p. 130). All three are west coast sites, where glacial scouring has been followed by coastal submergence, so that exceptionally deep water is available. In the case of Bantry Bay the navigable channel is more than 27 metres deep – a facility that can be matched by few harbours in Europe, and more than adequate to receive the largest vessels afloat.

Here, at Whiddy Island, near the head of the estuary, the American-based Gulf Oil Company has constructed a crude oil terminal with a storage capacity of a million tonnes. To reap the economies of large-scale shipment the company has built a fleet of six huge tankers, each of 326,000 tons d.w., and the largest vessels in the world. Since the inauguration of the terminal in October, 1968, the Gulf fleet has been bringing crude oil from Kuwait to Bantry Bay. From here the oil is distributed in 'small' tankers of up to 100,000 tons d.w. to Milford Haven and Gulf refineries on the Continent. So for the first time the Republic is brought squarely into the commercial net of the world oil industry.

External Relations

Politically the Irish Republic is an independent state within the British Isles, but outside the United Kingdom and the British Commonwealth. It maintains its own tariff system, which is designed to assist the home industries.

Plate 3.   PEAT-WORKING IN THE REPUBLIC OF IRELAND

A milling machine is scraping the surface of the bog to a depth of about a centimetre at a time, and is piling the broken peat to form a long rick for drying. The rick is being covered with a layer of polythene to protect it from wind and rain. The milled peat may be fed direct to generating stations or may be converted into briquettes.

Photo by courtesy of Dolphin Studios, Dublin

Yet there are strong cultural, social, and economic links between the Republic and the United Kingdom. In the sphere of learning 'the Border' is no barrier, and 'British' university conferences welcome the representatives of Eire. The Irish £ has the same value as the £ sterling, and for the purpose of postal charges the Republic is on the same basis as the United Kingdom. For many purposes the citizens of Eire are still regarded as British subjects, and there is no passport barrier between the two countries.

One of the most disturbing features of the economy of the Irish Republic is its consistent loss of population. This is due partly to the fact that the high natural increase cannot be absorbed either by the land or by the relatively few, though growing, industries; but the problem lies deeper than this, for there has been a substantial and continuous decline in the actual population of the state. In 1841 the 26 counties had a total population of 6½ millions. As a result of the disastrous potato famine of 1846 between one and two million people died of starvation and another million emigrated. By 1901 the population had declined to 3,222,000; in 1966 it totalled 2,884,002.

Irish emigration to Great Britain is at the rate of 20,000 to 30,000 annually; men and women are leaving in approximately equal numbers. The men engage largely in labouring[1] or agriculture, while the women for the most part enter domestic service (though many become nurses and teachers). There is a reverse movement in the rapidly growing tourist traffic from Britain to Ireland.

The Republic has very strong commercial links with the United Kingdom, which buys more than half her exports and supplies more than half her imports. Eire ships ten times as much material (by value) to the United Kingdom as she does to the nearest rival for her products (the United States); she receives more than five times as much from the United Kingdom as she does from the United States. It is clearly to the benefit of both countries that these links should be preserved.

In recent years the national product has increased by an average of 4½ per cent. annually, and the total value of Irish exports rose to form new records in each of the years 1966, 1967, and 1968. Translated into human terms, the statistics mean the gradual replacement of the donkey by the car, the use of electricity instead of paraffin, the introduction of modern sanitation, and the appearance of radio and television on the farm. These are welcome signs of an improvement in the Irish economy.

---

[1] Thus, it has been suggested, with some truth, that Coventry has been rebuilt with Irish labour.

FOR FURTHER READING

Books

CHARLESWORTH, J. K.: *The Geology of Ireland* (Oliver and Boyd, 1953).
FREEMAN, T. W.: *Ireland*, fourth edition, revised (Methuen, 1969).
'Republic of Ireland', *Financial Times* Survey, April 11, 1960.

Articles

BOAL, F. W.: 'Agriculture in Down and Wexford', in *Irish Geography*, Vol. IV, No. 1, 1959.
DWYER, D. J.: 'Peat Fuel Production in the Irish Republic', *Geography* (April 1958).
EVANS, E. E. and Others: 'Rural Settlement in Ireland and Western Britain', *Advancement of Science* (March, 1959).
FREEMAN, T. W., 'Galway, Key to West Connacht', *Irish Geography*, Vol. III, No. 4, 1957.
—— 'North Inishowen, Co. Donegal', *Irish Geography*, Vol. III, No. 2, 1955.
GILLMOR, D. A.: 'Cattle Movements in the Republic of Ireland' *Transactions, Institute of British Geographers* (March 1969).
HAUGHTON, J. P.: 'The Mullet of Mayo', *Irish Geography*, Vol. IV, No. 1, 1959.
O'BRIEN, M. V.: 'Economic Geology of Ireland', *Advancement of Science* (March 1958).
SWEETING, M. M.: 'The Enclosed Depression of Carran, County Clare', *Irish Geography*, Vol. II, No. 5, 1953.
SYNGE, F. M.: 'The Quaternary Period in Ireland – an Assessment', *Irish Geography*, Vol. IV, No. 2, 1960.
WALSH, T. and Others: 'The Use of Peatland in Irish Agriculture', *Advancement of Science* (June 1958).

Maps

Bartholomew's quarter-inch map of Ireland, in 5 sheets.
    Geological Map of Ireland, 1 : 750,000 scale, Ordnance Survey Office, Dublin.
    The one-inch geological maps are available, but they are uncoloured, and therefore rather difficult to interpret. There are colour-printed maps of a few areas of special interest.

CHAPTER EIGHT

NORTH AND CENTRAL WALES

WALES has a large measure of physical and cultural unity, which serves to distinguish it from the rest of the British Isles. It is physically distinct by reason of its location, climate, structure, and relief. In no other region outside Scotland is there so widespread a distribution of heavy rainfall. In a narrow coastal belt there is a rainfall of 900 to 1000 mm per annum: this is low for Wales. Almost everywhere else the rainfall amounts to more than 1300 mm, and in Snowdonia an area of about 260 square km receives more than 2500 mm. Snowdon summit, as we have seen, probably receives more than 5000 mm, and this is the rainiest place known in the British Isles.

This heavy rainfall has a profound effect on soils and agriculture, for even on moderately steep slopes the soils tend to be saturated, leached, and acid, frequently with the accumulation of hardpan below the surface. Much of the rainfall occurs not as violent downpours but as a long-drawn-out drizzle, which soaks the ground more thoroughly than would a heavy shower with its rapid runoff.

Like western Ireland, Cornwall, and the Hebrides, Wales shares in the mild winters, the delayed autumns, and early springs of the Atlantic fringe of Britain; and palms and fuchsia hedges are to be seen in Anglesey, in Lleyn, and along the shores of Pembrokeshire.

Structurally Wales is characteristically the meeting-place of the Caledonian and Armorican trends, and from this springs the fundamental contrasts between north and south Wales. In the north and centre the rocks range from Pre-Cambrian to Silurian in age, and were folded in Siluro–Devonian times by pressures from the south-east: the 'grain' of the structure thus runs north-east and south-west, and is well illustrated in the Lleyn peninsula and in the low ridges of Anglesey. The height of the Snowdonia area is largely a result of uplift in later times, but is partly due to the resistance of the masses of contemporaneous igneous rocks. Coal measures are present only on the fringes, and manufacture plays only a minor part in the life of the region.

In contrast, the structure of south Wales has resulted from pressures from the south and S.S.W., which took place in Carbo–Permian times. A major downfold was produced in the Carboniferous and Devonian rocks, so that the axis of the south Wales coal basin is arranged east and west. The Armorican trend is shown also in the Gower peninsula, in Carmarthen bay, and in the alignment of Milford Haven. South Wales is essentially a mining and manufacturing region, and recent developments at Milford Haven and elsewhere are reinforcing this traditional character.

Wales is culturally distinct from England in several ways. It was never thoroughly Romanized, never conquered by the Saxons. The Welsh were not town dwellers, and town life began only when it was imposed by the Norman kings. The remoteness of the hill farm, however, encouraged the survival of the Celtic genius for poetry and song. The Welsh language, on the other hand, has suffered severely from the competition of English. Under Tudor rule, in 1536, it was decided to unite Wales with England; and in spite of their own Welsh origin, the Tudors imposed English as the official language. In the State schools of 1870 English was the medium of instruction; indeed, it is only since 1943 that Welsh has been admissible in courts of law. Welsh, however, remains the normal tongue in the hills, in Anglesey and Lleyn – that is, in most of Wales except in south Pembrokeshire, in the two coalfields, and along the eastern border. But the ability to speak Welsh steadily declines, despite all the efforts to preserve it, and between the Census years of 1951 and 1961 the proportion of Welsh-speaking persons fell from 28·9 to 26 per cent. of the total.

North and Central Wales – Structure

In north and central Wales there is one of the most complete sequences in Europe of the Pre-Cambrian and older Palæozoic rocks. It has been estimated that in Anglesey as much as 6000 metres of Pre-Cambrian strata have accumulated: they include not only marine sediments, but in addition the products of four distinct periods of volcanism. During the course of Pre-Cambrian earth movements these strata were thrown into great folds, which were themselves refolded; and under heat and pressure the sediments were converted into gneisses, schists, and quartzites. The results can be studied at South Stack, off Holyhead Island, where sharp folds traverse the entire cliff-face of white quartzite.

On the floors of the Cambrian seas another 3600 metres of marine sediments were deposited. They comprised sands, grits, and pebbles (evidence of shallow water) and clays and silts (evidence of deeper

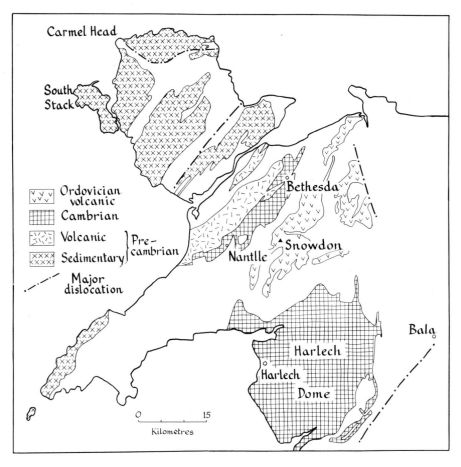

Fig. 24. A GEOLOGICAL MAP OF NORTH WALES

The Pre-Cambrian rocks of Anglesey form the largest exposure of that era in southern Britain; the Cambrian strata between Bethesda and Nantlle form the 'slate belt'. Ordovician volcanic material is exposed in the Snowdon Range. Blank areas consist mainly of bedded Ordovician rocks. Note the Bala-Towyn Fault and the Carmel Head Thrust.

water). The former have consolidated into the resistant sandstones and gritstones which now form the Rhinogs of western Merionethshire, the latter changed into the shales and mudstones which form the more subdued landscape on their borders.

The following Ordovician period witnessed violent volcanic outbursts in addition to quiet sedimentation. Sheets of lava and volcanic 'ash' accumulated to a thickness of 600 metres and now form some of the highest summits, including Snowdon itself (Fig. 24). Masses of igneous material were injected into joints and bedding planes; the larger bosses form rounded mountains such as Mynydd Mawr, while the dolerite sills stand out as narrow ridges, as in the area north-east of Portmadoc. The Silurian rocks were formed at the bottom of a sea, and now constitute the most widespread deposit in Wales: they occupy most of the plateau area south of Llandudno and east of Aberystwyth.

These varied deposits were at the end of Silurian times thrown into folds, squeezed, faulted, and overthrust during the course of the Caledonian earth movements. The Cambrian shales of Caernarvonshire were thrust against the resistant mass of Pre-Cambrian rocks to the north; heat and pressure re-oriented their minerals to produce slate, with its characteristic property of cleavage. Behind them the Ordovician rocks were compressed into a major downfold, now seen in the Snowdon range and in Lleyn. The rocks of Snowdon summit – now the loftiest element in the landscape – must in Devonian times have been overshadowed by mightier peaks on the crests of the upfolds (Fig. 25 and Plate 4).

In the Berwyns and Merionethshire two domes were raised, whose cores of older rock have been revealed by subsequent erosion: in the Berwyn dome the Ordovician rocks are exposed, while in the Harlech dome these have been pierced to reveal the underlying Cambrian strata. The domes are bordered to the south by two upfolds, which constitute the Clun Forest basin and the central Wales syncline.

Associated with these folds are great systems of faults. In the Carmel Head thrust in Anglesey masses of Pre-Cambrian material were forced over the Ordovician strata, so that the normal order of the rocks was reversed; and between the two domes there occurred a major fracture which can be traced almost continuously across Wales from Towyn in the south-west through Bala and Corwen to within 13 km of Chester. This, the Bala fault, now affords a useful through route followed by main roads.

In Devonian and Carboniferous times most of the area was probably land, and in only a few districts is there evidence of marine deposits of those periods; but where they occur the Carboniferous rocks have left their impression on the landscape: there are large limestone quarries at Llandulas and Penmon, and collieries in Flintshire.

The Carbo–Permian earth movements which in England raised the Pennines, the Malverns, and the Mendips, met in north and central Wales a resistant block of old rocks which had been packed tightly in Siluro–Devonian times. The existing structures were not greatly disturbed, but a mass of Silurian rocks was raised to form

Plate 4. SNOWDON FROM CWM DYLI

Snowdon (1085 m) is the highest mountain in England and Wales, and is believed to have the highest rainfall in the British Isles (over 5000 mm per annum). Consequently a view such as this is rather rare. Snowdon is formed of a resistant Ordovician volcanic rock, which has been compressed into a downfold and hence further strengthened: its present height, however, is due in part to an elevation of the land. The Quaternary glaciers have rounded the lower slopes; the sharp edges and peaks are the result of frost action. Notice the mountain wall (centre, right) which separates the higher summer pastures from the enclosed and improved lower slopes.

Photo H. Rees

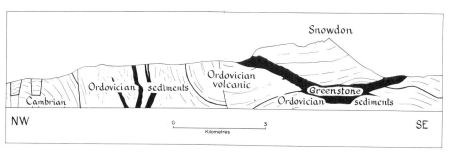

Fig. 25. GEOLOGICAL SECTION ACROSS THE SNOWDON AREA

Snowdon itself is in the core of a Caledonian syncline, and in Devonian times there must have been far higher summits on the crests of the anticlines. Igneous intrusions are shown in black.

the Clwydian range, while a corresponding belt to the west was dropped to form the straight trough of the vale of Clwyd. Lateral movement along the great Bala fault produced a remarkable shift in the position of a limestone belt near Llangollen.

The Tertiary earth storm largely passed by north and central Wales; but since that time the land surface has risen intermittently by as much as 600 metres. At each stage in the uplift the land or portions of it were reduced to a peneplain, now represented by platforms at about 600 and 300 metres. Lower surfaces, at 170, 120, and about 80 metres, are to be seen in Anglesey and Lleyn, and at the foot of Snowdonia, and cut right across the structures, irrespective of the age or resistance of the rocks; they are presumed to be true wave-cut platforms, backed by degraded lines of cliffs.

North Wales was one of the gathering grounds of the Quaternary ice sheets, and everywhere in the highlands the smooth outlines resulting from glaciation are evident. The Llanberis pass is one of many examples of U-shaped valleys; there are ribbon lakes in Nant Gwynant and elsewhere; and the south wall of the Nant Francon pass is adorned by a splendid row of corries. The lowlands are plastered with boulder clay, and it is this superficial cover which accounts for the relatively rich farming of the coastal fringe, particularly in Arfon, Lleyn, and Anglesey. The title 'Môn, Mam Cymru' ('Anglesey, Mother of Wales') recalls the former significance of the island, both as a granary and as a home of the Welsh princes.

Historical Geography

A wealth of prehistoric remains suggests that the region, and Anglesey in particular, was well known, peopled and farmed from at least the Bronze Age onward. The Romans built a road system and established camps at Caerhun, on the Conway, at Tomen-y-Mur, near Trawsfynydd, and at Segontium, near Caernarvon, together with a small fort at Holyhead. They worked extensively the copper ores of Parys Mountain, and 15 of their copper 'cakes', weighing 13 to 23 kg apiece, have been found in the region. At Dolau Cothy (seven miles south-east of Lampeter) they mined gold from the Silurian rocks and presumably transported it along Sarn Helen, the north-south road which passes through the area.

The Saxons did not penetrate far into Wales and the Saxon period of England corresponds with the age of the Celtic saints in Wales. Many Celtic holy men were travelling to and fro across the Irish Sea, and establishing coastal settlements in Wales. The present-day village church can often be traced back to a foundation on the same site by one of the Celtic saints, to whom it may be still dedicated.

The early Norman kings found in north and central Wales the strong kingdom of Gwyneth, ruled from the palace at Aberffraw, in south-west Anglesey. Edward I determined on the conquest of Wales, and to pursue his object built a chain of walled seaports guarded by castles. He peopled them with Englishmen, granted them a monopoly of trade, and hoped that they would form centres from which English culture might spread throughout Wales. Some of Edward's foundations have survived as towns: they include Flint, Conway, Beaumaris, Harlech, and Caernarvon – the last forming one of the finest medieval survivals in Britain (Fig. 26 and Plate 5).

From the Middle Ages until the coming of the railway there was an extensive movement of stock (particularly cattle) from Wales into England. The animals were collected at some 70 centres, driven eastward along a series of established hill routes, and sold for fattening in the Midlands and East Anglia, or for slaughter in London. In its essentials the trade continues today, but the animals move by rail or lorry instead of on the hoof.

The copper ores of Anglesey were rediscovered in 1768, and Parys Mountain quickly became the greatest producer in Europe, with an annual output between 1773 and 1785 of more than 3000 tonnes of metallic copper. The port of Amlwch was built to refine and ship the metal; but mining virtually ceased in 1883, and now the port is silent and the great quarries are derelict. Climbers using the Miners' Track to Snowdon summit will know the ruined buildings of the Britannia copper mine which overlook Llyn Llydaw: this mine closed in 1915.

It is not generally realized that until recently central Wales was a considerable producer of gold. Mining was actively practised in the second half of the nineteenth century, and the industry reached its peak production in 1904, when the output of Merionethshire was 19,653 oz. Scores of old shafts and levels are to be seen in the Cambrian rocks of the south-eastern flank of the Harlech dome, but almost the whole of the total came from three mines. These were the Gwynfynydd mine, 10 km north of Dolgellau, and the Vigra and St David's mines, 6 km W.N.W. of Dolgellau. The Queen wears a ring made from the gold of the St David's mine, and in the 1960's a company was in existence for the purpose of reopening this mine. One of the last to close was the Prince Edward mine, which was 4 km north-east of Trawsfynydd, and which was operating until 1935.

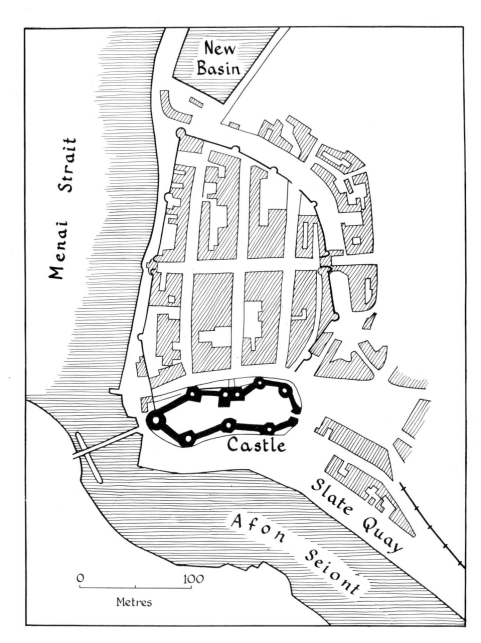

New Basin

Menai Strait

Castle

Slate Quay

Afon Seiont

0   100

Metres

Fig. 26. THE CENTRE OF PRESENT-DAY CAERNARVON

The site was a low hill protected by the Menai Strait on the west, the Seiont on the south, and the little river Cadnant on the north and east. The grid of streets was typical of the thirteenth-century 'bastide' towns, which were planned in imitation of the old Roman towns. Others which originated in the same period are Flint, Conway, Beaumaris, Hull, Liverpool and Salisbury.

Plate 5. CAERNARVON AND THE MENAI STRAIT

Castle and town were conceived and built as a unit by Edward I to further his conquest of Wales: notice the town wall with its row of bastions overlooking the Strait, whose western entrance the town was designed to control. In the background, to the right, is the nineteenth-century dock, which still receives small freighters. The expansion of the town during the nineteenth century was largely a result of the slate traffic. The photograph is taken from a turret of the castle, and the camera points north. Compare with Fig. 26.

Photo H. Rees

Farming

In the hills farming is directed essentially to the production of sheep, for either cross-breeding or fattening in the lowlands. It is based on two processes: on the downhill movement of stock on the farm-land with the approach of the cold weather, and on the wintering out of a proportion of the flock in near-by lowlands. As a subsidiary activity the farmer may also keep a herd of store cattle. We may illustrate the system from the farm of Mr W. R. Griffith, who operates on 160 hectares at Caeaugwynion, on the western face of the Snowdon range, overlooking Llyn Cwellyn (Fig. 27). The land rises steeply from the main road at 145 metres to the summit of the ridge at 592 metres. Since it faces south-west it receives most of the available sunshine, while the opposite slope has been planted by the Forestry Commission. In summer Mr Griffith allows the sheep to graze freely above the mountain wall, which is at about 460 metres; meanwhile the cattle are grazing the middle slopes (the *ffridd*) below the wall: here the land is divided by walls and the pastures improved – they are limed and treated with basic slag and other fertilizers, and the bracken is cut methodically.

About the end of September Mr Griffith chooses 100 of his 500 sheep and sends them off to the lowlands of Denbighshire for the winter, for the land cannot then support the whole of his flock. A month later he moves his herd of 65 Welsh Black cattle down into the lowest of his fields, and he pastures the remainder of his sheep on the *ffridd*: there they remain throughout the winter.

The sheep are of the Welsh Mountain breed: they are small, with coarse wool; but they are sturdy animals and good milkers, so that in spite of harsh conditions lamb losses are few (just before lambing-time the ewes are pastured on the richest grass on the valley floor). Mr Griffith keeps no poultry, he has no arable land, and he milks 'half a cow' – only sufficient for the home.

The hill farm thus plays an essential part in the economy of the United Kingdom: it is the source from which the flocks and herds of the lowland farmer are replenished. Yet it could hardly survive without Government support. There are grants for the clearing of scrub and eradication of bracken, for improving water-supplies and farm buildings; there are subsidies for liming and fertilizing, and for many other purposes. The prospect for the hill farmer is uncertain. An official investigation took place during 1954–55 in 120,000 hectares, stretching from the plateau near Aberystwyth eastward to the English border. The committee found that 'the established pattern (of agriculture) is disintegrating over wide areas: if the present rate of decline continues it is possible that the moor-

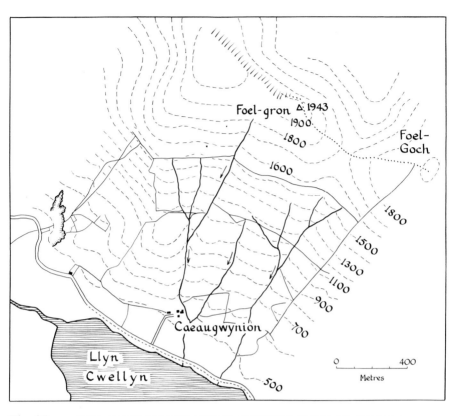

Fig. 27. A HILL FARM ON THE SOUTH-WESTERN SLOPE OF SNOWDON

Its land ranges from below 150 metres to almost 600 metres; it is entirely under grass. The farmer rears 500 sheep and 65 cattle on about 160 hectares. The mountain wall, at about 460 metres, marks the upper limit of the improved land. Heights are in feet.

land area will be virtually depopulated within comparatively few years'. They concluded that 57 per cent. of the farms in the area were definitely too small to be economic; that a further 31 per cent. were marginal; and that only 12 per cent. yielded a profit beyond the value of the farmer's own labour. The population of the area had declined from 12,200 in 1931 to 10,700 in 1951.

There are similarities here to western Ireland. The young people are leaving the farms in search of greater material comfort (55 per cent. of the farms were without piped water; 92 per cent. were without mains electricity). It is likely that more and more land in the heart of Wales will be acquired by the Forestry Commission and by the water undertakings.

The Coastal Fringe

The land in the coastal fringe is lower and more level, there is a smaller rainfall, and average temperatures are higher. The pastures are richer, they will support a greater density of stock, and in favoured localities will fatten them; arable farming is more practicable, and there are easily accessible markets for the produce. Throughout the area dairy farming is important. It is a recent and a growing activity, which has become established only in the last 30 years or so; and its main product is fresh milk. The demand springs from the coastal population – from the line of towns between Bangor and Rhyl and the many smaller resorts and caravan sites elsewhere, and there are five collecting stations in the area.

But dairy cows are still outnumbered by beef cattle, and most of these are destined for fattening in the English Midlands. Many farmers on the coastal belt also rear flocks of sheep: the rich pastures of Anglesey will fatten lambs; elsewhere the sheep are reared as stores. In addition, almost everywhere the farmers of the coastal fringe perform an important service in that they receive lambs from the hill farms for wintering. They draw on a very wide area: for example, farmers on the Brecon Beacons, about 70 km away, send their lambs for wintering near the Cardiganshire coast. A limited amount of arable farming is practised; the natural and improved pastures are supplemented by crops of oats, swedes, and mangolds, grown for fodder; and in Lleyn and Anglesey a beginning has been made in the cultivation of early potatoes.

Quarrying

The most significant mineral product of the region is coal, from the Flint and Denbigh coalfield; but this activity is so closely linked with the English Midlands that it is more conveniently mentioned in that connection (see p. 254).

There are large limestone quarries at Penmon, in Anglesey and at Llandulas, 6 kilometres east of Colwyn Bay; and 'granite' is quarried for road-stone at Trevor in Lleyn and at Penmaenmawr, west of Conway. Nevertheless, the most characteristic mineral of the region is slate.

The visitor can hardly fail to notice the great black spoil heaps from past and present slate-workings. Its exploitation has brought great changes to the landscape; and in spite of increasing costs and the competition of manufactured tiles, slate-quarrying is still of some consequence. Welsh slates can be seen in many parts of the world – in Denmark and Istanbul, in Argentina and Penang.

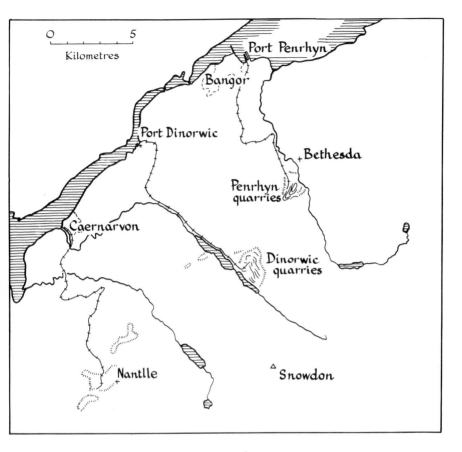

Fig. 28. THE SLATE QUARRIES OF SNOWDONIA

Quarrying is still active, though on a reduced scale, in the three districts indicated. Each was connected by rail to a port for shipment, but the ports are now deserted and the railways disused. Distribution of the slate is now by lorry. There are other quarries farther south.

Slate-working takes place largely on the two flanks of Snowdonia. The main belt follows the outcrop of the Cambrian rocks on the north-west side of the mountains from Nantlle to Bethesda (Fig. 28); here the Cambrian shales, thrust north-westward against a mass of Pre-Cambrian rocks, have been converted into slate.

From Nantlle in the early nineteenth century slates clattered down the 16-km narrow-gauge railway built by Robert and George Stephenson to the newly constructed slate quay at Caernarvon. The Atlantic crossing appears to have held no terrors, and in 1843 a local shipowner invited emigrants to sail to New York in his 600-ton barque 'with a ballast of slates'. The rapid development of Caernarvon in this period – it grew from a town of 4000 people in 1801 to one of more than 10,000 in 1851 – may be attributed largely to the slate industry in the hills behind it.

Ten km north-east of Nantlle are the Dinorwic quarries, once the most productive in Wales, but now derelict; it was these which in 1962 supplied the new slates for Nos. 10, 11, and 12 Downing Street. Five km beyond is the Penrhyn quarry, claimed to be the largest man-made excavation in the world: it is 2 km long, ·6 km wide, and 360 metres deep. Here a dozen artificial terraces have been cut, bounded by vertical cliffs 22 metres high (Fig. 29). The slate is loosened by explosives, raised by diesel locomotive, cut by circular saw, split by hand, and trimmed by guillotine. It is incredible to see a wedge driven in, and the solid rock open out like a book.

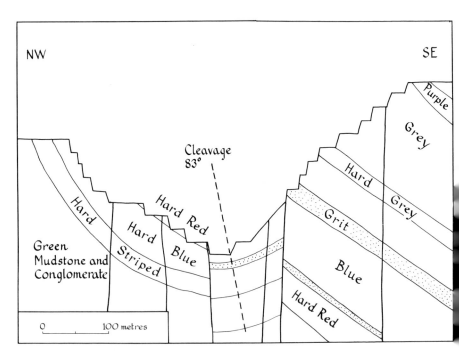

Fig. 29.   SECTION ACROSS THE PENRHYN SLATE QUARRY
This section illustrates the different qualities of slate which are obtained, and the structure of the slate beds. The cleavage has no relation to the bedding planes, and is more or less constant in direction throughout the quarry. The vertical lines represent dykes.

About 1000 men are employed in these quarries, and the annual output is of the order of 50,000 tonnes – about one-third of what it was in 1938. Then the outlets were Caernarvon, Dinorwic, and Penrhyn – busy little ports 60 years ago, but now virtually deserted. At Blaenau Ffestiniog, on the south side of Snowdonia, is a second group of quarries, working the slates of the Ordovician rocks. The six quarries now in operation produce together about 20,000 tonnes annually. They were linked by light railway to the coast, and a harbour was built at Portmadoc. The railway has now been converted for tourist use; the slates are distributed by road, and the harbour is deserted.

Power

North and central Wales possess several advantages for the production of hydro-electricity. There is a regular and heavy rainfall, with the possibilities of a considerable head of water, and the rocks are generally impermeable. There is no very large catchment area, however; there are few large high-level storage lakes, and there is only a small local demand for power.

Nevertheless, power has been developed at four places. The earliest plant to be built was the small one at Cwm Dyli, opened in 1905. It has a capacity of $5\frac{1}{2}$ MW, and draws on the water stored in Llyn Llydaw, on the east face of Snowdon. The catchment area is very small, but this is offset by the extremely high rainfall. There are two larger stations, at Maentwrog, in the vale of Ffestiniog, and at Dolgarrog, in the vale of Conway. The former is of interest in that a large reservoir was constructed to supply it – Trawsfynydd lake – to which we refer again later. The catchment area, about 130 square km, is again relatively small; the capacity is 24 MW. At Dolgarrog the capacity is a little greater (about 28 MW), and here the catchment area has been considerably increased by the construction of tunnels and aqueducts (Fig. 30); the resulting interference with the natural drainage is shown on the one-inch map. The power here was originally used locally for the refining of aluminium.

The newest hydro-electric station, opened in 1963, is at Tan-y-Grisiau, near the slate quarries of Blaenau Ffestiniog. It is unusual in that it is designed as a pump-storage scheme: power is generated during the peak periods of the day; but at night, when the demand is low, generation ceases, and instead water is pumped back into the reservoir. With a capacity of 300 MW, this is the largest station of its kind in Europe.

Greater than any of the foregoing are the two nuclear power-stations, the one, on Trawsfynydd lake in the north of Merionethshire; the other, at Wylfa Head on the north coast of Anglesey.

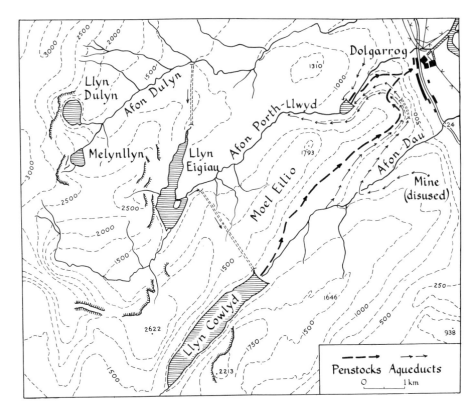

Fig. 30. THE DOLGARROG HYDRO-ELECTRIC STATION

The catchment area has been ingeniously extended by means of tunnels and aqueducts. A head of over 300 metres is utilized, and most of it is concentrated in the last kilometre, where the water plunges over the fault scarp which bounds the Conway valley. Contours at 250-foot intervals.

The Trawsfynydd station has a capacity of 500 MW; it is the only inland nuclear power-station in the United Kingdom, and draws its cooling water from Trawsfynydd Lake (Fig. 31). The Wylfa Head plant, with a capacity of 1180 MW, became the most powerful nuclear plant in the world when it began to feed power into the super-grid in 1971. Holyhead was chosen as the site for a new aluminium smelter partly to be near this important new source of power. These vast plants take five or six years to construct; they require considerable improvements in the local road systems, and their building provides temporary employment for some 2000 people.

Towns

There is space for only brief mention of some of the towns of the

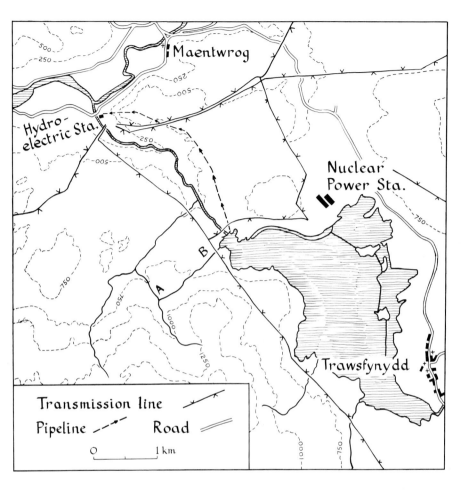

Fig. 31.   THE TRAWSFYNYDD AND MAENTWROG POWER-PLANTS

Trawsfynydd Lake, over 5 square kilometres in area, was formed by damming the Prysor river to serve the Maentwrog hydro-electric station (24 MW capacity), brought into service in 1928. The catchment area has been increased by the construction of artificial channels such as AB. Mean annual rainfall is 1800 to 2500 mm. Most of the head of 200 metres is concentrated in the last $\frac{1}{2}$ kilometre of the pipeline. The nuclear power-station draws on the lake for its cooling water, and the discharged warmer water is conducted around the lake by means of dams to facilitate cooling. The capacity of the nuclear power-station is 500 MW. Heights are in feet.

region. Bangor, the market centre for Anglesey and the coastal fringe, functions also as a scientific centre for north Wales. It is one of the bases of the Nature Conservancy, which conducts experiments in Snowdonia – for example, in sheep grazing; its university college includes Departments of Agriculture, Forestry, and Marine Biology. Aberystwyth too has a wide influence as a cultural centre: it contains the National Library of Wales, and its university college has a Department of Agricultural Botany; workers in Aberystwyth have gained wide recognition in the fields of plant-breeding and grassland improvement. Holyhead handles the mail and passenger traffic with Dublin, and in the United Kingdom is second only to Dover as a passenger port. A bustling town, it has little that is purely Welsh in its character or appearance.

We have referred in passing to the tourist industry. A row of resorts extends along the sandy north coast, and includes Rhyl, Colwyn Bay, and Llandudno. Conway, Caernarvon, Beaumaris, and Harlech attract many summer visitors, partly on account of their castles; Abergele, with over 6000 caravans, is probably the largest caravan site in Britain; there are other caravan sites at Harlech and Conway, and a large holiday camp at Pwllheli. The inland resorts are smaller, but still evident, as at Beddgelert and Betws-y-Coed; and these are in the midst of the magnificent scenery of Snowdonia. The smallest village is now within reach of the family car, and there is little doubt that the mountains and beaches of north Wales form one of its major economic resources.

FOR FURTHER READING

Books

BOWEN, E. G. (Ed.), *Wales* (Methuen, 1957).

DAVIES, MARGARET: *Wales in Maps* (University of Wales Press, 1958).

EMBLETON, C.: *Snowdonia* (Geographical Association, 1962).

Mid-Wales Investigation, Welsh Agricultural Land Sub-commission (H.M.S.O., 1955).

ROBERTS, E.: *The County of Anglesey,* Mem. Soil Survey (H.M.S.O., 1958).

SMITH, B. and GEORGE, T. N.: *North Wales,* British Regional Geology handbooks (H.M.S.O., 1961).

THOMAS, T. M.: *The Mineral Wealth of Wales* (Oliver and Boyd, 1961).

Prehistoric and Roman settlement is well discussed in the volumes on Anglesey and Caernarvonshire of the Royal Commission on Historical Monuments.

Articles

MOUNFIELD, P. R.: 'The Location of Nuclear Power Stations in the United Kingdom' in *Geography* (April, 1961).

REES PRYCE, W. T.: 'The Location and Growth of Holiday Caravan Camps in Wales' *Transactions, Institute of British Geographers* (December 1967).

Maps

The one-inch geological map of Anglesey was published in 1967, in both solid and drift editions; the quarter-inch geological map, sheets 9 and 10 (North Wales), for long out of print, was re-issued in 1968.

Most of the region is covered by Bartholomew's $\frac{1}{2}$-inch sheets 22 and 27.

The O.S. 1-inch sheet 107 well illustrates glacial landforms.

CHAPTER NINE

SOUTH WALES

BETWEEN south Wales on the one hand and north and central Wales on the other there are strong contrasts. North Wales contains most of the Welsh-speaking element in the population, the slate quarries, most of the sheep and cattle farms, the forests, the mountains, lakes, and reservoirs, and the hydro-electric and nuclear power stations. South Wales, populated mainly by immigrants from England, has the miners and the metal-workers, the seaports, the oil-refineries, and, more recently, the many light industries which have been established to offset the decline in the inland basic industries.

Physical Basis

As in southern Ireland, we see in south Wales the effects of both the Caledonian and the Hercynian earth movements. The Caledonian folds, ranging north-east and south-west, express themselves in the trend of the Cardiganshire coast and in the outcrops of Ordovician and Silurian rocks in the north and north-western parts of the region. Farther south the folds of Carbo–Permian (Hercynian) times are seen in the elongated basin of the South Wales coalfield. Between the two is a roughly triangular area of Old Red Sandstone where the strata, protected perhaps from the Hercynian earth storm by the Malvern Hills, remain almost horizontal. They reach their greatest elevations in the Black Mountain, Fforest Fawr, and the Brecon Beacons, which form the northern limit of the coalfield.

Since the pressure came from the south, it is here that the dips are steepest; the strata dip southward at 45 degrees or more, and the outcrops are accordingly crowded together. In the north the dips are gentle; the strata dip southward at about 10 degrees, the outcrops are broader, and the coal and iron seams were more accessible, and were first worked near the northern border of the coalfield (Fig. 32). Moreover, the Lower Coal Measures consist largely of soft shales, and their erosion has resulted in a natural

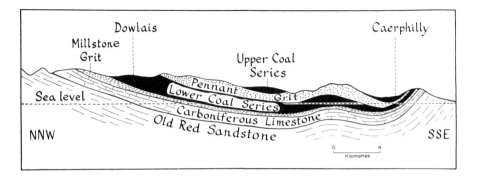

Fig. 32. GEOLOGICAL SECTION ACROSS THE SOUTH WALES COALFIELD
Since the pressures came from the south, here the dip is steepest (about 45°) and the outcrops are narrowest: this effect is accentuated by thinning of the beds. Most of the moorland in the middle of the coal basin is composed of the barren, resistant Pennant Grit. The faults have been omitted.

routeway running east and west from the neighbourhood of Abergavenny to the vale of Neath.

In detail the coalfield is complicated by minor structures. A central upfold (the Pontypridd–Maesteg anticline) raises the comparatively barren Middle Coal Measures to the surface over a wide area; here are the coarse and resistant Pennant Sandstones, which form a deserted moorland area rising to about 600 m in the heart of the coalfield. Powerful faults cross the region: the main series runs approximately north and south, and this has added greatly to the difficulties of mining. Two important cross faults, running north-east and south-west, have been picked out by the rivers Tawe and Neath; but apart from these, the river system has little connection with the underlying structure: it is apparently superimposed, and it seems likely that the parallel rivers of south Wales originated upon a gently sloping surface of Cretaceous rocks, which have since been completely removed by the forces of erosion (in support of this suggestion we may quote the strange remnants of Cretaceous strata which are to be seen far from the main outcrop, in Antrim and the Hebrides).

Farther west, in Pembrokeshire, the effects of the Hercynian earth movements were more violent. The coalfield narrows to a mere two or three miles and at Milford Haven there are tight folds, where the beds in places dip vertically. The line of the actual waterway of Milford Haven appears to be related to the Ritec fault (named after the river entering the sea at Tenby), for a narrow trench corresponds with its line from Tenby to Pembroke Dock.

The Quaternary glaciers scoured the valleys of south Wales and left on the lowlands a mantle of drift. A post-glacial subsidence of at least 23 metres has drowned the lower portions of the rivers of Pembrokeshire and Carmarthen bay; and as a result of these combined influences we see one of the finest natural harbours of Europe in Milford Haven.

Farming

While the special character of south Wales springs from its industries, the varied physical environment offers a range of opportunities to the farmer. The large industrial population provides a ready market for fresh milk, and specialized dairy farming is practised in the gently undulating Towy valley and its neighbouring lowlands, and in the rich pastures of the Vale of Glamorgan. Llandilo, Whitland, and Carmarthen are milk-collecting centres. In Pembrokeshire mixed farming is the rule; the mild winters encourage the growth of dairy pastures and allow the production of early. potatoes and vegetables. Oats, barley, wheat, and sugar beet are also grown, and most farmers rear pigs. The Brecon Beacons are given over to hill-sheep farming; but the moorland within the coalfield is unproductive, for it has lost its potentially fertile valley land owing to the spread of industry and settlement.

The Metal Industries

The basis of the modern steel industry of south Wales is formed by the local supplies of high-quality coking coal; but there were metal-works in the region long before there was any large-scale mining of coal; and while tinplating is now the special interest of the metal-workers, the first non-ferrous metal to be refined in the region was not tin but copper.

In 1584 the owner of the Trewoorth copper-mines in Cornwall decided to establish a copper-smelter at Neath, where there was plenty of timber available for conversion into charcoal. From the first, successful experiments were carried out to supplement the use of charcoal with 'sea-coal', though this was not used on a large scale until the eighteenth century. When in the seventeenth century the copper ores of Parys Mountain, in Anglesey, were being exploited south Wales found itself midway between what were then the two chief sources of copper in the world. The first works in Swansea were opened in 1719, and the town rapidly developed into the centre of the copper-smelting industry of Europe. During the greater part of the nineteenth century copper-smelting remained the chief source of wealth in Swansea.

Inland, at Merthyr Tydfil and Aberdare, small ironworks had

been operating since the late sixteenth century, utilizing the ores of the north-eastern part of the outcrop of the Lower Coal Measures. At first the fuel in regular use was charcoal, and the coal itself was neglected. But in 1730 Abraham Darby discovered the secret of converting coal into coke; gradually the new fuel was adopted, and the iron industry expanded, using water-mills to drive grindstones, to power hammers, and to work bellows. Merthyr Tydfil gained the reputation of being 'the most populous town in Wales'.

Tinplating was introduced into south Wales at an ironworks in Pontypool about 1670, and after a lapse was resumed in 1720. About 1760 sulphuric acid came into use for the purpose of cleaning the iron plates before tinning, and since this acid was a by-product of copper-refining there was an incentive to the tinplaters to set up their works at Swansea. A century later the researches of William Siemens at Landore (3 kilometres north of Swansea – see Fig. 33) resulted in the development of the open-hearth steel furnace. The new alloy soon replaced iron as the basis of tinplate; but now the local Coal Measure ores were replaced by higher-grade material, some of it imported, and coastal sites clearly offered economies in transport. Thus the most characteristic feature of the twentieth-century steel industry has been its migration to the ports. Only in a few instances (and then largely for sociological reasons) have new plants been set up inland.

Copper-smelting has now disappeared completely from Swansea: its works were unable to compete against those set up near the newly developed orefields overseas; but the tradition of copper-working continues at the Imperial Chemical Industries works at Landore, where copper plates and sheets are produced, together with pans for the brewing industry.

Some of the old copper works were converted to zinc-smelting, and Swansea (pop. 172,566) has become one of the chief centres of the zinc industry in the British Isles, with the works of the Imperial Smelting Corporation at Llansamlet, in the lower Tawe valley. The concentrates are imported, largely from Spain and Australia. Zinc-manufacture has its place in the local industrial structure, for an important branch of the plating industries is the production of galvanized sheets (steel coated with zinc) for the manufacture of commodities such as buckets and corrugated roofing, designed for harder wear than tinplate. Sulphuric acid is a by-product also in zinc-refining, and this again is utilized in the tinplate industry.

At Clydach, 8 km north of Swansea, are the largest nickel-refineries in the United Kingdom. Here Dr Ludwig Mond set up

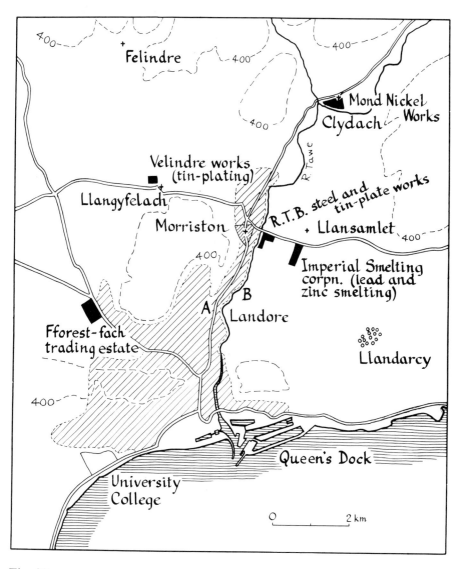

Fig. 33. THE SWANSEA DISTRICT

The lower Swansea valley showing some important sites mentioned in the text. A – the site of the first copper-smelting works in the eighteenth century; B – the site of the Siemens works; R.T.B. – Richard, Thomas & Baldwin. The approximate extent of the built-up area is indicated by oblique shading. Heights are in feet.

his works in 1900, attracted by the acknowledged reputation of the district in metal-working, and by the possibility of using large quantities of local gas for fuel. Copper-smelting has thus left in its train several flourishing metal industries: but it has also blighted the countryside, for nothing will grow where its poisonous fumes have contaminated the ground.

Steel-making and Tinplating

Since 1930 the steel industry of south Wales has been completely remodelled, and the district is now the greatest producer in the British Isles, the bulk of its output being directed to the tinplate industry. The first of the modern plants dates from 1930, when the Dowlais Company transferred operations to Cardiff. Here imported ore is delivered direct to the four blast furnaces which tower above the port installations; and the coke ovens supply Cardiff with most of its gas.

In 1938 a new large plant for the manufacture of sheet steel was established at Ebbw Vale, in the district where the Welsh iron industry had its birth. Government-sponsored, it provided employment for 5000 people in an area where new opportunities were sorely needed. Though far from its ore port (Newport), it benefits from local coking coal and good rail communications with its markets in London and the Midlands, and the choice of site is justified in that the works are being expanded. The Ebbw Vale works are the chief suppliers of steel for car bodies in this country; in addition they supply sheet to a local tinplate mill.

At Margam an existing iron and steel plant has been extended and modernized, and a great 203 cm continuous strip mill has been built, the whole forming the largest integrated works in Europe (Fig. 34). The Steel Company of Wales operates here what is essentially a steel town, stretching for 7 km along the seashore and employing 20,000 people. In the strip mill an ingot weighing 6 or 7 tonnes is quickly rolled out into a sheet over a kilometre in length: it may reach the consumer in the form of a car body, an electric radiator, a sink unit, or a toffee tin. With an annual capacity of 3 million tonnes, this one plant produces more than a third of the steel plate of the United Kingdom; much of this is forwarded to the new tinplate works at Trostre and Velindre, sited inland once again for sociological reasons. Overlooking the docks at Port Talbot, where the ore carriers unload, are the five blast furnaces. One, with a hearth diameter of 9·45 m, is the largest in the world.

The latest of the south Wales steel plants was opened in 1962 at Llanwern (Newport), on a virgin site with ample room for expan-

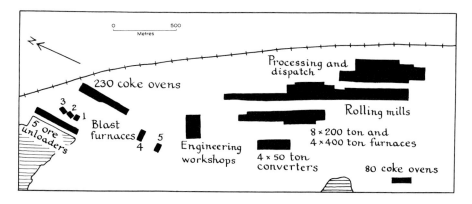

Fig. 34. THE WORKS OF THE STEEL COMPANY OF WALES, PORT TALBOT
Here is produced about 75 per cent. of all the tinplate in the United Kingdom. In 1970 blast furnace
no. 5 was the largest in the world. *By courtesy of the Steel Company of Wales.*

sion, close to coking coal, and with good rail connections to its
markets in London and the Midlands. The capacity of the works
is about $1\frac{1}{2}$ million tonnes a year, and it employs 6000 people.

The south Wales steel industry is now served by a new ore port
at Port Talbot, opened by H.M. the Queen in May 1970. This is the
largest tidal harbour to be built in Britain for 50 years, and the first
to accommodate 100,000-ton ore carriers.

Coal-mining

Two features distinguish the south Wales coalfield from other
British coalfields: the first relates to the character of the coal itself,
the second to the physical features of the region.

In this coalfield there is a wide range of coals, from steam coals
in the south and east, through coking coals to anthracite in the
north-west (Fig. 35). Each main type has had its effect on the
economic development of the coalfield. The coking coals have aided
the growth of the iron and steel industry; they were first worked at
the north-eastern outcrop, where many of the better seams are now
approaching exhaustion, but there are important and largely
untouched reserves in the south. It is calculated, for example, that
all the needs of the Margam works could be met if a single large
colliery were developed on the site, whereas today its coking coal
is supplied from seven different pits.

The steam coal of south Wales ('Cardiff coal') has in the past
enjoyed a wide reputation as bunker fuel. It is almost smokeless,

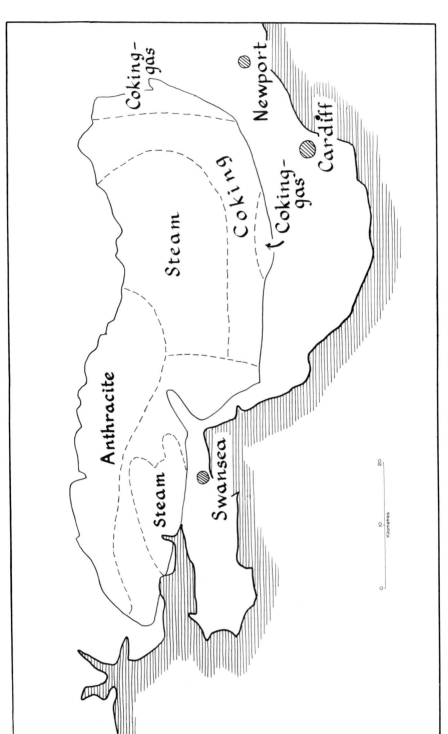

Fig. 35.   THE RANGE OF COALS IN THE SOUTH WALES COALFIELD   *By courtesy of the National Coal Board.*

keeps well in all climates, and is not easily broken in transit. The docks at Cardiff and Newport were built primarily to handle the export trade, and equipped with the characteristic coal hoists. But today only a quarter of the world's merchant tonnage is fuelled by coal; the coal traffic has dwindled to a trickle and so much of the dock capacity was idle that the Rochdale commission recommended closing the docks at Barry and the Bute Docks at Cardiff.

The demand for anthracite, on the other hand, remains more steady, for it is of great value in central heating. The outlet for the anthracite collieries is Swansea, and here coal shipments, though reduced, are far greater than those at Cardiff or Newport.

In its physical features the south Wales coalfield differs from all the others in Britain: it consists of a number of deep and steep-sided parallel valleys which have been trenched into a moorland plateau (Fig. 36). In the valley floors are the mines and the waste tips, the few terraces of miners' houses, the roads and the canals of the eighteenth century, and the later railway-lines. In each valley there are several collieries; the mining villages have grown so that they almost touch, and the valley is built up for virtually its entire course through the coalfield. Development is most intense in the east, where there is little room for playing-fields, let alone agriculture; in the west, however, the valleys are shallower, the plateau is lower, and the mines more widely spaced, so that the miners retain a link with farming and manage their small holdings.

In 1946, when the Coal Board was established, there were 203 pits in the coalfield. By 1958 71 of these had been closed; and the process is continuing – a recurrent threat to the security of the mining population. Even if the men are transferred to a neighbouring pit, this usually involves a longer journey; and in many cases there is no alternative employment to be had.

But reorganization has its brighter side. In the anthracite area two important new collieries have been developed: at Cynheidre, about 6 kilometres north of Llanelly; and the Abernant pit in a deserted valley which links southward to the Tawe valley at Pontardawe. At Cynheidre there are seven seams to be worked, and sufficient reserves for 200 years; this, the largest scheme undertaken by the Coal Board anywhere in Britain, provides employment for 945 men. Abernant is the deepest pit in the region: its shafts descend to 730 metres below the surface to work a virgin area of anthracite about 65 square km in extent, and it employs 1054 men. Both pits began producing in 1960, and reached full production in 1965.

The anthracite collieries, which in 1958 numbered 29, have

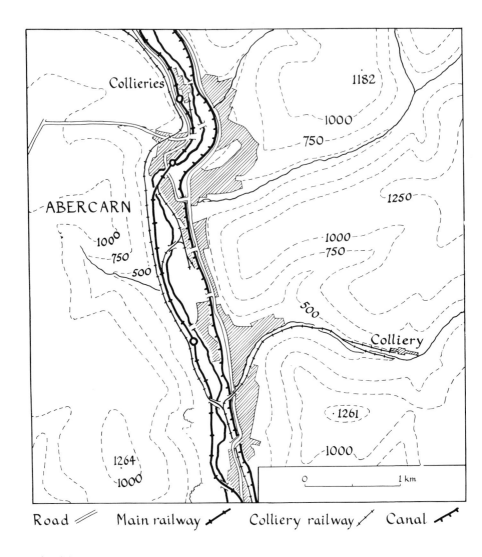

Fig. 36. A MINING VALLEY IN SOUTH WALES

This is part of the Ebbw Vale. The rivers have trenched deeply into a moorland plateau, and all human activity is cramped into a narrow corridor. Built-up areas are lined. Heights are in feet. *Based on the O.S. 1-inch map. Crown copyright reserved.*

gradually been reduced to 9 new or reorganized pits. In the process the total employment has been reduced from 15,000 to 9,000 men; but improved efficiency has limited the decline in output of anthracite. It is now about 2 million tonnes a year.

Reorganization extends also to the bituminous section of the coalfield, where almost every valley has its development scheme: this usually involves the closing of the older pits.

Since 1943 open-cast mining has been developed on an important scale. About a dozen main sites are jointly producing about $1\frac{1}{2}$ million tonnes annually, mainly from the northern outcrop. An important locality is at Glyn Neath, near the head of the Vale of Neath, where 200 men are scouring the cap of a hill to win what remains of the 5·5-metre and the 2·7-metre seams following shaft mining in the past. They are working at depths of up to 90 metres, and are using the world's biggest walking dragline.

In an attempt to absorb displaced miners and metal-workers the Government has encouraged the establishment of both heavy and light industries in the region. Trading estates have been set up at Cardiff, at Fforest-fach (Fig. 33, p. 123), at Bridgend, Hirwaun, and Treforest (west of Caerphilly); and in 1962 new estates were established at Maesteg and Caerphilly. An important single example of 'light industry' is the Hoover washing-machine factory at Merthyr Tydfil, which employs 3500 people – as many as some of the trading estates. The success of the Government efforts may be judged from the fact that since 1937 more than 100,000 people have found new employment.

The Oil Industry

In 1920 an undulating site between Swansea and Neath was chosen for the first major oil-refinery in the United Kingdom. To supply it with labour (it formerly employed 3000 people) a new village was built and named Llandarcy, after Mr W. K. D'Arcy, one of the founders of the British Petroleum Company (see Fig. 33, p. 123). The refinery is expanding: its 1963 capacity of $3\frac{1}{2}$ million tonnes has been raised to 8 millions. The installation plays an important part in the region: in addition to the normal distribution of refined products, it provides the fuel for the Margam and Newport furnaces and the raw materials for a new petro-chemical works near Briton Ferry; and for long oil was the staple cargo of Swansea docks.

But Queen's Dock cannot accommodate the large tankers that are currently in service, and for that reason the company built a new oil jetty and tank farm at Angle bay, on the south side of Milford Haven (Fig. 37). Here, as we have seen, is one of the finest natural harbours in Europe. The navigable channel provides 15 m of water at low water of extraordinary spring tides: sufficient in 1960 to receive the largest tanker in the world. A 95-km pipeline connects the jetty with Llandarcy.

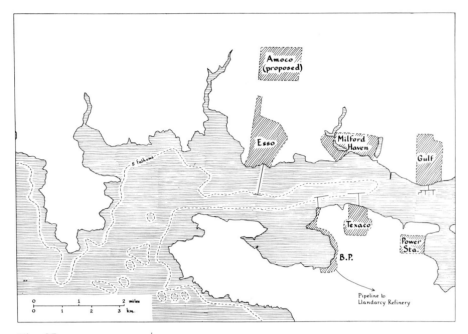

Fig. 37. MILFORD HAVEN

The Esso Refinery and B.P. Jetty were opened in 1960; the Texaco refinery was opened in 1964 and the Gulf refinery in 1968. A fourth is planned for Amoco. The generating station entered service in 1969 and is scheduled for completion in 1972.

On the north side of the Haven the Esso company opened a refinery in 1960; its capacity, initially 4·8 million tonnes per annum, has since been raised to 6·3 million tonnes.

Rapid developments took place during the 1960's. Texaco opened its first United Kingdom refinery in 1964 at Pwllcrochan, on the south side of the waterway: its capacity is 5·9 million tonnes. Four years later the Gulf Oil company opened its first British refinery in the area: this has a capacity of 4 million tonnes and is linked with a petro-chemicals plant. A fourth refinery, for the Amoco group, is planned (Fig. 37).

Advantage has been taken of the abundant supplies of oil for the construction of an oil-fired power station on the south shore of the Haven, near Pembroke. The plant produced its first electricity in 1969, and when complete in 1972 will have a capacity of 2000 MW: it will rank as one of the most powerful oil-fired power stations in Europe.

The depth of water in the Haven, which seemed ample in 1960, would have limited its use to 150,000 tonners. In 1967, however,

Plate 6. THE ESSO REFINERY ON MILFORD HAVEN

This formerly neglected corner of Wales has become a thriving industrial centre and a major oil port. The camera is pointing a little east of south (compare Fig. 37).

An Esso photograph

the port authority began to dredge the channel, and by 1971 the harbour had been deepened to accommodate 270,000 tonners, with a draught of 19 metres. Oil and power are highly mechanized industries, but the new works nevertheless employ nearly 2000 people and this formerly neglected corner of Wales has become Britain's second oil port.

Cardiff (pop. 278,221)

Cardiff was founded by the Romans, who established a military post on the east bank of the Taff. Six centuries later the derelict Roman fort was converted into a Norman castle, and by 1100 a burgh was in existence to the south of it. John Speed's map, drawn in the early seventeenth century, shows that the town even then remained essentially medieval in plan, protected by a moat and a wall pierced by four gates.

The rise of the city and port is related to the growth of coal-mining and iron-manufacture in the valleys which focus on it – the Rhymney and the Taff and their tributaries – and this in its turn led to the need for improved communication with the coast. The slow transport by pack-horse of coal and iron from Hirwaun and Aberdare, Merthyr and Dowlais, was superseded by the Glamorganshire canal, which in 1794 joined Merthyr and Aberdare to Cardiff. This was followed by the construction in 1841 of the Taff Vale railway – the first major railway in Wales.

Nearly 30 pits were sunk in the valleys tributary to Cardiff, and the city rose to become the greatest coal port in the world: the handling of 26 million tonnes of coal in 1913 apparently still stands as a world record. Today shipments are mainly coastwise, and they have shrunk to about $2\frac{1}{2}$ million tonnes, mainly handled at Barry. The imports of Cardiff include iron ore for the Dowlais steelworks, petroleum products, foodstuffs, and timber, including pitprops.

Cardiff contains the National Museum of Wales and one of the four constituent colleges of the University of Wales. In its spacious civic centre, where trees mingle with buildings, are also the administrative offices of Glamorganshire, easily the most populous county of Wales. Yet official recognition of its ranking has been tardy, and only in 1955 was Cardiff granted by letters patent the status of capital of Wales.

FOR FURTHER READING

Books

BOWEN, E. G.: *Wales, A Study in Geography and History* (Cardiff, 1952).
—— (Ed.): *Wales* (Methuen, 1957).
CUNDALL, L. B. and LANDMAN, T.: *Wales, an Economic Geography* (Routledge, 1925).
HOWE, G. M. and THOMAS, P.: *Welsh Landforms and Scenery* (Macmillan, 1965).
PRINGLE, J. and GEORGE, PROFESSOR T. NEVILLE: *South Wales*, British Regional Geology handbooks (H.M.S.O., 1948).
REES, HENRY: *British Ports and Shipping* (Harrap, 1958), Ch. 10.
THOMAS, T. M.: *The Mineral Wealth of Wales* (Oliver and Boyd, 1961).
TRUEMAN, SIR A. (Ed.), *The Coalfields of Great Britain* (Arnold, 1954), Ch. VI.

Articles

THOMAS, G. H.: 'The New Iron Ore Terminal at Port Talbot', in *Geography* (July 1969).
WATTS, D. G.: 'Milford Haven and its Ore Industry, 1958–69', in *Geography* (January 1970).

Maps

Geological map-coverage is patchy. The $\frac{1}{4}$-inch maps are still out of print, and there is only partial cover on the 1-inch scale.

The 7th edition 1-inch topographical maps 153 (Swansea) and 154 (Cardiff) are valuable, but some important works do not yet appear – for example, Llandarcy refinery, Velindre tinplate works, Abernant colliery, and the Newport steelworks.

Bartholomew's $\frac{1}{2}$-inch sheet 12 covers the coalfield; Milford Haven appears on sheet 11.

CHAPTER TEN

SCOTLAND: THE HIGHLANDS AND ISLES

SCOTLAND may be readily divided into three parts on grounds of both human and physical geography, and the two remarkably straight fault boundaries of the Central Lowlands provide unusually convenient limits. North of the line Stonehaven to Helensburgh are the Highlands and Islands: this division is the largest in area, the highest in relief, the wettest in rainfall, and the smallest in population. While there are several sub-regions, they have certain elements in common: ancient rocks, poverty of natural resources, remoteness, and dependence on the primary industries of farming and fishing. The region includes the crofting settlements and the only Gaelic-speaking area of Scotland; it contains two-thirds of the land area of Scotland but only 6 per cent. of its population.

Physical Basis

In the Highlands and Islands we find the most widespread exposure of the Pre-Cambrian rocks in Britain. They are divisible into three groups, which comprise, in order of age, the Lewisian Gneiss, the Moine Schists, and the Torridon Sandstone.

The oldest, the Lewisian Gneiss, occurs typically in the Outer Hebrides. Of sedimentary origin, it has been metamorphosed into an extremely hard material, forming the jagged peaks of Harris (rising to 800 m), exposing much bare rock in the high elevations, and giving rise to peat rather than soil in the lower parts. Only where the gneiss is covered with shell sand can the land be made at all productive.

The Moine Schists form the surface of most of the Highlands north-west of the Great Glen. These too are metamorphic rocks; but they break down more easily than the gneiss, and there are several potentially productive straths, such as those of Loch Broom, Strathnaver, and Halladale.

The Torridon Sandstone forms the coastal belt of the north-west Highlands, from Loch Alsh northward, around lochs Torridon and Broom to Cape Wrath. It consists of red and chocolate-coloured shales and sandstones, which appear to have accumulated in shallow water in a desert climate. They weather into gravelly, porous soils which easily dry out and are liable to over-grazing; but they offer limited possibilities for farming.

The Pre-Cambrian rocks were elevated, peneplained, and submerged below the Cambrian sea, receiving at least 600 metres of sediments. These now appear as grits, quartzites, limestones, and shales in a narrow belt east of the Torridon Sandstone, and present the unique feature in the Highlands of a series of west-facing scarps. The limestones, where present, offer decidedly better opportunities for farming, whether used as sheep pastures or as arable land.

During the Caledonian earth storm the enormous pressures were relieved not only by folding and faulting but by the sliding forward and sideways of great masses of rock. The extent of this displacement – the Moine Thrust – is estimated at about 16 kilometres; it usually forms the boundary between the Cambrian rocks and the Moine Schists. Of the same age are the granite intrusions of Caithness, of the north shore of Loch Linnhe and elsewhere, together with the remarkably straight fracture of the Great Glen, which traverses the entire Highlands from Loch Linnhe to the Moray Firth. In places there are two parallel faults, but generally the Glen has been carved along a single line of weakness, so that it is not, properly speaking, a rift valley.

W. Q. Kennedy has suggested that a lateral displacement has occurred along the fault to the extent of about 100 km – that the whole of the north-west Highlands has slipped south-westward! There certainly appears to be a lack of alignment in some of the granite masses each side of the fault, and an eastward displacement of the Kintyre coast in relation to the main highland edge (Fig. 38).

The great depth of Loch Ness (its floor descends to 240 m below sea-level) reflects its origin, and lends credence to the reports of a 'monster' there. Earth movements along the fault have not entirely ceased, and this is a British earthquake zone. The shocks of the Inverness earthquake of 1901 were felt all over the Highlands.

The Highlands south-east of the Great Glen are known as the Grampians; these, together with the Shetland Islands, are composed largely of old and varied metamorphic rocks – slates, limestones, and grits. Termed the Dalradian series, they cannot be precisely dated. Much of the highest land is composed of granite, and has summit levels at about 900 to 1200 metres. It includes the Cairngorms, Lochnagar, the Moor of Rannoch, the masses west of Aberdeen, and Ben Nevis itself (1343 m).

In Devonian times a gulf occupied what are now the eastern

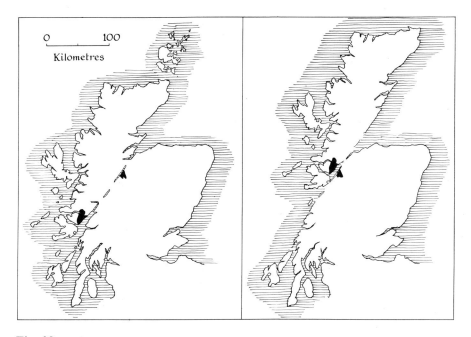

Fig. 38. A SUGGESTED DISLOCATION ALONG GLENMORE
The diagram on the right indicates the appearance of the coastline, other things being equal, if the (hypothetical) shift had not occurred. There is a more rational shape in the west of Scotland, and two masses of granite (here shown black), at present unrelated, come into alignment.

flanks of the Highlands and extended to the Orkneys. The Old Red Sandstone of these areas, in spite of its cover of glacial drift, shows itself in the remarkable extent of the cultivated land. There is a small coalfield near Campbeltown, in Kintyre; there are outliers of Triassic and Jurassic strata at Brora on the eastern coast of Sutherland, and in Skye; and there are Cretaceous rocks in Mull. All these are hundreds of miles from their main outcrops and are of great significance to the palæogeographer. More important in the human life of the region are the widespread exposures of Tertiary lava in Skye, Mull, Rum, Arran, and elsewhere, for they weather into what are potentially the most productive soils in the Highlands.

The Quaternary glaciers scoured and smoothed the surface and left their deposits on the lower land. The general pattern of relief and drainage, however, remains guided by structure. One pheno-menon of unusual interest is to be seen in Glen Roy, about 24 km north-east of Fort William. During a retreat phase the outlets of this and neighbouring glens were blocked by ice and lakes were formed, whose levels depended on the heights of the cols through which they overflowed. Three levels are known (350, 325, and 261 metres) and at each the lake waves cut a terrace or bench. These are the 'parallel roads' of Glen Roy.

Climate

The climate of the Scottish Highlands has several distinct characteristics: mild winters, heavy rain, strong winds, and abundant cloud. The rainfall ranges widely over quite small areas. It reaches a maximum where the highest ground faces the westerly winds. Ben Nevis receives 4090 mm annually, and even the low ground near by, if it has a westerly aspect, receives up to 2500 mm. In contrast, along the north and east coasts the rainfall is surprisingly low: the Caithness coast experiences less than 750 mm, while the sheltered coastal strip of Moray and Nairn has less than 635 mm, and grows even good crops of wheat.

The winter temperatures are exceptionally mild for the latitude: across the Atlantic in the same latitudes are the north of Labrador and the southern tip of Greenland! In lowland Caithness the mean January temperature is similar to that of East Anglia; but the humidity is higher, there is less sunshine (in spite of longer summer days), and in exposed situations there are strong winds. In the Shetlands there are on the average 180 gale days a year. Such places are almost treeless. In the sheltered valleys considerable planting by the Forestry Commission is taking place; and in the east, Moray and Nairn are the two most wooded counties in Great Britain.

From the point of view of human geography, we may divide the Highlands and Islands into three sub-regions: these are the crofting districts, the eastern fringe, and the main mass of the Highlands.

The Crofting Districts

Crofting is the usual type of farming practised along the whole of the intricately indented western coasts, in the Hebrides and in the Shetland Isles. It is characterized by a high degree of self-sufficiency, and by security of tenure. Almost every crofting settlement is on the coast, where there is most potential farm-land, where fishing offers a supplementary income, where seaweed is available for fertilizer, and where the soils are in places lightened by shell sand. The basis of crofting life is the co-operation of equals. Four men form a boat's crew, and the same four may form a work team on the land. The number of work teams, and hence the size of the 'township', depends on the amount of available arable land.

The homestead normally stands in or near its own arable land – often a plot of 1 to 2 hectares, running from the coastal road

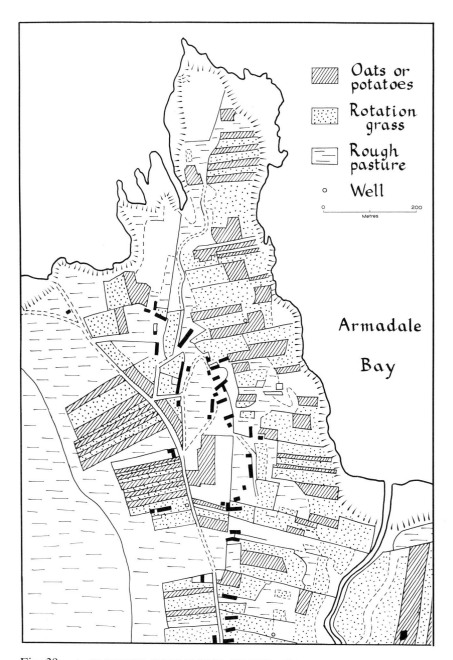

Fig. 39. A CROFTING SETTLEMENT ON THE NORTH COAST OF SUTHERLAND

This is Armadale, 13 km from the Caithness border. It has no shape: the dwellings (shown black) are scattered, and each crofter lives near or amid his holding. Many are part-time fishermen. There is an extraordinarily high proportion of arable land. *After E. T. Smith,* 1939.

up the lower slopes of the hillside. It is cultivated in strips on a five-year rotation, with two years under potatoes and oats and three under grass (Fig. 39); it is not enclosed, but the cattle are tethered for grazing on the rotation grass, and in winter are allowed loose to browse on the stubble. The summer hill grazing is held in common, but each crofter has a defined share (often exceeded!), expressed in terms of the pasturage for one cow.

The traditional 'black house' was a long, rectangular building with rounded corners, dry-stone windowless walls, and a hole in the roof to let out the smoke from the open peat fire. It was quiet; it was warm and draught-proof, and it was shared by the cow. Black houses are still in use; but the cow is housed separately, windows have been inserted, and a stove with a chimney replaces the open fire. Elsewhere there are 'model' cottages; but they are noisy and draughty and they do not blend with the landscape.

The crofter produces his own potatoes, fish, milk, and eggs, together with vegetables such as curly kale, red cabbage, leeks, carrots, turnips, and broad beans. Formerly barley bread was a staple food; today the crofter eats wrapped bread and cakes.

The Government provides grants to help the crofter to improve his dwelling; it assists in the development of piers and harbours; it supervises shipping services and encourages rural industries such as bulb-growing in the Hebrides and knitting in the Shetlands.

Nevertheless, crofting is a declining way of life. The population is falling; homesteads and piers lie ruined. In 1831 there were 200,000 people in the western Highlands and isles; since that time each census has revealed a successive decline in population, and in 1951 the number had fallen to 119,000. Some districts have fared worse than others: in Skye the population has fallen from 23,000 in 1841 to 7372 in 1971; in Mull, from 10,600 in 1821 to 1560 in 1971. More significant, the structure of the population has become unbalanced (Fig. 40); there is a preponderance of old people and a shortage of young people. In some townlands in the Shetlands there are no children at all; and in the remote bay of Sandwick in the island of Mainland (Shetlands) 26 of the 27 crofts are derelict.

The causes of this rural depopulation are complex. The introduction of sheep has led to the deterioration of pasture, over-grazing, and soil erosion; the crofter fishing industry has felt the competition of powered vessels; the young people have left the croft in search of a gayer life. For these there is no simple remedy.

The Outer Hebrides

The Outer Hebrides consist of one large island, subdivided ad-

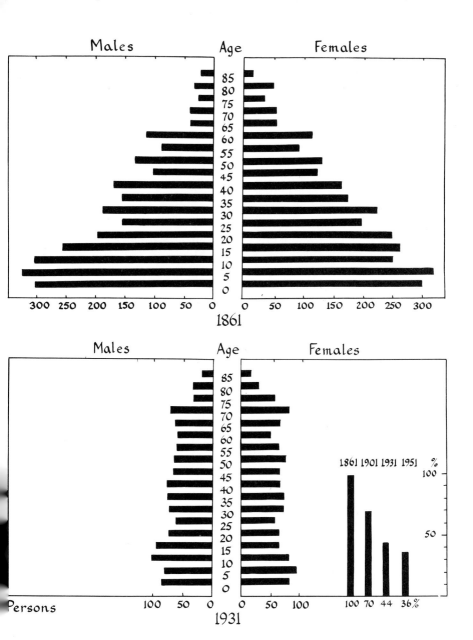

Fig. 40.   AGE STRUCTURES IN THE PARISH OF GAIRLOCH

In 1861 there was a balanced structure of population: apart from minor irregularities the age groups decrease as they progress from youth to age. By 1931 the population had become unstable. The proportion of children had greatly decreased while the older age groups were disproportionately large. The inset shows the change in total population expressed as a percentage of the 1861 figure. Gairloch is typical of many crofting parishes in the western Highlands and Isles. *After F. Fraser Darling*, 1955.

ministratively into Lewis (part of the county of Ross and Cromarty) and Harris (part of Inverness-shire), together with many smaller islands (also part of Inverness). The chief of these are North and South Uist, Benbecula, and Barra. Geologically the Outer Hebrides consist almost entirely of Lewisian Gneiss (Pre-Cambrian in age) and contemporaneous granite intrusions. Their special character springs from a relatively prosperous fishing industry, a comparatively high proportion of arable land (especially in the southern half), and the production of 'Harris Tweed' (mainly in the northern half).

The Outer Hebrides lie amid productive fishing-grounds, but the local industry has felt the competition of the powered vessel. Herring-fishing is centred on Stornoway, in Lewis. Lobster-fishing is more typically suited to the small boat: it has even increased in importance in recent years. Lobsters are trapped at Loch Roag, on the west coast of Lewis, and at other neighbouring inlets; Barra is famous for its cockle beaches.

At intervals along the western shores are cream-coloured beaches which indicate the presence of shell sand. Backing them is a narrow strip up to 3 km wide, where the lime from the shell 'sweetens' the soil and results in the growth of a rich natural pasture. When dressed with the abundant Laminaria seaweed from the shore this forms productive arable land, well seen in the western coasts of the Uists, Barra, and Benbecula: here nearly 12,000 people support themselves mainly by farming.

Lewis and Harris are agriculturally less favoured, and the people seek supplementary incomes in fishing and in tweed-making. Sheep are reared especially for their wool locally and in the Uists. Small quantities of heavy cloth of high quality are still produced in the Uists: the crofters spin and weave it by hand and colour it with vegetable dyes; but this is very expensive. Harris Tweed does not conform to such rigid specifications: officially it is 'made from pure virgin wool, produced in Scotland, spun, dyed and finished in the Outer Hebrides and hand woven by the islanders at their own homes. . . .' The yarn is produced at the mills at Stornoway; it is distributed to the crofters, who weave the cloth at home on semi-automatic looms, and return it to the mills for finishing. By farming, fishing, and tweed-making nearly 24,000 people support themselves in Lewis and Harris; the population is declining, but less rapidly than elsewhere.

The Shetland Islands

The Shetlands and the Orkneys, though often confused in popular imagination, are in reality quite different in character. The Orkneys, only 11 kilometres from the mainland, represent an extension of the Old Red Sandstone of lowland Caithness; they are well cultivated and relatively prosperous.

The Shetlands lie a further 95 kilometres away: they consist of granite and metamorphic rocks, eroded by ice, and almost completely mantled with peat bog. Arable land is scarce, and high winds prevent the growth of trees (cf. p. 24).

The Shetlands have cultural links with Norway: their 17,000 people are descended from Vikings, and till the fifteenth century the islands actually formed part of the Norse empire. As in the rest of the Highlands, the croft alone cannot support its family, and the men are part-time fishermen, or help in road-making or in other public works. But the local fishing industry has declined, and all around the coasts are the remains of disused piers. Commercial fishing is now centred upon Lerwick, the only town of the Shetlands, and their administrative and shopping centre. It has regular shipping links with Aberdeen, from which it draws fertilizers and provisions, and to which it sends the produce of the islands – in particular live animals and iced fish.

While the crofters of the Outer Hebrides have turned to cloth-making, the Shetlanders engage in knitting the fine, silky wool of the local sheep. So careful is the work, and so smooth the material, that a Shetland shawl will pass through a wedding ring. There are mineral resources on the islands: chromates, serpentine, and kyanite are all produced in Unst; but these industries cannot occupy more than a fraction of the inhabitants, and it seems inevitable that the population will continue to decline.

The Eastern Fringe

On the eastern coastal fringe of the Highlands there is a surprisingly high proportion of arable land. In most of the area the underlying rock is Old Red Sandstone: this influences the composition of the glacial drift, giving rise to a light, warm, well-drained soil; but this is only part of the explanation, since the arable belt continues into the Buchan peninsula, with its varied igneous and metamorphic rocks. The low relief and the relatively slight rainfall together with the cover of drift have allowed the development of an almost continuous belt of cultivation in lowland Caithness, and from the Dornoch Firth to Aberdeen.

The cool, humid conditions favour the growth of oats and turnips, and these are the two leading crops; but barley and even wheat are grown in appreciable quantities. A usual rotation is that which we have seen in the crofts of the west coast: oats, turnips, grass, grass, grass; but the turnips are sometimes replaced by sugar beet, potatoes, and cabbages. The crops are fed largely to animals – particularly to beef cattle, for this is a northern extension of the famous fattening belt of Aberdeenshire (p. 154). Elgin, Forres, and Nairn are market towns for the Moray Firth area, but the main centre for the whole region is Aberdeen, with a large cattle market.

The Main Highland Mass

By far the greater part of the Highlands consists of a virtually uninhabited moorland. This is not to imply that it is valueless, for real waste-land is confined to the bare summits and to the broken rocky slopes. Much of the surface lies at about 300 metres above sea-level, where there are remnants of an ancient peneplain. Its wetter portions form peat bog of little value; but the better-drained areas consist of heather moors, which are utilized as sheep runs, grouse moors, or deer 'forests'. Frequently the same land serves all three purposes, but it is noteworthy that in the higher and steeper areas only the more agile red deer can make use of the spells of fine weather for grazing.

A distinction may be drawn between the eastern and the western Highlands. In the west the mountains rise abruptly from the sea, with little or no coastal plain (Plate 7). Facing the prevailing winds, they receive over 2000 mm of rain per annum, compared with 750 to 1000 mm in the east. The rivers are short and swift; they erode rapidly, and soils, where they exist, are saturated and leached. In the east the rivers are longer, their gradients are more gentle, and owing to the colder winters much of the runoff is held back in the form of snow. These differences are reflected in the plant cover. Peat bogs are typical of the west, with damp oak woods in the sheltered hollows; in the east there are dry heather and grass moors, with pine and larch in the hollows.

The county of Sutherland claims the distinction of having the largest proportion of its surface in moorland – 96 per cent! Even here the straths were populated until the nineteenth century, though the farmers lived only at subsistence level. Between 1807 and 1820 about 15,000 people were moved – some forcibly – to the coastal areas, where they were given land to cultivate and encouraged to enter the fishing industry, or were enabled to emigrate to Canada. Several small ports were established, of which only Helmsdale has survived.

As in the Welsh hills, the upland sheep farm cannot support the

Plate 7. A HILL SHEEP FARM IN THE WESTERN
HIGHLANDS

*This farm is at the head of Loch Duich, opposite the Isle of Skye; the
valley floor is almost at sea level, while the mountains overlooking it
rise to over 760 metres. Aspect is important: the hillside in the background faces north and offers little pasture whereas the opposing slope
offers grass and heather. The farmer rears sheep, but cannot fatten
the lambs, so these are sold to lowland farms; he rears beef calves,
for there is little local demand for milk.*

Photo by courtesy of the Association of Agriculture

whole of its flock during the winter. There are large autumn sales,
and some of the remainder are wintered in the lowlands.

Even apparently useless land has its value as gathering grounds
for water-power, and the lot of the Highlander has been greatly
improved in the last generation or so by the widespread provision
of electricity. Since the establishment in 1943 of the North of
Scotland Hydro-electric Board the number of power-stations

(including diesel and steam-generating stations) has risen from 16 to 63 and their installed capacity has grown from 230,000 to 1·8 million kW. More than 90 per cent. of the premises in the region are now supplied with electricity.

There is little point in examining the details of specific schemes. Every river system in the Highlands is now harnessed, and the map (Fig. 41) indicates the widespread net of power-stations and distribution lines. The greatest head is of 415 metres, at Finlarig (Perthshire); the largest single station (Sloy) has a capacity of 130,000 kW, but about half the stations are small, with capacities of 1000 to 10,000 kW.

In some of the outlying islands the development of hydro-electricity is not feasible. There are diesel-electric stations at Lerwick, Kirkwall, and Stornoway, and at Daliburgh, in South Uist: all these are to be extended. In the Inner Hebrides Skye, Mull, and Arran have hydro-electricity, Islay has a diesel plant, while Jura is supplied by submarine cable from Kintyre.

There is little scope for the further development of conventional water power in the Highlands, and future expansion will probably be in the form of pumped storage and nuclear power. More than 7000 factories now depend on cheap electricity. The most significant addition will be the large aluminium smelter, now under construction, on a fine natural harbour at Invergordon (22 km north of Inverness). With an annual output of 100,000 tonnes, this will quadruple the output of the British Aluminium Company, whose existing works are at Fort William and Kinlochleven, near the southern end of the Great Glen. There is further discussion of electricity in the north of Scotland in Chapter 24, p. 380.

The lochs of the Great Glen were joined in the early nineteenth century by Thomas Telford to form the Caledonian Canal; this is still regularly used by fishing-vessels, small oil-tankers, and pleasure craft. Inverness, at its northern end, is the largest purely Highland town; it is the county town, a railway junction and market, a tourist centre and small port.

Aberdeen

The port and city of Aberdeen (pop. 182,006) is the third largest in Scotland. It is well situated to serve the relatively populous eastern fringe of the Highlands, and it maintains regular sea connections with the outlying islands – Stornoway, in Harris, Kirkwall, in the Orkneys, and Lerwick, in the Shetlands. In addition, coastal services join it with Dundee to the south, Wick and Thurso to the north, and even Liverpool, around the north of Scotland.

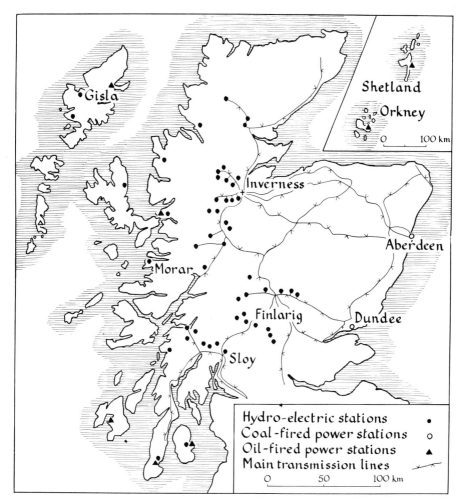

Fig. 41. ELECTRICITY GENERATION IN THE NORTH OF SCOTLAND
The Aberdeen station has now been closed down.
By courtesy of the North of Scotland Hydro-Electric Board.

Aberdeen is the chief fishing-port of Scotland, and benefits from its proximity to the North Sea fishing-grounds. During the herring season – from May to September – the port is busy with the work of fuelling, refitting, icing, and provisioning the fishing-vessels. The herrings are salted, dried or cured, or nowadays quick-frozen; and much of the catch moves by express train to Billingsgate. The whole of Albert Basin is devoted to the fishing industry, and it spreads on to the wharves of the Dee. The fuel requirements of the fishing-fleet are reflected in the unusually large imports of coal and petroleum.

In Aberdeen there is an old-established shipbuilding industry with a local flavour; it specializes in the construction of fishing-vessels, and in the general-purpose ships which serve the Orkneys and Shetlands – equipped to handle not only passengers and general cargo, but also live animals and frozen fish. Two other characteristic industries of the city are the quarrying and working of granite from the hills inland, and the manufacture of paper; to serve the latter, ships bring wood-pulp from the Baltic and china clay from Cornwall. The chief export, apart from bunker fuel, is oats for seed and fodder: this is shipped to most of the east-coast ports of England.

Aberdeen has the most northerly university in the British Isles, and its Department of Geography has a special interest in Scandinavia. Many of the activities of the whole Highland region are thus reflected in Aberdeen.

FOR FURTHER READING

Books

For the physical basis, see the British Regional Geology handbooks (H.M.S.O.).
PHEMISTER, J.; *The Northern Highlands* (1960).
READ, H. H.: *The Grampian Highlands* (1957).
RICHEY, J. E.: *The Tertiary Volcanic Districts* (1956).
The reports of the Land Utilisation Survey, though out of date, are still valuable. Among them are:
Part 2, *Moray and Nairn*, F. H. W. Green (1937).
Part 3, *Sutherland*, F. T. Smith (1939).
Part 15, *Caithness*, S. W. E. Vince (1944).
DARLING, F. FRASER (Ed.): *West Highland Survey* (Oxford University Press, 1955), is an essential work, and is acknowledged as an important source for this chapter.
Report and Accounts, North of Scotland Hydro-electric Board, annually.
O'DELL, A. C. and WALTON, K.: *The Highlands and Islands of Scotland* (Nelson, 1962).

Articles

LEA, K. J.: 'Hydro-Electric Power Generation in the Highlands of Scotland' *Transactions, Institute of British Geographers* (March 1969).
TURNOCK, D.: 'Evolution of Farming Patterns in Lochaber', *Transactions, Institute of British Geographers* (June 1967).
TURNOCK, D.: 'Regional Development in the Crofting Counties', *Transactions, Institute of British Geographers* (December 1969).

Maps

The only geological map for the entire region is on the scale of 1:625,000.
The O.S. Land Utilisation map on the same scale provides a valuable picture of the distribution of the arable land.
The region is covered by the O.S. ¼-inch maps, sheets 1–6.

CHAPTER ELEVEN

CENTRAL AND
SOUTHERN SCOTLAND

STRUCTURALLY this major region contains two contrasting units – the Central Lowlands and the Southern Uplands. In both the general alignment of the strata is from north-east to south-west, in conformity with the Caledonian trend. The most remarkable of the trend lines are the two prominent faults which bound the Central Lowlands: each is about 210 km long, and both continue into Ireland. They are virtually parallel, and yet are 70 km apart. The rocks between them are younger than those beyond them, and the land here must have subsided many thousands of feet to form a rift valley, one of the most striking elements in the structure of the British Isles.

The materials which form its upper surface are mainly sediments and lavas of Devonian and Carboniferous age. The Devonian rocks outcrop in a broad, continuous belt in the north (Strathmore) and in a narrow, interrupted belt in the south, and have been down-warped to form a major syncline. In Kincardineshire their various members – sandstones, shales, conglomerates, and lavas – combine to reach the astonishing thickness of 5500 metres, or over three miles. The Ochil and Sidlaw Hills are composed of volcanic rocks of Devonian age which have been raised to form an arch; erosion of its summit has exposed the underlying softer Old Red Sandstone sediments in the fruitful Carse of Gowrie, and has admitted the sea to form the Firth of Tay.

The floor of the Devonian syncline is occupied by the various Carboniferous strata, whose outcrops have been influenced by the position of minor intersecting earth folds and subsequent erosion. The Scottish coalfields, in common with those bordering the English Pennines, lie in separate basins, and have been greatly disturbed by faulting (Fig. 42).

The Scottish Carboniferous strata differ from those of England in several ways. In the lower part of the series sandstones are prominent, and these are mapped as the Calciferous Sandstone: in Fifeshire and the Lothians they include beds of oil shale, which

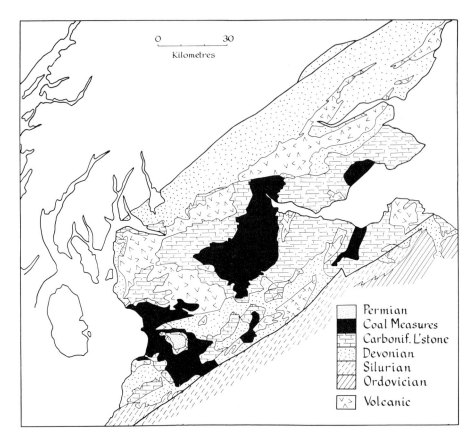

Fig. 42. THE SCOTTISH LOWLANDS: GEOLOGY

Essentially this is a structural trough, floored by Carboniferous rocks. The underlying Devonian strata outcrop on the north and south margins, and a line of volcanic hills extends between the Firths of Clyde and Tay. The remarkably straight fault boundaries are well illustrated.

have had an important influence on the activities of the region. The Upper Carboniferous Limestone contains valuable coal seams, so that the Scottish coalfields are greater in extent than the outcrops of Coal Measures might suggest. Finally, in Lower Carboniferous times there was widespread volcanic activity. The resulting lavas are well seen in the Campsie Fells, the Dumbarton Heights, and in the plateaux south of Glasgow, while the prominent hills of Arthur's Seat and the Castle Rock at Edinburgh represent the stumps of Carboniferous volcanoes.

The hilly country south of the southern boundary fault consists essentially of a plateau of older Palæozoic rocks whose summits rise above 600 metres. The outcrops run north-east and south-west, and the oldest strata – of Ordovician age – are exposed in the north-west, forming the Lammermuir and Moorfoot Hills. The apparently simple arrangement of the rocks masks a complex structure, for there are here a series of isoclinal folds which were formed during the course of the Caledonian earth movements (Fig. 43). They were planed off subsequently by erosion, and their existence is betrayed only by lens-shaped inliers which represent the cores of the upfolds.

Most of the plateau is formed of strata of Silurian age and of varied physical character: they comprise grits, shales, limestones, mudstones, and conglomerates. Among the Ordovician rocks are lavas, volcanic agglomerates, and 'ash'. In the south-west are other igneous rocks, for the wild and rugged moorlands of Loch Dee and the mountains Cairnsmore of Fleet and Criffel are composed of granite which was intruded into the Ordovician and Silurian sediments towards the end of the Caledonian earth storm, in Devonian times.

The structural grain of central and southern Scotland thus ranges north-east and south-west; but on climatic and human grounds it is useful to separate the wetter, mainly industrial west from the drier, mainly agricultural east. The respective regional capitals are Glasgow and Edinburgh.

SOUTH-WEST SCOTLAND

Climatically south-west Scotland may be defined as the region with more than 1000 mm of rain per annum. Arable farming yields place to grassland farming, and here is the home of the famous red-and-white milking breed, the Ayrshire cattle. Industrially, this is the major coal-producing region of Scotland; it contains the country's entire iron and steel industry, and most of its shipbuilding capacity. Here too is Scotland's largest city, and her chief port.

The industries of south-west Scotland cannot be explained solely in terms of the physical background. It is true that there were here two valuable raw materials – splint coal, a hard, slaty type of coal, which could be used 'raw' (that is, without coking) in the nineteenth-century iron furnaces, and useful iron ores which occurred in the Coal Measures themselves. But the industries of the region were in existence before the Industrial Revolution, and their origin may be traced, perhaps, to the union of the Scottish and English Parliaments in 1707. This opened the American colonies to Glasgow traders, so that sugar, cotton, and tobacco soon arrived in quantity in the Clyde.

The river, however, was untamed, interrupted by sandbanks and

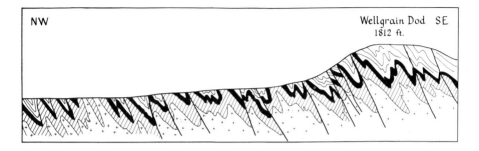

Fig. 43. A GEOLOGICAL SECTION IN THE SOUTHERN UPLANDS
This section, exposed in the valley of the Clowgill Burn (a tributary of the Clyde), about 15 kilometres north-east of Sanquhar, illustrates isoclinal folding in the lower Silurian strata of the Southern Uplands. The length represented is about 2 kilometres. *After J. Pringle*, 1948.

waterfalls, rich in salmon, and unnavigable at Glasgow (which, indeed, had originated as a fording-point). The trade of the district was handled at the outports of Irvine and Port Glasgow, the latter having been built specially for the purpose in 1662.

Three of the local industries had their origin in the colonial traffic: they are sugar-refining, tobacco-processing, and cotton-manufacture. The sugar trade is based on Greenock, where the port is equipped with grab cranes and hoppers for bulk handling, and where sugar forms 80 per cent. of the overseas imports. There are local refineries, and in Glasgow, sugar-refining machinery is manufactured: this is an industry with a world-wide reputation.

Glasgow (pop. 896,958), in common with other west-facing ports, has long had an interest in the import and manufacture of tobacco. Here the firm of Stephen Mitchell and Son was founded as early as 1723; this, together with three other well-known local concerns, is now combined within the Imperial Tobacco Company, with two large works in the city.

For the manufacture of cotton the Glasgow region possesses several advantages: it has exceptionally soft water together with a humid climate, and the Clyde and its tributaries offered the opportunity for the development of water-power. Between 1760 and 1830 the industry developed rapidly, and during the process the population of Glasgow expanded from 28,000 to 200,000. By 1860 there were 150 cotton-mills in the region. But the American Civil War interrupted the supplies of the raw material, and the cotton-masters were forced to look elsewhere.

Today the cotton industry survives mainly at Paisley, whose whole prosperity depends on the manufacture of thread. Here the mills of J. and P. Coats, Ltd., employ about 8000 people. They provide a good example of industrial momentum – where an activity survives owing to inherited skills and established reputation rather than physical advantages. The cotton is no longer imported locally, but is received from Liverpool; the reels are manufactured in Scandinavia, and are imported through Leith and Grangemouth.

The industry to which the cotton-manufacturers turned, about 1860, was shipbuilding; and shipbuilding was closely linked with the production of iron and steel and the mining of coal. This group of industries has for long formed the core of the manufacturing activities of south-western Scotland.

Coal-mining

Scotland is rich in coal, and the Glasgow region has been the focus of many large and productive pits. There are still 2 sizable collieries within a radius of 20 km of the city centre; 30 km to the east are another 3 pits, and in Ayrshire there are 3 workings, from which Belfast is supplied with coal through the ports of Ayr, Troon, and Ardrossan.

The supply of prime coking coal, however, is limited, and is supplemented from Durham; some of the better seams are approaching exhaustion, and the output of Scottish coal, especially that of the Glasgow region, is declining. In 1947 13 per cent. of the nation's coal was mined in Scotland; by 1970 the proportion had fallen to 8½ per cent. In order to reduce financial losses, the National Coal Board has closed many pits. The effect upon employment is bound to be serious, and is aggravated by the increased use of machinery. In 1957 about 87,000 people were engaged in mining; by 1970 the labour force had been reduced to 29,500. In the space of 13 years the mining population has been reduced to one-third.

Iron and Steel

In 1759 at Carron, near Falkirk, there was established one of the world's earliest large-scale ironworks. It drew on the local supplies of iron and coal, and it is still flourishing, though it now uses imported ores. The Scottish ironmasters pioneered many new techniques, as did also their contemporaries in engineering and shipbuilding. Here were witnessed many of the advances which marked the Industrial Revolution. In 1769 James Watt produced his steam-powered pumping engine. In 1802 this type of engine was embodied in the *Charlotte Dundas*, which ran successfully on the Forth and Clyde canal and constituted the first practical steamboat. In 1818 the lighter *Vulcan* was built on the Monkland canal, near Glasgow – and is claimed to be the first iron ship. In

1828 the hot blast was developed, improving the process of smelting and allowing the use of the local blackband ore; in 1842 the steam hammer was produced, and speeded up the work in the forge.

The production of local ore reached a maximum of 2·6 million tonnes in 1880; but as in most British coalfield areas output has declined virtually to extinction, and the modern steel industry depends upon imported ore.

The entire Scottish iron and steel industry is concentrated within a radius of 25 km of Glasgow. It has its own distinct character. It maintains close connections with shipbuilding and shipbreaking, for it supplies plates and castings to the builders and it draws large quantities of scrap from the breakers. The manufacture of alloy steels forms an important branch of the industry, and in this respect Scotland is second only to Sheffield. Nearly one-fifth of the output is destined for export: this is typical of Scottish manufactures in general, and stems from her relative isolation from the rest of the United Kingdom.

The oldest ironworks is the Carron works, whose two small blast furnaces produce foundry iron alone – that is, iron for castings. The largest and newest works are at Ravenscraig, on the eastern outskirts of Motherwell, and these form an impressive introduction to central Scotland for the visitor who arrives from England by rail. Here a fully integrated steelworks costing over £100 million has been established in what in 1954 were green fields. Their development was completed in 1963 by the commissioning of a new hot strip mill, and it is expected that 30 per cent. of its output will be absorbed by the new Rootes Group car factory at Linwood.

Four more steelworks, one of them specializing in tubes, operate in the same area; others are near Coatbridge and along the Clyde on the eastern outskirts of Glasgow. To supply all these with imported ore a new terminal has been constructed at Glasgow docks: it handles cargoes from many lands – from Sweden and Labrador, Newfoundland and Spain, north and west Africa and Venezuela. Iron is now by far the leading import of Glasgow.

Shipbuilding

Along the Clyde there are 11 shipbuilding establishments. Jointly in 1970 they launched 30 vessels, totalling 297,000 tons – nearly one-third of the total tonnage launched in the United Kingdom. How has this come about?

The growth of shipbuilding is not easily explained, but it clearly could not have happened without the improvement of the river. This important undertaking was carried out according to the plans of John Golborne in 1773. The river was confined between narrow walls to increase its scour; sandbanks were dredged, and rocky barriers were blasted away, so that (with later improvements) vessels drawing 10 metres of water can now reach the city docks at high tide. The Clyde is almost as artificial as the Suez Canal.

There are shipyards at Troon and Ardrossan, at Greenock, Port Glasgow, Dumbarton, and Bowling, and others within the city boundary. Most famous of all are John Brown's of Clydebank, where the mouth of a tributary stream widens the river locally and permits the launching of very large vessels. Here were built the giant Cunarders. Scott Lithgow, with new berths along the lower Clyde, can build even larger ships, and are currently constructing two vessels of more than 260,000 tons d.w.

The Clyde shipbuilders are versatile. In addition to orthodox vessels they produce icebreakers and dredgers, ferries and floating cranes. A whole range of related industries has developed in the region: they include marine engineering, the manufacture of navigational instruments, the production of ropes and canvas, carpets and furniture, ventilation and refrigeration equipment, and the construction of shipyard cranes and sluice gates.

But shipbuilding is one of the first industries to suffer in a trade recession, and the traditional Scottish industries are therefore particularly vulnerable. In 1933 for every 10 men working there were 3 unemployed, and even in recent years unemployment in Scotland has been nearly twice the national average. To offset the dependence on a single group of industries, industrial estates have been established similar to those of south Wales. By 1963 there were 21 Government-sponsored estates, employing about 100,000 people, and producing a great variety of light manufactures, such as clocks, typewriters and accounting machines, and electronic equipment. North American firms are well represented, and illustrate the international outlook of Scottish enterprise. A recent important advance has been the establishment of motor-car plants at Bathgate and Linwood, whose combined labour forces number about 8500 men.

SOUTH-EAST SCOTLAND

While south-west Scotland forms a single closely knit industrial region, south-east Scotland is more fragmented and more varied in its activities. The rivers Tay, Forth, and Tweed serve to demarcate four sub-regions. North of the Tay is a district which for want of a better name we shall call the Dundee region; between the Tay and Forth is the Fife peninsula; south of the Forth are the

Lothians; and beyond the Lammermuir and Moorfoot Hills is the Tweed basin. Each region has its distinct character.

The Dundee Region

The Sidlaw Hills separate a narrow lowland (Strathmore) in the north from a larger coastal lowland in the south. The Sidlaws consist of a plateau of volcanic rocks whose general surface is between 120 and 180 metres, but whose summits rise above 300 metres. Most of the surface is strewn with glacial drift, and only on the crest are masses of basalt to be seen. The higher land is clothed in heather, bracken, and rough pasture, together with plantations of pine; in the valleys, however, the volcanic rocks weather to rich soils which support valuable arable land and pasture.

North of the Sidlaws, the surface of Strathmore lies at about 60 metres O.D. and is traversed by meandering rivers with broad flood-plains. The soils are of alluvial or glacial origin, but, reflecting the underlying Old Red Sandstone, they usually consist of fertile reddish loams. These are extensively cultivated, and the arable land is interrupted only by the pastures of the river flats and by occasional patches of heath and woodland on morainic sands and gravels. This remarkably high proportion of cultivation is the most characteristic feature of the whole of the lowland area of south-eastern Scotland.

In Strathmore 90 per cent. of the improved land is under the plough, and only 10 per cent. remains permanent pasture. Rotation grass accounts for 30 per cent. of the arable area; it is followed by oats (about 25 per cent.), turnips and swedes (12 per cent.), and potatoes (9 per cent.). Wheat occupies about 6 per cent. of the arable land, and barley about 2 per cent. Arable farming is linked with the rearing and fattening of high-quality beef cattle, in particular the famous Aberdeen Angus breed, a black-polled animal which attains a great weight. It is pastured on the rotation grass in summer, and in winter is stall fed on turnips, oats, and hay. Its manure in turn nourishes the turnip and potato crops.

South of the Sidlaws is the coastal plain. Devonian sediments form its floor, but these are masked by estuarine clays in the Carse of Gowrie and by glacial material elsewhere. Again, this is predominantly an arable district. The most valuable crop is the potato, which is particularly important near the towns. It is usually followed in the rotation by wheat, which grows surprisingly well in spite of the fact that it is far north of the normal growing area of the United Kingdom. It is cultivated at up to 150 m on the southern flank of the Sidlaws, where volcanic soils and a southerly aspect are advantages. The climate is almost as favourable as that of East Anglia: on many summer days the temperature rises above 21°C; the average daily sunshine in June exceeds 6½ hours, and the rainfall is low. In these circumstances extraordinarily high yields are obtained.

Small fruits, chiefly raspberries, but also currants and strawberries, are cultivated around Dundee and Arbroath and between Brechin and Montrose, where there are sheltered sites with a southerly aspect. The acreage is comparatively small, but in favoured districts reaches 4 per cent. of the arable land. In the same areas market-garden produce is raised, including carrots, onions, cabbages, rhubarb, peas, and beans. There are jam factories and canning and bottling plants at Dundee and Montrose.

We may suitably illustrate the agriculture of the region from a farm in the Carse of Gowrie (Fig. 44). Its land comprises mainly the marine alluvium of the Carse itself, at about 15 metres above sea-level, but rises northward to include a small tract of the Old Red Sandstone of the Sidlaw foothills. The proportions of arable and permanent pasture in this instance are almost equal.

Of the arable crops, the most valuable is potatoes. The farmer raises a crop of early potatoes, and follows this by the main crop, which is grown for seed and sold in England. The potatoes of eastern Scotland are especially valuable as seed since the cool climate and the sea breezes discourage greenfly, which tend to be a pest to potato-growers elsewhere.

In point of area, however, potatoes are exceeded by oats. Like the main potato crop, the better oats are sold for seed, while the smaller grains are sieved out and fed to stock. Wheat is the third crop, and is all sold for milling; turnips and swedes equal the wheat acreage, and are both used for winter feed. In addition the farmer grows 2 hectares of sugar beet, on contract to the factory at Cupar, in Fifeshire.

The permanent pasture is exceptionally rich, and stock fatten up quickly on it. The farmer buys about 100 Irish Shorthorn cattle each year for fattening: these have been imported through Glasgow. He also buys about 180 Scottish Blackface lambs when they are half grown (about 5 or 6 months old), for this highland breed fattens rapidly on rich lowland pastures; and he rears his own lambs from a flock of about 40 Blackface ewes, crossing them with his Border Leicester ram: the resulting lambs combine the hardiness of the mountain breed with the rapid maturing of the lowland breed.

Formerly noted for apples, the Carse now produces only a little tree fruit. The main market for the farm is not Dundee, but Perth.

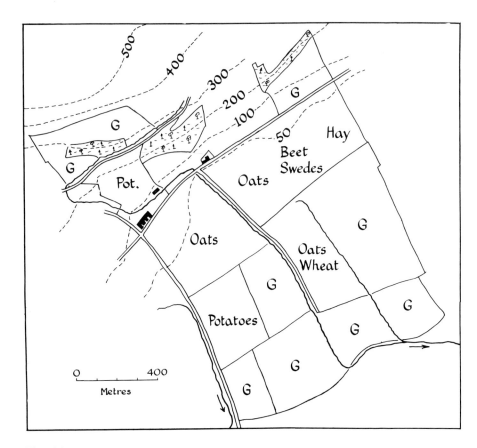

Fig. 44. A FARM IN THE CARSE OF GOWRIE
G = permanent grassland. Heights are in feet. *By courtesy of the Association of Agriculture.*

Dundee

The prosperity of Dundee (pop. 182,084) is closely bound up with the manufacture of jute, which employs about 18,000 people, or 20 per cent. of the working population. Here are nine-tenths of all the jute spindles of the United Kingdom. The jute industry, however, was a relatively late addition to the earlier textile manufactures of wool and linen; its rise was linked with the interruption of flax imports by the Crimean War (1854–56), and was aided by the growth of the local whaling industry (for whale oil was used to soften the jute fibres before spinning them).

The first full cargo of jute arrived from Calcutta in 1840. The annual import in 1846 was 19,000 tonnes, and in 1866, 63,000 tonnes; by the end of the century it had risen to 279,000 tonnes. During the course of a boom in jute Dundee doubled her population; new docks were laid out for the jute traffic, and related industries became established, including the manufacture of linoleum (which has a jute basis) and the production of jute-processing machinery. Today 40 separate firms engage in the industry; 70 per cent. of the overseas imports of Dundee consist of raw jute, and one-third of the total exports consist of manufactured jute. Jute has many uses: as sacks, bags, and binder twine; as reinforcement for upholstery and clothing; in carpets, tarpaulin, roofing felt, damp courses, and even ceilings.

The linen industry of Dundee survives and prospers, employing about 2000 people. It supplies in particular the local shipyard with canvas for hatch-covers, deck-chairs, and life-jackets. Dundee is not only the centre of the most specialized jute industry in Europe, it is also the regional capital of a wide area, and a centre for university education.

The Fife Peninsula

The Fife peninsula contains several contrasting physical elements, but it has an essential unity based on a prosperous and mainly arable farming. It is bounded to the north-west by the Ochil Hills, whose tilted lavas, rounded by the Quaternary ice, present a landscape of rough pasture and new plantations in striking contrast to the surrounding cultivated land. A second lower and interrupted belt of lavas runs parallel to the Ochils but farther south, and between the two uplands is a longitudinal valley, floored with Old Red Sandstone. Its western section is the basin of Kinross, containing the broad and shallow Lake Leven: this, perhaps, like Lake Victoria and Lough Neagh, is the result of subsidence of the surface following the emission of large quantities of lava. To the east is the Howe of Fife – drained now by the river Eden, but with a surface so level that it must formerly have been the floor of a lake.

Bordering the Firth of Forth is a broad belt of Carboniferous rocks. In the east these consist of the Calciferous Sandstone; in the west, of Carboniferous Limestone; and in the centre, of Coal Measures: this is the Fifeshire coalfield, which reaches the Firth in the broad bay between Kirkcaldy and Largo, and faces across the estuary the corresponding coalfield of Midlothian. Much of the surface is strewn with boulder clay, whose composition, though variable, generally reflects the character of the underlying rocks. Since the end of the Ice Age the land has risen in stages and there is a coastal fringe of raised beaches at 7·5, 15, and 30 metres: these offer fertile level terraces for cultivation and dry sites for settlement. The soils range widely in character. Among the richest are those derived from volcanic material, for these contain phosphate of lime from the mineral apatite; those derived from the Carboniferous Limestone, however, tend to be heavy and cold.

Fifeshire has a higher proportion of arable land than any other Scottish county. The spread of cultivation is interrupted only by the summits of the hills or by lowland moors, such as are found along the coastal tract between St Andrews and the mouth of the Tay: here there are heather-clad sand-dunes, plantations, the famous golf-links, and the oldest university in Scotland.

Cash cropping is combined with the fattening of sheep and cattle, and the following 7-course rotation, which is commonly followed, illustrates the range of crops: oats, potatoes, wheat, turnips, barley or oats, hay, and grass. Dairy farming becomes more important in the south-west, to supply the relatively large urban population with fresh milk. Barley is grown particularly in the north-east, where the soils are lighter, the rainfall lower, the winters milder, and where there is a high proportion of sunshine.

Potatoes are of special significance in the Howe of Fife. Here are produced some of the finest in Britain, on soils derived from the sands and gravels which overlie the Old Red Sandstone. In this district too, at Cupar, is the only sugar-beet factory in Scotland. Its presence has acted as a stimulus to the growing of beet locally, for here transport costs are at their lowest.

The Fifeshire coalfield is a rich one with about 30 workable seams and an under-sea extension whose seams total about 37 m in thickness. Compared with other Scottish fields, the costs of production are low and output per man is high; but the richest reserves are at great depth, and new large-capacity mines will be needed to tap them. The output, formerly 10 million tonnes per annum, has shrunk to a mere 2 million; the 40 collieries of a few years ago had dwindled to 14 by 1965, and 7 more of these were closed by 1967. Here are the usual spoil heaps, subsidence, light railways, and sprawling villages such as Cowdenbeath and Lochgelly; and here is the chief coal port of Scotland: Methil. Fifeshire has an old-established tradition of manufactures, which include paper-making, linen textiles, and linoleum. The linen industry originated in the fifteenth century from locally grown flax, and still flourishes at Kirkcaldy, Leven, Cupar, and other centres. To linen were added the manufacture of cotton, silk, rayon, and nylon, and it is significant that the Queen's silken wedding dress was produced at Dunfermline. Related industries include the manufacture of ropes, twines, and oilskins, and there is a remarkable specialization in Kirkcaldy of linoleum, the two basic raw materials for which are jute and linseed oil.

The Lothians

The three counties of East Lothian, West Lothian, and Midlothian correspond broadly with the belt of land which drains northward to the Firth of Forth. It includes a coastal lowland, which is backed by plateaux that rise above 460 metres. To the west is the Clyde basin; to the south-east is the basin of the Tweed.

Two mountain masses following the Caledonian trend thrust themselves into the coastal lowland and narrow it: these are the Lammermuir Hills, built of resistant, impermeable, and tightly folded Ordovician and Silurian sediments; and the Pentland Hills, formed of Devonian lavas. The lavas account in large measure for the strategic situation of Edinburgh, and outliers of similar material form the Castle Rock and the neighbouring heights, which give a distinctive setting to the capital.

The lowlands correspond with areas of Carboniferous sediments. In the lowest division – the Calciferous Sandstone – are the well-known oil shales, which are exposed to the west and south-west of Edinburgh. The Carboniferous Limestone contains some of the richest coal seams (there are 26 seams of 30 cm or more in thickness) and the remaining seams occur in the Lower Coal Measures, which are exposed in a belt about 6 km south-east of the capital.

The oil shales were first worked in 1858 near Broxburn, about 16 km west of Edinburgh; quarrying continued for over a century, and the familiar petroleum products were recovered in a refinery at Pumpherston, 5 km south of Broxburn. About 1950 the shale was being worked in 12 mines and a quarry, which produced 117,000 tonnes of shale; this was treated at 5 crude-oil works which yielded a total of 117,000 tonnes of oil – that is, rather more than the annual production of crude oil from wells in the United Kingdom. The total employment in the industry was about 4000 persons. In 1962, however, the Government preferential duty was discontinued, and this old-established activity was forced to come to an end.

The Midlothian coalfield contains up to 34 workable seams; over large areas these are comparatively level and free from faulting; a high degree of mechanization is thus possible, and costs are among the lowest in Scotland. This is an expanding coalfield, and there are hopes that both man-power and output will be raised.

There is a large unproved area below the Firth of Forth which is likely to contain vast reserves for future use.

In the lowlands both soils and landscapes bear the imprint of ice action. West of Edinburgh an intricate system of drumlins can be seen, whose alignment is reflected in the arrangement of the minor watercourses. Interesting 'crag and tail' formations have resulted where the advancing ice has scooped out a hollow in front of an igneous crag, but has left behind a gently sloping 'tail' on the lee side, as at the Castle Rock, Edinburgh, where the tail is of Carboniferous Limestone. A mantle of glacial drift covers the lowlands to a depth in places of 30 metres. It generally reflects the underlying 'solid' formation, 'staggered' a little eastward, in the direction of the ice advance; thus reddish gravel-like soils have developed above the Old Red Sandstone, while above the Carboniferous rocks there are often dark, heavy clays.

As in other parts of south-eastern Scotland, the climatic conditions favour arable farming. This is a region of bright sunshine, rather extreme temperatures, cold east winds, and low rainfall. A coastal strip receives less than 650 mm of rainfall per annum, and Leith, with 592 mm, has the same rainfall as Skegness, in Lincolnshire. The proportion of arable land is everywhere high in the coastal belt, but it decreases westward inversely with the amount of precipitation; thus in East Lothian it represents 76 per cent. of the improved land, in Midlothian 59 per cent., and in West Lothian 55 per cent.

Differences in farming practice are related to variations in climate and soil. Dairy cattle are most prominent in the damper west; barley is particularly important near the coast of East Lothian, where there are light soils and a high proportion of sunshine. Here the finest barley is used in the local breweries and distilleries, while the poorer qualities are fed to stock. Wheat is significant everywhere in the lowlands below 150 metres; oats are grown in rotation with wheat and potatoes, but extend up to 300 metres on the hillsides and as far as the damper parts of West Lothian, where the rainfall reaches 900 mm per annum. Sheep are reared in the remoter uplands, but are fattened in the lowlands.

Edinburgh

The rise of Edinburgh (pop. 453,422) is linked with the strategic importance of its site. The configuration of the Firth of Forth is such that it narrows rapidly westward from about 20 km to about 8 km, so that for the first time a ferry crossing becomes feasible. Near the same point on the south shore of the Firth, the coastal plain narrows between the Pentland Hills and their outposts on the one hand and the water of the Firth on the other, so that a strongpoint here could control the east-coast route from England into Scotland.

The opportunity was provided by nature in the shape of the Castle Rock – a volcanic plug whose western face has been sharpened by ice action to form a precipice – while marshy river flats to the north and south made the site additionally secure.

A settlement on the crag was first mentioned by Ptolemy in the second century A.D., and by Norman times a walled borough had been built. At the summit of the Rock was the castle; along the crest of the limestone 'tail' was the High Street and market-place. The dwellings of the burgesses fronted the High Street, and their long, narrow holdings extended down the sloping sides of the hill as far as the wall.

Edinburgh was the first important Scottish town on the east-coast route from England, and for centuries relations between the two neighbours were strained; thus Edinburgh developed trade and cultural contacts with the Continent rather than with England. Their modern representatives are seen in the imports of timber and woodpulp from the Baltic, and dairy produce from Denmark.

During the seventeenth century the growing population was housed in the High Street in 5- and 6-storey flats; these were superseded in the eighteenth century by the creation of an elegant 'New Town' including Princes Street to the north; in its design the Adam brothers played a part.

Modern Edinburgh is primarily a centre of education, administration, and finance; but it has also important and characteristic industries. Its paper manufactures date from 1675, and rely on the local supplies of pure water from the Esk and the Water of Leith. Edinburgh is accounted the second most important brewing centre in the United Kingdom, and in this the local barley has played its part. The city has a reputation for printing and publishing, and is the home of the well-known map-making firm of John Bartholomew.

Leith, which since 1920 has been incorporated in Edinburgh, is the second port of Scotland, and the chief of its east-coast ports. It had only slight natural advantages, for the Water of Leith opened on to a flat and muddy shore, and its modern trade springs from its position in relation to a productive hinterland. The port is almost completely artificial: it comprises the river mouth, a series of six enclosed basins, and a large new tidal harbour.

Leith imports grain for the whole of south-eastern Scotland; it imports timber from Scandinavia for pitprops, for the brewing and fishing industries, and for general construction. It maintains regular cargo services with Denmark and Finland, ships Scottish oats southward, and imports china clay for paper-making from Cornwall and cement from the Thames; it is also a centre for ship-building and until recently engaged in the whaling industry. The industries of the port include the manufacture of ropes and canvas, biscuits, and fertilizers – all of them related to local products or local needs.

The Tweed Basin

The Tweed with its tributaries drains a very wide area which comprises almost half the Southern Uplands. The hills which enclose it curve round in the shape of a horseshoe open to the north-east, and include the Lammermuirs and Moorfoot Hills to the north, built of Ordovician and Silurian sediments; the Cheviots to the south, formed of lavas of Devonian age; and in the west, a series of plateaux at about 370 metres whose isolated summits represent igneous intrusions into Silurian strata.

The plateau lands form a thinly peopled country of sheep farms with few roads or railways. They have their value as catchment areas for the cities of the Lowlands – the main Edinburgh reservoir is in the Talla glen, near the headwaters of the Tweed – and their wool 'crop' has provided the basis for the cloth-making industry of the middle Tweed towns.

'Tweeddale' corresponds largely with the county of Peebles; it consists entirely of upland country and is noted for its fine plantations of coniferous and deciduous trees. It has easy communication, both westward to the Clyde and Glasgow, and eastward to Berwick. At the county town of Peebles appear the first and the largest of the many woollen-mills which form the distinguishing characteristic of the Tweed basin; and there are others at Walkerburn, a few miles downstream. Water-power was an early factor of importance, and the mills still cling to the riverside.

'Teviotdale' forms the nucleus of the county of Roxburgh, and here are Hawick and Jedburgh, both in steep-sided valleys. Hawick is the largest of the Tweed towns – a river focus where the Teviot valley begins to widen out into a plain; it spins and dyes and weaves tweeds, but its speciality is knitwear. Farther east, Jedburgh (on the Jed) relied on rayon until the factory closed in 1957; this industry has in part been replaced by the manufacture of machine tools.

Another valley – that of the Ettrick – forms the core of the county of Selkirk, and the county town too has its woollen factories. Galashiels, in the same county, is larger and more industrialized; it is the centre of technical education for the whole Border woollen industry, and the source from which the craft spread to neighbouring valleys.

In general the mills are small; there is little or no mass-production; and the Border industry combats its isolation from the market by concentrating its skill upon the production of goods of outstanding quality. In this its outlook is similar to that of Scottish manufacturers in general.

The Whisky Industry

Whisky is prepared in over a hundred distilleries distributed around the margins of the Highlands, and in the Lowlands. To make whisky, the starch present in malted (partly germinated) barley is first converted into sugar, and then, by treatment with yeast, the sugar is fermented into other substances, including alcohol. The alcohol is then separated out by distillation.

The process was introduced from Ireland into Scotland about the fifteenth century; whisky was produced in the western Highlands and islands, and at first was purely a local drink, manufactured during the winter months when there was little work to be done on the farms. By the eighteenth century the activity had spread to the central and eastern Highlands (now the greatest producers), and had penetrated to the Lowlands.

The modern industry dates mainly from the 1860's. Its chief requirements are threefold: a copious supply of water which has drained through peat; a supply of peat for the malting process; and a supply of barley or other grain. Much of the grain is now imported from the Lowlands, from England, or from Australia.

Most of the distilleries are situated around and near the Moray Firth, with a major concentration in the lower Spey district: here are about 40 of the hundred or so distilleries in Scotland. In the west the outstanding district is Islay, in the Inner Hebrides, which has 7 distilleries. All these Highland establishments are small, employing 20 to 30 people; but they provide a secure occupation, often in distinct industrial villages, in a region which has suffered severe rural depopulation.

The spirit from these centres is blended with that produced in larger distilleries in the Lowlands – in Edinburgh, Glasgow, and elsewhere: each of these employs several hundred persons. In all about 3000 brands of whisky are available for home and export. Associated trades include the production of casks and bottles and distillery equipment. The chief exporting port is Glasgow.

The exports of whisky are far greater than the quantities consumed at home: they are steadily increasing in volume and now stand at more than double the pre-War total. The United States buys more than half the exports, and Scotch whisky is the largest single dollar earner of the United Kingdom.

FOR FURTHER READING

Books

JONES, S. J. (Ed.): *Dundee and District* (British Association, 1968).

MACGREGOR, M. and A. G.: *The Midland Valley of Scotland*, British Regional Geology Handbooks (H.M.S.O., 1948).

PRINGLE, J.: *The South of Scotland*, British Regional Geology Handbooks (H.M.S.O., 1948).

REES, HENRY: *British Ports and Shipping* (Harrap, 1958), Ch. 11.

SCOLA, P. M.: *The Lothians*, The Land of Britain, Parts 16–18 (Geographical Publications, 1944).

Scientific Survey of South-Eastern Scotland (British Association, 1951).

Articles

'The Scottish Steel Industry' (British Iron and Steel Federation).

STORRIE, MARGARET C.: 'The Scotch Whisky Industry', in the *Institute of British Geographers Transactions and Papers* (December 1962).

Periodical

Glasgow Herald Trade Review, annually each January.

Farm Study

Association of Agriculture, Farm Adoption, No. 3: Westmill, Inchture, East Perthshire, 1952 onward.

Maps

O.S. $\frac{1}{4}$ inch sheets 6, 7, and 8.

Geological Survey $\frac{1}{4}$ inch sheets 12, 13, 14, 15, 16, and 17.

Section B: The West Country

CHAPTER TWELVE

THE SOUTH-WEST PENINSULA

T HE SOUTH-WEST PENINSULA has a distinctive personality. Here is the classical example of a peninsula, bounded on three sides by the Atlantic, thrusting itself farther south and farther west than any other part of Britain, and bounded on the east by a narrow waist between Bridgwater bay and Lyme Regis, where the Somerset levels serve to isolate it from the rest of England. It possesses the longest coastline of any region in England; it exhibits the boldest cliffs; it retains the closest links with the sea; it has the greatest extent of granite moorland. Here are to be seen the clearest effects of past mineral workings; but today the region depends largely for its income on the tourist and the holiday-maker.

It forms a fitting bridge between the Celtic lands and Saxon England. It shared in the prehistoric cultures of Atlantic Europe, and possesses innumerable stone monuments: there are 90 stone circles and 90 burial chambers on Dartmoor alone! Until the late eighteenth century the Cornish branch of the Celtic tongue was still spoken, and it survives in the majority of the place-names. In many parts of the peninsula the small, squarish fields of the Iron Age are still under cultivation, and settlement is typically restricted to the hamlet or isolated farmstead. Only in the east do place-names and nucleated villages give evidence of a substantial colonization by the Saxons.

Physical Basis

A series of parallel dykes in the district between Mounts bay and Camborne in the far west perhaps forms evidence of the Caledonian earth movements; otherwise the framework of the south-west peninsula derives from Carbo-Permian times, when many thousands of feet of Carboniferous and Devonian sediments were crumpled and overthrust to form a series of lofty mountain ranges. These have been reduced by erosion to mere stumps; but the outcrops of the strata still range east and west, in common with those of the Mendip Hills, south Wales, and south-western Ireland.

Most of the peninsula is occupied by a major downfold, whose floor is occupied by Carboniferous strata named the Culm Measures. These correspond broadly with the Millstone Grit of other regions, but in age overlap both the Carboniferous Limestone on the one hand and the Coal Measures on the other. They consist of grits, limestones, sandstones, and shales, but are named from the bands of soft, sooty coal which are present in a few places. To the north and south are the Devonian rocks, whose age increases with their distance from the centre of the syncline. Both series have been intensely folded, as can be seen in many fine cliff sections.

During the course of the Carbo–Permian earth movements masses of hot granite were forced into the Carboniferous and older rocks, cooling at depth, altering the rocks in contact with them, and emitting vapours which have given rise to mineral deposits and china clay. Long-continued erosion has stripped off the sedimentary covers to expose the surface of the granite; and owing to its greater resistance the granite masses now surmount the sedimentary rocks to form the row of five dome-shaped moorland tracts which extend from Dartmoor to Land's End. Their ultimate representatives are the Isles of Scilly, which appear to form the remains of a collapsed boss of granite.

The river system presents its own problems. Today the two longest rivers – the Tamar and the Exe – rise near the north coast and flow southward, and the alignment of the north-flowing streams suggests that they have resulted from river capture on a large scale. The upper Camel, the upper Torridge, and a right-bank tributary of the Taw (the Bray) offer convincing evidence to this effect (Fig. 45). Thus the river system appears to have developed on a surface which was tilted in mid-Tertiary times to the south. In addition, an eastward trend can be discerned: it is seen in most of the valleys of Exmoor, in the middle Dart, the upper Teign, and the Teign estuary; and it has been suggested that these streams originated in early Tertiary times on an eastward-sloping surface of Cretaceous rocks, since eroded away. Here then may be an example of a superimposed drainage system.

The south-west is a region of level skylines and gentle slopes – a region of 'upland plains'. Three of these have long been recognized, at about 120, 230, and 300 metres; and recent work adds several others. They appear to be the result of marine erosion at successively lower levels, and they have important effects on the contemporary scene: over wide areas the rivers are sluggish, the drainage indeterminate, and the surface boggy, while the strong Atlantic winds blow without hindrance. The latest change in the

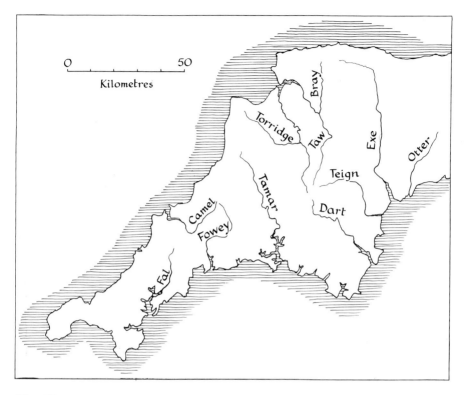

Fig. 45. THE RIVERS OF THE SOUTH-WEST PENINSULA

relative levels of land and sea has been a land subsidence, which has flooded the river mouths, provided many sheltered harbours, and brought the sea far inland.

In climate no less than structure the south-west is distinct. It forms part of an 'Atlantic' climatic province in common with Anglesey, Lleyn, and Pembrokeshire in Wales, western and south-west Ireland, and the Channel Isles.

The winters are exceptionally mild. The mean minimum temperature in January at Land's End is above 5°C (41°F), and equalled only by a narrow coastal strip in south-western Ireland. The mean January temperature in the Scillies is 8°C (47°F), and is unequalled in the British Isles. Temperatures generally are high: when averaged throughout the year the sea-level temperatures of Cornwall are higher than those of any other part of England or Scotland, while those of Land's End are equalled only by the Channel Isles. The range of temperature is low – only 5 to 5·5°C

(9 to 10°F) – and is similar to that of Anglesey, the Scottish islands, and south-west Ireland. Snow is rarely experienced below 60 metres, and for the three months January to March, south-western Cornwall is the only portion of the British Isles to average less than one snowy day per month.

All these elements are clearly related to the presence of the Atlantic, to the warm current which bathes our shores, and to the direction of the dominant winds (at Scilly westerly, north-westerly, and south-westerly in that order of frequency). For the same reasons the relative humidity is high (75 to 80 per cent,), except for the inland districts, and the rainfall is almost everywhere greater than 1000 mm per annum, rising to 1500 mm on the moorland summits. Other climatic features are less easily explained: the rain comes in downpours rather than drizzles, and the south-west is one of the sunniest regions in Britain; its average sunshine, and in particular its winter sunshine, is equalled only by the southern coasts of Kent and Sussex. Fog is distinctly rare: in most of the region there are fewer than 10 foggy mornings in the year.

This characteristic climate has impressed itself on the region in several ways. It accounts for the palms, the hydrangeas, and the fuchsia hedges around the coasts. It allows grass to grow for ten of the twelve months, so that the problem of winter feed for stock – acute elsewhere – is here virtually non-existent. It favours the earlier cultivation of flowers and vegetables; it encourages the tourist traffic,[1] and it has made the peninsula a favourite place of retirement for people of means.

Mining and Quarrying

It is believed that the tin of Cornwall was first worked in the late Bronze Age, when it joined the gold from Ireland in a trade route which ran from the Wicklow Hills across the south-west peninsula to the Continent. Certainly we possess an account of its extraction, refining, and export during the Iron Age, in the writings of the Roman Diodorus Siculus.

From the mid-fourth century A.D. till the mid-twelfth century, however, tin-working ceased. When it revived, in 1156, the south-west became the greatest producer in all Europe; and this proud position it appears to have retained until about 1870, when Cornwall was the leading producer of tin in the world.

The early workings were shallow, and confined to the river

---

[1] It is estimated that in 1970 for the first time tourism brought more money to Cornwall (£50 million) than farming (£40 million) – *The Times*, 14th September 1970.

gravels; but about A.D. 1500 shaft mining began. The metal was weighed, stamped, and assayed for duty at the stannary towns, which included Ashburton, Tavistock, and Chagford, in Devon, and Liskeard, Lostwithiel, Helston, and Truro, with at times Bodmin and Penzance, in Cornwall. Gunpowder was introduced in the late seventeenth century, and steam pumping in the eighteenth century allowed the drainage of a shaft 300 metres deep.

Copper as well as tin is associated with the granite intrusions. The veins of tin ore usually occur in the granite itself, while those of copper are found in the surrounding sedimentary rocks. In the zone of altered sediments ores of both metals occur. Copper is not normally found in the alluvial deposits, so that its exploitation was delayed until the deeper workings took place. The granite masses widen below the surface, so that a shaft which began as a copper mine often later yielded tin.

Mining was widespread in and around the igneous districts but was of special importance in a few localities. These included the St Austell and Tavistock and the Redruth–Camborne districts (Fig. 46), while in the Penwith (Land's End) peninsula there were nearly 300 mines. Here today the ruined chimney-stacks and engine houses make a desolate scene. To serve the Redruth–Camborne district the port of Hayle was developed, and here a limited amount of smelting was carried on with the aid of coal from south Wales. It proved more economic, however, to ship the ore to the fuel; and so arose the non-ferrous metal industries of the Swansea area (p. 121). Hayle also engaged in the manufacture of the famous Cornish pumping engines, and shipped them overseas until about 1900.

The mining of copper and tin was at its peak about 1850, when the Devon–Cornwall region was the leading producer in the world of both metals, and the mining industry employed about 100,000 people. The output of tin at this period was about 10,000 tonnes a year; and in copper the region had almost a world monopoly.

The deepest mine was Dolcoath mine, on the north-eastern outskirts of Camborne. At 1200 metres the shaft had penetrated the tin levels; but the mine closed down about 1920. One of the richest was the Devon Great Consols, on the lower Tamar: this produced copper and arsenic. In the 1850's it employed 1100 men; by the 1880's it was the world's greatest producer of arsenic; but in 1901 it failed. Near-by Tavistock grew essentially as a nineteenth-century mining town, and its population of about 6000 is still well below its peak of 8965 in 1861. Cornish engineers did not hesitate to follow the veins below the sea, and the workings of the Levant mine, near St Just, extend for a kilometre below the Atlantic.

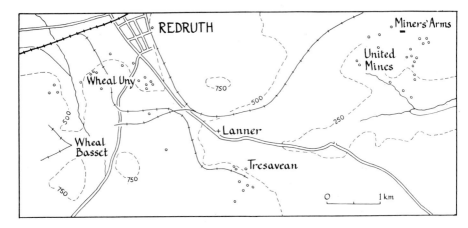

Fig. 46. THE LANDSCAPE OF MINING IN CORNWALL

The circles represent shafts (all now disused); they were served by a net of lanes and some main roads and by the railways. Two aqueducts are shown in the east and west margins of the area: they supplied water for sorting the ores. 'Wheal' is from the Cornish *hivel* and signifies 'mine'; Uny is a saint's name. The rounded summits are of granite; the lower slopes are of Old Red Sandstone, and the district is traversed by mineral veins. Heights are in feet. *Based on the O.S. 1-inch map. Crown copyright reserved.*

Decline set in about the 1870's, following the development of overseas deposits such as those of the Lake Superior region, of Rio Tinto, in Spain, and, later, those of Malaya and the East Indies. However, during the 1960's the high price of tin resulted in a renewed interest in the Cornish mines and by 1970 eleven former mining areas were being investigated. The two remaining active mines, Geevor (10 km north of Land's End) and South Crofty (between Redruth and Camborne), have been re-equipped and expanded, and a major new mine, the Wheal Jane, near Truro, was opened in 1971. The three enterprises employ a total of about 1000 men and produce over 40,000 tonnes of concentrate annually.

The emphasis in mineral-working, however, remains in china-clay quarrying: this is a vital raw material, rather rare in the world, yet present in great quantities in the granites of the south-west peninsula. The industry dates only from the middle of the eighteenth century, when a Plymouth potter, William Cookworthy, seeking the white clay from which the Chinese had made their porcelain, discovered it at Tregonning, a few kilometres west of Helston.

There were links between the newer and the older industries. Some of the china-clay deposits were discovered during the course of ore-prospecting. Expanding at a time when ore-mining was on the decline, the china-clay industry was able to absorb some of the

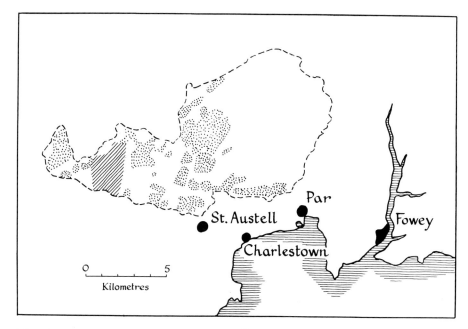

Fig. 47. CHINA CLAY IN CORNWALL

The broken line encloses the St Austell granite mass; the stippled areas yield china clay, and the shaded area china stone. Both are used in the manufacture of porcelain, and china stone is used also in the production of earthenware, while china clay is utilized in paper-making. The three ports supply the paper industry, but the potteries receive their materials by rail. The headquarters of the china-clay industry are at St Austell.

labour and even the equipment of the tin and copper mines. Cookworthy himself opened up the Hensbarrow Moor area, north of St Austell (Fig. 47), and this is still the chief producing district – surmounted by grey conical tips, and scarred by vast open-cast workings with walls where clay is washed down by jets of water.

The output of china clay (586,000 tonnes in 1938) has expanded steadily to reach a record total of 2,784,000 tonnes in 1969. In paper-making there is no substitute for it, and it has many other uses. Two-thirds of the total is exported: indeed, china clay forms our greatest export raw material; and it has given rise to the small but flourishing ports of Fowey, Par, and Charlestown. A regular stream of small ships carries the clay along the coast to all the paper-making areas of Britain – to the Thames and Medway, to the Mersey, to Leith and Aberdeen; but clay for the Staffordshire potteries travels by rail.

In 1969 Fowey shipped more than 800,000 tonnes of china clay, virtually the whole of it representing exports. Nearly one-third of it crosses the Atlantic to the United States and Canada; more than one-fifth goes to the paper mills of Scandinavia; Italy and the Netherlands are also important customers. Britain is second only to the United States in world production of china clay, and the whole of the British output is derived from Devon and Cornwall.

From time to time other minerals have been raised in the south-west peninsula, but the only remaining one of significance is slate. The major producer is the great quarry at Delabole, near the north coast of Cornwall, west of Camelford. Here the Devonian mud-stones have been metamorphosed by the granite intrusion of Bodmin Moor; and they are quarried in what is claimed to be one of the largest man-made excavations in the world.

Farming

In the south-west peninsula the farmer tends to concentrate on stock-raising. Arable land, permanent pasture, and rough grazing each account for about one-third of the total surface; but the ploughed land is used largely for the growing of fodder crops. Owing to the high rainfall and humidity, the acreages under wheat and barley are well below the national average, and oats is the chief cereal: it is fed largely to stock.

Cattle are reared for beef rather than milk, for the region is rather remote from the centres of population. Small quantities of milk, nevertheless, *are* sent daily by express train to London, even from western Cornwall, from farms which can maintain high-quality Guernsey herds. Most of the local milk, however, is either sold fresh to holiday-makers or converted into cream. We may elaborate this general account by looking more closely at three specimen sub-regions – Exmoor, the Penwith (Land's End) penin-sula, and the Scilly Isles.

Exmoor is a windswept moorland of Old Red Sandstone, whose level summits form marshy tracts of bright green sedge-grass. Much of the lower moor was enclosed from 1820 onward, when John Knight and his son constructed new roads and enclosed the land with high walls of stone and turf, planted with beech in order to provide shelter from wind and snow. They drained, ploughed, and limed the land and converted the moor into farms, whose holdings usually ran from valley bottom to hill crest, with the farm-stead itself usually on the middle slope of the sunny side of the valley (as we have seen, most Exmoor valleys run east and west). Sheep and shepherds were brought from Scotland, and Exmoor has become essentially a sheep-rearing district, in which good fodder crops of oats, barley, and roots are raised in the sheltered valley floors. In addition, most Exmoor farms rear their North Devon cattle, and sell the bullocks for finishing in the lowlands.

In the far south-west the Penwith peninsula has exceptional climatic advantages, but even here there is local variety. The Penzance area faces south, and is sheltered from strong winds; calcareous sea sand and fish fertilizer are available locally, and are widely used to improve the soils, and the district has good rail connection to London. Here is a district of intensive cultivation of flowers and early vegetables. It is enclosed by a belt in which the farmer concentrates on dairying, and devotes his arable land to fodder crops or grass leys.

The land still bears the marks of former mining activity. Once the mine had closed the miner's smallholding alone could not support him. He moved to one of the growing coast resorts; or he sought a fortune in the Rand or the Klondyke, and his smallholding reverted to rough pasture. During the late 1950's much of this neglected land was reclaimed for dairy farming.

In the Scilly Isles the Atlantic climate reaches its ultimate development, and here flowers will ripen three weeks earlier than on the mainland. The granitic soils are acid, but they are tempered by the lush vegetation, and seaweed is used liberally as a fertilizer. The commercial growing of daffodils began in 1879, and has expanded so greatly that bulbs now occupy more land than all the other crops combined, and account for one-third of the farmland.

The bulbs are planted in late summer and oversown with grass. They bud in late December or early January, and are then picked by hand to ripen under glass; they are packed in boxes, shipped to Penzance, and forwarded by express train to Covent Garden market. All other farm operations are subsidiary to flower-growing. Other crops are grown only on land unsuited to the daffodil, and labour is applied to them only after the flower-picking season (January to April). Holdings are small, and the land is farmed intensively: the same field which produces daffodils in the spring yields pasture or a hay crop in the summer.

A typical farm on St Mary's covers 5·5 hectares and is operated by the farmer with one hired labourer (Figs. 48 and 49). Daffodils occupy 2·2 ha; 2·4 ha are under permanent or ley pasture. On the remaining ·9 ha or so there are small plots of oats and early potatoes, fodder crops such as kale and mangolds, or garden produce such as tomatoes, peas and beans, and cabbages. There are 3 Guernsey cows and about 50 head of poultry. The permanent pasture occupies the higher, more exposed land to the south.

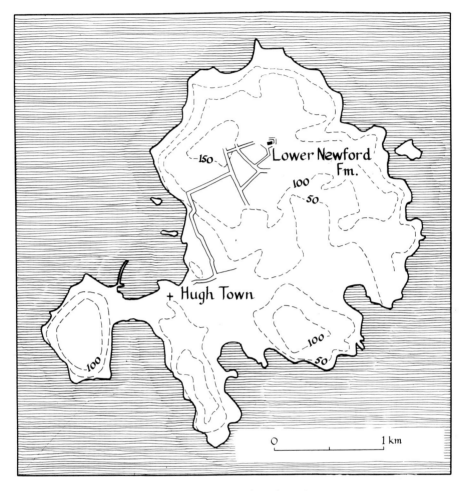

Fig. 48. THE SETTING OF LOWER NEWFORD FARM, SCILLY
Heights are in feet. *Based on the O.S. 1-inch map. Crown copyright reserved.*

Cities

There are two regional centres of the south-west peninsula: Exeter
(pop. 95,598) and Plymouth (pop. 239,314). The site of Exeter was
shrewdly chosen by the Romans about A.D. 50. Here a volcanic
hill dominated an almost level gravel terrace at the lowest crossing-
point of the Exe and near its head of navigation; and Exeter
provided a fitting southern terminus for the Fosse Way. The
Normans confirmed its importance by building a castle and a

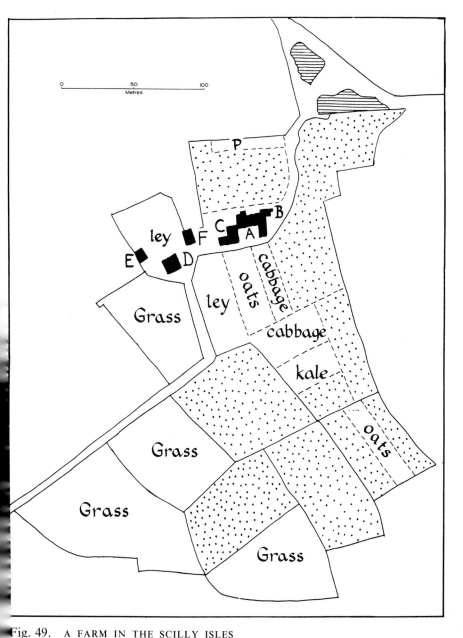

Fig. 49. A FARM IN THE SCILLY ISLES

Stippled areas are growing bulbs; P – new potatoes. The key to the buildings is as follows: A – dwelling-house; B – wash-house; C – glasshouse, packing-shed, and bulb-sterilizer; D – milking-shed, store, and garage; E – poultry-house; F – implement shed and store. The shaded areas are ponds. The location of the farm is indicated in Fig. 48. *After A. Downes, 1957.*

cathedral, and the city grew as the centre of a populous and productive agricultural region. Exeter became and remains a port, and
its regional functions enabled it to survive the loss of its woollen
industry. It is essentially a market and shopping-centre, a county,
cathedral, and university town.

Plymouth is much larger than Exeter; yet the reasons for its
growth are less tangible The Roman road system did not penetrate
this far, and the earliest mention of a settlement in the district is in
the Domesday Survey, relating to Sutton, at the head of Plymouth
Sound. The Tamar was and is a barrier rather than a routeway,
and its estuary has been bridged only in the last few years. The
district boasted no important agricultural surplus; the woollen
industry was concentrated farther east, while tin-mining was
farther west.

Plymouth folk therefore turned to the sea: they engaged in the
herring fisheries and in the coasting trade, and in the fifteenth
century they played an important part in colonial expansion: there
are many 'Plymouths' scattered over the New World. Towards
the close of the seventeenth century a dockyard was established on
the eastern side of the estuary, where the deep-water channel
approaches the shore. The site was somewhat exposed, and it was
necessary to import the timber for shipbuilding from the Forest
of Dean; but the situation was strategic, for it commanded the
entrance to the Channel. The rise of the city was linked with the
expansion of the dockyard. Largely rebuilt since the Second World
War, Plymouth is a passenger port, and engages in varied manufactures, but it remains essentially a town whose interests are
national rather than regional.

Other urban centres of the south-west include market towns
such as Okehampton, Launceston, and Bodmin; tourist resorts
such as Torquay, Ilfracombe, and Newquay; and fishing-ports such
as Newlyn, Mevagissey, Polperro, and Looe. The last group engages particularly in the pilchard fisheries, which are confined in
the United Kingdom to this row of ports, at virtually the northern
limit of range of this subtropical fish.

FOR FURTHER READING

Books
BALCHIN, W. G. V.: The Making of the English Landscape series, *Cornwall* (Hodder
    and Stoughton, 1954).
BARLOW, F. (Ed.): *Exeter and its Region* (British Association, 1969).
EDMONDS, E. A., McKEOWN, M. C. and WILLIAMS, M.: British Regional Geology
    Handbooks, *South-West England* (H.M.S.O., 1969).

HOSKINS, W. G.: *Devon* (Collins, 1954).
SHORTER, A. H., RAVENHILL, W. L. D. and GREGORY, K. J.: *South-West England* (Nelson, 1969).

Articles

BLUNDEN, J. R.: 'The Renaissance of the Cornish Tin Industry', in *Geography* (July 1970).
DAVIES, ARTHUR: 'The Personality of the South-West', in *Geography* (November 1954).
DOWNES, A.: 'Farming the "Fortunate" Isles', in *Geography* (April 1957).
FREY, A. E.: 'Bristol and its Future', in *Geographical Magazine* (February 1967).
GOODRIDGE, J. C.: 'Renewed Interest in Cornish Tin', in *Geography* (January 1962).
— 'The Tin-mining Industry: A Growth Point for Cornwall', *Transactions, Institute of British Geographers* (June 1966).
— 'Untapped Wealth of Britain's Tin Mines', in *Geographical Magazine* (December 1967).
HILTON, N.: 'The Land's End Peninsula: the Influence of History on Agriculture', in *Geographical Journal* (March 1953).
SHORTER, A. H.: 'The Site, Situation and Functions of Exeter', in *Geography* (November 1954).
SHORTER, A. H. and WOODLEY, E. T.: 'Plymouth: Port and City', in *Geography* (December 1937).
WOOLDRIDGE, S. W.: 'The Physique of the South-West', in *Geography* (November 1954).

Maps

Geological Survey, ¼-inch sheets 21, 22, and 25.
  Bartholomew's Revised ½-inch maps: 1 (Cornwall), 2 (Dartmoor), 3 (Exmoor), 4 (Dorset).

CHAPTER THIRTEEN

THE BRISTOL–MENDIP REGION

ESSENTIALLY the Bristol–Mendip region comprises the land which is drained westward to the Severn estuary. It is a region of varied rocks, of erratic river-courses, of high tidal ranges; and its unity springs from the fact that it is tributary to Bristol. In the south we include the Plain of Somerset but not the Quantock Hills, whose geology links them more closely with Exmoor and the south-west peninsula. We place the eastern boundary at the junction of the Cretaceous and Jurassic rocks, so that Bath and the Cotswolds fall within the region. In the north the West Country merges imperceptibly into the Midlands, and we place the boundary tentatively between Gloucester and Tewkesbury, so as to leave the Vale of Evesham in the Midlands.

Physical Basis

In the main this is a land of Keuper Marl, bordered to the east by a scarp-foot belt of Lias Clay, which widens southward and sends a narrow tongue to the west in the Polden Hills. These, together with similar outliers of Lias such as Brent Knoll and Glastonbury Tor, rise abruptly from the recent alluvium of the Plain of Somerset, and give character to this part of the West Country. They form the remnants of downfolds, whose rocks, strengthened by pressure, have resisted erosion, so that they have become the highest elements in the landscape.

Masses of Carboniferous strata rise like islands from the 'sea' of Keuper Marl, to form undulating lowlands such as the Somerset coalfield or plateaux such as the Clifton Downs and the Mendip Hills: these represent the denuded stumps of lofty mountains raised during the Carbo–Permian earth storm. The folding seems to have originated from the south, and the Mendips present a striking contrast in the angles of dip of the strata to the north and to the south of the core of Old Red Sandstone. Thus to the north of Black Down the Carboniferous Limestone dips northward at about 70°, while to the south it dips southward at about 22° (Fig. 50). Faulting and thrusting reminiscent of the Alps has been

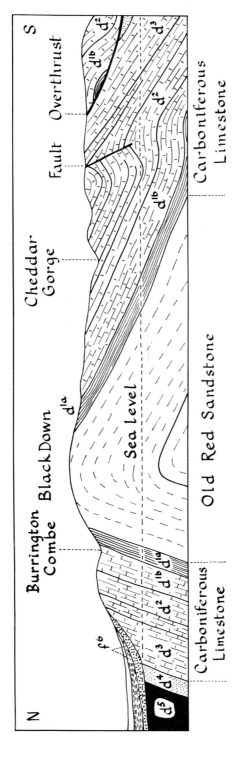

FIG. 50. GEOLOGICAL SECTION ACROSS THE MENDIP HILLS

The line of the section passes through Burrington Combe and Cheddar Gorge. On the north side the rocks dip steeply, on the south side more gently: this suggests that the pressures originated from the south. The overthrust is reminiscent of Alpine structures. Key to the symbols: f⁶: lined, Keuper Marl; stippled, Dolomitic Conglomerate; d⁵: Coal Measures; d⁴: Millstone Grit; d³: Hotwells limestone; d²: Burrington and Cheddar Oolites; d¹ᵇ: Black Rock Limestone, d¹ᵃ: Lower Limestone Shales. The bed above the Keuper Marl is 'Head' – a deposit of material which has slipped downhill under the influence of semi-glacial conditions. The length of the section is 84 km; vertical exaggeration is ×3.

discerned, so that in the Priddy district and east of Clevedon there is repetition of the rock sequences, while in the remarkable gorge of the Avon at Clifton one can see that the Carboniferous Limestone has been forced over the Trias.

Several contrasting sub-regions suggest themselves: the Plain of Somerset, the Mendips, the Cotswolds, the lower Severn valley.

The Plain of Somerset

After the Fens, the Plain of Somerset is the second largest alluvial area in Britain. A small portion lies north of the Mendips, but the main extent of the plain is to the south, where, if we neglect the intervening 'islands', it stretches for about 26 km from north to south, and about the same distance from east to west. The low hills break the monotony of the plain and divide it into separate basins: these are drained by the Axe (between the Mendips and the Wedmore ridge), the Brue (between the Wedmore ridge and the Poldens), and King's Sedgemoor Drain (south of the Poldens), while the section north of the Mendips is drained by the Yeo.

As in the Fens, deposits of clayey silt stretch well inland from the coast; and beyond the silt there are accumulations of peat. The surface of the peat is as low as 2·1 metres above mean sea-level; the silt is usually about 6 metres above sea-level. Since, however, the level of high spring tides in the Bristol Channel is about 7·6 metres O.D., the whole of the plain would at times be inundated if it were not for the protection of the sea wall. In some places, as at Brean, this is formed naturally by the sand-dunes; at others, as at Huntspill, it is man-made, of concrete and stone.

Unlike the Fens, this is almost completely permanent pasture, utilized for dairy herds. A large dairy near Highbridge bottles and processes much of the milk from the south-western part of the plain. The sea wall is believed to date from Saxon times, but the present regular network of drains dates only from the eighteenth century: it reclaimed much valuable pasture-land, but could not prevent flooding of the peat lands after heavy rainfall in the catchment areas. Accordingly the Somerset River Authority constructed 7 large pumping stations and several smaller ones to lift the water so that it will gravitate to the sea. The largest of them is at Gold Corner, 6 km south-east of Highbridge: at full capacity its pumps can lift 1000 tonnes of water each minute, which is discharged into a large and straight new cut called the Huntspill river (Fig. 51).

The small field ditches with their simple sluices are the responsibility of the farmer; the rhynes (or more important channels) are administered by local committees of farmers; and the main drains

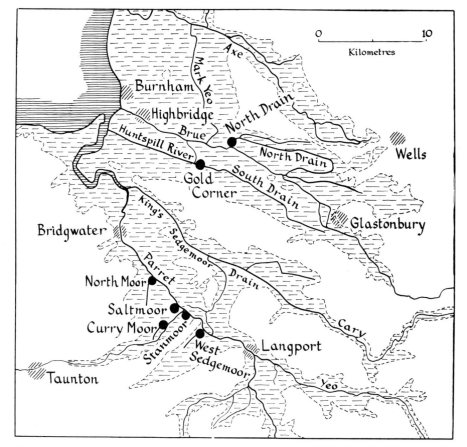

Fig. 51.   DRAINING THE SOMERSET LEVELS

The land requiring drainage is shaded; it amounts to 640 square km including a district north of the Mendips beyond the north margin of this map. The major pumping stations are represented by black circles. The largest, at Gold Corner, was constructed in 1945; the newest, the North Drain pumping station, was opened in 1958. Together they raise the water in the Brue valley sufficiently to allow it to gravitate to the sea. All the sea outlets are protected by sluice gates, for the tide in the Bristol Channel rises to 7·6 metres O.D. *By courtesy of the Somerset River Board.*

are controlled by the River Board. All the coastal outlets are protected by automatic tide flaps, which open on the ebb tide and close when the flood tide builds up a pressure in front of them. In addition there are sluice gates which normally impound the water during the summer, for then the pastures dry out and the problem is to supply sufficient water. Some farmers irrigate their pastures in summer by sprays, but all need an adequate level of water in the drains, for these supply drinking-water to the cattle, and also act as field boundaries to prevent the cattle from straying.

Peat has long been cut in the plain – for example, in Tadham and Westhay Moors. It is dried, and has been used on a limited scale for fuel; but it is now mostly milled and bagged for use in horticulture.

A Marshland Farm

We may illustrate the farming activities in the Plain of Somerset from Brean Down Farm, which is situated immediately to the south of the eastern tip of the limestone mass of Brean Down, south-west of Weston-super-Mare (Fig. 52). Here Mr Vowles farms 99 hectares, all of it flat, low-lying alluvial clay standing at about 6 metres above mean sea-level, and including 18 hectares of saltmarsh. At spring tides the saltmarsh is submerged for two or three hours, and so would the whole farm be without the protection of the sea wall, part of which bounds the farm to the east.

The farm is completely pastoral, and the entire farm income is derived from the pedigree herd of Friesian cattle, which numbers about 90 milking cattle and 45 other young cattle. From May to September the cattle are grazing the pastures or the salt-marsh – to which they have free access. They find the salt herbage quite palatable, but return to the fresh-water pastures as soon as they become thirsty. From October to April the cattle are stall fed, and Mr Vowles normally reserves about 40 hectares for hay; but he finds it profitable to supplement the grass by 'cake' throughout the year, and in this way secures a high milk yield.

Since the farm is so close to the sea, drainage presents little difficulty, and if the sluice gates were opened at low tide the ditches would soon be empty. The problem is more to retain sufficient water in them for stock and pasture: the rainfall is rather low (just 750 mm a year, on the average) and a strong wind in summer quickly dries out the turf. Hence sheep as well as cattle can be reared and formerly brought in 10 per cent. of the farm income. To economize in labour, Mr Vowles has sold his sheep, has modernized his dairy, and aims to expand his herd to about 120 milking cows.

This is a remote farm, but it is surprisingly well equipped. Milking machines deliver direct to churns fitted with internal water-cooling systems; and there is mains water and electricity. The stock are marketed at Highbridge; the milk is bottled or converted into Cheddar cheese at a dairy at Edingworth (8 km to the south-east as the crow flies). All this work is carried out by Mr Vowles and two full-time workers.

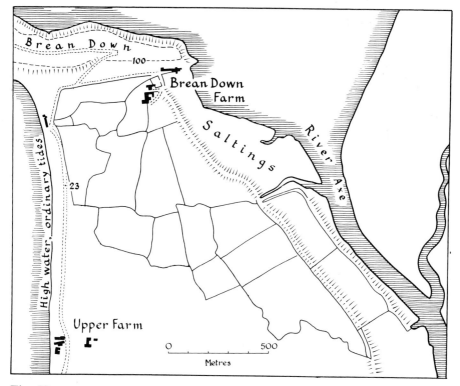

Fig. 52. BREAN DOWN FARM: A MARSHLAND FARM
The fields are divided by ditches, the outlets of which are protected by tide flaps. The saltings are covered at spring high tides. The entire farm is under grass. Heights are in feet. *Based on the O.S. 2½-inch map. Crown copyright reserved.*

The Mendip Hills

The Mendips form a grassy, level plateau at about 250 metres, composed mainly of dry, permeable Carboniferous Limestone. The level surface masks a complex structure, in which the crests of elongated domes have been eroded to reveal in five districts the cores of Old Red Sandstone. Here, as in Black Down and North Hill the rounded, bracken-covered summits reach 270 or 300 metres.

The steep edges of the plateau are broken by a series of deep, dry gorges, whose precise origin is debatable. Possibly they have been cut by rivers which have subsequently disappeared from the surface; or they may have been formed by the collapse of the roofs of a series of water-cut caverns. Caverns there are in plenty: there are seven in Burrington Combe alone, and in the whole of the Mendips possibly 100. Cheddar Gorge is the most famous of the ravines, and in places the bare cliffs rise almost vertically to over

120 metres above the floor; but others too, such as those of Ebbor, Wookey Hole, and Shipham, have their wild beauty. While water is scarce over the greater part of the plateau, it is present in small quantity over the Limestone Shales, which form the lowest member of the Carboniferous Limestone series, and normally provide an encircling band around the Old Red Sandstone exposures. Here we find many of the present-day Mendip farms, together with the remains of past settlement. Around the plateau edges the water issues in the form of springs or as fully fledged rivers (such as the Axe at Wookey Hole), and supports a whole ring of towns and villages, from Chewton Mendip in the north-east through Blagdon, Banwell, and others in the north, to Axbridge, Cheddar, Wells, and their neighbours in the south.

Depressions in the hills tend to be occupied by the Dolomitic Conglomerate (an old scree) or by the Keuper Marl. Both of them weather to reddish soils favourable to cultivation; similar red soils are to be seen on the Mendip flanks, and where they face south they are cultivated for strawberries and anemones.

There is evidence in the Mendips of a very long sequence of human occupation. Aveline's Hole in Burrington Combe has yielded evidence of Palæolithic family hearths; there are Mesolithic burials in Hay Wood, near Hutton; and three long barrows in the Priddy district suggest that Neolithic men lived here. Bronze Age barrows are characteristic of Mendip summits, and the enigmatic earthen-bank Priddy Circles are also assigned to this period. Iron Age hill forts guard the gaps in the northern rampart of the Mendips, and there are others on the limestone outliers of Brean Down and Worlebury Hill. In places such as Bleadon Hill the grassy slopes are terraced, and signs of the small, squarish Celtic fields are still evident, particularly when the setting sun reveals the shadows of their banks. In the plain to the south are the sites of the only two Iron Age lake villages known in Britain – near Godney and at Meare.

Four Roman villas are known in or near the northern flank of the Mendips, and the Romans are known to have smelted lead at Priddy and Charterhouse, though the only remains of their mining settlement at Charterhouse is a forlorn grassy amphitheatre on a bleak hillside. The town was linked by road to the Fosse Way, and recent discoveries farther west, including a temple on Brean Down, suggest that the road continued to Uphill, where (or at Rackley) there may have been a port to ship the lead.

As the new one-inch geological map indicates, lead veins are scattered over wide areas east of Charterhouse and north and east of Priddy. The Mendip ore – galena (lead sulphide) – contains small quantities of silver, and the Romans were able to separate the two metals by a preliminary heating over beds of bone-ash: this absorbs the lead while rejecting the silver. The Romans valued silver highly, both for ornamental purposes and for coinage, and they may well have regarded the silver as the main product and the lead as the by-product.

Mining ceased with the departure of the Romans, and was revived only in Norman times; it was practised actively throughout the Middle Ages, and reached a peak about 1650. There followed a gradual decline: the more accessible veins were becoming exhausted; the price of lead was falling as new overseas sources were developed, and about 1850 lead-mining became extinct.

The smelting branch was limited to the areas where running water was available to sort the ores, and the two main districts were in the shallow valleys carved by tiny streams in the Limestone Shales at Charterhouse and Priddy. Even when mining ceased the metal industry was not dead, for a few enterprising men had discovered that the cast-off slags of the Roman and later smelters were still rich in metal, and because they were so accessible, were well worth reworking. Roman slag was found to contain up to 27 per cent. of lead, and there were vast quantities of it: at Priddy the dumps were 180 to 270 metres wide, 4 to 6 metres deep, and 1600 metres long.

Accordingly in the 1850's a new phase of the industry began. Cornishmen with smelting experience arrived; they dug rows of pits ('buddles') and they built 'modern' furnaces with long horizontal flues, in which much of the lead accumulated as a sooty deposit. At Charterhouse the Mendip Mining Company even erected a plant for the recovery of silver; and the newcomers proceeded to extract wealth from the waste-products of ancient and medieval times. The following figures speak for themselves:

Lead produced at St Cuthbert's Works, Priddy (in tonnes)		Silver produced at Charterhouse (in ounces)		
1883	99	1858	1295	(36·7 kg)
1884	132	1859	950	(26·9 kg)
1885	117	1860	850	(24·1 kg)
1886	94	1861	850	(24·1 kg)
1887	87	1862	1025	(29·0 kg)
1888	87	1863	1000	(28·3 kg)
		1864	2660	(72·5 kg)
		1865	1300	(36·8 kg)
		1866	1488	(42·1 kg)
		1867	1700	(48·2 kg)

Sorting and smelting continued into the early years of the present century, but has now long ceased, and the works have been dismantled. The remains of a once flourishing industry are to be seen in the ruined flues, the overgrown buddle pits, and masses of heavy, black, glassy slag.

Zinc-smelting was confined largely to the Shipham district, where veins containing calamine (carbonate of zinc) traverse the Dolomitic Conglomerate in all directions. Mining began in the reign of Elizabeth I, and reached a peak about 1800, when there were 400 to 500 miners in the district, and 4 roasting ovens in the village. Most of the zinc was forwarded to Bristol for use in the brass industry. But the veins did not extend to great depth (the Dolomitic Conglomerate itself is only a shallow deposit), and with their exhaustion the industry faded away about 1850. Today its remains are seen in the areas of disturbed ground around Shipham and the occasional lilac bush which marks the site of a demolished miner's cottage.

The Mendips have thus reverted to farming, but they also act as an important gathering ground for water-supply. We have noticed the line of settlements around their flanks, which depend on Mendip water. In addition, boreholes at Priddy supply the central district; others at Winscombe supply the Burnham area, and three large reservoirs store water for Bristol and the region in general.

Mendip farms are oriented towards stock-rearing, particularly sheep farming, but there is a surprising amount of cultivation for so elevated a region. We may illustrate the productivity of the Mendips from Lower Pitts farm, at Priddy, standing at 250 metres above sea-level. Here Mr R. Dyke farms 214 hectares and concentrates on stock-rearing (Fig. 53).

The enterprise is remarkable for the variety of its output. Virtually the whole of the land is capable of cultivation, and most of it is in fact ploughed every third year and re-seeded to grass. In spite of the altitude, corn crops flourish, and Mr Dyke normally grows about 12 ha of barley and 8 of oats, together with 6 of kale. All these are fed to the stock, and additional winter feed is provided by about 40 hectares of hay and 12 of silage.

Mr Dyke runs a milking herd of 80 Ayrshires with about 180 young cattle. His sheep flock comprises about 150 Kerry Hill breeding ewes, with 250 lambs; and he has 17 sows with their piglets. He no longer keeps laying hens, for it seems that only the specialists can now operate profitably. Much of Mr Dyke's produce finds its way to Bristol. The milk, collected daily, is pasteurized at Chew

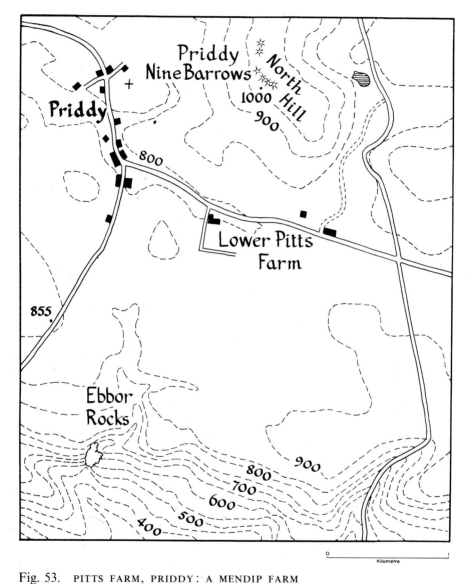

Fig. 53. PITTS FARM, PRIDDY: A MENDIP FARM

Although the farm lies on the plateau top at 250 metres, it is surprisingly productive. Heights are in feet. *Based upon the Ordnance Survey 1-inch map. With the sanction of the Controller of H.M. Stationery Office. Crown copyright reserved.*

Stoke (11 km to the north) and forwarded to Bristol. The lambs are sold at Farrington Gurney (13 km north-east of Priddy); the cattle are sold off the farm, and the ewes are traded at the famous sheep fair on the village green at Priddy.

The Cotswold Hills

The Cotswolds extend from the Frome district in the south to the neighbourhood of Moreton in Marsh in the north. They form a level plateau of almost horizontal strata – mainly limestones – which present a bold west-facing scarp, deeply dissected by small but swiftly flowing streams. The plateau surface slopes down very gently to the south-east, and is scored by deep, dry valleys which must have been cut by rivers when the water table stood at a higher level.

The scarp is highest east of Cheltenham, where its summit stands at 300 m above the sea, and about 210 m above the Lias lowland to the west. The height of the scarp is related to the differences in thickness of the members of the Jurassic rocks, and in particular to variations in the Inferior Oolite, which attains its greatest development near Cheltenham. The changing *direction* of the scarp is related to the axes of minor earth ripples and their later erosion.

Thus the remarkable Vale of Moreton, floored by the Lower Lias and overlooked on all sides by Jurassic scarps, represents a denuded upfold whose axis runs north and south. To the west is the corresponding downfold, with an axis passing through North-leach and Chipping Campden: here the rocks have been tightened and strengthened; the limestone extends to its most northerly point, and the Lias, brought to the surface, thrusts a broad tongue into the heart of the Midlands. Other parallel folds to the west account for the recessions and advances of the scarp. Many fractures occur, trending W.N.W. and E.S.E. and explain the complex pattern of the outcrops, though they do not greatly affect the plateau surface.

Traditionally this is sheep country, and the woollen trade and industry has left its mark on the countryside. As early as 1100 it was recorded that the nuns of Holy Trinity Abbey at Caen had flocks numbering 1700 on Minchinhampton Common in Gloucestershire. The Cotswolds developed their own sheep breed, which yielded heavy fleeces of long staple, and contributed largely in the early Middle Ages to British exports of wool to Flanders. The woolmen amassed large fortunes; they endowed churches, alms-houses, and grammar schools, and built pillared and roofed market halls. The results of their labours are seen in many Cotswold towns, such as Cirencester, Chipping Campden, Tetbury, North-leach, and Fairford.

About the sixteenth century a cloth industry developed in those Cotswold towns which had access to streams for power. Leland, who wrote in the early sixteenth century, remarked, 'All the town of Bradford-on-Avon standeth by cloth-making'. Malmesbury at this time was producing 3000 cloths annually. The deeply incised tributaries of the Severn provided ideal sites for power to drive the fulling mills, and soft water was contributed by the Cotteswold Sand, which attains 60 metres in thickness in the Stroud area; in addition, local deposits of fuller's earth provided the material for cleansing the cloth.

The Cotswold woollen industry reached its peak in the early eighteenth century; but was then overtaken by the West Riding, which could draw upon local supplies of coal at a time when steam was replacing water-power. Nevertheless, mills in Stroud and Nailsworth survive and flourish by dint of specialization in materials of high quality: they include red hunting cloth, 'bearskins' for the Guards, blazer cloths, billiard cloth, and covers for tennis balls.

Stone-quarrying in the Cotswolds dates at least from the time of the Romans, who used it to pave the Fosse Way and to build their villas. The lower portion of the Inferior Oolite consists of a freestone (a stone which can be cut in any direction), and has been quarried in the north under the names of Cheltenham and Campden stones, and in the south as the Dundry Freestone (seen in many Bristol churches). The Great Oolite has been worked as the Minchinhampton and Taynton stones, and the more famous buff-coloured Bath stone. This is quarried around Corsham, between Bath and Chippenham.

On the Cotswold farms wool has given place to the production of lamb and beef and the growing of cereals, and pasture is now interspersed with fodder crops and grain. The overgrown quarries, the dry-stone walls, the mellow, buff-coloured towns and villages, the tidy and colourful gardens, and the long, narrow plantations for windbreaks – these form characteristic elements in the Cotswold scene.

The smaller towns such as Chippenham, Cirencester, and Malmesbury are essentially markets; but Gloucester, Bath, and Cheltenham have wider connections. The first two are of Roman foundation. Gloucester commanded the lowest bridge over the Severn, and stood at the head of sea-going navigation; it also formed an important route centre in the Roman road system. Its later growth stemmed from its location in the productive Vale of Severn. Engineering industries have developed, in particular aero-engineering, and Gloucester is still the lowest bridge point. Congestion in the city has been reduced by the Severn bridge, which was completed in 1967. Gloucester remains a port by virtue of the 26-km Berkeley Canal, which avoids the tortuous navigation of the lower Severn. It is used by lighters and coasters of up to about 750 tons capacity, which carry petroleum and general cargoes into the docks at Gloucester.

The hot springs at Bath indicate that Britain is not entirely free from volcanic activity; their medicinal properties were recognized by the Romans, whose elaborate bath area forms one of the most striking archæological monuments in the country. During the eighteenth century Bath was developed as a spa for leisured folk, and its elegant squares and crescents – all built of the warm-looking Bath stone – provide fine examples of Georgian architecture and town planning. Cheltenham has something of the character of Bath, but lacks its Roman links and its abbey. Both are centres for retired people; Cheltenham has acquired a reputation as a centre for education.

Bristol and the Bristol Avon

The Bristol Avon originates from two headstreams which rise in the central Cotswolds near Sherston and Tetbury: these aim south-eastward as if to join the Thames, and should be classed as 'consequent' (they follow the *dip* of the strata). At Malmesbury, however, the river turns south and glides past Chippenham in a broad flood-plain: here it is a 'subsequent' stream (it follows the *strike* of the strata). At Bradford the Avon turns west and trenches into and through the Cotswolds: from here onward it must be classed as 'obsequent' (it flows against the dip of the strata). Below Bristol the river achieves the apparently impossible, and in the Clifton Gorge it cuts a deep gash across the entire thickness of the Carboniferous Limestone and the underlying Old Red Sandstone to reach the sea through a marshy plain.

How is such an enigmatic course to be explained? A river will flow round an obstacle if it is present, so the gorge section must have been initiated at a much higher level, presumably on a cover of younger rocks, which have since been eroded away. A river valley is like a saw-cut: once begun its position cannot be changed; uplift or tilting has rejuvenated the Avon and allowed it to cut more and more deeply into the limestones which were formerly hidden by newer strata. The same rejuvenation, perhaps, has enabled it to capture some of the headstreams of the Thames. At a later stage, swollen by meltwaters during the Ice Age, the river was able to cut the deep and wide valleys which are apparent even near its headwaters at Malmesbury and Tetbury.

Bristol (pop. 425,203) was founded on a hill of Keuper Sandstone in the angle at the junction of the Frome with the Avon. Two silver coins in the Royal Collection at Stockholm provide the earliest evidence of its existence: they date from the reign of Ethelred the Unready (978–1016), and bear the inscription 'Aelfwerd on Bric'. Aelfwerd was the minter; Bric is an abbreviation of Bricgstowe (bridge-place). It is clear that Bristol was an important centre before the Norman Conquest.

The site is of great interest: marsh and the gorge prevented any settlement lower downstream; here was the limit of navigation (it still is) and the lowest bridge point (it remained so until the nineteenth century). The site was well defended by nature, and approachable only from the east: here the Normans built a massive castle and ringed the city by a wall. From the first Bristol was a port, and its harbour was improved as early as 1240 by the digging of a new mouth for the Frome. But the wharves could be reached only on the rising tide, owing to the high tidal range of the lower Avon.

Early trade links were with Ireland, Gascony, Spain, and Portugal, and familiarity with the sea led Bristol men to engage in the search for new markets. Bristol merchants financed the voyage of John Cabot in 1497–98 which resulted in the discovery of Newfoundland, and set the pattern for the later transatlantic commerce. The city prospered as a result of the notorious slave trade; but this paved the way for the legitimate commerce in tobacco, cocoa, and bananas: though relatively small in volume, this forms a characteristic part of the imports of Bristol. In 1809 Bristol citizens took the bold step of converting the lower Frome and part of the Avon into a great enclosed dock – the Floating Harbour (Fig. 54); but during the course of the century the rapid increase in the size of vessels made even these works inadequate; large new docks were excavated in the marshland at Avonmouth, and these now handle the bulk of the overseas trade of the port, and the whole of the oil traffic.

The leading import is refined petroleum products, which Bristol distributes over a wide area; second is grain, and lofty flour-mills at Avonmouth mark the important trade links with the St Lawrence ports. The tobacco, cocoa, and bananas, together with animal feeding-stuffs, are handled at Avonmouth too, while

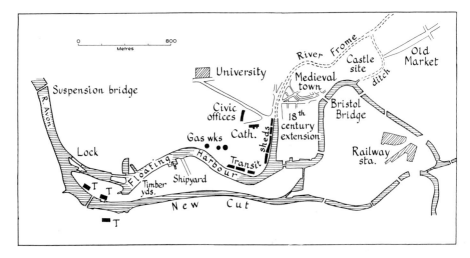

Fig. 54.   SOME ELEMENTS IN THE DEVELOPMENT OF BRISTOL

The town originated on a sandstone hill in the angle between the junction of the Frome with the Avon.
Originally the rivers joined immediately below Bristol Bridge, but in the thirteenth century the mouth
of the Frome was straightened to provide an improved quay. In the early nineteenth century a long
stretch of the Avon was impounded to form the Floating Harbour (essentially a huge wet dock).
T = tobacco warehouse.

the City Docks specialize in coal from south Wales, timber and
wood-pulp from Scandinavia, and general cargoes from France
and the Low Countries.

Bristol is normally our fifth or sixth port in terms of tonnage of
goods handled. It is also an important centre of manufacture,
producing cigarettes, chocolate, paper, cardboard, and aeroplanes.
Above all, Bristol is the regional capital for religion, commerce,
and culture for the whole of the West Country.

FOR FURTHER READING

Books
Bristol and its Adjoining Counties (British Association, 1955).
COYSH, A. W., MASON, E. J., and WAITE, V.: *The Mendips* (Robert Hale, 1962).
GOUGH, J. W.: *The Mines of Mendip* (David and Charles, 1967).
GRINSELL, L. V.: *The Archaeology of Wessex* (Methuen, 1958).
KELLAWAY, G. A. and WELCH, F. B. A.: British Regional Geology Handbooks,
   Bristol and Gloucester District (H.M.S.O., 1948).

Maps
Bartholomew's ½-inch maps: most of the region is on sheet 7; the Cotswolds
appear on sheet 14.
   O.S. 1-inch map, sheet 165, Weston-super-Mare.
   Geological Survey, ¼-inch map, 'The Bristol District', 1955.
   Geological Survey, 1-inch map, 'The Bristol District', 1962.

Section C: The North Country and the Midlands

CHAPTER FOURTEEN

THE LAKE DISTRICT
AND THE ISLE OF MAN

WE DEFINE THE LAKE DISTRICT in generous terms so as
to include not only the central hilly mass of north-west
England, but also the surrounding coastal plains and the
Eden valley to the east. It comprises the counties of Cumberland
and Westmorland, together with the Furness district of Lancashire;
excluded is the narrow belt of Crossfell in the extreme east, for
this forms an integral part of the north Pennines.

The region is one of the smallest natural units of the British
Isles, yet it possesses a distinct character. A dome both in topography and in structure, it offers the most complete example of
radial drainage in Britain. Nine long and narrow valleys are
occupied by ribbon lakes rather like the spokes of a wheel, and
these together with their dividing fells offer some of the finest
mountain scenery in the United Kingdom. To the east of the hill
country is the structural trough of the vale of Eden, and to the
north is the Carlisle lowland: these form the largest areas of agricultural land in the region. In the north-west is the Cumberland
coalfield and its associated iron-mines and heavy industry; to the
south is the isolated industrial centre of Barrow-in-Furness.

Structurally two distinct elements can be recognized. In the
central area of older Palæozoic rocks the outcrops range north-east
and south-west and reflect the Caledonian trend which we have
already seen in Scotland; but around this core, and especially on
the northern side, the younger rocks are arranged in concentric
rings in order of age: this is the mark of an eroded dome. Three
major periods of mountain-building have in fact contributed to the
structure of the region.

The oldest rocks are the Ordovician: they comprise a sedimentary
series in the north – the Skiddaw Slates – and a volcanic series in
the centre – the Borrowdale Volcanic series. In these two belts are
the highest peaks: Skiddaw (931 m), Helvellyn (950 m), and
Scafell Pike (979 m). They weather into contrasting forms. The

slates are impermeable, so that streams develop close together and erosion is rapid, and the existing ridges and peaks are likely to have been produced in pre-glacial times. During the Ice Age the innumerable small joints in the slates assisted the grinding action of the ice, and the result is a landscape of steep but smooth, regular slopes, which now generally bear a close cover of vegetation.

The volcanic rocks, on the other hand, are more permeable and the streams are farther apart. Joints are well developed and widely spaced, so that the plucking action of the ice sheet detached large fragments and strewed them along its path as erratics. In the resulting landscape there are many projecting rocky knobs separated by boggy hollows: it is irregular, exciting country compared with the tamer surface of the slates.

To the south are the Silurian rocks, in whose hollows are set Lakes Coniston and Windermere; they are less resistant than the Ordovician rocks, and present a more subdued landscape. All these older Palæozoic deposits were sharply folded during the Caledonian earth movements of Siluro–Devonian times; they were then planed off by erosion and submerged below the Carboniferous seas, so that Carboniferous strata rest unconformably upon the older rocks. During Carbo–Permian times the rocks were again folded and once more eroded, so that the Trias in its turn rests unconformably upon the Carboniferous strata.

Then in Tertiary times, while the Pennines were receiving their final uplift, the whole area was raised to form a dome. It evidently possessed a complete cover of newer rocks (there is a suggestive outcrop of Lower Lias to the west of Carlisle, 120 km away from the nearest main exposure in east Yorkshire), and on this cover the present rivers presumably had their origins. Subsequent erosion has revealed the older core of the region (Fig. 55), so that the rivers now bear little relation to the structures over which they pass, and provide one of the clearest examples in the British Isles of superimposed drainage.

Lakeland Proper

In the central hilly mass are to be found some of the finest examples of glaciated landscapes in Britain. The western hilly knot centred on Scafell receives a precipitation of over 3800 mm per annum, and here in the Quaternary Ice Age a thick sheet of ice established itself. The main valleys were scoured and straightened and the tributary valleys left 'hanging'. Corries, which are especially numerous on the colder, east-facing slopes, mark the heads of tributary glaciers: a row of them drains eastward into Ullswater,

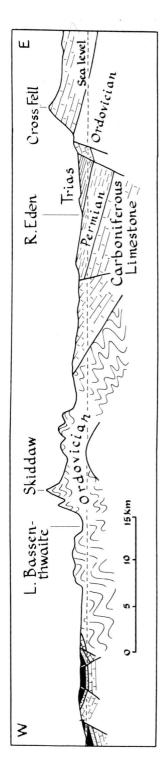

Fig. 55. GEOLOGICAL SECTION ACROSS THE LAKE DISTRICT

It passes from Harrington (on the coast south of Workington) across the Cumberland coalfield through the northern part of the Lake District, to Cross Fell. Coal Measures are shown in black. Millstone Grit is stippled.

and an exceptionally regular one is occupied by the tarn of Blea Water, which flows into the head of Hawes Water.

With the retreat of the ice from the encircling lowland, the valley glaciers deposited their debris in the form of terminal moraines, and on the final melting of the ice the blocked valleys were flooded to form the ribbon lakes which we now see. Good examples of later moraines can be found north and west of the village of Borrowdale (south of Derwentwater). The ribbon lakes, however, like all lakes, are only temporary features of the landscape: the streams which enter them are extending their deltas, while those which leave them are cutting more and more deeply into the morainic dams. Pairs of lakes, such as Buttermere and Crummock Water, have been separated by the growth of a delta from the sediment brought down by a stream in a side valley.

Closer study of the distribution of the hill masses reveals a central depression, occupied in part by Windermere, Thirlmere, and Bassenthwaite. Here an easy pass (Dunmail Raise) allows a main road to traverse the heart of the Lake District and connect Ambleside with Keswick, without climbing higher than 238 metres above sea-level.

To the west lie the highest summits – a series of peaks and craggy ridges which include Scafell and Great Gable, and bear all the marks of intense glaciation. The surface is broken and rugged, strewn with erratics, and exposing much bare rock. From their western flanks descend the three most regular of the radial valleys, containing Wastwater, Ennerdale Water, and Crummock Water; they are separated by triangular wedges of hill country.

East of the Windermere–Thirlmere depression is the drainage basin of Ullswater – a great amphitheatre whose high rim is shaped like a horseshoe. Its western side is dominated by Helvellyn, and its eastern side is the High Street ridge, followed by a Roman road to Carlisle. This drainage basin lies far enough east to receive a decidedly lower precipitation than that of the western knot, and its mean annual rainfall is about 2500 mm. Here the ice sheet appears to have been much thinner. The basin was occupied by a glacier, but the rim is smooth, rounded, and subdued, with few erratics, and in places with a mantle of broken-down parent rock which supports a cover of vegetation. There are thus few signs of intense glaciation, and this surface appears to be a relic of the pre-glacial landscape.

Ores of copper and lead have been known in the Lake District at least since the fourteenth century, but they were not actively worked until the mid-sixteenth century, when the Government encouraged German miners to settle and organize the industry. The mines were in the hillsides to the west of Derwentwater, in the hills north-east of Skiddaw, and in the valleys north-west of Coniston. Smelting began at Keswick, and the forests were felled systematically to provide the charcoal for fuel. For a time mining flourished, and it is recorded that between 1564 and 1570 the output reached a value of £31,000. The industry did not survive the Civil War, however, when royal support ceased; and though sporadic mining continued until the nineteenth century, it is now extinct.

Of greater interest is the graphite-working of Borrowdale, since it gave rise to pencil-making, which continues to flourish at Keswick. Graphite – so-called blacklead – was discovered by shepherds about 1550, on the side of Glaramara (south-east of Seathwaite), exposed after a violent storm had uprooted some trees. This was the first of its kind ever known, and within a few years the cottagers of Keswick were making primitive pencils by hand. The modern industry dates from 1832, with the establishment of the Cumberland Pencil Company, which claims to be the first in the world: it drew upon the local deposits of graphite from Wad mine, north of Seathwaite, until their exhaustion about 1880. Graphite is now imported from Ceylon, Mexico, and Korea, while the cedarwood, cut to size in slats, is drawn mainly from Kenya. For the production of the well-known 'Lakeland' coloured pencils the raw materials for the core include talcum and china clay. The factory overlooks the river Greta, employs about 150 people, and is one of the largest producers of pencils in the United Kingdom.

As in north Wales, the hill farmer concentrates on sheep-rearing and sells the lambs to lowland farmers for fattening in richer pastures. The Lakeland breed is the Herdwick – a small, hardy, sure-footed animal which can thrive on the hillsides throughout a normal winter, scraping through the snow to reach the pasture below. Only in the severest weather are they brought down to the lower pastures.

A Lakeland flock will number about 1000 sheep. At lambing time, which is five or six weeks later than in the lowlands, the ewes are brought into the shelter of the fields near the farmstead. Twins are rare, but in compensation the Herdwick yields a lean and sweet mutton. Shearing is in June and July, and neighbouring farmers co-operate for this and other tasks, such as collecting and dipping the sheep. Herdwick wool is coarse but strong, and suited for carpet-making and for blending with other wools.

The farmer may keep a few dairy cows to supply nearby hotels with fresh milk, and he sets aside a field or two for hay or oats: these are used as winter feed for the cattle, and only in cases of emergency will they be fed to sheep. Most likely there will be no hired labour on the farm.

As in· north Wales, the Lake District has been utilized for afforestation, and as a source of water-supply. The Forestry Commission has planted large areas in Ennerdale and in the valleys west of Bassenthwaite and elsewhere; but since the establishment in 1951 of a National Park covering the entire district further planting has ceased so that the natural beauty of the landscape may be preserved.

The heavy rainfall, together with the existence of natural reservoirs, have made the region a valuable source of supply of soft water for the neighbouring towns. Thirlmere and Hawes Water supply Manchester, Workington draws upon Crummock Water, Kendal is supplied from the Kenmere reservoir, and Barrow from the Seathwaite reservoir.

Summer visitors substantially contribute to the income of the inhabitants, for the towns and villages are tourist resorts: in this relatively small region there are about 25 Youth Hostels.

Barrow and the Cumberland Coalfield

Compared with its counterpart east of the Pennines, the Cumberland coalfield is a small one. During recent years the number of pits has been reduced from a dozen to two, which jointly produced in 1969–70 nearly half a million tonnes. The strata dip gently seaward; they include about ten seams of commercial importance, among them the Main Band, which attains 5 metres in thickness under the sea west of Whitehaven.

They are interrupted, however, by a complicated system of faults trending north-west and south-east; and both the northern and southern limits of the Coal Measures are set by faults. The coal is used for coking, gas-making, steam-raising, and in the home. The most accessible deposits of land coal have now been largely tapped, and most of the output is from undersea workings. These began at Whitehaven as early as 1731, and they now extend as far as 8 kilometres from the shore.

The coalfield is conveniently situated for trade with Ireland, and there is a regular collier traffic from Whitehaven and Workington to Belfast and Dublin.

The occurrence of rich hematite ironstone quite close to the coalfield led to the development of iron and steel industries. The ores are 52–55 per cent. pure, and are virtually free from phosphorus. They occur in two districts: at Egremont and Cleator, close to the southern border of the coalfield, and around the Duddon estuary to the south. The important Hodbarrow mine in the latter district was opened about 1864, and the iron industry reached its peak in the 1870's. Between 1871 and 1881 the population of Millom parish rose from 4300 to 7700, while that of Cleator rose from 7100 to 10,400. People flocked in from far and near, but there was an interesting influx from the mining districts of the south-west: in 1881 there were nearly 3000 men from Devon and Corn-wall living in the region, and there were 43 furnaces in blast.

By 1969 the output of west coast hematite had dwindled to 143,000 tonnes annually. Cleator and Cleator Moor consist mainly of abandoned shafts, disused mineral lines, and overgrown tips; but mining continues at Egremont and on a small scale at Hodbarrow. The local ores are supplemented by imports of foreign hematite. But the workings are declining in this area.

The iron and steel works at Workington are of interest in that here are the only acid Bessemer converters in the United Kingdom. The process is suitable only for non-phosphoric ores, but is parti-cularly appropriate for the manufacture of rails; accordingly almost the entire output is devoted to this product. At Barrow-in-Furness the steelworks help to supply the shipbuilding yard, which is on an adjoining site. Both industries have been established about a century, and during that period the population of the town has grown from less than 1000 to 65,000 people. The shipyard of Messrs Vickers-Armstrongs is one of our major establishments: it builds submarines and cruisers, oil tankers, aircraft-carriers. and large passenger liners.

The Eden Valley and the Carlisle Lowland

The lowland belts to the north and east of the hill masses of the Lake District are floored by Triassic and Permian material, and though this is extensively strewn with glacial material, the super-ficial deposits reflect the parent rocks and are generally reddish in colour and light in texture.

The Eden valley forms one of the most remarkable structural troughs in Britain. It is overlooked from the north-east by the fault scarp of Crossfell – a steep and straight mountain wall of limestone which rises from the valley floor at about 180 metres to a maximum height of 894 metres. Its western edge is less spectacular, but there is a rise in the surface where the Permian rocks give way to the Millstone Grit, and the geological boundary for over 16 km is so straight that it implies a fault junction here too. The

Romans, with a lively appreciation of the physical geography, constructed their road from Penrith to Carlisle parallel to the fault, and less than a mile to the east of it.

Sheltered by the hills to the west, the Eden valley has a surprisingly low rainfall – almost everywhere below 900 mm per annum; this, aided by the light soils, favours arable farming, and even wheat and barley are grown in small quantities. Below Appleby arable crops account for half the farm areas: they comprise mainly oats and rotation grasses, but include also swedes, turnips, and potatoes. Virtually all are fed to stock.

In the Carlisle lowland farming is essentially similar, but owing to lighter soils, lower elevation, and easy communications there is a greater emphasis on market-gardening and milk production. South-west of Carlisle is one of the best examples in England of drumlin landscape. The boulder clay here is arranged in oval mounds whose long axes run east and west between Aspatria and Carlisle, but in conformity with the topography, change to north and south in the basin of the Caldew, south of Carlisle. They have a clear influence on the distribution of farms and hamlets, which cling to the better-drained slopes and summits (Fig. 56).

Bordering the Solway Firth is a low-lying tract of peats, marine silts, and salt marshes, intersected by drains. It is virtually all permanent grassland, and provides valuable pastures for sheep and

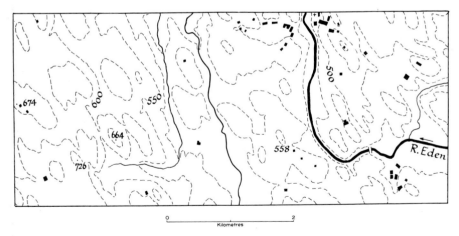

Fig. 56. DRUMLINS IN THE EDEN VALLEY

These oval hillocks give a characteristic pattern to the surface, and their influence is seen in the drainage and settlement. Farmhouses are sited mainly on the summits or slopes of the drumlins, where the land is better drained. The town whose outskirts appear in the north is Appleby. Heights are in feet. *Based on the O.S. 1-inch map. Crown copyright reserved.*

cattle. This is where many of the sheep from the fells are grazed in the winter; the local farmers in addition raise dairy herds and rear pigs and poultry. The market for this district and for the whole of the lowland is Carlisle.

Carlisle (pop. 71,497) is situated where the Caldew and Petterell rivers join the Eden, and remains, as in Roman times, the lowest crossing-point of that river. The actual site was occasioned by the narrowing of the belt of alluvium between banks of boulder clay. Its nodal situation was appreciated by the Romans, who focused on this spot their roads from the south (over Shap Fell), from the west (along the Lakeland foothills), from the east (by way of Tyne Gap), and from Scotland (through the valley of the Nith). The military settlement, one of the forts of Hadrian's Wall, was on the north side of the river; but a civilian offshoot developed to the south, and it was this site that the Normans chose to fortify by castle and wall.

Carlisle remained small until the construction of railways widened its catchment area. Today, however, it possesses one of the largest markets for store and fat sheep and cattle in the whole of England and Wales. Its textile industry originated in the eighteenth century from the spinning and weaving of local wool and flax, aided by the pure water of the Caldew; in addition it manufactures biscuits, has railway workshops, is the county town and cathedral city, and is a tourist centre for the Lake District.

The Isle of Man
Though it possesses only about 50,000 inhabitants, the Isle of Man has its own distinct character among the British Isles. Like the Channel Isles, it does not form part of the United Kingdom, but ranks as a dependency of the British Crown, with a large measure of self-government.

Physically the Isle of Man has affinities with highland Britain. It is built mainly of older Palæozoic grits and slates, but owing to the absence of fossils these cannot be precisely dated, and are provisionally regarded as of Cambrian age. The island was completely covered by the Quaternary ice sheets, and its soils, particularly in the lowlands, are mainly derived from glacial drift.

Almost equidistant from Cumberland in England, Wigtown in Scotland, and county Down in Northern Ireland, the Isle of Man is centrally placed in the Irish Sea, and has been open to Atlantic cultural influences at least since Neolithic times. A dozen elaborate Megalithic tombs testify to the settlement there of Neolithic folk; during the Bronze Age it lay on the trade route between Ireland

and the Continent. Remains of the Iron Age are scanty, perhaps on account of a deterioration in the climate; but during Roman times the Celtic inhabitants of the island lived peacefully in remarkably large round houses, some of which were as much as 27·5 m in diameter. Celtic Christian missionaries were active in Man, and many of the 160 ancient church sites date back to the early Christian period.

The island attained its greatest influence in Atlantic Britain under the Vikings. From about A.D. 800 onward the Norsemen arrived, first as raiders and later as settlers. From about 1080 to 1266 the Isle of Man formed the base of a Norwegian sub-kingdom – that of the Sodreys or Southern Isles – which included the Hebrides, centred on the isles of Lewis, Skye, Mull, and Islay. The Norsemen demarcated the existing parishes of the Isle of Man (each with a stretch of coastline); they organized the diocese of Sodor and Man, with a cathedral on St Patrick's Isle at Peel under the Archbishop of Trondheim; and they established a system of government centred on an assembly on Tynwald Hill (4 km south-east of Peel). So originated the Tynwald court which, together with the elected House of Keys, still forms the Manx Parliament.

Mining for lead and silver no longer occurs, fishing is of little account, and the island now depends on farming and the tourist industry. Agriculturally the most striking feature is the high proportion of arable land: in this respect Man compares with the neighbouring coastal lowlands of Scotland. About 45 per cent. of the island is under crops (mainly oats, turnips, and potatoes), and another 25 per cent. is under temporary grass. There is virtually no permanent pasture, and almost the whole of the remainder of the area consists of mountain moorland.

The tourist industry is of vital importance to the island, and about half a million visitors arrive annually. There are daily steamer connections with Liverpool, and an exceptionally busy airport at Ronaldsway, in the south of the island.

FOR FURTHER READING

Books

EASTWOOD, T.: *Northern England*, British Regional Geology Handbooks (H.M.S.O., 1946).

JONES, LL. RODWELL: *North England* (1926). A pioneer work, still well worth reading.

SMAILES, A. E.: *North England* (Nelson, 1960).

STAMP, L. D. (Ed.): *The Land of Britain*; Part 49, *Cumberland*; Part 50, *Westmorland* (Geographical Publications, 1943).

Articles and Booklets

BAINBRIDGE, T. H.: 'Cumberland Population Movements', 1871-81, in the *Geographical Journal* (July–Sept., 1946).

HAY, T.: 'Mountain Form in Lakeland', in the *Geographical Journal* (June 1944).

KINVIG, R. H.: 'The Isle of Man and Atlantic Britain' (Transactions, Institute of British Geographers, 1958).

MONKHOUSE, F. J.: 'Some features of the Historical Geography of the German mining enterprise in Elizabethan Lakeland', in *Geography* (December 1943).

—— *The English Lake District*, British Landscape through Maps (Geographical Association, 1960).

THORPE, H.: *Lancastria, A Pictorial Survey of England and Wales* (G. Philip, 1958).

Maps

O.S. 1-inch Tourist Map, Lake District.

Bartholomew's ½-inch map, sheets 34, 38.

Geological Survey ¼-inch sheet 3.

CHAPTER FIFTEEN

NORTH-EAST ENGLAND

BOTH PHYSICALLY and from the human standpoint, north-east England forms a distinct unit. Rich in resources of coal, iron, and salt; isolated by hills to the north, west, and south; remote from the main body of England – the region has preserved an individuality and a measure of self-sufficiency such as few others can show.

Physically the region comprises the north Pennines together with the southern slopes of the Cheviots and the flanking coalfield to the east. Its southern boundary may be placed at the Jurassic scarp of the Cleveland Hills of north Yorkshire, and at the Northallerton Gate, where it joins hands with the Vale of York. These limits coincide closely with those of a group of drainage basins: they include the Tees, Wear, Tyne, Blyth, and Aln. All are east-flowing streams, and they emphasize the importance which the east coast has had throughout the economic development of the region.

Politically the counties of Northumberland and Durham form the core of the region; industrially this is a major coalfield of Britain, the chief shipbuilding area of England, and one of its main iron and steel districts. Population and industry, however, cling to the coast, and inland are some of the most remote and lonely moorlands to be seen in the British Isles.

Physical Basis

Essentially the north-east is a region of Carboniferous rocks: these form the whole of the north Pennines and much of the Cheviot Hills, as well as the coalfield. Only towards the south-east do younger rocks outcrop: here occur successively Permian, Triassic, and Jurassic strata, each of which has provided important raw materials for industry (Fig. 57).

The Tyne Gap separates two differing structures: to the north is a series of domes and basins; to the south a tilted block. The Cheviot (816 m) is the most prominent of the domes. Its core is a granitic intrusion, whose surface outcrop, however, is quite restricted in area. This is surrounded by basalt and ringed by concentric bands of lower Carboniferous strata. As in the south-west

Fig. 57. THE NORTH-EAST COAST: GEOLOGY

While the general structure is simple, local folds and faults have resulted in the complex boundaries seen in the west of the region. The boundary between Magnesian Limestone and the Trias is occasioned by a fault. The structure along the line of section is shown in Fig. 58.

peninsula, the intrusion is reflected in the bulging coast between Holy Island and the mouth of the Coquet river.

The Cheviot dome is matched by a smaller upthrust to the west, and erosion has revealed in its core the earliest of the Carboniferous rocks. Here are the Bewcastle Fells, which overlook the Carlisle lowlands and form the western bastion of the region. Two basins oppose the domes, and the younger strata preserved in their floors present a more subdued landscape: south of the Cheviot is Redesdale, with its centre at Otterburn; north of the Cheviot a second structural hollow shows itself as the Tweed basin.

The Tyne corridor itself has resulted from crustal sagging along an east-west line, emphasized by a series of faults which generally trend in the same direction. To the south is the tilted block of the north Pennines. Its western edge is formed by the lofty fault scarp of Cross Fell; eastward the strata dip gently (Fig. 58), and are succeeded by younger formations which cut the coast at sharp angles. The lower Tyne and middle Wear trench deeply into the Coal Measures, and their valleys have aided the transport of coal.

From South Shields to West Hartlepool and ranging south-westward is the narrow outcrop of the Magnesian Limestone. It is of significance in the life of the region in several ways: it presents a west-facing scarp; it forms a 'nose' on the coast between South Shields and Sunderland; it is quarried to provide the linings for steel furnaces; and by hindering dredging at the mouth of the Wear it has prevented Sunderland from becoming a major port. The Magnesian Limestone conceals the south-east corner of the coalfield; the seams here are deeper, more expensive to tap, and economic only by large-scale development – here, then, are the newer collieries of the Northumberland and Durham field.

To the south-east a fault abruptly terminates the Magnesian Limestone and presents the Trias of the Vale of Tees. Below the surface are deposits of salt and anhydrite – valuable chemical raw materials – while the drift-covered lowland itself forms the most productive farming district. This is an area of progressive farming stimulated by the near-by urban market: it produces cereals, dairy cattle, good-quality bacon pigs, and vegetables. Beyond, in the Middle Lias of the Jurassic scarps, the exploitation of ironstone bands gave new life to the industries of the region in the middle of the nineteenth century.

Traversing rocks of all ages are many igneous dykes. Some of them point towards the great dyke swarm in the Isle of Mull, and are probably of Tertiary date. Others, confined to the Carboniferous Limestone, are earlier, and among them is the persistent Whin Sill (from which the 'sill' of geology took its name). Of a bluish-grey dolerite, it is 20 to 30 metres thick; and, more resistant than the limestone into whose bedding plane it was injected, it now outcrops as a ridge, in places many miles long. Bamburgh castle is built on its crags, and its weatherbeaten fragments form the Farne Isles. In the Tyne corridor the Romans aligned part of Hadrian's Wall along it; in modern times it has been put to more prosaic use, and is quarried at convenient points for road metal.

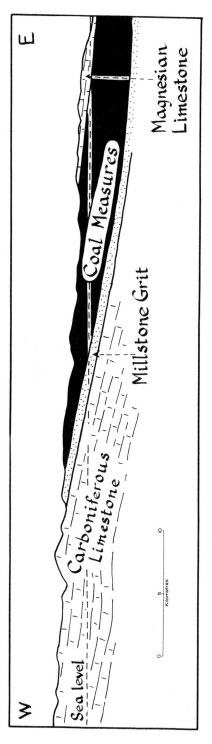

Fig. 58. GEOLOGICAL SECTION ACROSS THE NORTH-EAST COAST

It passes across the north Pennines from near Stanhope to the sea at Easington Colliery, and illustrates the gentle tilting of the strata down to the south-east, and the concealment of the Coal Measures below the Magnesian Limestone. At Easington the coal seams are worked below the sea for a distance of nearly 5 kilometres from the shore.

As in the Lake District, the surface features have been modified by ice action. The highlands have been scoured and strewn with erratics; the lowlands have been mantled with drift, and the drainage system has been modified by haphazard depressions in the drift cover.

Of the early phases of settlement perhaps that of the Romans has had the most lasting influence. Newcastle and Durham, as well as smaller settlements such as Brough and Chester-le-Street, have grown around Roman sites; the trunk road between Borough-bridge and Catterick retains the Roman line, and so does its western fork across the saddle of Stainmore into the Eden valley. The most direct route between Newcastle and Carlisle still runs along the Roman line parallel to but north of the Tyne.

The North Pennines

The sparse population of the remote moorland of the north Pennines is confined to the deep valleys cut by the southern headstreams of the Tyne and by the upper Wear and Tees. In these dales farming and settlement persist to remarkably high altitudes, roads provide an unusually complete network of communications, and even railway lines have been built well into the highland.

The explanation lies in the working of lead, which at its peak about 1860 provided employment for about 4000 miners. As in the Mendips, the industry declined when the competition of overseas deposits forced down the price of lead, and by the opening of the twentieth century mining and smelting activities had virtually ceased. The lead-workers had engaged in part-time farming, and though there was a considerable decline in the population of the valleys, a few families remained there grazing their flocks of hardy sheep on the hillsides and selling the lambs for fattening elsewhere. In some districts, such as Allendale in the north, cattle are reared as well as sheep, and the output of milk is increasing. In the early days the lead was smelted by charcoal, and the land cleared of natural woodland: only recently has the Forestry Commission replaced some of the timber by planting on the moorland edges.

The tradition of quarrying continues, however, in a few isolated areas. The Whin Sill is worked for roadstone at Middleton in Teesdale, and in Weardale; on a far larger scale are the quarries for fluxing limestone in Weardale between Stanhope and Frosterley. The bed being worked is known as the Great Limestone – the thickest of the limestone bands (about 18 metres thick) and the bed richest in lead. Here the Great Limestone is closest to the Tees-side blast furnaces and most accessible for lorry transport.

The Northumberland and Durham Coalfield

The Northumberland and Durham coalfield was the earliest to be worked in Britain on any important scale. There is a record of continuous shipment of coal from this region to London from 1316 onward. The traffic remained small until coal became an accepted fuel, but in the second half of the sixteenth century the trade multiplied fivefold. At a time when transport by land was difficult and expensive, this coalfield possessed the vital advantage that its seams outcropped close to navigable water.

In their natural state the rivers were shallow, but could be used by the flat-bottomed craft known as keels. Wagon-ways equipped with wooden rails were constructed from the pits to the riverside loading points: these were the forerunners of the railway system. By the 1820's there were 570 keels operating on the Wear, and they transhipped their cargoes to about 20 sailing colliers which carried about one million tonnes annually.

During the course of the century the arduous business of loading by hand was replaced by gravity loading, by means of staiths. A staith is a jetty or wharf provided with railway tracks, and so arranged that the railway wagons can discharge into the collier waiting below. This speedy method of loading is characteristic of the north-east coast: it is possible only because the rivers have been rejuvenated, and have incised their beds deeply below the general level of the land (Fig. 59).

There are about 20 commercially important seams in the coalfield, but they are scattered through nearly 600 metres of otherwise barren strata. The following table shows the position and thickness of the first eight coal seams which would appear in a shaft at Newcastle:

	Metres
Closing Hill Seam	0·5
Strata	140
Hebburn Fell Seam	0·8
Strata	75
Five-quarter Seam	1·2
Strata	80
Three-quarter Seam	0·6
Strata	15 to 55
High Main Coal	1·8
Strata	10 to 45
Metal Coal	0·5
Strata	10
Stone Coal	0·5
Strata	18 to 30
Yard Coal	0·9
Strata	18 to 30

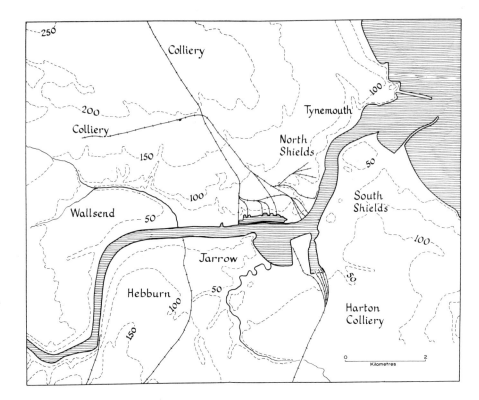

Fig. 59. THE LOWER TYNE

The remarkably steep banks of the river have allowed the development of gravity loading by means of staiths – an important asset to the region. The area shown includes three collieries, and there are two others just beyond the south margin of the map. They are almost ideally situated for coal shipment. In addition to the coal staiths there are shipbuilding and repairing yards on both banks along this stretch of the river (see Fig. 61). Heights are in feet.

Three or four seams in the coalfield attain a thickness of 1·8 to 2·5 metres, but most of them hardly reach 1 metre. We have already mentioned the concealed portion of the field in the south-east; in addition the seams extend below the water of the North Sea, and at Easington colliery, south of Seaham, the workings stretch for nearly 5 kilometres from the shore.

The coal ranges widely in character, and this has its effects on the nature of the trade. All types are to be found, with the exception of anthracite (Fig. 60). Coking coal – reputedly the finest in the world – occurs in south-west Durham, and much of this is transported by rail to the steel district of Tees-side. Northward and eastward the carbon content decreases, through gas coal to steam coal and house coal. Gas coal is shipped from Sunderland, steam coal from the Tyne, and house coal from Blyth.

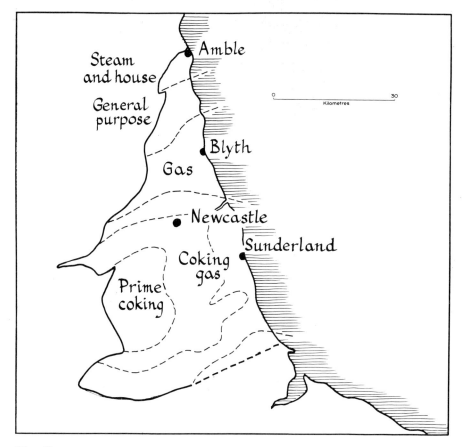

Fig. 60. THE RANGE OF COALS IN THE NORTHUMBERLAND
AND DURHAM COALFIELD   *By courtesy of the National Coal Board.*

Forty years ago the Tyne shipped steam coal to coaling stations
in every sea. With the growth of oil-burning vessels the export
trade has drastically declined; but the coastal coal traffic with
London is as great as ever. Thames-side power-stations and gasworks, cement-works and paper-mills depend almost entirely on
coal from the north-east coast. On any day about 40 colliers are
likely to be on their way in or out, with many others loading or
discharging in port. Coal is still the outstanding cargo shipped
from the Tyne; it is virtually the only export of Blyth, Sunderland,
Seaham, and the Hartlepools.

Pit closures are being offset by the construction at Lynemouth
(10 km north of Blyth) of a new aluminium smelter. This will be
coal-fired: it will employ directly 900 people and indirectly a further
1000 miners.

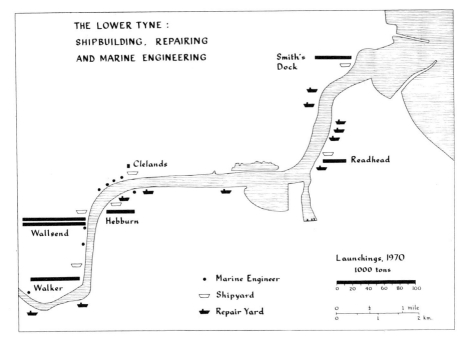

Fig. 61. TYNESIDE: SHIPBUILDING AND ASSOCIATED INDUSTRIES
In 1968 the Wallsend, Walker, Hebburn and Readhead establishments merged to form the Swan
Hunter Group. The output of each individual shipyard during 1970 is indicated by the length of its
respective black bar.

Shipbuilding

With the development of coal-mining came the need for colliers,
and so originated the shipbuilding industry. Until the nineteenth
century the vessels were built of timber, and for this purpose trees
were felled in the deep wooded valleys which joined the coast. As
the century progressed, first iron and then steel was used in place
of wood, and the shipyards benefited from the proximity of the
iron and steel industry. In return they supplied the works with
scrap metal.

The Tyne, like the Clyde, is now largely artificial. In 1850 at
low-water spring tides there were only 1·8 m of water at its mouth:
now there is a dredged channel allowing 7 metres of water at low-
water spring tides as far as the staiths at Derwenthaugh, over 22 km
from the mouth of the river. Five large and famous shipyards
border the river below Newcastle (Figs 61 and 62), and from their

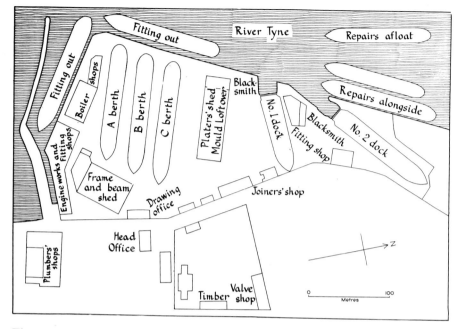

Fig. 62. A TYNESIDE SHIPYARD

This is the shipyard of John Readhead (Fig. 61). The hull is constructed in a building berth, and the vessel is completed in a fitting-out berth. The dry docks are for repair work. Shipyards involve a variety of activities, only a few of which are indicated here. *By courtesy of John Readhead & Sons, Ltd.*

35 berths come one-sixth of the total tonnage of the United Kingdom launchings. In addition there are 16 ship-repairing establishments with about 30 dry docks. Every type of vessel is built and repaired here, but there is a special interest in oil-tankers. The Tyneside shipbuilding and repairing industry employs directly about 20,000 people: there are also important shipyards on the Wear and Tees.

Iron and Steel

The early iron and steel industry, based on ores extracted from the Coal Measures, and using charcoal as fuel, was established inland. In the Consett district a colony of German metal-workers was producing knives and swords as early as the seventeenth century: doubtless they were using the water of the Derwent to operate their bellows and hammers and to turn their grindstones.

With the depletion of the forests and the exhaustion of the Coal Measure ores the inland sites lost their advantages, and the works at Consett are the sole survivor of a once widespread group. Consett now relies completely upon imported ore, which arrives from a Tyneside quay near Jarrow. Specially designed hopper wagons, each holding 57 tonnes, run from the dockside over the 40 km uphill to the Consett blast furnaces.

With this exception, the modern iron and steel industry is concentrated on Tees-side (Fig. 63). There are important contrasts with the Tyne. The Tees winds through a low-lying, drift-covered plain, with abundant space for large-scale works. Industry arrived late, and in 1831 Middlesbrough could muster only 134 people.

The early head of navigation on the Tees was Yarm; but by 1800 coal was being shipped from Stockton, which offered a greater depth of water. In 1825 there was opened Stephenson's famous railway from Darlington to Stockton, and the Tees became, temporarily, the outlet for the coal of south Durham. Five years later, the railway company, seeking a shipping point with even deeper water, extended the line to Port Darlington, and built the nucleus of modern Middlesbrough.

By 1850 Middlesbrough was a coal port of 7000 people; then in that same year a 5-metre seam of ironstone was found to outcrop in the near-by Cleveland Hills. Situated midway between the coking coal of south Durham and the newly found deposits of iron, Middlesbrough was seen to be an ideal site for the erection of steelworks. Within five years 35 furnaces had been built and a million tonnes of ore was being won annually; by 1870 there were 40,000 people in the town and 10,000 iron-miners in the district.

During the 1880's steel began to replace iron; the output of Cleveland ore reached nearly 7 million tonnes, and Tees-side produced much of the steel for the growing railway system. Local ore production then gradually declined as the more accessible deposits were exhausted, and with the closing of the North Skelton mine early in 1964 iron-mining in the Cleveland Hills came to an end. But steel-making prospers owing to its coastal situation, which has allowed the easy import of foreign ore.

Unlike other towns of nineteenth-century growth, Middlesbrough exhibits a measure of zoning. The residential areas lie on the slightly higher land south of the flood-plain of the Tees; the iron and steel works have been built close to the river, and each has its own wharf. The large new works at Lackenby and north of Redcar utilize reclaimed tidal flats for the building of long jetties to the deep-water channel of the Tees. A single great organization – that of Dorman Long and Company – controls almost completely the Tees-side steel industry. Its works include 11 blast furnaces,

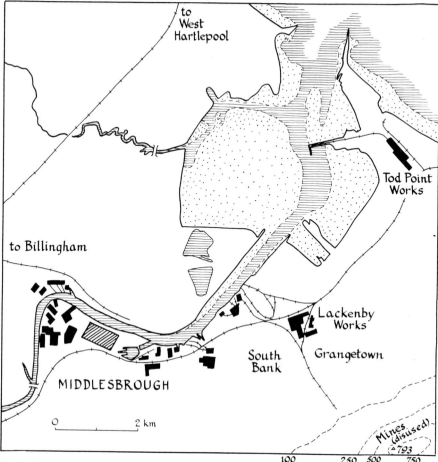

Fig. 63. TEES-SIDE

The shaded (lined) area one mile north-east of the bridge at Middlesbrough was the original nucleus of the town, built in 1830, and the early steelworks were in the 'Ironmasters District' immediately to the west. Modern works have been built nearer the sea. Large areas of formerly tidal land have been reclaimed in the estuary. Stippled areas represent foreshore exposed at low tide; steelworks are shown in black. Heights are in feet. *Based on the O.S. 1-inch map. Crown copyright reserved.*

and the firm employs about 31,000 people. The company is well known as the producer of two famous bridges: those spanning Sydney harbour and Auckland harbour; but its links are perhaps closer with shipbuilding and marine engineering. About three-quarters of the entire output consists of plates and other heavy rolled products, including railway lines.

The Chemical Industry

Chemical manufacture is a normal accompaniment of steel-making, for in the coking process there emerge three important raw materials which form the basis for a whole range of chemical processes: these are ammonia, tar, and benzole. In Tees-side there is the additional advantage that the Triassic deposits contain salt and anhydrite (sulphate of lime). The latter, first worked in 1923, is now mined to the extent of about one million tonnes annually.

The vast chemical works of Imperial Chemical Industries at Billingham, on the north shore of the Tees estuary, covef 400 hectares and employ about 16,000 people. Their products include acids, cement, fertilizers, and synthetic petroleum products. The same organization is developing a second large site on the south side of the river, at Wilton. Here chlorine and caustic soda are being prepared from the local salt deposits, and a petroleum chemicals industry is being established, using imported oil.

Both plants are served by deep-water wharves, where there are imports of petroleum, creosote oil, phosphates, and potash. Paradoxically, potash is known to exist below the North York Moors in Eskdale, in a bed 8 metres thick at a depth of 1200 metres. In 1967 a potash-mining project was announced; by 1971 two shafts had reached a depth of 610 metres and commercial production is expected to begin in 1973.

Newcastle

The Romans bridged the Tyne at the spot now occupied by the Newcastle swing bridge, and guarded the crossing by a camp built on the north side of the river. So originated Newcastle. For long the site had immense strategic value. Here the east-coast route from the Midlands into Scotland is confined between the Pennines and the sea to a corridor less than 20 km wide; this corridor is joined from the west by the Tyne Gap, which provides the only easy communication between east and west in northern England. Newcastle controlled both these routes.

The 'new castle', of earth and timber, was established in 1080 by Robert, the eldest son of William the Conqueror, and the stone keep which replaced it a century later stands today overlooking the river in the centre of the city. The low early bridge formed the limit of seagoing navigation, and though specially designed colliers now penetrate well beyond the bridges, Newcastle remains the lowest bridge point and the port for ocean freighters.

The shape of the medieval walled town is still reflected in the street plan of the central area. Its growth as the market for a wide area was aided by a distinct focus of river valleys on the site. From the south the middle portion of the Wear is continued by the Team; from the Consett area in the south-west comes the Derwent; and from the north is the smaller Ouse Burn. Roads and, in later times, railways emphasized these routeways and added to the growth of the city; and with the exploitation of the coalfield and the development of shipbuilding and engineering, Newcastle has become the shopping and administrative centre, the cathedral and university town for the whole of the north of England.

The general trade of the port is handled mainly below the bridges. Here, on the Newcastle side, are more than 2 km of quays, with another 300 metres of quays on the Gateshead side of the river. Grain ships from Canada and Australia berth at the lofty flour-mills, timber from Scandinavia, and dairy produce from the Low Countries are discharged at the wharves, with other varied cargoes. Characteristic connections are with Scandinavia: Newcastle is the normal passenger port for Norway, and there is still a considerable export of coal to Denmark, which possesses no local source of fuel or power. As a general port and regional capital, Newcastle has no rival in northern England.

Durham, the county town to the south, stands apart from mining and manufacture. It occupies a magnificently defended site in a loop of the deeply incised river Wear, and is dominated by its cathedral and castle (the latter has been appropriated by the university). The city has expanded, but not greatly beyond its original site, and it is characteristic that the parent University of Durham has been outstripped in size by her 'daughter' college, now the University of Newcastle.

FOR FURTHER READING

Books

EASTWOOD, T.: *Northern England*, British Regional Geology Handbooks (H.M.S.O., 1946).

JONES, LL. R.: *North England* (1926).

REES, HENRY: *British Ports and Shipping* (Harrap, 1958), Chapters 8 and 9.

SMAILES, A. E.: *North England* (Nelson, 1960).

Article

ELLIOTT, N. R.: 'Hinterland and Foreland as illustrated by the Port of Tyne' *Transactions, Institute of British Geographers* (September 1969).

Maps

Bartholomew's ½-inch maps, sheets 35, 36, 39, and 42.

The solid geology is covered by Geological Survey ¼-inch sheets 1/2 and 4.

The Geological Survey 1-inch sheet 6, drift (Alnwick) illustrates the extensive drift cover and the outcrop of Whin Sill.

Ordnance Survey 1-inch sheet 78, 7th series (Newcastle-upon-Tyne) illustrates the incised valleys and the distribution of collieries.

CHAPTER SIXTEEN

YORKSHIRE, DERBYSHIRE, AND NOTTINGHAMSHIRE

THIS VERY LARGE REGION, unwieldy in many respects, possesses nevertheless a measure of physical unity in that it corresponds with a single drainage basin – that of the Humber – and has a degree of economic unity in that it is served by a single major port – Hull. But its sub-regions differ widely one from another, and there is no single capital for the whole region: Leeds is the largest city, but Sheffield and Nottingham are regional centres for the south, while York and Hull exercise certain regional functions for the east.

The region includes the sparsely peopled central and south Pennines and the populous coalfield on their eastern flanks; in the east are the fertile vales of York and Trent, and beyond them, in the north-east, the Jurassic and Cretaceous scarps and vales.

Physical Basis

Complex in detail, the structure in its essentials is simple. The strata range in age from the Carboniferous Limestone of Derbyshire and the central Pennines to the Chalk of the York Wolds. For the most part they outcrop in their correct order without important omissions; and they dip gently eastward or southward so that their resistant members form bold west- or north-facing scarps.

A threefold division of the Pennines into north, central, and south is perhaps to be preferred. The north Pennines we have already noticed (p. 212); they are bounded southward by the valley of the Tees. From here to the Aire gap the hills constitute the central Pennines; and from the Aire gap southward, the south Pennines.

The central and south Pennines stand in sharp contrast to each other. The former consist of a rigid, elevated block of Carboniferous Limestone, bounded by faults to the west (the Dent Faults) and south (the Craven Faults). In the south Pennines, however, the strata yielded to the pressures of the Carbo–Permian earth movements by folding. The pressures seem to have acted from the east, for on this side the dips are gentle, while those to the west are steep. The main axis of the upfold runs well to the west of the centre of the hills (for the most part a little west of longitude 2° W.), and its steeply dipping western limb is dislocated by a series of strong faults – which, indeed, are characteristic of the whole length of the western edge of the Pennines. In general the south Pennines retain their cover of Millstone Grit, with its distinctive landscape and land use; but in Derbyshire the strata have been raised to form an elongated dome, from whose crest the Millstone Grit has been stripped to reveal the underlying Carboniferous Limestone.

Eastward the Millstone Grit dips gently and regularly and its grit bands stand out from the softer shales to form prominent west-facing scarps. Such is the rampart of the Chatsworth Grit whose almost vertical face rises 15 metres above the shales to form Stanage Edge and Burbage Rocks, and continues far to the south to overlook the Derwent valley.

The Coal Measures rest upon the Millstone Grit and dip in their turn below the Magnesian Limestone, whose narrow outcrop continues from Durham (p. 210) through Yorkshire and as far south as Nottingham. It presents a west-facing scarp, yields useful building stone, and weathers into fertile, limy soils – traditionally sheep and barley land.

Beyond are the vales of York and Trent. Carved alike from the soft Triassic rocks, they differ in that these 'solid' deposits are exposed only in the Nottinghamshire portion: in Yorkshire the vale is floored by varied glacial and post-glacial deposits, and it is these rather than the Trias which are reflected in the agriculture of the district.

The uplift of the Pennines appears to have been completed in Tertiary times, and at the same time the Jurassic deposits of north-east Yorkshire were raised into a dome, whose effect is now seen in the Cleveland Hills. These present a north-facing scarp to the Vale of Tees, and west and south-west facing scarps to the Vale of York (the Hambleton and Howardian Hills).

To the south the Cleveland Hills are truncated by a powerful fault with a throw of nearly 150 metres, passing through Helmsley and Pickering. The Hambleton and Howardian Hills are separated by a remarkable rift valley (the Gilling Gap), and the Gilling fault extends as far east as Malton. The Vale of Pickering is thus a structural trough: it is floored by Kimmeridge Clay, and partially filled by old lake sediments.

Farther south the Jurassic strata thin out, and at Market Weighton they are represented on the surface only by the Lower Lias. The virtual disappearance of the Jurassic belt here was occasioned by a persistent tendency to uplift in Jurassic times.

In the Chalk of the York Wolds the structures are simple: faulting is absent and the strata dip gently, at angles usually less than 10 degrees. The crescent-shaped scarp suggests the existence of a basin whose centre lies below Holderness. In our description of the sub-regions we move from older to newer rocks, beginning with the Pennines in the west and ending with Holderness and Hull in the east.

The Pennines

The structural contrasts between the central and south Pennines are reflected in landscape and land use. Into the central Pennines, or 'Askrigg block', the Wharfe, Nidd, Ure, and Swale have cut long and deep valleys: these are the Yorkshire Dales. From 150 to 275 metres deep, they are steep-sided and flat-floored, and have evidently been modified by ice action. The Carboniferous Limestone here consists of alternate bands of limestone and shale, and the latter are sufficiently extensive to produce impermeable subsoils over wide areas. The limestone outcrops form benches along the valley sides, and yield better grazing-land.

The intervening moorlands provide summer pasture for sheep: this is the home of the Swaledale – a large animal, hardy and resistant to damp, with a valuable fleece. In the lower dales the Swaledale is crossed with the Wensleydale to produce lambs more suited to fattening.

The valleys usually trend east and west, so that aspect plays an important part in farming possibilities. Improved pasture is confined to the valley floors; but there is virtually no arable land, and Professor Wooldridge, when helping in the first Land Utilization Survey, remarked on a single ploughed field in Wensleydale, which he could see from the surrounding heights many miles away.

In the Malham district, near the Craven faults, are excellent examples of karst phenomena, with deep gorges, swallow holes, limestone pavements, and emergent streams such as the headwater of the Aire, which escapes from the foot of a limestone cliff.

The south Pennines are lower, their Millstone Grit subsoil is largely impermeable, and the peaty moorland is unsuited to sheep. In the far south, however, the limestone district of Derbyshire offers further examples of karst landscape: there are dry ravines such as the Winnats; caves as at Castleton, and deep river-cut gorges such as Dovedale. Both here and in the central Pennines are signs of the old lead-mining industry, which reached its peak about 1850. The veins, or 'rakes', were followed, sometimes for a mile or more, and were pierced by shafts to depths of 165 metres. The miners went to great lengths to drain their shafts, and their levels, or soughs', driven far into the hillsides, have left their mark on the existing drainage pattern.

The Derbyshire Dome is bounded by minor earth ripples. A downfold to the north has compressed, strengthened, and preserved a triangular mass of grit to form the flat-topped moor of Kinder Scout (637 m) in the misnamed High Peak. To the east upfolds have affected the shape of the coalfield: the Brimington anticline restricts the width of the exposed field west of Sheffield, and the Ashover anticline restricts it in Nottinghamshire.

The abundant and pure water-supply of the Millstone Grit areas aided the growth of the domestic woollen industry, and many weaver's cottages remain, in remote areas and on steep hillsides; some are now occupied by smallholders who rear poultry and a few dairy cattle. The fulling mills were built in the valley bottoms to use the power offered by the swift streams.

Today the grit areas form important sources of water-supply for the large populations on both flanks of the Pennines. The narrow, steep-sided valleys are easily dammed; and the heavy rainfall and the impervious subsoils are additional advantages.

The Coalfield

The so-called York, Derby, and Nottinghamshire coalfield extends also into Lincolnshire and Leicestershire; it is by far our largest and most productive coalfield. The exposed coalfield covers 2300 square km, and to this we must add a further 5200 square km at least for the concealed coalfield. Coal has been proved at depth near York, in the north-east, near Grantham, in the south-east, and beyond Lincoln, in the east, where the base of the Coal Measures lies at more than 900 metres below sea-level.

In the exposed coalfield there are 30 workable seams, and some of these, together with clayband ironstones, were worked in Roman times. Records of medieval mining date back to the thirteenth century. Until 1859 all the workings were in the exposed field; but in that year a large colliery was established near Worksop in the concealed coalfield. Its shafts pierced the Magnesian Limestone and reached the famous Top Hard seam (or Barnsley Bed of Yorkshire) at 467 metres; the project successfully demonstrated the potentialities of the concealed coalfield.

The Top Hard seam, usually 1·8 metres thick, has been found to extend over a wide area, and today there are 54 pits in the concealed coalfield, most of which are working that seam. For this newer part of the coalfield Mansfield is an important centre.

As in the Northumberland and Durham coalfield, there is a wide range of character in the coals. Generally speaking, the rank increases downward and westward, so that the best coking coal is found in the west of south Yorkshire, while house coals are found in the higher seams and in Nottinghamshire. Between these two extremes are gas coals, and these account for about two-thirds of all the coal mined in Yorkshire. There are vast reserves, estimated at 10,000 million tonnes of workable coal.

A slow movement of mining activity has taken place eastward, away from the western outcrop zone towards the deeper seams in the east, and towards the concealed coalfield. In Nottinghamshire an important coal-producing district is the valley of the Erewash: here the river follows the crest of an anticline which brings near the surface some valuable seams, including the Top Hard itself. Roads, railways, and canal follow the valley, which is lined by collieries and mining villages.

Leeds and the Woollen Industry (Fig. 64)

The woollen industry of west Yorkshire has arisen through a combination of favourable physical elements – advantages which few other places in the United Kingdom could provide.

The neighbouring limestones offered good sheep pastures, though the grits of the immediate locality were too damp to carry large flocks: these on the other hand provided the abundant lime-free water which was essential in the washing and dyeing processes. The textile machines of the eighteenth century were designed for operation by water-wheels, and the steep gradients of the moorland streams presented ideal sites for such mills. With the perfection of the steam-engine in the late eighteenth century, the wealth of coal in the region confirmed the location of the industry, and the West Riding soon outstripped its rivals in East Anglia and elsewhere.

The mill was now no longer tied to the stream for its power; many mills could be established in the same district, and so the factory town made its appearance. In striking contrast to most other industrial districts, the woollen towns are almost in the heart of the moors: gradients are steep, transport is difficult, and there is no single valley focus. In these circumstances each town tends to carry out all the processes, and specialization is by product rather than by stage.

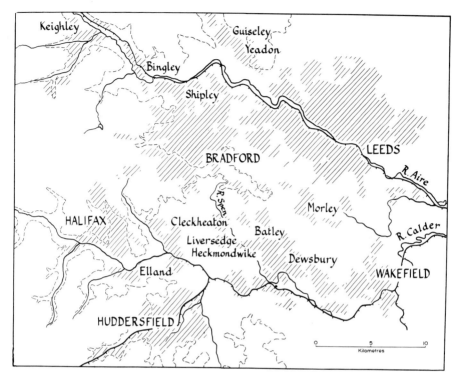

Fig. 64.   THE WEST YORKSHIRE CONURBATION

The towns originated as valley settlements. Leeds in the Aire valley, Halifax in the Hebble valley, Huddersfield in the Colne, Bradford in that of the Bradford Brook. But their outskirts now spread into the hills, and the suburbs of Bradford, Halifax, and Huddersfield climb well beyond the 600-feet contour (here shown as a broken line).

Halifax (pop. 91,171) is the carpet centre, and its fortunes are linked with a single firm which operates about 30 mills; Huddersfield (pop. 130,964) is the centre for woollens, Bradford (pop. 293,756) for worsteds, Leeds for ready-made clothing, and the Spen valley towns (Liversedge, Heckmondwike, and Cleckheaton) for textile machinery – an activity descended from an early iron industry. Far from any major port, the industry imports most of its raw wool through London.

Leeds (pop. 494,971) owes much of its growth to its natural nodality. Eastward the river Aire links with the Humber, and morainic ridges provide dry routes across the Vale of York; westward the Aire Gap allows easy communication with industrial Lancashire; southward roads and railways follow the foot of the

Magnesian Limestone to Wakefield and Rotherham, and eventually reach the Erewash valley and Nottingham.

Leeds became a port in 1659 when the Aire was made navigable as far as the city; its westward links were strengthened when the Leeds–Liverpool canal was opened in 1816, and the water traffic continues, though on a small scale. Modern Leeds is the cultural and commercial centre for almost the whole of Yorkshire.

Sheffield (pop. 519,703)

Iron has been worked in the Sheffield district certainly from Roman times, possibly in prehistoric times. Medieval furnaces are known, but the chief development dates from the sixteenth century, by which time Sheffield was exporting its cutlery overseas. The main source of iron was the Tankersley ironstone, which outcrops between Rotherham and Dewsbury: it was smelted by charcoal, and by repeated forging it gained sufficient carbon to take a good cutting edge.

When water-power was harnessed to the industry the Sheffield region possessed the outstanding advantage that it lay at the focus of five streams, whose beds descended so steeply from the Millstone Grit that they offered sites for water-wheels every few hundred metres (Fig. 65). In 1794 there were 83 water-wheels in the district, and this had become the chief centre in the country for the manufacture of edged tools such as scythes, files, saws, and cutlery. For export they were carried by packhorse eastward across 32 km of hilly country to Bawtry, on the river Idle, transferred to boats, and again transhipped to seagoing vessels at Hull.

Arthur Young in the late 1760's described vividly the use of water-power to work the bellows, and drive the hammers and grindstones:

> . . . do not forget the tilting-mill, which is a blacksmith's immense hammer in constant motion on an anvil, worked by water wheels, and by the same power the bellows of a forge adjoining kept regularly blown . . .
>
> The mechanism of these grinding wheels is very curious; many grindstones are turned by a set of wheels which all receive the motion from one water wheel, increasing in velocity from the first movement to the last, which is astonishing; in the finishing wheels it is so great, that the eye cannot perceive the least motion.

The remains survive of some of these old mills, such as the tilt-hammers and grinding wheels of the Abbeydale works – a scythe-making establishment on the banks of the Sheaf.

Sheffield had grown around a twelfth-century castle overlooking the junction of the Don and Sheaf, and was the most convenient

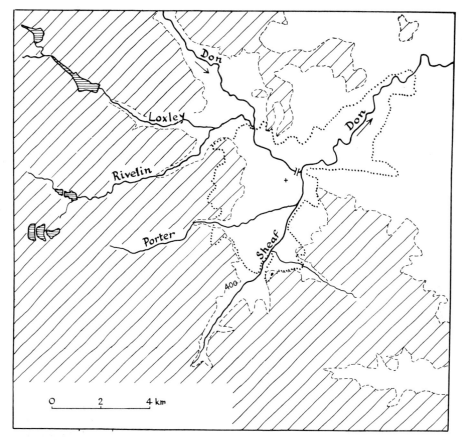

Fig. 65. THE SITE OF SHEFFIELD

The city grew round a twelfth-century castle on a hill in the angle between the junction of the Don and the Sheaf. The bridge and parish church (now the cathedral) are indicated, but the castle has vanished. Five streams focus on the town, and it grew in the early Industrial Revolution as a market for the products of the valley ironworks. The land above 400 feet is shaded. Modern reservoirs are ruled horizontally. The dotted line indicates the approximate limit of the built-up area.

centre for the assembly and marketing of the products of the valley forges. Many inventions and improvements were initiated there. About 1740 Benjamin Huntsman developed the production of crucible steel, and two or three years later Thomas Bolsover first produced 'Sheffield Plate' by fusing silver with a copper alloy. After a century this was superseded by electroplating. In 1858 Sir Henry Bessemer opened his works in Sheffield, demonstrated his 'converter,' and made a fortune; and in 1913 Harry Brearly discovered the secret of making stainless steel.

There are still small workshops in the centre of the city where craftsmen assemble penknives for a world-wide market. More characteristic today, however, are the large works in the Don valley, where the flood-plain allows more space for modern furnaces and rolling mills. Among the products are stainless steels, heavy-duty steels, plated steels, and cutting steels. A unique feature is that the smelting branch is absent: there are no blast furnaces nearer than Rotherham; and for its specialist products Sheffield depends largely on the electric furnace.

Far from any port, hemmed in by hills, lacking in raw materials, Sheffield nevertheless prospers owing to accumulated skills and an acknowledged reputation. It is the supreme example of industrial inertia.

The Vales of York and Trent
These vales, which merge to form a single lowland, are clearly defined by the geological structure: to the east are the Jurassic and Cretaceous scarps, to the west the dip slope of the Magnesian Limestone. The limits to the north and south are less precise, but may be placed at the constrictions of the vales at Northallerton and Nottingham. This large lowland has a uniform relief, rainfall, and structure. Much of it is below 30 metres O.D., and hardly any of it is above 60 metres. It is well defined by the 660 mm isohyet, and the central district receives an average of less than 610 mm of rainfall annually, so that climatically it is suited to cereal crops. Structurally it is a 'strike' vale, carved from the easily eroded Triassic deposits – the older Bunter Sandstone and Pebble Beds in the west, and the younger Keuper Marl in the east.

The 'solid' deposits, however, appear on the surface only in the Nottinghamshire portion of the sub-region; in Yorkshire they are masked by a variety of drift. North of Northallerton the whole width of the vale is occupied by a spread of boulder clay, which is here gathered into drumlins; farther south the boulder clay is confined to the flanks of the vale, and differences in texture are a result of different origins. The westerly clay was brought by Pennine ice, and the soils derived from it contain limestone fragments; that on the eastern flank was brought by Scottish ice, which had passed over Keuper Marl and Lias, and here the soils are heavier and tend to be acid. On both flanks the land is suited to pastoral rather than arable farming.

West of Thirsk, however, are extensive sheets of outwash gravel, in places forming esker ridges which run north and south. The gravels offer light, easily worked soils, and dry sites for settlement.

They were singled out by the settlers who founded Thirsk and Northallerton and a host of villages, by the builders of the Roman road between Boroughbridge and Catterick, and in later times by the engineers of the York and Newcastle railway. Today this is arable land, dominated by root crops such as sugar beet, potatoes, and carrots, together with rye and peas. All grow well on light, sandy soils.

The centre of the vale is the floor of the former Lake Humber, and laminated clays provide evidence of the increase in melt-water which regularly took place each summer. The clays contain a proportion of sand, and this is productive land, occupied by an even spread of farmsteads.

Rising from the lake floor are two of the finest examples of terminal moraines in this country. They extend east and west in lobes, one crossing the vale at York, the other a few kilometres south, through Escrick. Like the outwash gravels, they proved attractive to settlers, and are followed for most of their lengths by roads. Other less prominent moraines, recording later stages in the ice retreat, have been discerned at Raskelf (13 km south-west of Thirsk) and at Well (16 km west of Thirsk).

South of the Yorkshire–Nottinghamshire boundary the drift cover is missing. The Bunter soils, in the west, are porous, and in places consist of coarse gravels; they lack lime, and tend to dry out. Large areas are wooded or have reverted to heath; in the north is the district of private parks known as the Dukeries, and in the south are the remnants of Sherwood Forest. Given adequate lime and manure, however, these soils can be productive of root crops.

The Keuper soils are heavier and better watered, and support a balanced agriculture: the farmers rear sheep and cattle, they produce milk, wheat, sugar beet, and potatoes, or they grow fruit and market-garden produce. This is indeed the most fertile land in Nottinghamshire.

For the greater part of the vale York is the natural centre. Its site is of exceptional interest (Fig. 66). Here the Ouse has cut a narrow passage through the York moraine and this has provided a suitable bridging point. Near by it receives a tributary – the Foss – from the north-east; and in the angle of the river junction stands a detached portion of morainic clay. It was this easily defended site that the Romans chose for Eburacum.

The town thus stood at a crossroads, where the north-south river route was crossed by the east-west moraine route. The Ouse was formerly tidal as far as York, and river barges still reach the city

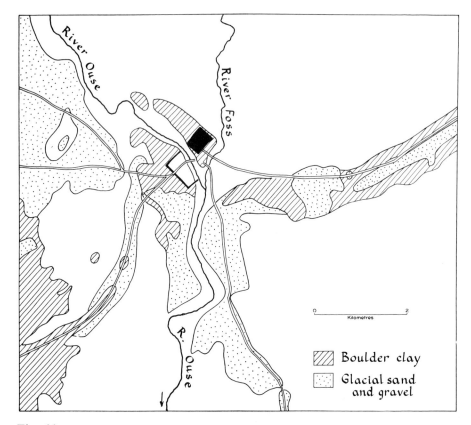

Fig. 66. THE YORK MORAINE AND THE SITE OF YORK

The Roman legionary fortress (shown in black) was built on a hill of boulder clay in the angle at the junction of the Foss with the Ouse. Here the Ouse breaches the York moraine and the flood-plain narrows between cliffs of boulder clay sufficiently to allow bridging. The site was admirably defended by Nature, and could be reached by sea-going vessels. The minster now occupies the centre of the Roman site. Medieval York spread to the opposite bank of the Ouse, and its walls are indicated. The diagram shows clearly how the main roads cling to the moraine ridges. Areas left unshaded consist of lake deposits and river alluvium. *Based on the Geological Survey 1-inch map.*

today. Medieval York spread on to the western bank of the Ouse, and its piety and power are evidenced by the almost complete circuit of walls, the city gates, and the magnificent minster.

Modern York (pop. 104,513) is largely a product of the railway workshops and the chocolate industry. For the latter there is no convincing geographical explanation. The firm of Rowntree traces its origin to a local family grocery business, established in 1725. Today Rowntree's employ about 10,000 people, or almost one-tenth of the population of the city.

The Eastern Scarps and Vales

The four sub-regions in the east of Yorkshire have a common structure in that the strata dip south-eastward, the more resistant of them forming bold scarps. While all bear the marks of glaciation, the effects have been different from place to place.

The North York Moors (which include the Cleveland Hills) may be defined by the 600-foot contour; they present steep scarps to the north and west, and rise to summits of over 360 metres. Though classified by the geologist as part of the Inferior and Great Oolite, the major part of the moorland surface in fact is formed of sandstones and shales, with only thin intervening bands of limestone. The moors are largely heather-covered, but the soils in the valleys are cultivated for roots and oats, which are fed to sheep. Here is an important contrast with the Yorkshire Dales, which is occasioned by a distinctly lower relief and a smaller rainfall.

During a late stage in the glaciation of Yorkshire (Fig. 4, p. 15) ice sheets blocked the natural drainage to the north and east and the meltwater was trapped to form a series of small lakes in Eskdale. These overflowed southward, and in the process cut a deep and narrow winding trench, now known as Newtondale: it provides a low-level route through the hills which was utilized by the railway from York to Whitby.

The Newtondale spillway led into the structural trough of the Vale of Pickering, which in pre-glacial times must have drained eastward. But this exit was blocked by ice: the evidence is provided by a mass of boulder clay which plugs the former gap at Filey and spreads north over the Jurassic rocks and south over the Chalk of the Wolds. Behind this barrier a lake formed – 'Lake Pickering'. Its deposits vary in texture: they are peaty in the centre, clayey and gravelly in the north, and of chalky sand and gravel in the south.

A high proportion of this land is under the plough, for the soils are relatively rich in lime. The farmers grow wheat and rear beef cattle. A long line of villages all but encircles the vale: their sites offered well-water or water from springs; they stand beyond the level of floods; and the villages are often the centres of long, narrow parishes which run across the strike of the strata and share in all the qualities of land.

The Derwent, which now drains the Vale, thus has a most erratic course. A headstream rises close to Filey, less than 2 kilometres from the sea; but its water flows westward and southward through a course of over 160 kilometres before reaching the mouth of the Humber: it provides one of the clearest examples in Britain of a glacial drainage diversion.

The chalk scarp of the Yorkshire Wolds rises 150 m above the vale in the north and 180 m above the plain to the west, to reach a summit of 239 m near Pocklington. The scarp, the summits, and the higher dip slopes are free from drift, and here are the familiar dry valleys and convex slopes of chalk country. Until the early nineteenth century this was indeed open downland grazed by sheep. But pioneer farming families enclosed the land and introduced a new farming system based on the growing of fodder crops for sheep. Today the sub-region is remarkable for the extremely high proportion of arable land: even the scarps are cultivated. The soils are too light for wheat, and the farmers usually follow a rotation consisting of barley, clover, oats, and turnips (or swedes).

The lower parts of the chalk dip slope are masked by boulder clay, and there are ribbons of gravel in the valley bottoms. This country merges into the hummocky lowland of Holderness, which is again strewn with drift. At these lower elevations wheat becomes more important, at the expense of oats and barley. Over the whole district – scarp, dip slope, and Holderness – the only significant break in arable farming is in the flood-plain of the river Hull, and in the neighbourhoods of Hull and Bridlington, where there is an incentive to raise dairy cattle to provide fresh milk.

Hull

Hull (pop. 285,472) originated as a haven of refuge at the mouth of the river Hull, for small craft trading with the ancient wool port of Beverley. In 1293 Edward I, seeking a base for his Scottish wars, bought the little village from the monks of Meaux abbey (5 km east of Beverley), renamed it Kingston-upon-Hull, and built a new and fortified town. He reserved a central plot for the church and market, constructed a rectangular grid of streets, and surrounded the town by a wall with a moat fed from the river (*cf.* Caernarvon, Fig. 26, p. 108).

The medieval plan can still be discerned in the central area, and the nineteenth-century dock-builders used the site of Edward's moat for their first basins (Fig. 67). But the real growth of Hull began in the eighteenth century, when, thanks to its extensive water connections, the port became the outlet for the products of one-sixth of the area of England and Wales. The configuration of the Humber estuary aided its development, for the deep-water channel impinges on the concave bank at Hull.

With 94 trawlers based on the port (1970), Hull possesses one of the largest deep-sea fishing fleets in the world. At St Andrew's dock

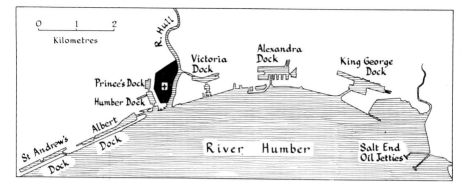

Fig. 67. THE PORT OF HULL

The site of the new town built by Edward I is shown in black. This is inserted from W. Hollars' plan of about 1660. Prince's and Humber Docks now occupy part of its moat. King George and Alexandra Docks handle the coal traffic; Victoria Dock specializes in timber; St Andrew's is the fish dock; the petroleum traffic is handled at Salt End. An important physical advantage of the site is the concave bend in the Humber which throws the deep-water channel to the north side of the estuary. *By courtesy of the Port Authority.*

are the ice factories, the cod-liver-oil plant, the fishmeal and manure works, the herring-curing and smoking houses, and the repair shops. Nearly a quarter of the population of Hull is dependent on the fishing industry.

Hull is not only our greatest fishing-port, but is also the leading British port for the import of oilseeds, and the chief centre of the crushing industry. Many types of seeds are handled: groundnuts, palm kernels, and cotton seed arrive from West Africa; linseed and castor seed from South America; and linseed and castor seed together with rape seed and copra from India. Large mills along the banks of the Hull process these seeds and in turn supply the margarine and soap industries, and the manufacturers of animal feeding-stuffs and paints.

One of the chief claims to unity of the wide region we have described lies in the fact that it forms the hinterland of Hull. Hull ships coal along the coast from the York, Derby, and Nottinghamshire coalfield, and in return imports its pitprops. From large installations at Salt End, Hull supplies the whole of the Trent and Ouse basin with its petroleum products. Hull is one of our major grain ports, and supplies millers as far south as Nottingham and Derby, and as far north as Middlesbrough.

But, as we have seen, Hull possess her own characteristic industries; to these we must add the production of castor oil and cod-liver oil. In both of these Hull is the world's leading centre.

236 *Regional Geography*

FOR FURTHER READING

Books

BERESFORD, M. W., and JONES, G. R. J. (Ed.): *Leeds and its Region* (British Association, 1967).

EDWARDS, K. C.: *The Peak District* (Collins, 1962).

EDWARDS, W. and TROTTER, F. M.: *The Pennines and Adjacent Areas,* British Regional Geology series (H.M.S.O., 1954).

LINTON, D. L. (Ed.): *Sheffield and its Region* (British Association, 1956).

REES, HENRY: *British Ports and Shipping* (Harrap, 1958), Chapter 4.

STAMP, L. D. (Ed.): The Land of Britain (Geographical Publications).

Part 46, Yorkshire (West Riding), by S. H. Beaver (1941).

Part 48, Yorkshire (East Riding), by L. D. Stamp (1942).

Part 51, Yorkshire (North Riding), by S. W. Wooldridge (1945).

Part 60, Nottingham, by K. C. Edwards (1944).

TRUEMAN, SIR ARTHUR: *The Coalfields of Great Britain* (Arnold, 1954), Chapter IX.

WILSON, V. *East Yorkshire and Lincolnshire,* British Regional Geology series (H.M.S.O., 1948).

York, A Survey (British Association, 1959).

Articles

HENDERSON, H. C. K.: 'The Agricultural Geography of North Derbyshire', in *Geography* (July 1957).

KIRK, M.: 'The Vale of York, The Evolution of a Landscape', in *Geography* (November 1955).

PEEL, R. F. and PALMER, J.: 'The Physiography of the Vale of York', in *Geography* (November 1955).

REES, HENRY: 'Leeds and the Yorkshire Woollen Industry', in *Economic Geography* (January 1948).

Maps

Bartholomew's ½-inch maps: Sheets 24, 29, 32, 33, 35, 36.

Many useful 1-inch geological maps illustrate parts of the region. The following will be found especially useful:

Sheet 54 (drift), for the Vale of Pickering, the North York Moors, the bare Chalk and the boulder clay 'plug'.

Sheets 63 (drift) and 71 (drift) for the York and Escrick moraines.

Sheet 42 (drift) for the drumlins and eskers of the Northallerton area.

Sheet 77 (drift) for the west-facing scarps of the Millstone Grit and Coal Measures in the Huddersfield area.

CHAPTER SEVENTEEN

LANCASTRIA

THE TERM 'LANCASTRIA' is convenient to describe the industrial region which lies between the Lake District and the Midlands on the one hand and the Pennines and the sea on the other. Its fortunes were founded on cotton manufactures; but today these are matched by other industries, notably engineering. The region includes two of our major ports and our largest ship canal, together with our chief saltfield and our greatest chemical district.

Physical Basis

Essentially Lancastria is a lowland and foothill region. The lowland is developed upon Triassic deposits, which form the north-westerly extension of the Trias of the Midlands. It is bounded to the east and west by older rocks, and it is those to the east which have been most significant in the life of the region. Here are the Coal Measures of south Lancashire, which in point of output constitute the third coalfield of England; beyond is the Millstone Grit of the south Pennines, which has been and still is of vital importance in connection with the water-supply for the region. The underlying Carboniferous Limestone is more restricted in its outcrop; but where it appears it has a negative influence, in that here the water is unsuited to the cotton industry and textile towns are absent.

The Trias of Cheshire occupies a broad and shallow basin whose rim is composed of Bunter Sandstone and whose floor is of Keuper Marl. The latter reaches here its greatest thickness in Britain – about 900 metres, near Northwich – and contains in its upper portion the beds of rock salt which have meant so much to industrial Cheshire.

The Coal Measures of south Lancashire dip steeply southward and westward and are broken into a patchwork of faulted blocks: hence the intricate outline of the coalfield. Some major fractures have displacements of a thousand metres. While the main axis of the upfold of the south Pennines ranges north and south, a subsidiary fold (the Rossendale Anticline) trends east and west,

237

and erosion of its crest has separated the Burnley section of the coalfield from the main outcrop. Other parallel earth-ripples explain the arrangement of the strata to the north: denudation of a second upfold has exposed the Carboniferous Limestone in the Ribble valley, while downfolding has preserved a large outlier of Millstone Grit to form Bowland Forest. The latter name is misleading, since this is a bare, peat-covered moorland.

These structures date from Carbo–Permian times, and later earth movements appear to have played little part in the evolution of the region. Rocks younger than the Trias, if they were present, have left no trace in the existing landscape. An extensive cover of drift, however, masks the solid deposits: this includes the peats of Chat Moss (west of Manchester), old lake floors at Bolton and Rochdale, and large tracts of gravels, and more especially, boulder clay.

On the map of the river systems of Lancastria the streaming surface of the Millstone Grit provides a striking contrast to the almost waterless limestone of the central Pennines and the Derbyshire Dome. Rossendale Forest and the Peak District form a crescent of hills, and their valleys and streams focus on a point near the centre of Manchester. Here, throughout history, has been the regional capital for Lancastria.

Historical Geography

The Romans recognized the main physical elements in the north-west: they built Chester as the legionary centre and port for Watling Street, and established Warrington, Preston, and Lancaster in similar sites at the heads of their respective estuaries. Joining these towns was the direct road to Carlisle. Farther east, between the Mersey marshes and the Pennine moorlands, they noticed that the valleys of the Mersey headstreams converged near a dry site, and here, in the angle formed at the junction of the Irwell and the Medlock, they established Mamucium (or Mancunium). Roman Manchester, on its sandstone hill, was the focus of 7 roads, and the fort was of more than local importance. A fragment of its east wall can still be seen. During the Danish raids the Mercians repaired the Roman walls; but the medieval town grew around a smaller and perhaps more easily defended site a little to the north, at the junction of the Irwell and the Irk: here the cathedral now stands. Joining the two sites, Roman and medieval, is Deansgate, the oldest street in Manchester.

Manchester probably grew as a rural market town, but by the fourteenth century the textile industries had achieved some importance; they began not with cotton but with wool and flax. The latter was cultivated on the level flats to the west of the town, the fleeces being provided by the flocks reared on the limestone Pennines. Rochdale, with its felt industry, and Manchester, with carpets, are reminders of this early phase of the textile industry. Cotton, when it first appeared, early in the seventeenth century, was woven across a warp of flax, and the combined cloth was known as fustian; the new fibre was imported from the eastern Mediterranean through the port of London. The foundation of the modern Lancashire textile industry may be placed after 1750, when American cotton replaced that from the Levant, and when a revolution occurred in both methods of transport and methods of manufacture.

Transport by land was characteristically difficult in pre-railway days, and the need for improved communication provided a challenge to the early industrialists.

It was the Lancashire roads which drew from Arthur Young his classic indictment:

> I know not, in the whole range of language, terms sufficiently expressive to describe this infernal road . . . [the road to Wigan] . . . let me seriously caution all travellers to avoid it as they would the devil; for a thousand to one but they break their necks or their limbs by overthrows or breakings down.

This was in 1770. The road between Newcastle-under-Lyme and Preston was no better:

> I would advise all travellers to consider this country as sea, and as soon think of driving into the ocean as venturing into such detestable roads. I am told the Derby way to Manchester is good. But further is not penetrable.

The pioneer manufacturers met the challenge boldly: here were built successively the first canal in the modern world (the Bridgewater Canal, 1764); the first passenger railway (the Liverpool and Manchester railway, 1830); and the only major ship canal in Britain (the Manchester Ship Canal, 1894).

Until about 1770 cotton manufacture was a cottage industry: the yarn was produced on the spinning-wheel and woven on the hand loom. During the late eighteenth century, however, came the successive invention of the water frame (1769), the power loom (1787), and the mule (1789), all of which were designed to work from water-wheels. Manufacturers now established mills at suitable waterside sites, and the factory made its appearance. The valleys became industrialized, and since these focused upon Manchester, that town developed into the marketing centre for the industry. So long as the motive force was water-power, the industry remained dispersed, for by its nature only one water-mill can operate at any given spot.

By the end of the eighteenth century virtually every potential water-power site was occupied by a mill, and it seemed as though further progress would be stifled. Just when it was needed came the successful application of steam to textile machinery, and by a convenient accident the cotton industry found itself situated upon a major coalfield.

The early engines were hungry for fuel, and while coal was cheap at the pit-head, a land journey of only 10 to 13 km was sufficient to double its cost. The manufacturer now aimed to build his works within about 500 metres of a colliery; many of the old water-mills became uneconomic, and new mills were built lower down the valleys where coal was accessible.

Twenty or thirty mills, intermingled with small brick houses for the employees, formed the nucleus of the nineteenth-century cotton town. There was no town hall, church, or school: all had to be inserted later. Lewis Mumford has called this 'the no-plan of the no-town'. So were built the spinning towns of Bolton, Bury, Rochdale, Oldham, and Ashton, forming a crescent around Manchester; and the weaving towns of Blackburn, Burnley, Nelson, and Colne, beyond the Rossendale moors. Almost every town on the coalfield developed its cotton industry, while Preston was the only centre away from the coalfield to retain it: here an established textile tradition together with cheap food and labour managed to outweigh the disadvantage of expensive coal.

In the second half of the nineteenth century a railway network was built, which served to confirm the dominance of Manchester. Cotton became the chief export by far of the United Kingdom: cotton was king.

The Natural Advantages of the Cotton Industry

At all stages the physical environment in south Lancashire has proved favourable to the industry. While the humid climate has been overrated (Lancashire is no more humid than East Anglia!),[1] the relatively high rainfall in the south Pennines is fundamental. The south Pennines receive 1300 to 1500 mm of rainfall per annum, and since the Millstone Grit is largely impermeable, there is a high proportion of runoff. The peat bogs of the plateau act as natural

---

[1] See the *Climatological Atlas of the British Isles* (Meteorological Office), 1952, p. 113. Each has a mean annual relative humidity of 70–75 per cent.

reservoirs and ensure an even flow of water. Its quality too is important: free from lime, it permits economies in soap, it allows dyes to act properly, and it does not clog boilers or pipes with deposits of 'scale'. The line separating the soft- from the hard-water areas passes through the centre of Manchester, and in this district coincides broadly with the junction of the Coal Measures and the Trias; in the Rossendale area it passes to the west of Blackburn and Bolton. To the east are districts whose water is of 3 to 6 degrees of hardness on Clark's scale; to the west the hardness is 13 to 20 degrees. It is significant that all the textile towns are found to the east of this line.

The production and refining of salt has long played an important part in the economic life of the region, and since salt is a basic raw material in the production of soaps and bleaches, it has had close connections with the cotton industry. Above the beds of rock salt is a reservoir of brine: this brine is pumped to the surface, and the salt is prepared by evaporation. The mining of rock salt has never formed a significant branch of the industry.

By 1700 salt had become a staple export of Liverpool. In the early industry the largest single cost of production related to fuel; and two of the earliest inland waterways of this country were developed in order to link the saltfield with south Lancashire coal. The Weaver Navigation, opened in 1732, joined the saltfield to the Mersey estuary; and the Sankey canal, opened in 1755, completed the link with the coalfield around St Helens. The Weaver Navigation still carries considerable quantities of coal southward and chemicals and salt northward: with a working depth of 3 metres, it accommodates barges and coasters of up to 400 gross tons.

At Northwich the beds of salt are only 60 m from the surface, and this was the traditional centre of the salt industry until a violent subsidence in 1880 destroyed many of the mines and works (Fig. 68). From this disaster the industry never recovered, and Northwich now depends on chemical manufactures rather than salt-production. The district, however, still yields brine for the chemical industry, and a pipeline from Holford (a few km east of Northwich) conveys it to Weston Point on the Manchester Ship Canal for use in the salt and chemical works there. The modern salt industry, equipped with vacuum evaporators in place of the older open pans, is concentrated at Middlewich and Sandbach.

We have already stressed the importance of the coalfield in the development of the cotton industry, and must now notice its more recent exploitation. Parallel with the expanding textile industry, the output of coal increased rapidly during the nineteenth century,

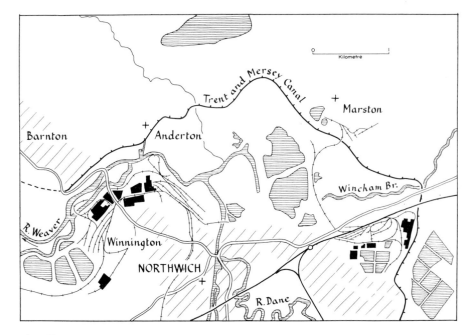

Fig. 68. PART OF THE CHESHIRE SALTFIELD

In this area the beds of salt are only 60 metres from the surface and subsidence is a serious problem. On the map its presence is revealed by water-filled hollows (though the regular-shaped areas in the south-east are reservoirs); on the ground there are cracked walls and sloping floors. The works (indicated in black) are chemical plants, and the extent of the railway sidings emphasizes the need to move large quantities of bulky materials. The Weaver has been canalized and straightened and will accommodate coasters of up to 400 gross tons. There is a link with the Trent and Mersey Canal at Anderton. Water is indicated by horizontal shading, and the approximate extent of the built-up area is shown by oblique lines. *Based on the O.S. 1-inch map.*

to reach a maximum of 27 million tonnes in 1907. The exhaustion of the better seams has resulted in a decline in production; nearly 300 pits have been closed since 1914, and the output at present is at the rate of about 6·5 million tonnes per annum (1969–70).

There is a southerly extension of the coalfield below the Trias of Cheshire, but the steep dips effectively limit the exploitation of the field in this direction. Here we find the deepest shafts in Britain: a few miles east of Wigan coal has been worked at more than 1200 metres from the surface. So great is the demand for coal in Lancastria that it can be met only by a considerable shipment across the Pennines from Yorkshire.

No two cotton towns are alike in their manufacturing activities: a regional specialization which had developed at least by 1830 remains today. It seems that the more northerly group of towns attached themselves to the weaving branches because they were expanding just at the time when the power loom was spreading. Other specializations, such as Bolton's fine spinning, Oldham's coarse spinning, and Blackburn's tropical-type cloths, can be explained only as the accidents of history.

During the post-War period there has been a drastic contraction in the cotton industry. Since 1938 the output of the Lancashire industry has shrunk to one-third of its pre-War level, while the national imports of unbleached cloth have multiplied by 14. In 1959 the United Kingdom for the first time in history became a net importer of cotton cloth; in the same year a reorganization plan was inaugurated. Rationalization, however, has brought little comfort, and in the decade 1958–67 over 1000 mills were closed and employment fell from nearly 250,000 to 100,000.

The Port of Manchester

The city of Manchester, 58 km from the sea, was converted into a port by the construction of the Ship Canal in 1894. While the chief focus of shipping is on the terminal docks in the heart of Manchester, there are wharves at many points along the canal, and the whole waterway constitutes the Port of Manchester.

The lowest section of the canal, between the entrance locks and Stanlow, is concerned particularly with the oil traffic, and has been dredged to 9 metres: elsewhere the ruling depth is 8·5 metres. At the canal entrance is the Queen Elizabeth II Oil Dock, opened in 1954 and the largest in the country; at Stanlow are additional oil docks, storage installations, and one of our major oil-refineries, the second largest in Britain (Fig. 69). Rapid changes are taking place in the oil industry, however, and tankers have outstripped the facilities provided by the canal docks (the Queen Elizabeth II dock accommodates tankers of up to 30,000 tons d.w.) so that the Shell Company is now supplying its Stanlow refinery from Tranmere, in Liverpool.

Large ocean freighters such as those used in the trans-Atlantic grain trade regularly use the whole length of the canal, passing through the five sets of locks, which give a combined lift of 18 m. At the city terminus there are two groups of basins: the smaller group (Pomona Docks) are used mainly in the coastwise and near Continental trade; the larger in the more distant traffic. Dock No. 9, the most westerly, handles much of the grain and cotton trade of the port and forms one of the major docks in Britain (Fig. 70).

The Ship Canal has attracted many important industries. Three kilometres from the entrance are the Bowater Mersey Paper Mills:

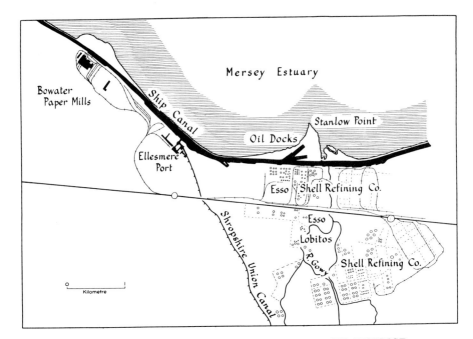

Fig. 69. THE MANCHESTER SHIP CANAL: THE STANLOW DISTRICT

In this diagram the Ship Canal together with the docks at Ellesmere Port are in black. *By courtesy of the Manchester Ship Canal Company.*

the canal brings them wood-pulp from Scandinavia and Canada, and china clay from Cornwall. At Ellesmere Port there are flour mills, chemical and metal works; and at Irlam there is a large iron and steel plant. But much of the industry of the region is concentrated at the industrial estate of Trafford Park, on the western outskirts of Manchester. This was the first to be opened in the United Kingdom (in 1896), and with about 200 firms, employing 5000 people, it is still the largest in the country. As in lower Thames-side, water transport is particularly attractive to industries which use bulky raw materials, and at Trafford Park there are six petroleum companies, several flour-millers, and soap and chemical manufacturers as well as many metal-working and engineering establishments.

Petroleum and its products form by far the leading import and export of Manchester, and account for more than half of its overseas commerce. Nearly all the other imports consist of bulk cargoes: in order of value these are raw cotton, copper (used in electrical engineering), wood-pulp (for paper-making), and raw wool (for the West Riding of Yorkshire), together with grain, timber, tea, and tobacco. On the export side, in addition to

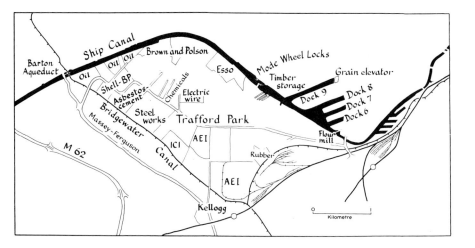

Fig. 70. THE SHIP CANAL: TRAFFORD PARK AND THE TERMINAL DOCKS

The Bridgewater Canal was the earliest in the country and still carries a heavy traffic. The numbered docks serve the large ocean-going vessels: the smaller docks to the east (Pomona Docks) serve smaller craft. Only a few representative railway links are shown. The key to the initials is as follows: AEI – Associated Electrical Industries; ICI – Imperial Chemical Industries. *By courtesy of the Manchester Ship Canal Company, Ltd.*

petroleum are chemicals from Merseyside and the saltfield, cotton and woollen manufactures, textile machinery, and aircraft engines. Coal is shipped to Ireland from Partington wharf, midway between Manchester and Warrington, and the nearest point on the canal to the south Lancashire collieries.

In addition to its port functions, Manchester is the organizing centre for the cotton industry, it possesses important engineering and chemical industries, and with its university and cathedral and shops is the regional capital for what has been described as the busiest tract of land in all the world.

Merseyside

The mouth of the Mersey is built up on the Lancashire side from Garston to Great Crosby (a distance of 19 kilometres), and on the Cheshire side from Bromborough to Wallasey (about 11 kilometres). This site, which provides for the livelihood of more than a million people, has offered remarkable physical advantages for the growth of a great port (Fig. 71).

The Mersey here cuts through a ridge of Triassic sandstone, whose relative resistance to erosion accounts for the narrow entrance to the estuary. Five km wide at Ellesmere Port, at its mouth the estuary is less than a kilometre across. At the same time

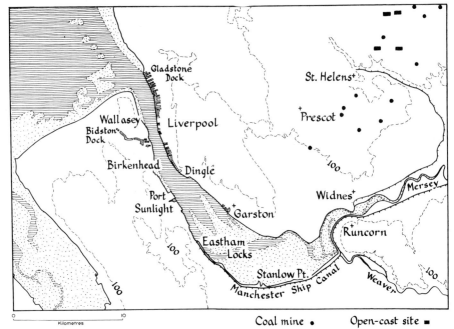

Coal mine •   Open-cast site ■

Fig. 71. MERSEYSIDE

The map illustrates the narrow entrance to the Mersey, which produces a tidal scour so that there is deep water at Liverpool. In contrast, the estuary of the Dee (in the south-west corner of the area) is subject to extensive silting. The narrowing of the Mersey is due to the existence of a ridge of Triassic sandstone revealed by the 100-foot contour. This outlines the diamond-shaped 'Liverpool Plateau'. which stands up, high and dry, from the surrounding lowland. For long Liverpool was confined to the plateau and linked to the rest of Lancashire only by the narrow ridge west of Prescot. Runcorn and St Helens are other old-established high sites; Garston and Widnes, however, are nineteenth-century creations. Widnes was built as a centre for chemical manufacture; Garston developed as the port for the neighbouring coalfield (some of whose pits are indicated). Gladstone Dock is one of the largest in Britain; Bidston Dock specializes in the discharge of iron ore for the steel industry of Deeside; Dingle handles the petroleum imports. *Based on the O.S. 1-inch map. Crown copyright reserved.*

there is an unusually high tidal range along these shores, amounting to 8·4 metres at spring tides. The combined effect of these two elements is to produce an active tidal scour in the port: twice a day the great reservoir formed in the upper estuary empties and fills itself, so that no dredging is needed at the docks. On the other hand, dredging *is* needed in the approaches to the port, and the high tidal range has made it necessary for the port authority to construct expensive enclosed docks.

That same sandstone ridge presents elevated and dry sites attractive to settlement on both banks of the river. The 100-foot contour at Liverpool encloses a diamond-shaped plateau which is all but surrounded by low-lying ground, formerly marsh: only a narrow neck of higher land, the Prescot ridge, joins this plateau to the rest of industrial Lancashire, and for many centuries this was the only land approach to Liverpool.

Yet the site of Liverpool went unnoticed until the reign of John, who sought a harbour more suitable than Chester for the embarkation of troops engaged in the subjugation of Ireland. In 1207 his builders laid out a new town where a small creek joined the estuary and offered safety to small ships. Modern Liverpool still centres on the site of this creek: here are the passenger-landing stage, the Royal Liver building, Cunard House, and the offices of the port authority. To the north and south stretch the long line of docks which handle the commerce on the Lancashire side. Facing them on the Cheshire side of the river are the docks of Birkenhead, which form an integral part of the port.

In common with our other west-facing ports, Liverpool has built up close trading connections with Ireland, the Americas, and West Africa.

The Irish traffic consists mainly in the carriage of livestock inward and coal outward. Cattle, sheep, and pigs arrive in comparable numbers, and are landed at Birkenhead, which has more space than Liverpool and easier communication with the pastures of the Midlands. Here there is lairage for 6000 cattle and 8000 sheep. Over half the cattle and sheep and nearly all the pigs are forwarded for fattening in lowland Britain; the rest are slaughtered locally, and give rise to associated industries such as the manufacture of glue and gelatine and the preparation of leather, and sausage-skins. A constant service by 13 cattle-ships is maintained across the Irish Sea, and livestock are carried in other general-purpose vessels too.

Coal destined for Dublin and Belfast is shipped from Garston, a railway port operated by the British Transport Commission and in close connection with the south Lancashire coalfield.

In the Atlantic traffic the chief commodities are iron ore, grain, sugar, and oilseeds. Imports of iron ore have expanded rapidly, and are linked with the establishment of large integrated steelworks at Shotton, on the lower Dee: this traffic is therefore handled on the Cheshire side of the estuary, at Bidston Dock, Birkenhead. Here also much of the grain trade is concentrated, though there are large mills in Liverpool too. The port handles 20 per cent. of all our imports of grain, and forms the largest milling centre in Europe.

The specialist wharves for sugar are at Huskisson Dock, where grab cranes handle it in bulk; near by is the Tate and Lyle sugar-refinery, the largest in the world. It is instructive to look more closely at Huskisson Dock. Opened in 1852, it set new standards in size and design which were followed by later dock-builders. It consists of an outer vestibule, large enough to allow vessels to turn, and two arms (originally there were three) bordered by transit sheds, where vessels can discharge and load. The dock is still sufficiently large to accommodate some of the biggest ships using the port – the Cunarders.

Oilseeds arrive particularly from West Africa and the Pacific islands; they include groundnuts, palm kernels, and copra, and these form characteristic cargoes imported at Bromborough Dock, close to Port Sunlight: this does not form part of the Port of Liverpool, but is owned privately by Unilever, Ltd. The establishments served by Bromborough Dock include the Stork margarine and Sunlight soap works, each the largest of its kind in the world.

The refined and reconstituted oils have a variety of industrial applications, and are used in margarine and candle making. To produce soap they are combined with caustic soda, itself a product of the salt-based chemical industry of Cheshire. The fibrous residues are converted into cattle cake and fertilizers, so that a whole range of related industries has arisen in the Port Sunlight district.

We have not mentioned cotton among the imports: formerly a leading commodity, it now ranks about ninth by tonnage. The exports consist almost entirely of manufactured goods; in order of tonnage they are iron and steel, chemicals, machinery, vehicles, soaps and oils, pottery and glass. The hinterland of Liverpool stretches far into the Midlands.

The industries of Merseyside thus include flour-milling, sugar-refining, oilseed crushing and the associated manufactures of soap, candles, and margarine: all are based on imported raw materials. To these we must add shipbuilding at Birkenhead. Here is the yard of Messrs Cammell Laird and Company, whose launchings in 1969 totalled nearly 56,000 tons, together with a nuclear submarine.

For long isolated from the rest of Lancashire, Liverpool has developed into a self-contained social unit, with its own cathedrals and university. It remains a regional capital for Merseyside, the Welsh border, and a wide area in Cheshire and north Wales.

FOR FURTHER READING

Books

CARTER, C. F. (Ed.): *Manchester and its Region* (British Association, 1962).

EDWARDS, W. and TROTTER, F. M.: *The Pennines and Adjacent Areas*, British Regional Geology Handbook (H.M.S.O., 1954).

FREEMAN, T. W., RODGERS, H. B. and KINVIG, R. H.: *Lancashire, Cheshire, and the Isle of Man* (Nelson, 1966).

LAWTON, R. and GRESSWELL, R. KAY: British Landscape through Maps, No. 6: *Merseyside* (Geographical Association, 1964).

REES, HENRY: *British Ports and Shipping* (Harrap, 1958), Chapters 2 and 3.

TRUEMAN, SIR ARTHUR: *The Coalfields of Great Britain* (Arnold, 1954), Chapter X.

Articles

COOK, NORMAN: 'Heart of the North-West' [Liverpool], in *Geographical Magazine* (August 1967).

ESTALL, R. C.: 'Industrial Change in Lancashire and Merseyside', in *Geography* (January 1961).

LAWTON, R.: 'Vital Liverpool', in *Geographical Magazine* (August 1967).

REES, HENRY: 'Evolution of Mersey Estuarine Settlements', in *Economic Geography* (April 1945).

——'A Growth Map for the Manchester Region', in *Economic Geography* (April 1947).

RODGERS, H. B.: 'The Lancashire Cotton Industry in 1840', *Transactions, Institute of British Geographers* (1960).

WALLWORK, K. L.: 'The Cotton Industry in North-West England, 1941–1961', in *Geography* (July 1962).

—— 'The Mid-Cheshire Salt Industry', in *Geography* (July 1959).

Maps

The core of the region is covered by Bartholomew's $\frac{1}{2}$-inch sheet 28; to complete it requires sheets 31, 32, and 23.

The region is well covered by the available 1-inch geological maps, both in the solid and drift editions, which are completely different. The following is of particular interest: Sheet 85, solid (Manchester), for the intricate faulting and the large number of coal seams shown.

CHAPTER EIGHTEEN

THE MIDLANDS

THE MIDLANDS form the only major region of Britain without a sea-coast, and their boundaries are not everywhere clear. To the west are the Welsh hills, and from Prestatyn to Bewdley we may use the western limit of the Coal Measures as our boundary. Farther south a great extent of Old Red Sandstone stretches between the Malverns to Mynydd Eppynt, in the heart of southern Wales. Here the Black Mountains form a physical barrier, so that almost the whole of Herefordshire and the eastern half of Monmouthshire belong to the Midlands. To the north the Pennines present a clear geological and topographic boundary, and we have no hesitation in including in the region the Potteries and the cities of Derby and Nottingham. To the south-east the Jurassic scarps provide a useful limit, though the feature is not formed by the same member throughout: south of Stratford-on-Avon, for example, the Lower Lias forms a dramatic scarp which introduces one to the Cotswolds and the West Country; yet Rugby, Evesham, and even the outskirts of Leicester stand on the same formation and must be counted part of the Midlands.

Three gaps remain. That in the south-west we have already discussed (p. 180); we place the north-eastern boundary beyond Nottingham, to leave Lincolnshire for separate treatment; in the north-west we share Cheshire with Lancastria, leaving the salt industry in Lancastria but reserving its dairy lands for the Midlands.

In climate, in relief, in geology, and in human geography the Midlands form a transitional region. They are neither wet nor dry: the 750-mm isohyet passes through the centre of the region, winding from the neighbourhood of Derby around the Birmingham plateau, skirting Hereford to reach Gloucester. They experience neither the extreme temperatures of East Anglia nor the oceanic climate of Atlantic Britain, though a hint of the latter is to be found in the Vale of Evesham.

Topographically the Midlands are neither plain nor uplands. Much of the surface is around the 90-metre level, and typically the landscape presents an alternation of river valleys such as those of the Trent and Avon, and low plateaux such as those of Charn-wood Forest and the Lickey Hills. Geologically the Midlands are based mainly on the Triassic system – neither old nor young. In its human geography the region offers examples both of specialized farming and distinctive manufactures. The geography of the Midlands is not easily condensed into a few pages.

Physical Basis

Over the greater part of the Midlands the 'solid' rock consists of the Keuper Marl or Upper Trias, horizontally disposed or only gently inclined. Towards the east in particular, it is largely masked by drift; but elsewhere there are many places where reddish soils betray the existence of the stiff red clay below. More restricted are the outcrops of the Lower Trias, consisting characteristically of Keuper and Bunter Sandstones. They are seen, however, in the crags of Nottingham castle and of Bridgnorth, in the hill on which Warwick has been built and in the fabric of its castle, and in the red sandstone of the new Coventry cathedral, which was brought from Hollington, in south-west Derbyshire.

The Trias rests upon the stumps of an earlier mountain system which was raised by the Carbo–Permian earth storm; and where the older rocks protrude they are seen to be rent and crumpled. Powerful faults bound the two Staffordshire coalfields, and at the eastern edge of the Warwickshire coalfield the seams rise steeply and rest upon Cambrian shales which overlook the Triassic plain to the east in a 60-metre fault scarp.

Coal basins jostle anticlines in whose cores older rocks are exposed. Close to the Leicestershire coalfield are the Pre-Cambrian ridges of Charnwood Forest; amid the Coal Measures of south Staffordshire are the Silurian rocks of Dudley; and the Welsh Border coalfields are interleaved with the older ridges of Long Mountain and Wenlock Edge (Silurian), the Long Mynd (Pre-Cambrian), and the Pre-Cambrian volcanic mass of the Wrekin. All these, with a predominantly north and south grain, form the remnants of Carbo–Permian mountain systems.

While the coal seams form the most valuable mineral deposits, the older rocks too have been widely quarried. The Silurian limestone of Dudley is honeycombed with old workings which formerly supplied the Staffordshire ironmasters with flux. In the Nuneaton Ridge gaping quarries have eaten into the Cambrian rocks, for these are the nearest supplies of roadstone to eastern England. The Etruria Marl of south Staffordshire, which occurs above the Middle Coal Measures, has been extensively quarried for the manufacture of the famous Staffordshire blue bricks – strong and impermeable. In the south-east of the region the Trias dips gently below the Lower Lias, the oldest of the Jurassic deposits. Mainly a stiff clay, it contains, however, beds of limestone, and these have been quarried for cement-making at Rugby, Harbury, and Long Itchington.

The ice sheets of Quaternary times covered the Midlands, and have left a varied series of deposits. As many as 16 successive fronts of the ice have been recognized north-west of Wolverhampton, together with the sediments of 'Lake Newport'. In the east of the region, between Coventry and Leicester, are extensive tracts of featureless clay classified by the Geological Survey as 'boulder clay'. In places a band of gravels separates the clay into an upper and a lower series, and there are excellent examples of how the Saxon and Danish settlers sought out the gravels as dwelling-sites (Fig. 72).

Penetrating studies of the superficial deposits by Professor F. W. Shotton have revealed that the so-called boulder clay is in fact the deposit of a lake ponded back at a late stage of the Ice Age between the ice fronts and the Jurassic scarps. 'Lake Harrison', as it has been called, occupied the area between Leicester, Birmingham, Redditch, and Stratford; its water stood at a height of 131 metres above sea-level, and it overflowed through gaps in the Edge Hill scarp before overcoming the ice front in the south-west. So the Warwickshire Avon was born.

Historical Geography

Palæolithic and Neolithic folk passed through the Midlands, following tracts of sandstones and gravels, which permitted easier travelling than the forested clays, and left behind them the stone tools which identify them. Centuries of cultivation have presumably destroyed most of the Bronze Age barrows which may have existed in the Midlands. Hill forts, owing to their strength and elevated sites, have usually escaped destruction, and more than 20 remain in the Midlands; though few have been excavated, they are presumably of Iron Age date.

The Romans reached the Midlands within three or four years of the Claudian invasion, and erected a temporary frontier for the Roman Empire along the line of the Fosse Way. A study of its location in relation to the drift geology reveals the remarkable understanding possessed by the Romans of the physical geography of the region. They built tribal capitals at Leicester and Wroxeter and smaller towns such as High Cross (at the intersection of Wat-

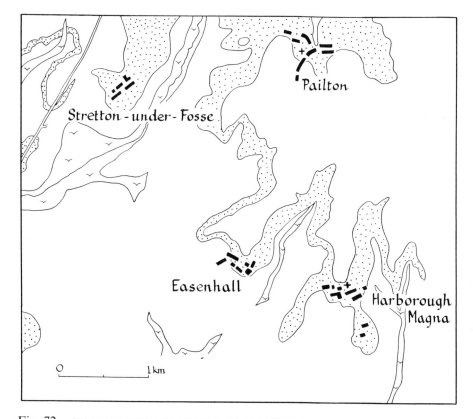

Fig. 72. VILLAGE SITES IN EAST WARWICKSHIRE

This district is about 20 km east of Coventry. Areas left blank represent clay – the so-called boulder clay of the Geological Survey. Stippled areas represent sands and gravels, which outcrop in narrow bands along the hillsides; these were chosen by early man for settlement in preference to the sticky clays.

ling Street and the Fosse Way), Alcester (an agricultural market), and Droitwich (a centre of salt-mining). Remains of an early fort can be seen in the grounds of the Birmingham University medical school; there appear to have been furnaces for the smelting of iron and lead at Tiddington (Stratford-on-Avon), and important potteries have been excavated recently at Hartshill (near Nuneaton) and Mancetter (near Atherstone).

The Saxons and Danes entered by the rivers and settled on the terrace gravels, and on the so-called glacial sands and gravels. Only later did they attempt to clear the forested clay lands. The great majority of the villages and towns originated in the so-called Dark Ages; and in the Anglo-Saxon Kingdom of Mercia the region for the first time became politically conscious.

Industrialization came early. The cradle of the Industrial Revolution is at Coalbrookdale, in Shropshire: here in 1709 the first Abraham Darby established great ironworks, smelting the local ores with charcoal produced in the near-by forests. He and his son, faced with declining timber resources, successfully used coke for the first time in iron-smelting, and laid the foundation of the modern iron industry. In 1773–79 Abraham Darby the third constructed the first bridge in the world to be made of iron, and it still spans the Severn close by, at Ironbridge. The Coalbrookdale site is still occupied by ironworks, and the remains of the Darby workshop are preserved as an industrial museum.

In 1762 Matthew Boulton built a small iron-mill at Soho in Smethwick, a few miles west of Birmingham, and made small metal wares. Thirteen years later he was joined by James Watt, and now the Soho Foundry began to make the massive castings needed by Watt's improved steam-engine. The Soho Foundry too remains a metal-works, which now produces weighing equipment.

Economic Geography

Within the region are many distinct units, some agricultural, others industrial, but each with its own character. We examine the in-industrial areas next, and begin in the south-west, with the *Forest of Dean*: this is at once a forest and a coalfield, and has in the past also been an ironfield. Iron was worked here at least as early as Roman times; this was an important source of metal in the early stages of the Industrial Revolution, and at the same time its oaks provided charcoal for the ironmasters and shipbuilding timber for the Royal Navy.

Mining is now at an end. Recent policy on the part of the Forestry Commission is to replace the oaks by the faster-maturing conifers, so that the character of the Forest is changing. The output of the small coalfield has ceased: Cinderford, whose livelihood once depended on the now derelict 'Eastern United' colliery, is a town of ex-miners, and the last remaining colliery was closed in 1967. The future perhaps lies in the organization of the tourist traffic, and in this connection the district has the benefit of the improved access afforded by the new Severn bridge.

In the far north-west of the region is the *Flint and Denbigh coalfield*. With an output of about a million tonnes a year, this is a small but active field with sufficient reserves for about a century. We have already noticed (pp. 104, 106) the existence of dislocations along the Bala-Towyn line and at Llangollen; these have separated the coalfield into three separate producing districts. In Flintshire the main seam is of limited extent, and is worked below the Dee estuary. Coal-mining here is subsidiary to paper-making, chemical manufacture, and the large iron and steel works at Shotton (p. 247). In Denbighshire coal-mining is the major activity, and deep pits are producing from below a great thickness of unproductive Upper Coal Measures.

It is probable that this coalfield represents the western rim of a large basin whose floor is occupied by the Trias of Cheshire; if so, its extent and depth are unknown. However, 56 km to the east the Coal Measures are again at the surface: this is the north Staffordshire coalfield, or *Potteries*. This south-western corner of the Pennines is a hilly area which has been deeply dissected by the headstreams of the Trent. Its triangular shape is explained by the existence of a downfold whose axis ranges N.N.W. and S.S.E., and which pitches southward. Here are 11 large pits, which produce the greater part of the output of about 6 million tonnes annually.

The firing of pottery requires large quantities of fuel, and, unlike the iron-smelting industry, coal has been used since early times. Since pottery clays are fairly widespread in occurrence, and coal was so difficult to transport, it was natural that the industry should develop on a coalfield. In south Staffordshire suitable clays were found in the Upper Coal Measures close to the outcrops of seams of coal. Other advantages were the nearness of Cheshire salt and Derbyshire lead – materials which were needed in the glazing process.

Pottery has traditionally been a family industry, and Josiah Wedgwood, who established his first kilns at Burslem in 1759, represented the fifth generation of a family of potters. It was he who introduced classical art into pottery, he who founded, and named appropriately, Etruria (west of Hanley). Wedgwood was a pioneer of improved transport: he encouraged the turnpiking of roads, and was one of the sponsors of the Trent and Mersey canal. Much of the raw material is brought from a distance – bones from Argentina, china clay and china stone from Cornwall, and ball clay from Dorset – but the industry remains where it was established, and is still in the hands of family concerns, such as Wedgwood's (now at Barlaston), Minton's (founded in 1793); and Copeland's (inheritors of the Spode traditions).

The Pottery towns are Tunstall, Burslem, Hanley, Fenton (Fig. 73), and Longton; they extend in a line following the strike of the rocks and are equally accessible to the raw materials. Their administrative centre is based on the former village of Stoke-on-Trent. Newcastle-under-Lyme, farther west, and away from the productive coal seams, is a residential and shopping town.

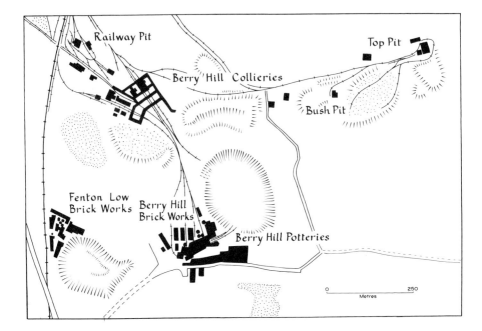

Fig. 73. THE LANDSCAPE OF THE POTTERIES

In this small area north of Fenton there are three coal-pits, two brickworks, and a pottery. The brickworks are responsible for the great excavations in the Etruria Marl, exposed in the west of the area. The collieries give rise to ugly tips, and the potteries pile up their waste into extensive 'shrap heaps'. This is from a pre-War survey. Changes have occurred: many brickworks are closed, and the marl holes are gradually being filled in. The collieries are being reorganized into larger units and their tips are being 'quarried' for road metal; potteries are combining and turning from 'bottle' ovens to larger kilns. But it is clearly a difficult task to restore such a landscape. *N.B.* Berry Hill Collieries are now closed. *Based on the O.S. 6-inch map. Crown copyright reserved.*

Nottingham (pop. 299,758) first appears in history in the *Anglo-Saxon Chronicle*, which under the year 867 describes how the Danes sailed up the Trent and encamped on the north bank of the river. By 924 the Saxons had recaptured the site and had spanned the Trent by a bridge. The Normans, arriving in their turn, built a castle on the sandstone crag a kilometre to the west, and settled around it. For centuries two rival walled towns thus existed side by side, with a great market-place between them: so originated the large town square in the city centre.

The home of Boot's pharmaceutical products, Raleigh bicycles, and Player's cigarettes, Nottingham has varied interests. The chief industry, however, comprises textiles: today the finishing branches outweigh hosiery and lace-making, but it is important to examine the origin of hosiery manufacture, since it was this activity which introduced textiles into a region extending west to Derby and Belper and south to Leicester and Hinckley.

In 1589 the Rev. William Lee invented the stocking frame (or knitting machine) at Calverton, 10 km north-east of Nottingham. So long as stockings were made of silk the local demand was small, and the main centre of the industry remained in the Spitalfields district of London, from which it could supply the gentry. When in the eighteenth century wool was substituted for silk the cost of the labour became more significant than the cost of the raw material. Now the east Midlands offered a distinct advantage, for in the villages were numbers of dispossessed farm-workers, unemployed owing to the enclosures, a reservoir of cheap labour.

A wholesale migration of the industry took place: between 1732 and 1750, 800 stocking frames were moved bodily from London to Nottingham, while others went to Leicester. By the middle of the nineteenth century Nottingham, Leicester, and Hinckley had become the chief centres of the hosiery industry, but within the district 250 towns and villages engaged in framework knitting. Lace-making, using cotton as its raw material, developed later, and became mechanized after 1808, when John Heathcoat of Nottingham produced the first lace net machine.

Fifty-six km south-east of Leicester, on the eastern fringe of the Midlands, are the iron quarries and steel-works of Messrs Stewart and Lloyd, at Corby. The ore bed here lies in the Northampton Sand (Fig. 78, p. 275); it is 2 to 2·5 metres thick and about 30 per cent. pure; but to reach it 15 to 30 metres of overburden must first be removed. To assist in this task three of the world's largest excavators – 'walking draglines' – are in use: their buckets can move 27 tonnes of earth in a single 'bite'.

Corby is the only major iron and steel works in Britain to be supplied exclusively by home-produced ore. The whole of the steel produced is used to manufacture tubes; and this establishment constitutes the largest integrated tube works in Europe. When the firm arrived in 1933 Corby was a village of about 1200 inhabitants; now there are about 12,000 employees in the works, and the town has a population of about 48,000 – almost completely dependent on the steelworks.

The Warwickshire and Leicestershire coalfields yield mainly house coal and have never produced iron ore, so that coal-mining has remained independent of the heavy industries. *Leicester* (pop. 283,549), founded by the Romans where the Fosse Way crossed the Soar, engages mainly in the production of hosiery and other knitwear, and to serve this an important textile machine industry has been developed. The manufacture of footwear, based on the hides of local cattle, forms an additional old-established industry.

In *Coventry* the workings of a colliery spread below the city, and in 1963 plans were announced to extend the area southward, so that by 1980 coal would be dug near the city centre 600 metres below the surface. To minimize the danger of subsidence extraction is to be limited to strips of the top third of the rich Warwickshire Thick Coal seam, which ranges between 6 and 9 metres in thickness.

Coventry grew around a Saxon priory founded upon a sandstone hill, and partly protected by the marshy valley of a small stream, the Sherbourne. In the Middle Ages it developed a prosperous cloth industry; fine churches and almshouses were built, and the town was encircled by a wall pierced by 12 gates (two of which survive). The origin of the city's ribbon-weaving industry is obscure, but it was flourishing by the middle of the eighteenth century, and at its peak in 1860 over 18,000 people were dependent on it, while watchmaking employed 2000 men and 3000 boys.

Both activities were sorely hit by the commercial treaty with France of that year, and the opportunity to adopt a new industry was provided when James Starley in 1868 persuaded his firm to turn from the manufacture of sewing-machines to the production of bicycles, which he had seen in France. Success was immediate. Starley himself pioneered many improvements, new firms were established, and within a generation Coventry had become the world centre of the bicycle industry.

A characteristic of Coventry is the speedy abandonment of a declining industry and the adoption of a growing one. The first British commercial motor-car was produced in Coventry in 1896, and within 10 years the new industry employed 10,000 people. From the car developed the tractor, the aeroplane, and the rocket; and parallel with these activities went electrical engineering, first in telephones, later in radio and television, while the textile traditions were maintained by the rayon industry, established in 1904.

Coventry has thus grown from about 70,000 inhabitants in 1901 to 334,839 in 1971, representing a rate of growth unparalleled in Britain. Its new status was recognized by the Government, which conferred upon it a Lord Mayor in 1953 and approved a university (for the city and county) in 1962; meanwhile the rebuilding of the city centre after wartime devastation, coupled with the consecration of the new cathedral, has attracted many visitors (Fig. 74).

We may define the *Black Country* as the group of metal-manufacturing towns which has arisen on the south Staffordshire coalfield.

Structurally the district consists of an eroded dome bounded to the east, west, and north by powerful faults, and exposing near its centre inliers of Silurian and igneous rocks. The latter, more resistant than the surrounding Coal Measures, form a ridge trending north-west and south-east, which constitutes part of the main watershed of England. To the south-west are the swift, incised tributaries of the Stour; to the north-east are the sluggish headwaters of the Tame, and here a broad valley provides the setting for most of the Black Country towns. Birmingham and Wolverhampton lie beyond the boundary faults, and are excluded from the group.

The major coal seam of south Staffordshire is the remarkable Thick Coal, 9 to 11 metres thick in places, and over wide areas less than 120 metres below the surface. This has proved a source of immense wealth to the district, and in addition, the productive Coal Measures contained beds of ironstone nodules yielding 35–40 per cent. iron: these were widely worked and locally smelted.

Coal-mining, however, has declined, while the iron-mining industry is extinct. In 1860 over 400 coal pits were operating, and produced about $7\frac{1}{2}$ million tonnes; by 1913 the output had fallen to 3 million, and it is now less than 1 million tonnes, and concentrated at 3 collieries. The Thick Coal is now exhausted except at considerable depth in the concealed portions of the coalfield. Similarly, iron-production reached 2 million tonnes in the 1850's, when there were about 180 furnaces in blast; it remained important until the 1880's, but now, together with the smelting industry, it has ceased. The Black Country now concentrates on the finishing branches of the metal industries, and as in south Lancashire a remarkable specialization has emerged, though its origins are not easily explained.

In Willenhall about 200 firms are engaged in the manufacture of locks and keys, and produce about 90 per cent. of the total in the country. Around Cradley Heath about 75 factories make anchors and chains. West Bromwich specializes in springs; Walsall claims to be the world centre for leather goods and saddlers' ironmongery and more recently has turned to the manufacture of car upholstery. Smethwick is renowned for the production of figured sheet glass and glass tubes, though its formerly renowned manufacture of lighthouse equipment has now ceased.

In this district, across the watershed, there was little possibility of river transport, and here was constructed the closest net of canals in Britain. It totals about 260 km, and contains 216 locks. Today the greater part of the canal system is disused or derelict.

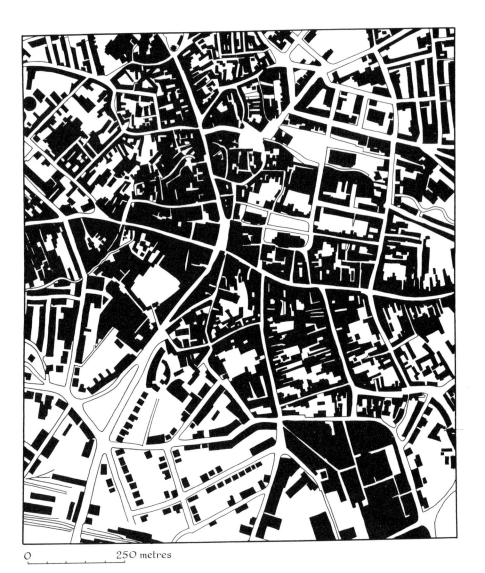

O   250 metres

Fig. 74a.   COVENTRY: THE CENTRAL AREA (A) IN 1923

There is much congestion through the building of cottages in former gardens and hence the striped appearance in the area south-east of the centre. The large black areas represent car and cycle works. Those in the south-east comprise the Maudslay, Parkside, Quinton, and Armstrong-Siddeley motor-works. In the south-west is the station; in the north-west, the gasworks. *Based on the Ordnance Survey 25-inch map with the sanction of the Controller of H.M. Stationery Office. Crown copyright reserved.*

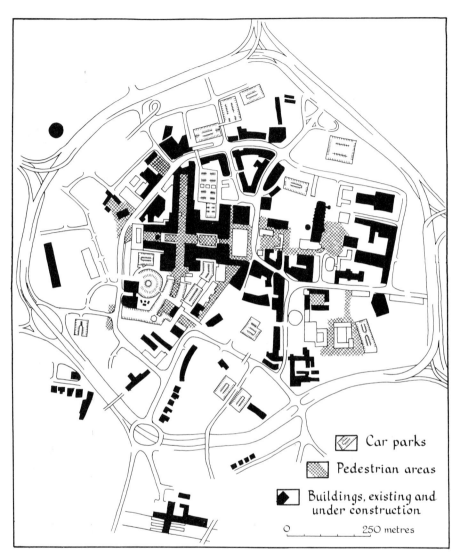

Legend:

⊞	Car parks
▨	Pedestrian areas
◆	Buildings, existing and under construction

0   250 metres

Fig. 74b.   COVENTRY: THE CENTRAL AREA (B) REDEVELOPED

This plan is on approximately the same scale and covers the same area as 74a (note the railway station in the south and gasworks in the north-west). The city centre – Broadgate – is the meeting-place of several zones. To the east are cultural buildings and the churches; to the south, administration; to the west, the shopping precinct. There is liberal provision for car-parking, both on roof-tops and in multi-storey parks. To the north-west is a zone of light industry. The whole is enclosed by an inner ring road. *By courtesy of the City Architect, Coventry.*

Other elements in the Black Country landscape are the abandoned colliery tips, water-filled gravel- and marl-pits, and acres of railway sidings (Fig. 75). On a slight rise, usually, is the town centre; around it the factories and works. The Industrial Revolution has scarred the face of Britain, and its traces are not easily removed.

Farming

Parallel with the developments in manufacture, specialization has taken place in farming. We examine here the market gardening and orchards of the Vale of Evesham, the beef-fattening of Leicestershire, and the dairy farming of Cheshire.

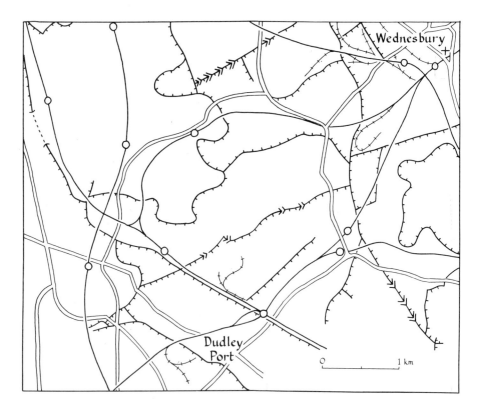

Fig. 75.   COMMUNICATIONS IN THE BLACK COUNTRY

This area lies between Walsall and Dudley in the heart of the Black Country. The canals are a legacy of the past, and most are now disused. The multiplicity of railways with eleven stations in this small district is uneconomic, now that the real arteries of commerce are the roads. Such areas form a planner's nightmare. *Based on the O.S. 1-inch map. Crown copyright reserved.*

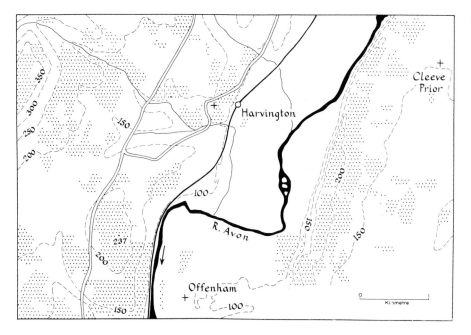

Fig. 76. ORCHARDS IN THE VALE OF EVESHAM

This district lies immediately north-east of the town of Evesham. The Vale of Evesham is open to mild Atlantic influences, and orchards are found at all heights up to and beyond 100 metres. The lowest land, however, is avoided owing to the danger of frost. Road and rail lead to the industrial Midlands, which form the chief market. The characteristic fruit here is the plum. The stippled areas represent orchards. Heights are in feet. *Based on the O.S. 1-inch map. Crown copyright reserved.*

The Vale of Evesham was the pioneer district in Britain for the intensive cultivation of fruit and vegetables; this industry is, however, of comparatively recent origin, dating only from the connection by rail to the rapidly expanding population of the Birmingham area. The soils are varied, and alone are insufficient to account for this market garden and orchard industry. More significant is the climate: the rainfall, about 635 mm per annum, is unusually low for the region; open to Atlantic influences, the Vale enjoys mild winters, yet is sheltered from strong winds in spring, so that crops are two or three weeks ahead of the surrounding districts (Fig. 76).

Almost every type of vegetable is grown, but there is a special interest in asparagus, and this is the home of the Pershore plum. Fields and holdings are unusually small (often a grower works about a hectare), and a distinct method of land tenure has evolved: according to the 'Evesham custom' a departing tenant can claim compensation for growing crops and unexhausted manures, and in addition has the right to nominate his successor. The scientific side of the industry is investigated at the National Vegetable Research Station at Wellesbourne, on the north-eastern outskirts of the district.

The south-eastern quadrant of Leicestershire contains some of the finest beef-fattening land in the country. The soils, based upon Lias clay largely overlain by boulder clay, are stiff and heavy, and until recent developments in farm machinery, could not easily be ploughed. The best pastures consist of over 30 per cent. rye-grass, and will fatten one or two bullocks and up to four sheep to the hectare. The cattle are bought in the spring and sold fat at intervals from July onwards. In the extreme case there are no stock on the land during the winter and there is no need for the cultivation of root crops: thus the farmer has the leisure for hunting, and his land suffers little damage when the pack crosses it.

The foremost hunting counties are Leicestershire, Rutland, and Northamptonshire. Fox coverts are maintained, hunting rights are reserved in tenancy agreements, and the 'hunt' even pays a small compensation to farmers whose poultry have been killed by foxes.

Beef-fattening remains the main source of income, but recent changes have reduced its relative importance: dairy cattle supply milk for London, sheep are kept on many farms, and the cultivation of wheat is a permanent result of the war-time ploughing campaign.

Cheshire has long been renowned for the quality of its dairy pastures, which extend into the lowland portions of Flint and Denbigh, Shropshire and Staffordshire. Climate has little voice in this specialization, for the fairly low rainfall (less than 750 mm per annum) is suitable equally for arable and grass farming. More decisive are the soils, which over wide areas are based on alluvium or boulder clay, and are therefore heavy and ill-drained. The ready supply of moisture in the soil favours the growth of a rich grass sward, and these are the most heavily stocked dairy pastures in Britain. Cheshire has nearly three times the national average density of dairy cattle. Intensive grazing is liable to deplete the fertility of the soil, and for generations this has been maintained by liberal dressings of bone manure and basic slag.

So great a cattle density can be maintained only by supplementary fodder. Before the War this was imported, but the Cheshire farmer has perforce become more self-sufficient: he grows mixed corn for cattle fodder, and he converts large quantities of grass into silage; moreover, he has increased the milk yield by turning more completely to the use of Ayrshire and Friesian herds.

Pigs are kept on most farms: they were fed formerly on the skimmed milk left over from the making of Cheshire cheese. Now the cheese is factory-made, but the piggeries remain, and the fodder is produced on the farm.

With such a variety of farming in the Midlands it is difficult to find a 'typical' example. We choose, however, a farm in Warwickshire, set compactly within a loop of the Avon opposite Stoneleigh Abbey, Kenilworth (Fig. 77). Grove Farm comprises 105 ha, much of which consists of a level tract of high terrace gravels in the 'core' of the loop, part of the fourth terrace of the Avon. In

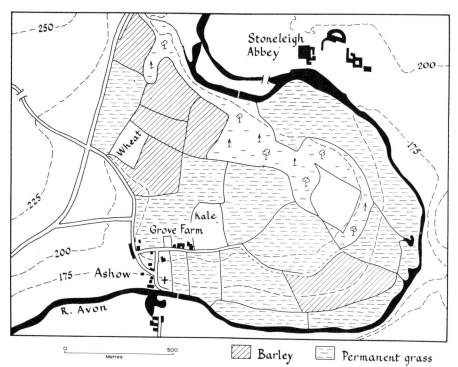

Fig. 77. GROVE FARM, KENILWORTH

This compact farm, set in a loop of the Warwickshire Avon, lies 3 km south-east of Kenilworth. The soils are light, derived from terrace gravels, and well suited to barley, which is the chief cereal. The farmer rears sheep, beef cattle, and poultry, and travels to the Welsh border to buy his sheep. Warwickshire is predominantly rural and accessible from all parts of the United Kingdom: partly for these reasons the grounds of Stoneleigh Abbey have been chosen by the Royal Agricultural Society as the setting for the Royal Show. Heights are in feet. *Based on the O.S. 2½-inch map. Crown copyright reserved.*

the steep slope overlooking the river the solid rocks are exposed, here composed of reddish Coal Measure marl and sandstone; and flanking the Avon is a strip of alluvial flood-plain.

This is a mixed farm with an emphasis on beef production: unlike its neighbours, it produces no milk. The farmer has 93 Hereford-cross cattle, 180 Welsh hill sheep, 6 sows with about 60 piglets, 100 hens, and 200 turkeys. About half his land is under pasture, and this includes the flood-plain; of the remainder, 14 hectares are mown for hay and 28 are cropped. Almost the whole of the arable land is under barley: it grows well in these light gravel soils, and with appropriate fertilizers can be cropped four years in succession before reseeding to grass. Barley makes a valuable fodder crop, but more than half is surplus to the needs of the farm and is sold. The main market is at Warwick, but to buy his sheep the farmer finds it worth his while to travel to Hay, just inside Wales, at the meeting-point of Hereford, Radnor, and Brecknockshire. Here then is an actual example of the movement of sheep from the Welsh hills to the English lowlands.

Birmingham

Of this large region, with its varied occupations, Birmingham is the undisputed capital. Its built-up area covers about 200 square km, and it harbours over a million people.

Birmingham (pop. 1,013,366) originated in Saxon times at a fording point of the little river Rea, and where the lower slopes of a fault scarp of Keuper Sandstone (the Keuper Waterstones) provided a firm foundation for settlement. At the time of the Domesday Survey it contained only 10 families, and it is not easy to explain why this place, far from navigable water, should become the second largest city in Britain.

A town grew up to supply the needs of the farming community, with iron and leather industries. It possessed an assured water-supply from the Keuper Sandstone, it was close to the Staffordshire iron ores, to timber for charcoal and oak bark for tanning. John Leland in 1538 found Birmingham manufacturing knives and cutlery, 'echoing with forges and occupied by many smiths'. Its population in 1600 was only about 3000. Manufactures of swords and guns, buttons, and metal trinkets expanded during the following century, and during the civil war the town was able to supply the Earl of Essex with 15,000 sword-blades.

In 1689 five leading gunsmiths of Birmingham contracted to supply muskets to the Government, and from this developed an association of master smiths who in 1861 established themselves as the Birmingham Small Arms Company. The B.S.A. group now comprises 28 subsidiaries, of which ten are situated in Birmingham: these manufacture small arms, motor-cycles, and scooters, small tools and machine tools and precision castings.

As in other large cities, Birmingham activities have clustered into zones. The original market-place (the Bull Ring) was close to the parish church, and this remains the district of the wholesale markets. The civic area, with the town hall, museum, and library, has grown up on the sandstone plateau to the west. Between the markets and the civic zone is the commercial core, with its large departmental stores and ten or so banks.

Old-established industries remain near the centre. The jewellery quarter is in the north-west, centred on Vyse Street, and here are about 250 firms, most of them small family concerns. The gun district is in the north-east, the brass district to the south-west. Pins, pens, and tubular bedsteads are well-known Birmingham wares; so are food products such as sauces and custards. Birmingham is one of the major British centres for the production of motor-cars, and associated activities include the manufacture of rubber tyres, parts, and accessories. Away on the south-western outskirts the Cadbury brothers in 1879 built a model factory and a garden village based on chocolate-manufacture, and set new standards for industry. Sweeping changes are taking place in central Birmingham: Victorian opulence is giving place to the more utilitarian architecture of the twentieth century, and an inner ring road is thrusting its way through the townscape.

FOR FURTHER READING

Books

ALLEN, G. C.: *The Industrial Development of Birmingham and the Black Country, 1860–1927* (Allen and Unwin, 1929).

Birmingham and its Regional Setting (British Association, Birmingham, 1950).

DIX, H. M. and HUGHES, D. R. (Ed.): *The Coventry District* (Coventry and District Natural History and Scientific Society, Coventry, 1960).

DURY, G. H.: *The East Midlands and the Peak* (Nelson, 1963).

EDWARDS, K. C. (Ed.): *Nottingham and its Region* (British Association, 1966).

FOX, LEVI: *Coventry's Heritage* (Coventry, 1957).

HAINS, B. A. and HORTON, A.: *Central England*, British Regional Geology Handbooks (H.M.S.O., 1969).

POCOCK, R. W. and WHITEHEAD, T. H.: *The Welsh Borderland* (British Regional Geology Handbooks (H.M.S.O., 1948).

STAMP, L. D. (Ed.): The Land of Britain (Geographical Publications).

Part 57, Leicestershire, R. M. Auty, 1943.

Part 61, Staffordshire, J. Myers and S. H. Beaver, 1945.

TRUEMAN, SIR ARTHUR: *The Coalfields of Great Britain* (Arnold, 1954), Chapters VII, XI, XII, and XIII.

Articles

CHEW, HILARY C.: 'The Post-War Land Use Pattern of the Former Grasslands of Eastern Leicestershire', in *Geography* (November 1953).

JOHNSON, B. L. C.: 'The Distribution of Factory Population in the West Midlands Conurbation', *Institute of British Geographers, Transactions and Papers* (1958).

RAWSTRON, E. M.: 'The Employment Structure of Nottingham, Derby and Leicester', in *East Midland Geographer* (December 1957).

REES, HENRY: 'Birmingham and the Black Country', in *Economic Geography* (April 1946).

―――― 'Rebuilding the Centre of Coventry', in *East Midland Geographer* (December 1959).

SHOTTON, F. W.: 'The Pleistocene Deposits between Coventry, Rugby and Leamington' (*Phil. Trans. Royal Soc.,* 1953, Series B, pp. 209–260).

SIMPSON, E. S.: 'The Cheshire Grass-Dairying Region', *I.B.G. Transactions and Papers* (1957).

SMITH, D. M.: 'The British Hosiery Industry at the Middle of the Nineteenth Century', *I.B.G. Transactions and Papers* (June 1963).

STEDMAN, M. B., 'Birmingham Builds a Model City', in *Geographical Magazine* (August 1968).

WISE, M. J.: 'Some Factors influencing the Growth of Birmingham', in *Geography* (December 1948).

WOOLLCOMBE, JOAN: 'Staffordshire Pottery', in *Geographical Magazine* (August 1938).

Maps

Bartholomew's ½-inch sheets 18, 19, 23, 24.

The ¼-inch geological map is out of print, and there are gaps in the coverage of 1-inch geological maps, but the following sheets are valuable: 168, solid and drift, (Birmingham), 169, solid and drift, (Coventry), 156 (Leicester), 126 (Nottingham).

Section D: The Scarplands and the Metropolis

CHAPTER NINETEEN

LINCOLNSHIRE AND THE FENS

LINCOLNSHIRE forms an appropriate introduction to the scarplands of eastern England. Here the Jurassic and Cretaceous rocks – the two major scarp-formers in England – are sufficiently close to be represented in the same county. In three directions Lincolnshire has clear boundaries: to the east is the sea; to the north is the Humber; and to the west is the Vale of Trent. Only in the south is the boundary artificial, for a large proportion of the Fens district falls in fact within the county. For the sake of convenience we include in this chapter the whole of the Fens.

The region is almost completely rural and agricultural, and its industries depend upon or have sprung from the needs of farming. The single important exception is the iron and steel industry: at various places in the Jurassic scarp iron ore is mined or quarried; at Scunthorpe in the north are important iron and steel works, and to serve them is the specialized port of Immingham Dock. There is fishing at Grimsby, and some development of resorts; otherwise the inhabitants of the region gain their livelihood from the land.

Physical Basis

The special character of Lincolnshire springs from the regular, almost unbroken, and nearly parallel chalk and limestone ridges. The main limestone scarp – Lincoln Edge or The Heath – is formed of the Inferior Oolite, here represented mainly by the 30-metre-thick Lincolnshire Limestone. Straight, regular, and rising abruptly to more than 60 metres above the marshy plain to the west, it forms one of the most impressive scarps in England. About half-way down the cliff is a bench or terrace formed by the resistant Marlstone, the topmost member of the Middle Lias: it is sometimes a source of ironstone, and it has influenced the siting of villages (Fig. 80, p. 279).

The Jurassic belt is at its simplest in the central section, for at both its northern and southern extremities its character is modified by the structure. In the north a second scarp is to be seen, west of the main one and quite close to the Trent. It is formed by certain limestone bands of the Lower Lias; and it is highly important,

271

since it contains the iron ore on which the steel industry of Scunthorpe is based (Fig. 78, p. 275). In the far south the ridge becomes broader and higher. This is due partly to an increase in the thickness of the strata, but mainly to a reduction in the angle of dip. Even in the north the dip is only about 26 metres per km, or about $1\frac{1}{2}°$; but this is sufficient to restrict the width of the ridge to 4 km. South of Grantham, however, the strata are virtually horizontal, but are disturbed by gentle folds ranging east and west. As a result the ridge broadens to nearly 20 km, and its height increases to between 120 and 180 metres.

East of Lincoln Edge the Middle Jurassic beds dip below the Oxford and Kimmeridge Clays: soft and easily eroded, these floor the Lincoln clay vale, drained by the Ancholme northward and the Witham southward. The solid deposits, however, are largely masked by boulder clay and Fen alluvium.

In their turn the Jurassic clays dip below the Cretaceous beds. Only in the north, beyond the village of Clixby, is there a simple Chalk scarp, with a regular cliff to the west rising to about 90 m, and a gentle dip slope to the east scored by dry valleys. South of Clixby is a complete contrast. The Wolds widen rapidly from about 7 to 15 km; the western border is broken and irregular, and in the south it is formed not by the Chalk but by a resistant member of the Lower Cretaceous beds known as the Spilsby Sandstone. Above this formation is softer material which has been eroded to form the valley of the Lymn. To the east is a second parallel scarp whose base is formed by the Carstone (*cf.* p. 294) and whose crest is formed by the Chalk. It is, indeed, a foretaste of the parallel scarps to be seen in south-east England, though the scarp-formers are different.

Geologically speaking, the whole of the land between the Wolds and the sea is Chalk. This may seem odd when we see a flat coastal plain everywhere to the east of the hills, and more so when we notice the abrupt eastern edge to the Wolds. This steep eastern margin is in fact an old sea cliff cut into the Chalk, and the Chalk continues eastward as a wave-cut platform a little below the present sea-level. Resting upon it are the boulder clay and marine alluvium which rank as superficial deposits, and do not appear on the maps of solid geology.

The almost triangular shape of the northern half of Lincolnshire is a result of the divergence southward of the two main scarps: in the north the Wolds and the Heath are only 3 kilometres apart; yet at the border of the Fens they are separated by 40 kilometres. The divergence continues as we trace them farther southward, and only in the West Country do they again approach each other. These changes are related to variations in the thickness of the intervening deposits of clay, and these in turn are linked with movements of the sea floor which were taking place when those clays were accumulating. While the Oxford Clay belt in the north of the county totals less than 75 metres in thickness, a greater subsidence in the south allowed over 250 metres of clay to accumulate.

The drainage of the region presents many problems, to which we can refer only briefly. The drainage of the clay vales on each side of the Heath is longitudinal – that is, northward and southward, following the strike of the rocks. In both the ridges, however, and across the coastal plain the drainage is transverse, cutting from west to east, across the strike.

The course of the Witham is erratic: rising in the extreme south-west of the county, it flows north as if to reach Lincoln; opposite a gap in the Heath at Ancaster it turns west as if to join the Trent via the Devon; instead it turns north, reaches Lincoln, and traverses the Heath by means of one of the most remarkable gaps in Britain. It then completes a semicircle by entering the Wash from the north-west. How can such an enigmatic course be explained?

It is clear that different parts of these river systems are of different ages. The latest changes are probably a result of river capture, in the course of which the Devon has lost its headstreams. The gaps at Ancaster and Lincoln can have been formed only at a much higher level than at present, before the Lincoln cliff existed. The clue is provided by the remains of a surface in the Wolds at about 140 to 150 metres, to which Professor Linton has drawn attention. This surface is assigned to Pliocene (late Tertiary) times, and on it a watershed is assumed to have ranged east and west, in about the latitude of Market Rasen. On this the original river system developed, and its remains are still to be seen in the Bain and the lower Witham (flowing south) and the Ancholme and upper Barnoldby Beck in the Wolds (flowing north).

Farming in the Scarps and Vales

Lincolnshire has a surprisingly high proportion of arable land. On the limestone and Chalk plateaux, on the drift-covered slopes, even in the low-lying plains, the main element in the landscape is the ploughed field.

This has not always been so. The very name of the Heath suggests its former character, and here in the mid-eighteenth century there were sandy commons abandoned to the rabbits and nettles. But from Norfolk the new agriculture spread into Lincolnshire, and in the late eighteenth and early nineteenth centuries the land was enclosed, by hedges in the Wolds and by stone walls in the Heath; the soils were ploughed and limed, and then planted with barley, clover, and turnips.

Today the farming remains essentially the same. The northern portions of both Heath and Wolds are the most fertile, and are exceedingly productive of sugar beet, potatoes, and green vegetables: these deep and stoneless loams form potentially first-class market-garden land. In the higher and broader central and southern Wolds the soils are thinner, stonier, and sandier, and this is traditionally sheep and barley land; in times of agricultural depression, however, the farmer returns it to grass. In the south-western Wolds and on the wave-cut platform alike the solid deposits are masked by boulder clay: the soils are deeper and more retentive of moisture, and the proportion of permanent pasture is higher. The products range between potatoes and sugar beet on the lighter land and wheat and beans on the heavier.

In the Scunthorpe district of the northern Heath is a remarkable spread of blown sand: this extends over a triangle whose corners are marked by the villages of Normanby, Broughton, and Laughton. There is much dry and sterile heath, but the Forestry Commission has planted large areas with conifers.

South of the blown sand district the soils are derived from the Lincolnshire Limestone, and again the Norfolk rotation essentially is still practised, with barley as the chief grain crop and sheep as the main stock. A modern tendency, however, is to replace the turnips by sugar beet. Large arable fields are the rule, with the grassland confined mainly to the homestead meadows. Since water is scarce on the plateau, the villages are situated on the margins along the spring lines. On the western side the marlstone bench provides a level site, and between Lincoln and Ancaster, for example, is a long row of 18 villages about a mile apart – perhaps the best examples of spring-line settlements in Britain. The parishes are long and narrow, ranging east and west so as to share in land of contrasting character; and the Roman Ermine Street is the dividing-line between the two rows of parishes (see Fig. 16, p. 64).

In the southern part of the Heath the soils are derived from boulder clay rather than the bare limestone: there is running water, the soils are heavier, and suited to wheat rather than barley. There is more permanent grass, more woodland, and the stone walls are replaced by hedges.

Between the Heath and the Wolds is the main clay vale of Lincolnshire: it is floored, as we have seen, by Oxford Clay, but

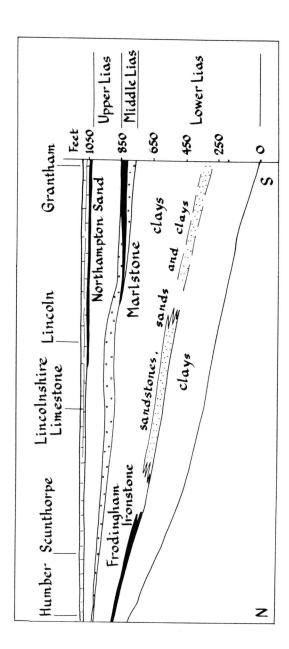

Fig. 78. GEOLOGICAL SECTION : THE JURASSIC IRONSTONES

This section illustrates the relative positions of the three Jurassic ironstones, which are shown in black. The Frodingham Ironstone is worked at Scunthorpe. The Marlstone ores are worked in South Lincolnshire, Leicestershire, and Oxfordshire, and until 1964 in the Cleveland Hills. The Northampton Sand provides the iron for the steel industry at Corby. The section represents a distance of 65 km. *After 'Guide to the Geology of the Midlands', University of Nottingham,* 1948.

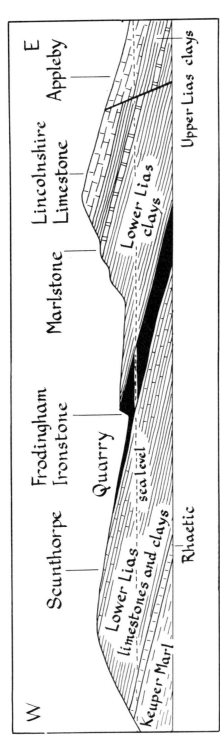

Fig. 79. GEOLOGICAL SECTION ACROSS THE SCUNTHORPE DISTRICT

Here the Jurassic rocks form a double scarp; and the Frodingham Ironstone outcrops along the dip slope of the more westerly scarp. It is worked in great open-cast quarries to the east of Scunthorpe, where an important iron and steel industry has been established. The local ore is supplemented by imports through Immingham Dock. The section represents a distance of 10 km.

this is largely masked by glacial drift and alluvium. Parts of the Ancholme basin in the north are below the level of high spring tides, and have been drained with the aid of sluice gates at Ferriby. This is a region of mixed farming, based upon wheat and cattle, and even here about half the land is under crops.

The coastal alluvial plain possesses a stiff clay soil, and the region is exceptional for Lincolnshire in that about 60 per cent. of the surface is under permanent pasture. Were it not for the unusually low rainfall (570 to 635 mm per annum) it would probably all be grassland. The crops consist of wheat, beans, and rotation grass, and are found on the lighter soils. Essentially this is cattle-fattening land; in recent years the unattractive prices offered for beef have encouraged the farmer to turn to dairying.

The Iron and Steel Industry

Lincolnshire is the largest iron-ore-producing county in the United Kingdom and her output of about 7 million tonnes annually represents 58 per cent. of the total British production. This ore is obtained from two different horizons of the Jurassic rocks: in the north from the Frodingham Ironstone of the Lower Lias; in the south from the Northampton Sand at the base of the Inferior Oolite (that is, just above the Upper Lias). The relationship of these two bands to the rest of the Jurassic strata is shown in the section (Fig. 78), which also indicates the southward thickening of the strata.

The Frodingham Ironstone outcrops in a band midway between the two Jurassic scarps of north Lincolnshire (Fig. 79), and, as is typical in the belt of Jurassic ironfields, is worked by open-cast methods. The ironstone band is about 8 metres thick, the ore is self-fluxing, and its iron content ranges between 17 and 35 per cent., averaging about 20 per cent. These, then, are not rich ores, but they are easily extracted, and the high transport costs associated with imported ores are avoided.

The quarries extend for about 11 km along the outcrop, but beyond Bottesford (about 14 km from the Humber) the ironstone is replaced by clays, and here is the southern limit of the ironfield. The beds are free from faults, and although they are almost horizontal, as they are followed eastward into the scarp face the thickness of the overburden increases, so that mining (as opposed to quarrying) will become more and more necessary. The first underground mine was opened to the north of Scunthorpe in 1949.

Since the ore is lean it is more economical to transport the fuel to the ore, so that the steelworks have been built on the orefield.

Four companies are established at Scunthorpe, which has grown since about 1860 parallel with the industry, and in 1961 had reached a population of 70,880. Here are four of the largest blast furnaces in the country; and in spite of the growing town, workers are travelling daily from as far afield as Doncaster, Goole, and Grimsby. The local ores are supplemented by imports from Sweden and elsewhere by way of Immingham Dock, which is equipped with a battery of grab cranes for the purpose.

In contrast to the Scunthorpe district, the ironfield of the Northampton Sand to the south has not in the main given rise to heavy industry, but is worked in scattered quarries. It has been quarried in the Greetwell district, east of Lincoln, and farther south into Rutland and Northamptonshire where it forms the basis of the steel industry at Corby (p. 257). The ore bed is up to 4·6 metres thick and contains between 31 and 38 per cent. iron.

Lincoln (Fig. 80)
Lincoln (pop. 74,207) occupies a remarkable site. A tongue of the Fens borders the Witham and extends as far upstream as Lincoln, so that here was the focus of all traffic between the Midlands and the east coast. At this place, in addition, is a complete breach of the limestone cliff, followed by the river. The Romans arrived at this spot only three years after landing in Kent, and they focused upon the site two of their trunk roads – Ermine Street, from London, and the Fosse Way, from Exeter. Their legionary fortress they placed, not down by the river, but on the summit of the cliff to the north, at a height of 60 metres. Later they extended the town downhill. The Roman walls have left their mark on the present-day town plan; their Foss Dyke canal, joining the Witham to the Trent, still carries timber and grain from Hull to the city; and modern traffic moves along the roads planned by the Romans.

The Roman street plan was obliterated by the Normans, who constructed the castle and cathedral: like many another city, its medieval prosperity was based on the manufacture of cloth, of which the 'Lincoln Green' of Robin Hood is a reminder. From the fifteenth to the eighteenth century the city languished, but revived after the improvements in agriculture and the draining of the Fens.

The modern industries of Lincoln have arisen from the needs of the district. They include the manufacture of grain-driers and crop graders and cleaners. Fundamental to the Fenland drainage is the production of pumping equipment, and 200 pumping stations in the district are supplied with plant manufactured in Lincoln. The same industry produces pumps for graving docks, and has

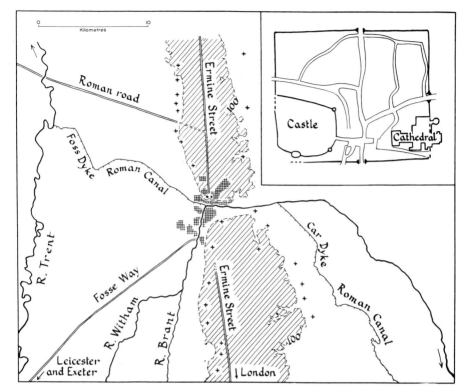

Fig. 80. THE SITE OF LINCOLN

The roads and the two canals are of Roman origin. The lined area represents the Lincoln cliff as out-lined by the 100-foot contour. Saxon and Danish settlers avoided the Roman roads and built their villages close to springs. These sites (deduced from the present-day villages) are shown by crosses. The cross-hatching indicates the approximate extent of the built-up area of Lincoln. The inset shows the medieval town enclosed by Roman walls; the length of its north wall is about 440 metres. *Based on the O.S. 1-inch map. Crown copyright reserved.*

equipped docks at Southampton, Liverpool, and overseas ports. Land drainage involves the use of earth-moving machinery, and established in the city is the largest manufacturer of excavators in Europe. Here are made the huge walking draglines which are used to remove the overburden in opencast coal and iron ore sites. More closely related to agriculture is the manufacture of potato crisps, which draws its material from 3500 ha of potato land in the Fens.

The Fens

The Fens form the largest single extent of alluvium in Britain, and are geologically of Recent (post-glacial) origin. There is little doubt that here in earlier times was a wide valley which formed a breach in the Chalk of Norfolk and Lincolnshire, and was occupied by the combined Witham, Welland, Nen, and Great Ouse. In Neolithic times the land subsided and the valley was submerged. From Roman times onward there has been gradual, if intermittent, reclamation, and the sea is still being forced to retreat.

The $\frac{1}{4}$-inch geological map does not particularize, but it is known that the Fenland soils may be divided broadly into peats and silts. The dividing-line passes between Crowland and Downham Market, silts to the north, and peats farther inland, to the south.

The two deposits are different in origin and utilization. The silts are of marine or estuarine origin, while the peats have resulted from the decay of land vegetation. Stratification in the peat beds has made it possible to date these deposits, and the lowest layers are assigned to the Mesolithic period. For centuries the peats were waterlogged, and only recently have they been brought into cultivation. Today both peats and silts are intensively cultivated, and wheat, potatoes, and sugar beet are characteristic of both. Vegetables, however, grow best on the peats, while fruit-growing is almost confined to the silts.

Although the peat is normally farther inland than the silt, it is at first sight surprising that the peat areas are lower than the silts, and in fact large tracts are actually below mean sea-level. This introduces one of the fundamental problems of the Fens, for when peat is drained it shrinks, so that the level of the land falls. Waterlogged peat contains up to 8 times its own weight of water, and when it is drained is likely to shrink as much as 30 cm in the first year. The dried surface then oxidizes, and this process continues indefinitely, causing a further reduction of the surface level of 3 to 5 cm each year. The surface of Whittlesey Mere has fallen 3·4 metres since it was drained in 1848, and is now below sea-level. Clearly, only by powerful and continuous pumping can such land be rendered fit for cultivation.

Reclamation of the Fens began in Roman times. Wide canals were constructed around the margins of the Fens to trap the water from the surrounding uplands, and to receive local water from a complex series of minor drains. In Roman times many hundreds of thousands of hectares in the southern Fens were thus under cultivation, and air photographs have revealed the positions of granaries, lanes, and farmsteads. The Car Dyke of Lincolnshire is one of the most striking remains of the Roman drainage system: serving the double purpose of drainage and navigation, it ran at least from the river Glen south of Bourne to the Witham near Lincoln, a distance of more than 115 km (Fig. 80, p. 279).

After the departure of the Romans the Fens reverted to swamp and lake. Medieval abbeys were founded on islands in the marsh, as at Ramsey, Thorney, Crowland, Ely, and Peterborough. Boston and King's Lynn became wool ports; but the Fens themselves were neglected. Serious drainage waited until the seventeenth century. In 1630 the fourth Earl of Bedford, together with 13 'co-Adventurers', engaged Sir Cornelius Vermuyden to drain the Great Level in accordance with methods of reclamation current in the Netherlands, and in 1653 the work was complete.

Vermuyden made two great parallel cuts on the river Ouse from Earith (near St Ives) to Denver (near Downham Market), and so bypassed the long sweep of the river by Ely. At Denver he constructed a tidal sluice, which prevented sea-water from penetrating into the Ely loop. The new cuts shortened the Ouse by 16 km, improved its gradient, and removed half the volume of water from the Old Ouse. These straight cuts – the Old and New Bedford rivers – remain as important features in the modern drainage system of the Fens, and the 'washland' that Vermuyden left between them forms an additional outlet for the water in time of flood.

Vermuyden had proposed a cut-off channel which would trap water from the upper Ouse tributaries and conduct it round the levels to Stowbridge: he was here following the principle which had been adopted 1500 years earlier by the Romans. This part of the work was not carried out, but forms an essential part of the modern flood-protection scheme (Fig. 81). This includes a new flood-relief channel 60 metres wide and 18 km long, terminating in a tidal sluice at King's Lynn. The vast project was inaugurated in 1954, has cost £10 millions and has taken 10 years to complete. It is justified by the extraordinary fertility of the land which it is designed to protect from flood.

In the Fens one sees thousands of hectares of land under the plough, with hardly a field of grass. The fields are rectangular, and their boundaries are not hedges but drains (Fig. 82). It is a monotonous, flat landscape, with hardly a tree to break the force of the wind. Wheat, potatoes, and sugar beet are staple crops on the silts and peats alike, and there are sugar factories at King's Lynn, Wissington, Ely, Peterborough, and Spalding. On the peat soils in addition vegetables are grown – in particular, celery, carrots, and onions. The peat fens of Norfolk alone grow one-third of the entire celery crop of the United Kingdom.

Winding among the peats are raised banks of silt known as roddons. Several feet higher than the surrounding land, they are

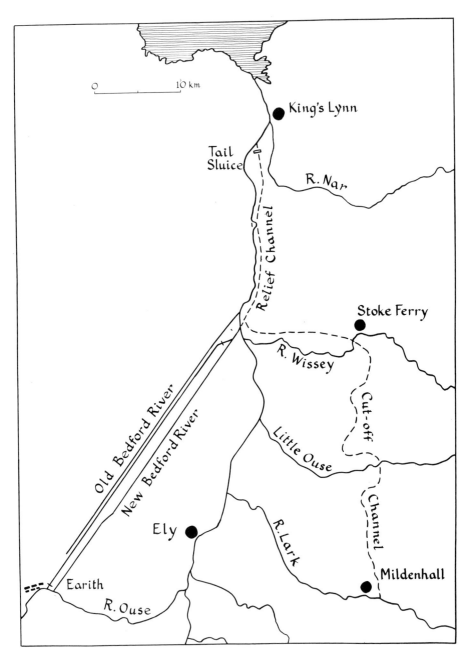

Fig. 81.   THE GREAT OUSE FLOOD PROTECTION SCHEME

A large new relief channel is provided for Vermuyden's Bedford Rivers, and water from the Ouse tributaries is trapped before reaching the main stream. *After W. E. Doran, 1956.*

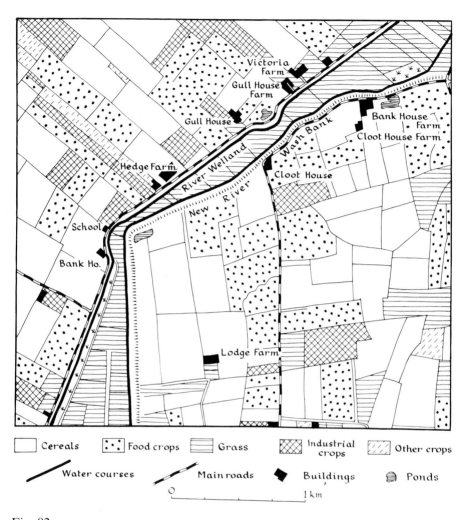

Legend:

☐ Cereals · ☐ Food crops · ☰ Grass · ☒ Industrial crops · ▨ Other crops

— Water courses · ⟋ Main roads · ◆ Buildings · 🖅 Ponds

0 _____ 1 km

Fig. 82. THE LANDSCAPE OF THE FENS

This is based on a portion of Sheet 499 of the Second Land Utilisation Survey of Britain. It illustrates part of the river Welland between Spalding and Crowland, about 19 km from its outfall, and is in the region of the Fenland silts. The surface is only 1·2 to 2 m above mean sea-level, so that it is below high-tide level. The main watercourses are embanked, and water from the smaller drains, which form the field boundaries, can join them only with the aid of pumping. To allow a quick runoff the drains are as straight as possible, and since the roads follow the drains, a rectangular grid of communications is produced, though in this figure only the main roads are shown. The main cereal is wheat; the chief food crop, potatoes; the 'industrial crop' is sugar beet. The land between the Welland and the New River is mainly under permanent grass and is preserved as 'washland'; in case of need it can be used as a flood-relief channel.

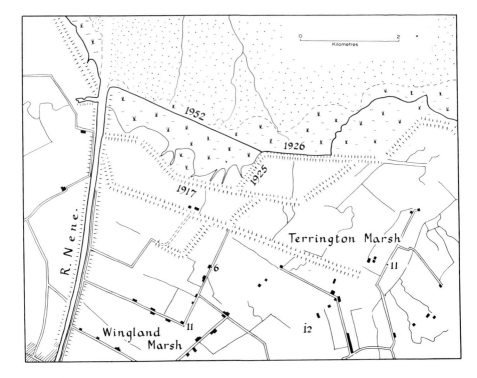

Fig. 83. RECLAMATION ALONG THE WASH

Successive sea walls provide evidence of the progress of reclamation along the borders of the Wash. First the new land provides cattle pastures; after three or four years it grows wheat. Heights are in feet. *Based on the O.S. 1-inch map. Crown copyright reserved.*

better-drained, and the farmsteads are frequently situated on them. They were originally the beds of rivers, at a lower level than the peats; but owing to the shrinkage of the latter they now stand above the general level of the land.

In the silty Fens fruit, bulbs, and flowers are grown, with concentrations of fruit around Wisbech and flowers and bulbs around Spalding. The Wisbech district specializes in apples (Bramleys), but there are also large areas of plums and pears, together with strawberries and gooseberries. Nearly two-thirds of the bulb area consists of daffodils and narcissi, with tulips accounting for most of the remainder. Bulbs are grown in rotation with wheat, potatoes, and sugar beet. Over 12,000 people are employed in the industry, and in addition to the bulbs, 25,000 boxes of flowers are dispatched from Spalding each day in the spring.

The Wash

All round the Wash the process of reclaiming land from the sea has long continued. Thus, at Holbeach Flats successive tracts became dry land in 1660, 1793, 1838, and 1948. Now the saltmarsh is again growing in front of the sea wall, and will soon be ripe for more reclamation. One of the latest extensions has been made at Wingland Marsh, north of Wisbech, and has not yet found its way to the maps. Here in 1951 a King's Lynn company which specializes in land reclamation built a sea wall 18 metres wide and 3 kilometres long east of the Nene outfall, and reclaimed 280 ha (Fig. 83). The salt-loving plants die down, drains are cut, cattle arrive to graze the land, and after three or four years wheat is growing. So the erosion of the east coast is being balanced by reclamation around the Wash.

FOR FURTHER READING

Books

Guide to the Geology of the East Midlands (University of Nottingham, 1948).

STAMP, L. D.: The Land of Britain (Geographical Publications):

Part 69, *Lincolnshire* (*Parts of Holland*) by G. I. Smith (1937).

Parts 76–77, *Lincolnshire* (*Parts of Lindsey and Kesteven*), by L. D. Stamp (1942).

STEERS, J. A.: *The Cambridge Region* (British Association, 1965).

WILSON, VERNON: *East Yorkshire and Lincolnshire*, British Regional Geology Handbooks (H.M.S.O., 1948).

Articles

DORAN, W. E.: 'The Great Ouse Flood Protection Scheme', in *The Dock and Harbour Authority* (April/May 1956).

—— 'The Fens', in *Geographical Magazine* (October 1965).

EDWARDS, K. C.: 'Changing Geographical Patterns in Lincolnshire', in *Geography* (April 1954).

KESTNER, F. J. T.: 'The Old Coastline of the Wash', in *Geog. Journ.* (December 1962).

LINTON, DAVID L.: 'The Landforms of Lincolnshire', in *Geography* (April 1954).

Maps

Bartholomew's ½-inch maps, sheets 20, 25, and 30.

Geological Survey, ¼-inch sheet 12. There are no 1-inch sheets available.

New Land Use Survey 2½-inch sheets 481 (Downham Market) and 499 (Crowland Fens).

CHAPTER TWENTY

EAST ANGLIA

T HE NAME of East Anglia derives from the Anglo-Saxon kingdom which was established during the first half of the sixth century A.D. The unity of the region had, however, been recognized earlier, for here during Roman times was the tribal territory of the Iceni. On all sides its boundaries are clear: to the north and east is the sea, to the west are the Fens. In the south the region is cut off from the London Basin by a series of valleys, formerly marshy, which merge eastward into estuaries. Of these the largest is that of the Stour: this no doubt formed the southern limit of the East Anglian kingdom, and still forms the boundary of Suffolk. Access was possible only in the south-west, where a narrow belt of bare chalk was probably only lightly wooded, and here the defensive works of Devil's Ditch and Fleam Dyke controlled the gateway.

Throughout its history East Anglia has been a region of consequence. The most easterly part of Britain, it has benefited from Continental contacts. Its medieval cloth industry decayed, but eventually was followed by such far-reaching improvements in farming that here indeed is the birthplace of the Agrarian Revolution in Britain. The region remains today one of the most purely agricultural in England. We define it as the counties of Norfolk and Suffolk, excluding the Fens, but including the chalk hills to the east of Cambridge.

Physical Basis

In its solid geology and structure East Anglia presents a simple pattern; but the superficial deposits by which this is masked tell as complex a story as is to be found anywhere in the country.

The foundation of the region is seen in a broad, plateau-like dip-slope of Chalk, which presents a scarp to the west and is overlain by Tertiary deposits to the east. The scarp exhibits a distinct change in direction near Brandon, and a structural weakness may account for the existence here of the vale occupied by the Waveney and the Little Ouse. Its human significance was early recognized, and here is the boundary between the 'North Folk' and the 'South Folk'.

The bare Chalk reaches heights of about 80 m in Norfolk, and a dissected scarp overlooks the Lower Cretaceous rocks to the west. Farther south, in eastern Cambridgeshire, it reaches 100 metres; it forms, however, a relatively narrow zone, and rarely exceeds 16 kilometres or so in width (Fig. 84). Between the Chalk scarp and the Fens in north-west Norfolk is a triangular zone of older Cretaceous rocks. Here clays and sands which correspond broadly with the Lower Greensand of south-east England account for the heathy country to the east of King's Lynn, while valleys filled with gravel and hills capped with boulder clay add to the diversity of this small corner of East Anglia.

Resting upon the Chalk in the east of the region, but largely obscured by drift, are the Tertiary rocks. The London Clay is present at depth but does not appear on the surface, and the period is represented by reddish and yellowish shelly sands and clays known as the Norwich Crag: these are marine deposits which accumulated near the estuary of a large river, perhaps the proto-Rhine.

For the most part it is not the 'solid' rocks but the drift deposits which have influenced the work and life of the region. They are the result of four distinct ice invasions, and here is the most complete and varied series of glacial deposits to be found in the British Isles. Along the coast between Happisburgh and Cromer as many as twelve successive beds have been recognized, and though these are not all present at any one spot eight of them are to be seen in the cliffs at Trimingham.

The region was first invaded by the North Sea ice sheet, which brought igneous rocks from Scotland and Scandinavia; but its deposits have been largely obscured by later advances of the ice. Next came the Great Eastern ice: this has been of fundamental importance to the region, for its deposit is seen in the great sheet of chalky boulder clay which covers most of East Anglia and forms the basis of its soils and agriculture, while the glacial sands of East Suffolk may represent its outwash material.

The third glaciation was by the Little Eastern ice sheet. It has left behind a prominent moraine of sand and gravel in the Cromer Ridge, extending between Fakenham and Cromer. Its crest is wooded, and, with a summit of 98 metres, this is the highest land in Norfolk. Its northern slope was in contact with the ice, and is appropriately abrupt. The outwash material from the Little Eastern ice may perhaps be seen in the loams of north-east Norfolk. The

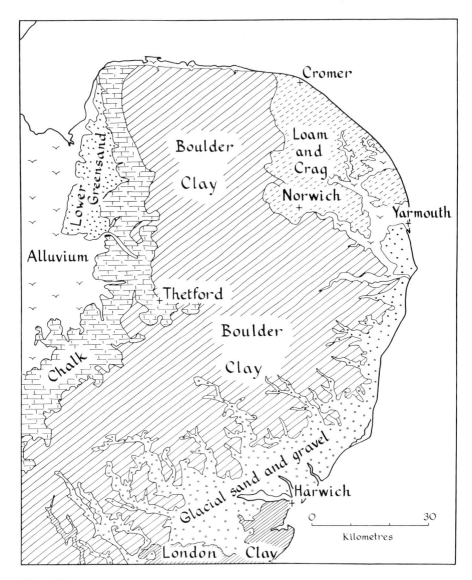

Fig. 84. EAST ANGLIA: DRIFT GEOLOGY

The solid geology is almost completely masked by glacial and alluvial deposits, and these form the basis of most of the agricultural sub-regions. Two of them, however, cannot be traced from the geological map: these are the Good Sands and Breckland. The former is a roughly triangular area in the north-west of the boulder clay of Norfolk; the latter centres on Thetford. The sub-regions are described in the text. *Based on the Geological Survey ¼-inch map.*

fourth and final ice sheet did not penetrate far into East Anglia, but its reddish-brown boulder clay, containing erratics from the Cheviot Hills, is seen at various points along the north Norfolk coast.

The Coasts

East Anglia has an exceptionally regular coastline, but it is by no means simple in origin or structure. In the south-east the estuaries of the Alde, Orwell, Deben, and Stour provide evidence of subsidence: these are drowned valleys. Similar evidence is lacking elsewhere; but at Brancaster (10 km east of Hunstanton), on the north coast of Norfolk, remains of a submerged forest are seen from time to time, suggesting that here too there has been a relatively recent submergence.

How then are we to explain the belt of marshland up to 2·5 km wide along this stretch of coast? It appears to be due to a change in the direction of longshore drift. From Sheringham eastward and southward the drift is in that direction, in agreement with the movement of beach material in Lincolnshire. But, for reasons not yet known, between Sheringham and Hunstanton the drift is westward. This is the only part of eastern England with a westerly longshore drift, and it is precisely this stretch which displays a belt of marsh in front of an old cliff-line. Professor Steers suggests that in effect we have here a great groyne which is trapping the material from Lincolnshire and beyond, and banking it against the coast.

In this North Norfolk Marsh reclamation has been in progress at least since the eighteenth century (*cf*. Fig. 85, p. 296): thus the straight bank forming the western side to the harbour of Wells was built in 1859, and resulted in the reclamation of about 260 hectares. This whole stretch of former saltmarsh, 7 km long and up to 1500 m wide, is now rich pasture-land; but reclamation of the marshes has assisted in the decay of a row of ports, including Cley, Blakeney, Salthouse, and Kelling.

South-east of Cromer erosion is the problem, for here whole villages have been washed away. Until the fourteenth century the village of Shipden existed below the cliffs of Cromer: now there is no trace of it. Whimpwell village (formerly near North Walsham) has vanished; so has the church of neighbouring Keswick. Eccles too, about 3 kilometres to the south-east, has gone, and the sorry foundations of its church are seen from time to time on the beach.

South of Yarmouth the coast is characterized by the growth of sandspits. Yarmouth, Lowestoft, Southwold, Aldeburgh, and Felixstowe all occupy similar positions on or near the bases of southward-growing sandspits. The most prominent of these is Orford Ness, south of Aldeburgh, where the mouth of the little river Alde is deflected southward for about 18 km. Its growth has been rapid and recent, and has been traced by comparison between seventeenth-century and modern maps; during the seventeenth, eighteenth, and nineteenth centuries the spit grew nearly 4 km – an average rate of about 14 metres a year. There is much still to be learnt, however, concerning the evolution of sandspits.

Climate
The westerly winds have lost much of their moisture before reaching East Anglia. The regular coastline minimizes the effect of the sea on temperature; while the relatively large spreads of light soil retain little heat. All these elements combine to produce the nearest approach in Britain to a continental climate. The rainfall is low: about half the region receives less than 635 mm per annum, and a higher proportion falls in summer than elsewhere. The summers are warmer and the winters are cooler than in other parts, and East Anglia has the highest range of mean monthly temperatures in the British Isles. In these circumstances frosts are frequent, though the region enjoys a high proportion of sunshine.

From the farmer's viewpoint there is a danger of drought in areas of light soil, and commercial fruit-growers need to avoid planting in frost hollows; but in general the climate of East Anglia is clearly favourable to agriculture and horticulture, and it is not surprising to find here the most extensive region of arable farming in Britain.

Historical Geography
Throughout prehistoric times the greater part of East Anglia consisted of high forest. Only on the lighter soils of Breckland and the Chalk plateaux was penetration easy, and it is in these districts that the remains of early Man are most readily seen.

In Palæolithic times a land bridge existed across the North Sea, and as the glaciers waxed and waned so primitive man retreated and advanced. His flints have been found at Mildenhall and Barnham on the borders of Breckland, and at Hoxne, in the upper Waveney valley. About 6000 B.C., during Mesolithic times, the melting of the great ice sheets produced a rise in sea-level and Britain became an island. Tiny flints and barbed harpoons characteristic of the time have been found at Thetford and elsewhere. Neolithic culture is represented in the area by a village site at Mildenhall and by flint-mines, the most famous of which is Grimes' Graves, about 8 kilometres north-west of Thetford. Here one can descend 6 metres into a Neolithic shaft and see the band of black flints which the miners prised out with the aid of antler picks.

About 250 round barrows in west and north Norfolk testify to the presence of Bronze Age folk; pile dwellings in Breckland may date from this time, and there were cremation cemeteries in the area between Ipswich and Colchester. The valleys of Breckland were occupied in Iron Age times, and a farmstead has been examined at West Harling, in the valley of the Thet, 16 kilometres above Thetford. When the Romans arrived the region was occupied by a tribal group styled the Iceni: they introduced chariot warfare, were gifted artists and craftsmen, and issued their own coins. A long trackway, the Icknield Way, following the crest of the Chalk ridge, linked their territory with Salisbury Plain, but may have had an earlier origin.

During Roman times virtually the whole of East Anglia was opened up to settlement, excepting only the Broads. At Colchester the native capital of the Trinovantes was replaced by a walled town according to the usual Roman pattern, and at Caister, 5 km south of Norwich, the Romans organized a capital for the Iceni: its streets and buildings can occasionally be seen in the form of crop marks in the ripening corn. These towns were joined by a main road to Londinium, which was paralleled by a second road farther west (Peddars Way); the latter points into the Wash near Hunstanton, and may have linked by ferry with the coast of Lincolnshire. About a dozen smaller settlements, as many potteries, and 20 villas are known in East Anglia; yet, apart from Colchester, on the southern fringe of the region, not a single present-day town or village can trace its origin back to Roman times.

In the fifth and sixth centuries A.D. wave after wave of Saxons and Angles from north-west Germany swept up the rivers of East Anglia and occupied the land. The Norwich and Ipswich districts, together with the Chalk outcrops and the Fenland margins, were soon settled, and by about A.D. 550 the kingdom of East Anglia was established. At the height of his power King Raedwald (who died in 624–625) was acknowledged as the overlord of all southern England, and it is possibly he whose death was commemorated in the magnificent ship-cenotaph at Sutton Hoo, on the east bank of the Deben, opposite Woodbridge in Suffolk.

With the details of the Danish raids we cannot concern ourselves;

but the region was one of active colonization. More interested than the Saxons in urban life, the Danes contributed largely to the growth of Thetford and Norwich. By 1066 Norwich boasted about 5000 inhabitants, while Thetford was little smaller, and contained 12 churches; and East Anglia generally was one of the most populous regions of the kingdom. Norwich has prospered as the regional capital, but Thetford has remained only a small market town, the centre for the relatively unproductive district of Breckland.

During the Middle Ages the prosperity of East Anglia was based largely on wool. At first the raw wool was exported to Flanders for manufacture; but during the fourteenth century the inhabitants, strengthened by the arrival of Flemish weavers, turned more and more to the production of cloth. Hadleigh, Colchester, Lavenham, and Bury St Edmunds became important centres of the industry. Suffolk was the chief county in England for woollen cloth, while the Norwich district, lacking in water-power, specialized in the worsted branch (named after the village of Worstead, 20 kilometres N.N.E. of the city). Lavenham, with its towered church, its guildhall, grammar school, almshouses, and inns, is a typical survivor of the East Anglian woollen industry. During the fourteenth century it produced annually 500 to 1000 broadcloths. To the south-east is the little village of Kersey, which gave its name to the coarse ribbed cloth which the district produced.

The Industrial Revolution spelt the end of the East Anglian cloth industry, for the district had little water-power, no coal, and no iron, and it could not compete successfully with the West Riding of Yorkshire. Fortunately, however, the decay of textiles coincided with a complete reorganization of agriculture which in large measure was due to the adoption of Flemish techniques. Two Norfolk landowners were prominent in popularizing the new agriculture; both had their estates in the district of light soils of north-west Norfolk.

Charles Townshend, the second Viscount ('Turnip' Townshend), of Raynham, near Fakenham, retired to his estate in 1730, and during the remaining eight years of his life introduced two vital reforms: he marled his land – that is, he mixed the light surface sands with the underlying clays and produced a valuable loam – and he abandoned the medieval 3-course rotation in favour of a 4-year rotation. Instead of wheat, wheat, fallow there now appeared turnips, barley, clover, wheat. Under the old system one-third of the land was idle and there was no winter food for animals: under the new there·were roots and hay for animals (the turnips were fed directly to sheep, in the arable fields); the clover restored nitrogen to the soil; there was more stock and more manure, and the whole of the land was in use.

Thomas Coke, later Earl of Leicester, succeeded to his estate at Holkham, near Wells, in 1776, and during his long life he drained his section of the North Norfolk Marsh, he anchored the sand-dunes with conifers, he improved the land with bone manure, he fed his stock with rape and linseed cake, and he transformed the quality of the local sheep and cattle out of all recognition. From Norfolk the improved farming spread to all parts of eastern England, and the Norfolk rotation is still the basis of modern arable farming.

Today East Anglia has an exceptionally high proportion of its area under cereal crops, and of these the chief is barley. It contains large numbers of sheep and cattle, in spite of a small proportion of permanent pasture, for the stock are either stall fed or folded on root crops. An important relative newcomer to the farm economy is sugar beet, which was introduced in the 1920's. It has been of great benefit to the farmer, since it can take the place of other roots in the rotation, and it brings an immediate cash return. Yet the feeding value of the tops and the pulp is as great as that of the same acreage of mangolds.

Sugar beet was pioneered by the Director of the Norfolk Agricultural Station, and the first factory in England was opened at Cantley on the Yare (16 km south-east of Norwich) in 1912. It was followed by two more on the Fenland border, at Wissington (1925) and King's Lynn (1927), and there are now factories too at Ipswich and Bury St Edmunds. Norfolk alone produces about one-fifth of the entire sugar-beet crop of the United Kingdom.

Sub-regions

In no other major region of the United Kingdom can we distinguish so many and such varied sub-regions. In our description we begin on the periphery, proceed clockwise from Breckland, continue with the boulder clay plateau in the heart of the region, and conclude with the bare Chalk.

Breckland is unique in Britain. Here is the spectacle of a forest ringed with heath set amid some of the most productive farm-land in Britain. The geological map gives little clue to this strange phenomenon, for it indicates Breckland as a district of Chalk, in places mantled by boulder clay, and similar to the neighbouring districts to the north and south.

But the glacial cover of Breckland differs from the surrounding deposits in that clay is largely absent. Professor Steers[1] describes at least two chalky boulder clays separated by sand, loess, and brickearth. Leaching has left the insoluble sand on the surface in places; elsewhere layers of stones result from the erosion of the sand with which they were mingled. These surface conditions are aggravated by strong winds and an exceptionally low rainfall, of about 580 mm per annum, together with the almost continental temperatures which result from the poor conductivity of heat on the part of the sands. In June the 2.0 P.M. temperatures are likely to be 3°C higher in Breckland than at Yarmouth; but late frosts are frequent, and the minimum temperatures are at times 8° lower than on the coast. Here we find the nearest approach in Britain to the Continental steppes: sand-dunes are to be found, dust storms have occurred, and much of the land is left in heath which until the arrival of myxomatosis about 1954 was infested with rabbits.

The central core of Breckland has, however, been planted by the Forestry Commission, and Thetford and Swaffham forests, totalling about 18,600 hectares, form one of the largest plantations in the kingdom. The main species are the Scots and Corsican pines, which grow well in Breckland conditions. Agriculture is not entirely absent: it takes the form of intensive, often experimental enterprises. On these light soils carrots and parsnips are grown, and it is found that peas for canning ripen early here. The cultivation of asparagus and the propagation of hop sets are other unusual activities practised in Breckland, while the sandy soils of the district are found to be suitable for the rearing of ducks; here, indeed, originate three-quarters of the national population of ducks. The market centre for the products of Breckland is Thetford: it has canneries, and light industries are being attracted to the town since its development as an overspill for London.

The *'Greensand' belt* is varied geologically, but its soils are in general sandy and leached. The surface is undulating, with a high proportion of woodland and heath, and well-watered valleys. A row of spring-line villages occurs at the foot of the Chalk scarp. The strata cannot be correlated with those of the Greensand of Kent, but are similar in that their sandy soils are suited to fruit-growing. The royal estate at Sandringham produces dessert apples and blackcurrants. Building stone is scarce in East Anglia, but the Greensand belt yields a suitable sandstone known as the Carstone which is used locally in the villages.

[1] *Norwich and its Region* (British Association, 1961), page 33.

Until the end of the seventeenth century the *Good Sands* consisted of poor heath and supported only occasional patches of rye and a few sheep. When Viscount Townshend settled on his Raynham estate in 1730 he is said to have found 'two rabbits fighting for a single blade of grass'. The district was the home of the farming pioneers; and Arthur Young, seeing the vast improvements that allowed wheat and barley to flourish, named it in 1804 the 'Good Sands'. Today this is prosperous farm-land, with extensive tracts under the plough, even in the 'parks' of Raynham and Holkham. Small patches of woodland and common are the only reminders of the former desolation.

The North Norfolk Marsh is separated from the Good Sands by one of the clearest geographical boundaries to be seen anywhere in Britain (Fig. 85). To the north of the old sea cliff which terminates the Good Sands there is hardly a road or a habitation. Some salt-marsh remains, but much of it has been reclaimed for pasture, and is used as an adjunct to farms in the Good Sands. We illustrate from a farm on the Holkham estate close to Wells.

This is a large farm, totalling 308 hectares, of which 29 are on the 'marsh' and the remainder on the Good Sands. It is almost entirely an arable farm, and even the marshland fields are under wheat or temporary grass. Cereals occupy about one-third of the land, and of these the chief is barley for malting (59 ha). Wheat follows, for milling (24 ha), with oats third, mainly for stock-feeding (14 ha). About one-fifth of the land is under vegetables: these include carrots and peas in roughly equal areas, both largely for canning, with some of this produce carted by lorry as far as Sheffield. In addition are sprouts and cabbages, destined for the London market. Sugar beet occupies 37 ha, and is crushed at the King's Lynn factory; there are 8 ha of roots, and most of the remaining land is under temporary pasture, for hay.

The farmer keeps a milking herd of 60 Friesians, and the milk is bottled in King's Lynn. In addition to his home-bred calves he sends to Devon for nearly 300 steers each year, and fattens them: these are mainly stall fed. In order to make full use of his grass leys he keeps a flock of 100 ewes to produce fat lambs. The farmer requires the full-time services of 26 men, including a lorry-driver, bricklayer, and carpenter. The farm was not inherited, it was built up by hard work and skilful management from one of 24 hectares with about 8 milking cows in 1936, and it well illustrates the potential productivity of the Good Sands. It is a far cry from the farmer in county Kerry (p. 93).

The Loam region occupies most of the triangle whose corners lie

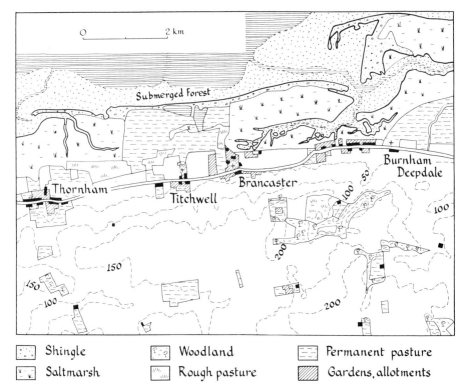

⠿	Shingle	░	Woodland	═	Permanent pasture	
⋎	Saltmarsh	⋃	Rough pasture	▨	Gardens, allotments	

Fig. 85. 'GOOD SANDS' AND MARSH

The road runs parallel to and just south of one of the clearest geographical boundaries to be seen anywhere in Britain. To the south are the Good Sands – the scene of the agricultural improvements of the Agrarian Revolution. It is almost completely arable (on this map all land not otherwise designated is arable). To the north is land recently won from the sea, in part salt marsh, elsewhere good pasture. The land utilization is from the survey of 1931–32, but is unlikely to have changed in its essentials. The farm described on p. 295 lies 10 kilometres east of this area. Heights are in feet.

at Sheringham, Cromer, and Caister-next-Yarmouth. It is a region of diverse geology, and its soils are derived from such varied material as glacial gravels, loam, brickearth, and Crag. The loam and brickearth are sufficiently widespread to give character to the region, and all the soils are light, warm, easily worked, and retentive of moisture. Consequently this is an exceedingly fertile and productive district; it is densely peopled, containing half the population of the county; it has many fine churches and mansions which testify to a traditional prosperity.

The crops include barley, wheat, and sugar beet, which together account for two-thirds of the arable area: in addition are potatoes and peas. The latter are designed for quick-freezing, at plants in North Walsham, Westwick, or Yarmouth. Many farms in the loam region are now growing tulip and daffodil bulbs, which equal in quality those grown in the Fens.

The Broads comprise about 20 lakes which drain to the river Bure or to its tributaries, the Ant, Thurne, and Muckfleet (Fig. 86). Long regarded as the remnants of a wide bay formed by a submergence of the land in Neolithic times, they are now known to be flooded peat diggings of the twelfth and thirteenth centuries. Rectangular in section, and originally 3 metres or more deep, the basins gradually become filled with organic matter. When they shallow to about a metre they are invaded by reedy plants, and the spreading vegetation converts the marsh into dry land. The Broads, like all lakes, are doomed to disappear.

The land separating the Broads is often 6 to 9 metres above the water-level, and in reality forms outliers of the Loam region. Farmers in the loam district can therefore share in the pastures of

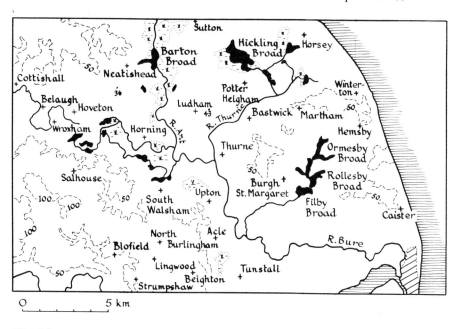

Fig. 86. THE NORFOLK BROADS

The broads are shown in black. As the contours suggest, the intervening areas are quite high: these are outliers of the loam region and are agriculturally very productive – hence the large number of villages. The area in the south-east shaded obliquely is part of Yarmouth. Heights are in feet. *Based on the O.S. 1-inch map. Crown copyright reserved.*

Broadland, and many of them grow blackcurrants, whose native habitat is the reedy borders of the Broads. In addition a harvest of reeds is gathered in each winter for thatching purposes: this is a declining pursuit, for it is cold, damp, and uncomfortable work; but there is a good demand for Norfolk reeds, which are reputed to last for centuries. More significant in the life of the region today is the tourist industry, and many villages help to supply the needs of visitors who come to enjoy the yachting and fishing.

Yarmouth (pop. 50,152) is not so much the centre of Broadland as a fishing-port, resort, and industrial town in its own right. The site, on a south-pointing sandspit, is restricted, and the immediate hinterland is of only limited productivity. The town rose to importance as the port for the worsted cloths of Norwich; but from the sixteenth century onward its prosperity was based upon the herring fishery. In the early twentieth century over a thousand drifters landed their catches there each season, a quarter of them based on Yarmouth itself. The herring fishery has declined; but Yarmouth remains a commercial port trading regularly with Antwerp and Rotterdam. Its products have a local flavour and include frozen foods, malt and beer, and potato crisps. The town is now the base for the North Sea gas operations (p. 374): a new quay has been built, and 47 companies have made Yarmouth their headquarters.

The East Suffolk Sands form a distinctive sub-region whose soils are derived from outwash gravels and, at lower elevations, from the underlying Crag. From a narrow coastal strip between Lowestoft and Aldeburgh the region widens and extends as far south as Ipswich and Hadleigh and beyond Colchester. Farther west the gravels are overlain by boulder clay, but are exposed in long tongues in the river valleys, so that the western boundary of the sub-region is complex.

The soils are not naturally fertile, but respond well to fertilizers and are particularly suited to root crops. Here carrots are grown for the London market. The areas of coarser soils have been afforested, but there remain tracts of heath and common. Coastal submergence has drowned the river mouths, and at the heads of the estuaries are the old-established ports of Woodbridge on the Deben, Ipswich on the Orwell, and Colchester on the Colne. Founded when land transport was difficult, they were placed as far inland as possible.

At Harwich the reverse is seen: rail transport is quicker than sea, so the port is placed on the coast. A freight-train ferry links Harwich with Zeebrugge, while the passenger service joins with the

Hook of Holland. In addition there are regular cargo services to Antwerp, Rotterdam, and Esbjerg, which results in a surprisingly large volume of overseas trade.

Ipswich (pop. 122,814), at the lowest bridge over its river, and in close touch with the boulder clay soils of central Suffolk, has become the administrative centre of the county, and its chief market, manufacturing town, and port. Its industries are closely connected with farming: they include flour-milling, the manufac-- ture of fertilizers and animal food, and agricultural engineering. From the last has developed the specialist activity of Messrs Ransomes and Rapier, producing mobile cranes, excavators, and fork-lift trucks. Ipswich imports coal, petroleum, and wheat (mainly transhipped in London), fertilizer materials (including ammonium sulphate, basic slag, phosphates, and potash) and roadstone and building stone; but like others with farming hinterlands, its exports are small.

The Boulder Clay, by far the largest sub-region of East Anglia, forms the core of its agricultural life. Only a thin skin in the west, the boulder clay thickens eastward to reach 30 to 45 metres. Southward and eastward it becomes heavier, but everywhere it contains a proportion of chalk, so that it is described as 'chalky boulder clay'. Consequently, its soils are more suitable to arable farming than are those derived from the boulder clay of the Midlands. Other favourable elements are the dry and sunny summers and the level surface, which assists in the large-scale use of machinery.

In a state of nature this was oak-ash woodland, and in spite of many centuries of clearance of the woodland it retains a wooded appearance. The level surface is dissected by a series of south-east-flowing streams, and these have excavated steep-sided valleys which are filled with gravels. Here for the most part are the villages, for clean water is available from springs and shallow wells. As one travels across the plateau it appears deserted in spite of the cultivated fields; and the first sign of habitation is the tip of the church spire in the distance: the village itself is out of sight in the valley (Fig. 87).

There is perhaps less specialization here than in the peripheral regions. Barley and wheat remain important crops, but dairying and poultry farming take their place in the farm enterprise, since the relatively heavy soils produce good pastures. No major town has arisen in the boulder clay region: instead it is dotted with small market towns such as Attleborough, Wymondham, and East Dereham in Norfolk, and Debenham, Stowmarket, and Lavenham in Suffolk. They are placed about 16 km apart, so that each serves

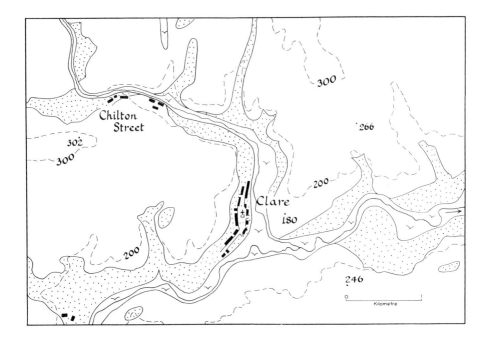

Fig. 87. A GRAVEL-STREWN VALLEY ON THE SUFFOLK-ESSEX BORDER

A level plateau at 250–300 feet, whose surface is composed of boulder clay (here shown blank), is deeply incised by the rivers. The plateau is devoted mainly to arable farming (wheat, sugar beet, and roots), but it has a deserted appearance since most of the people live in villages in the gravel-filled valleys. As one approaches the village from the plateau the first sign of the settlement is the tip of the church spire. This landscape is typical of much of Suffolk and north Essex. The gravel valleys may be regarded as western extensions of the East Suffolk Sands (Fig. 84, p. 288). In the figure the gravels are stippled. The river is the Stour. Heights are in feet. *Based on the Geological Survey 1-inch map.*

a radius of about 8 km – the distance which in former days could be conveniently covered to and fro on horseback in one day.

The *Bare Chalk* forms a narrow belt, only 7 or 8 kilometres wide, in Suffolk and Cambridgeshire south of Breckland. Here the boulder clay is absent, and in place of the featureless plateau are the broad swellings and dry valleys characteristic of the Chalk. Clumps of beech and occasionally long, narrow plantations (windbreaks) are to be seen, and the springy turf has favoured the horse racing at Newmarket. Much of the chalky soil, however, is under the plough. From prehistoric to Saxon times this formed the only gateway into East Anglia, and its strategic value is indicated by the linear earthworks which traverse it.

Norwich

With a population (including the suburbs) of about 150,000, Norwich is the largest city in East Anglia, and its obvious regional capital. Situated at the junction of the loam region and the boulder clay of Norfolk and easily accessible to the Good Sands, it has become a great agricultural market: Norwich is the classic example of a route centre, and on it focus no fewer than a dozen major roads and five railways (the importance of some of the railway lines has diminished in recent years).

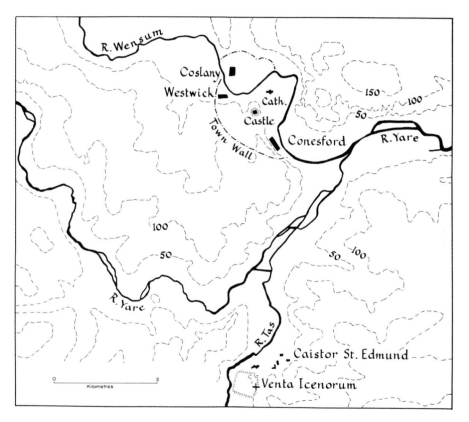

Fig. 88.   THE SITE OF NORWICH

The Roman centre for East Anglia was Venta Icenorum, and from here a road ran northward to the site of the later castle, to reach the Wensum where the flood-plain is at its narrowest. Norwich grew around this river crossing. The city is unusual in that it has resulted from the fusion of three pre-Norman settlements: Coslany and Westwick (both Saxon), and Conesford (Danish). The castle is of Norman origin; the wall was built in the fourteenth century. Today almost the whole of the area north of the river Yare is built up. Heights are in feet. *In part after D. Howard and C. A. Pratt, 1941.*

The city stands close to the junction of the Wensum and the Yare – two of the largest rivers of East Anglia – and is unusual in that it has resulted from the fusion of three distinct village nuclei – two of them Saxon, the third Danish (Fig. 88). They were placed just above the confluence where the alluvium of the Wensum narrows between gravel terraces, so that it was possible to ford the river. Apart from the bridge at Yarmouth, there is still no road across the river below Norwich.

The medieval town clustered around its castle and cathedral and was ringed by a wall in the fourteenth century; as a result of its prosperous cloth industry the city rose to become the third in England. Woollen textiles remained of consequence until the eighteenth century; they were replaced by silk-weaving in the nineteenth century, and in 1851 textiles remained the chief industry of the town, employing over 5000 people.

Decline continued, however, for the city was far from sources of power; and in its place there came a remarkable expansion in the manufacture of footwear. For this craft Norwich was well suited: there was local raw material and abundant skilled labour seeking employment; and by 1931 well over a third of those engaged in manufactures were producing boots and shoes. From the first there was a concentration on women's and children's shoes, in which skill and craftsmanship are at a premium. Today the industry employs about 9000 people in 23 factories; it produces eight million pairs a year, and forms the third shoe-making district in Britain, after Leicestershire and London. Associated industries are tanning and the manufacture of cardboard boxes.

Other characteristic products of Norwich are based on farming. Colman's, best known as millers of the locally grown mustard, produce also various cereals, baby foods, and barley water, and there are two other grain-millers in the city. All possess riverside sites, and Norwich remains a port, with connections with London and the near Continent. Local barley forms a raw material for an important brewing industry which sends its beer as far as Lincolnshire and Cambridgeshire. Among many others we may single out the manufacture of metal fencing and wire netting, which has developed in response to the needs of the local farms. Two Norwich firms now produce about half the entire output of the United Kingdom in this product: much of it is exported to Commonwealth countries.

With its Norman castle, its flint-built medieval churches, its elegant eighteenth-century Assembly House, its influential corn exchange and cattle market, and its modern factories, Norwich presents a harmonious blend of old and new. Its status as the cultural and commercial focus of a wide region was recognized in 1959 by the granting of a university to the city.

FOR FURTHER READING

Books

CHATWIN, C. P.: *East Anglia and Adjoining Areas*, British Regional Geology Handbooks (H.M.S.O., 1961).

Norwich and its Region (British Association, Norwich, 1961).

STEERS, J. A.: *The Coastline of England and Wales* (Cambridge University Press, 1946), Ch. IX.

Article

HOWARD, D. and PRATT, C. A.: 'The Evolution of Norwich', in *Geography* (September 1941).

Farm Study

'An Arable Farm in North Norfolk' (Association of Agriculture, 1962 onwards).

Maps

Bartholomew's ½-inch maps, sheets 21 and 26.

¼-inch geological map sheet 12 indicates the drift deposits of Norfolk. The only 1-inch geological maps available are in the south of the region, where sheets 206, 207 and 208 illustrate the boulder clay and East Suffolk sands regions.

The new 2½-inch Land Use Sheet 442 (Thetford) illustrates Breckland.

CHAPTER TWENTY-ONE

SOUTH-EAST ENGLAND

I N T H E W H O L E of the British Isles there is no better-defined region than south-east England. Its special character springs both from its regular geological structure, and from its proximity to Continental Europe. The pattern of its curving bands of strata is reflected in its relief and drainage, and in its systems of farming. It has experienced successive waves of invaders from Bronze Age to Norman times, and many of them have left traces of their cultures. Here was the birth of the British navy in the shape of the Confederation of the Cinque Ports; yet by a curious twist of fortune some of these historic towns now foster rather than hinder the Continental traffic, and Dover is by far the greatest passenger port in Britain. The region has produced two major breeds of sheep and one of cattle, and is the foremost producer of fruit and hops. Finally, as its alternative name of 'the Weald' suggests, south-east England is still one of the most thickly wooded areas of the British Isles.

It is usual to define south-east England in terms of the three counties of Kent, Surrey, and Sussex; this simple definition is suitable providing that we omit the built-up areas of London from Surrey and Kent.

Structurally the area consists of an eroded dome, elongated in an east-west direction and partially invaded in the east by the English Channel. Its eastern end is seen beyond the Strait of Dover in the country behind Boulogne, and the white cliffs of Dover have their counterpart in the Chalk 8 kilometres to the west of Calais.

The uplift was slight compared with the folding of the Alps (which took place at the same time), and the tilt of the strata is often of the order of only one or two degrees – far too small to be represented correct to scale on any diagram. Locally, however, the dips are much greater; and in the Hog's Back, west of Guildford, the Chalk dips at 60 degrees, so that its outcrop shrinks to a mere 275 metres in width.

Vast quantities of the Chalk and underlying strata have been eroded from the higher parts of the dome, and in three small areas even the uppermost layers of the Jurassic beds – the Purbeck

– are exposed. Over most of the region, then, the outcrops of today represent the edges of beds whose upper surfaces are concealed by the strata which rest on them. These outcrops form roughly concentric narrow bands around the core of older strata in the central Weald (Fig. 90), and their relation one to another is seen in the generalized section (Fig. 89).

Since the various strata differ in resistance to erosion, they have been removed at different rates. The Chalk, Lower Greensand, and Hastings Beds stand out as ridges or hills largely because they are porous: the water percolates before it has a chance to erode – hence the prominent inward-facing escarpments of the North and South Downs and of Ragstone Edge, and the hilly central area of the Forest Ridges. Conversely, the Gault and Weald Clays have been worn away more quickly to form the Vale of Holmesdale and the North and South Clay Vales. The symmetry of the relief is broken by the absence of a Lower Greensand scarp in the south, for the outcrop here is too narrow to have much effect on the surface.

When examined in detail the 'dome' resolves itself into a large number of discontinuous, parallel upfolds: the Isle of Thanet owes its existence to an upfold which brings the Chalk to the surface again north of the main escarpment of the North Downs; and about 70 km to the west another upfold exposes the Chalk again in the Hoo Peninsula, where it is quarried for the cement works at Cliffe. In the South Downs an upfold whose axis runs south of Lewes and north of Eastbourne substantially increases the width of the Chalk outcrop there. The long westward-pointing finger of Weald Clay south-west of Haslemere results from the erosion of another upfold, so that the country around Petersfield is almost a Weald in miniature. Other folds account for the erratic shapes of the outcrops north-east of Haslemere. Detailed mapping in the

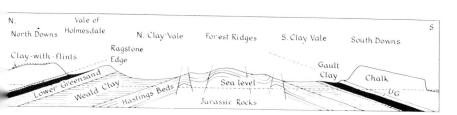

Fig. 89. GEOLOGICAL SECTION ACROSS SOUTH-EAST ENGLAND

The faults and folds in the Hastings Beds are diagrammatic. The length of the section is about 65 kilometres. UG signifies Upper Greensand.

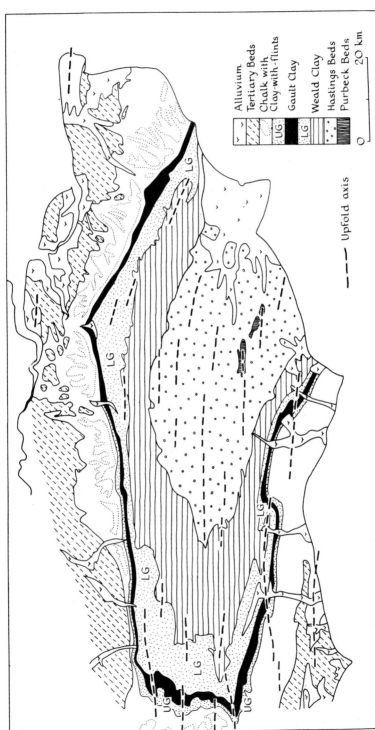

Fig. 90. SOUTH-EAST ENGLAND: GEOLOGY

The upfold axes are reflected in the shapes of the outcrops. The apparent absence of folds in the Weald Clay is due to the fact that major structures cannot be recognized there. UG signifies Upper Greensand; LG, Lower Greensand.

Alluvium
Tertiary Beds
Chalk with
Clay-with-flints
UG
Gault Clay
LG
Weald Clay
Hastings Beds
Purbeck Beds

0   20 km

— — — Upfold axis

central Weald has indicated the existence of many faults as well as folds; but it has not proved possible to locate these structures in the soft Weald Clay.

The rivers at first sight pursue strange courses, for they cut across the structure rather than follow it: both in the north and in the south the main streams have cut gaps right through the Chalk. Yet the original drainage on the newly uplifted dome must have been generally east and west, conforming with the pattern of folds which we have noticed: relics of this original drainage are seen in the two Rothers of Sussex. As Professor D. L. Linton has pointed out, most of the early river system was obliterated by the sea of Pliocene times, whose waves cut a new level surface over much of the south-east. When this surface was raised and slightly arched the ancestors of the present rivers began their northerly or southerly courses irrespective of the underlying structure.

The rivers have had considerable influence on human affairs. The Medway is used by ocean vessels as far as Rochester, by coasters as far as New Hythe, and by barges as far as Maidstone. The river gaps are utilized by roads and railways, and the concentration of traffic has aided the rise of towns such as Dorking, Leatherhead, and Guildford in the north, and Arundel and Lewes in the south.

Historical Geography and the Changing Coastline

A wealth of remains from all the major periods suggests that south-east England was well known to early man. The Thames gravels at Swanscombe have yielded one of the few discoveries to date from Palæolithic times. A Mesolithic settlement and boat have been found at Murston (near Sittingbourne), and many other sites of the same age are known in the Lower Greensand areas and in the High Weald. An interesting and isolated group of megaliths (monuments consisting of huge stones) adorns the southern entrance to the Medway gap, and show that Neolithic man appreciated the geography of the area: the Pilgrims' Way, which passes close to the group, probably originated at this time. The many round barrows which survive on the Sussex downs are evidence of Bronze Age occupation. In the same area Mr E. C. Curwen has drawn attention to the remarkable concentration of settlement in Iron Age times: in the stretch of downs between the Adur and Ouse there are 32 sites and remains of cultivation at all heights from 60 to 180 metres (see Fig. 14, p. 59); and the defensive needs of the whole tribe may have been met by the hill fort of the Caburn, south-east of Lewes.

The coming of the Romans marks a new phase in the human occupation of the south-east: a network of military roads was laid out, lowland towns were established, and the region gained a measure of unity. The Romans founded Canterbury, Rochester, Chichester, and Dover, where they guided the Channel crossing by twin lighthouses; they worked the iron ores of the Weald (about ten of their furnace sites are known), and threaded the area by four parallel roads; they established the dip-slope route along the North Downs from Canterbury to London – still used by the present A2; and they built about 50 villas as the centres of farming estates.

The traditional landing-point of the Saxon invaders of Britain is placed at Pegwell Bay, at the southern entrance of the Wantsum – the strait which then separated Thanet from the mainland. Early place-names suggest that north Kent and the Sussex coast were soon occupied by settler groups; and by the sixth century Kent and Sussex had emerged as separate kingdoms. In their turn Danes and Normans invaded the south-east: by the time of the Domesday survey the pattern of village settlement as we know it today had been established: whole strings of villages followed the foot of the Chalk and Lower Greensand scarps, where water was available from springs; in the Chalk downs the settlers clung to the lower slopes of the dry valleys, where the water table was nearer the surface; they sought out the river gravels, which were near the streams for water, yet out of reach of flood; they penetrated the woodland of the High Weald to settle in the valleys; but the sticky clay soils of the Weald Clay they avoided almost completely.

Nowhere are the effects of a changing coastline on human activities better illustrated than in south-east England. Several factors, physical and human, have acted in combination. In Neolithic times, what is now Romney Marsh was then a wide bay, whose cliff, forming the inner edge of the Marsh, can still be traced. A rise in the level of the land relative to the sea allowed the Romans to drain part of the marsh by the construction of Rhee Wall, now followed by the road between Appledore and New Romney; and the reclamation of the marshes to the west took place in Saxon and Norman times in the shelter of the shingle ridges of Dungeness, and in spite of a fall in the land surface of about 1·5 metres between Roman times and 1300.

Since that time the land has been stationary in relation to the sea and the longshore drift has been allowed full play. Along the south coast this is normally from west to east, in accordance with the direction of the dominant winds. Shingle banks tend to grow across the mouths of the rivers, deflecting them eastward, and a striking example of this is seen at the mouth of the Adur, by Shoreham. Bays turn into lagoons; rivers clog up the lagoons; and the process is speeded up by man, who drains the marshes, so that Pevensey Levels, Romney Marsh, and the Wantsum now all form valuable pastures.

The closing of the Wantsum is of some interest. In Roman times it provided a sheltered waterway forming a short cut to London, protected by the forts of Regulbium (Reculver) and Rutupiae (Richborough). But a southward drift built up a shingle bank and diverted the navigable channel to the south, so that Richborough gave place to Stonar (farther south), and Stonar to Sandwich. Then the current appears to have reversed its direction to build up an outer ridge pointing northward, and even Sandwich was deserted by the sea. Small ships used the Wantsum until the end of the fifteenth century; but the removal of the tidal scour led to the accumulation of river mud, so that Thanet soon ceased to be an island.

In Romney Marsh the fortunes of several towns have been influenced by coastal changes. Old Romney at the time of the Domesday survey had a fine harbour and five churches; but continued reclamation of the marsh pushed the Rother, which fed its harbour, farther and farther west, so that now the village is 5 kilometres from the sea.

Old Winchelsea, on the other hand, now lies beneath the waves. It had become more and more exposed to south-westerly gales owing to the erosion of the cliffs at Fairlight (east of Hastings), and it was finally destroyed by a tempest in 1287. Fortunately the far-sighted Edward I had already prepared a new town for the inhabitants (the present Winchelsea), which prospered for 150 years. But the eastward drift has clogged its former harbour, and the still unfinished town now lies a mile inland, with one of its fine gates astride a country road.

It is difficult now to imagine the bustle which must have characterized the ports of the south-east in the Middle Ages. Their inhabitants built and manned the ships which in time of need served the king: in the twelfth century they were expected to supply between them 55 vessels for the fleet. The original Cinque Ports were Hastings, Dover, Romney, Hythe, and Sandwich; but during the course of the thirteenth century Rye and Winchelsea became equal to them in status. These head ports were aided by 'limbs' which numbered about 30: most of them have decayed. Some, like Tenterden, are now quite inland and deserted by their creeks; others, like Bekesbourn and Bulverhythe, we cannot even trace.

By the early sixteenth century the naval services of the Cinque Ports had ceased, and south-east England had become primarily a farming region.

Land Use

There are important links between the geological outcrops and the types of farming practised in south-east England; but the relationship is not the simple one of cause and effect. Physical conditions provide opportunities to the farmer; but what use he makes of them is sometimes a matter of economics or tradition. This is well illustrated in the fruit-growing areas; but for the moment we will examine the differences which can be seen in farming as one moves from the younger to the older rocks.

The Chalk rim varies in width, in elevation, and in surface cover; but everywhere water is scarce. It is available in the dry valleys from fairly shallow wells; but the plateau surface is 60 to 90 metres above the water table. Here the animals are supplied from 'dew ponds': these have prepared clay bottoms, and are doubtless fed by rainfall rather than by the dew. It is not surprising that the few villages of the Chalk country lie deep in the sheltered valleys.

The rolling Chalk hills, with their smooth, convex slopes, their dry, thin soils, and springy turf are best illustrated in the South Downs. The sheep breed of that name was developed in the small isolated Chalk area east of Lewes (where we have already noticed the hill fort of the Caburn). As in East Anglia, the sheep were associated with mixed farming: they nibbled the grass on the downs during the day for most of the year; but at night they were herded into the low-lying fields of turnips or clover grown specially for them. Owing to increasing labour costs, this traditional system has declined in favour of grass feeding, and sheep are giving way to cattle in view of the growing demand for fresh milk from the coast resorts. Nevertheless, at Findon (north of Worthing) the old-established sheep fair survives.

The North Downs stand in sharp contrast owing to their extensive cover of Clay-with-flints. This sticky, reddish clay containing masses of stones represents the insoluble material which remains after rainwater has dissolved away the Chalk, but includes also the remnants of a former cover of Tertiary material. The highest parts of the North Downs, together with the slopes that are too steep for cultivation, are largely left in woodland. Beech is the characteristic tree: it tolerates limy soils, though it will not grow in waterlogged conditions, and its dense foliage prevents the growth of all except shade-loving species such as yew, box, elder, and ivy. A fine belt of woodland thus extends along the crest of the North Downs in an almost unbroken line from Guildford to Folkestone: the tracts north and east of Ashford are managed by the Forestry Commission.

On the lower dip slopes the Clay-with-flint soils are successfully cultivated for wheat and roots in mixed farms, and lower still these areas have been invaded in places by orchards.

The Chalk scarp everywhere faces the Weald in a bold rampart. At its base is the Chalk Marl, a soft variety of Chalk which contains a relatively high proportion of clayey matter. This rests on the Upper Greensand which, though a thin formation, outcrops everywhere at the foot of the Chalk scarp in Sussex and Surrey, but fades out just over the Kent border, near Otford. In places the Upper Greensand is only one field wide; but it forms a characteristic bench at the foot of the scarp (Fig. 89, p. 305), and its easily worked soils, leavened by downwash from the Chalk Marl, are usually under the plough.

The Gault Clay rings the Weald with an outcrop about a mile wide on the average. A bluish clay, it gives rise to cold and sticky soils which are almost everywhere left either in permanent pasture for cattle or in woodland. They can be improved only by careful drainage and liberal application of lime, and it was for this purpose that in the past so many small pits were opened up in the Chalk scarps. Near Paddlesworth, in the Medway valley, the Gault is being worked for cement-making.

The Gault forms a prominent longitudinal valley in the north (the Vale of Holmesdale), but in the south it merges with the Weald Clay to form the Southern Clay Vale, or Vale of Sussex. It is of great significance in water-supply, for the Gault provides the impermeable seal below the Chalk and Upper Greensand, so that their accumulated water reaches the surface in a line of springs near the junction of Gault and Upper Greensand. Here the Saxon village was built; and the parish boundaries of today still reflect the varied types of land which were available close at hand. The manor was often long and narrow in shape running across the outcrops: the village was close to the spring and set amid the cultivated fields (Upper Greensand); above it were the sheep pastures (Chalk) and below it the cattle pastures (Gault), while farther afield was the woodland which supplied fuel and pannage for swine (Lower Greensand) (*cf.* Fig. 16, p. 64).

The Lower Greensand comprises four beds which not only differ among themselves but change their character as they are followed around the Weald. The combined outcrop is widest in the west (14 km, west of Haslemere): this is due partly to the existence of local upfolds and partly to an increase in the thickness of the beds. In the north the average width is about 5 km (for example, at Sevenoaks), but in the south it shrinks to less than 2 km. The major components of the Lower Greensand are porous sands, and it is this rather than their hardness which allows them to resist erosion and to stand up as hills. In Kent, however, hard bands of sandy limestone – ragstone – appear, and form one of the most useful building stones of the region, and the nearest to London. 'Kentish Rag' has been used in the building of the Tower of London, and in the castle, cathedral, and town walls of Rochester, and is still being quarried north of Maidstone.

The sandy, leached soils of the Lower Greensand give rise to one of the most extensive tracts of heath-land in southern England: it includes Leith Hill, the Farnham district, and the hilly area around Hindhead. Heather is in many parts accompanied by small pines, oaks, and birch, with gorse and bracken. East of Maidstone, however, the sandy beds are thinner and the water table is sufficiently near the surface to allow the soils to be cultivated, and here the Lower Greensand forms part of the fruit belt of mid-Kent.

The Weald Clay is a thick mass of brownish or bluish clay, reaching a maximum thickness of more than 300 metres. In contrast to the Lower Greensand, it is threaded by many streams, which are fed by the springs at the base of the Greensand. These are the agents which have removed vast quantities of the clay, excavating a broad vale around the central Weald. Its level floor is in places only 18 to 21 m above sea-level; and before the construction of modern sluices there was serious flooding each winter; for example, around Headcorn (north-east of Cranbrook).

In the natural state the clay soils supported damp oak woodland, together with individuals of many other species, such as birch, alder, aspen, poplar, ash, hazel, and willow; and these were the oak woods which supplied the shipbuilding industry of Saxon and medieval times. Today, however, the woodland has been cleared and virtually all the Weald Clay is farmed. The emphasis is on permanent pasture for grazing or mowing, and the object is fresh milk for use in London and the coast resorts. Along the Medway and its tributaries there are deposits of river gravels and loams, and these provide productive arable soils; and even the clay soils are cultivated in places, after careful drainage, liming, and manuring. Typical farms in the Weald Clay belt of north Kent have 50 per cent. of their land under permanent grass and another 11 per cent. under temporary grass. The chief cereals are wheat (9 per cent.) and oats (7 per cent.), while fruit and hops account for a further 6½ per cent. of the area.

The Hastings Beds consist of four members in which clays alternate with sands or soft sandstones, and the general result is that the sandy strata have resisted erosion more than the surrounding Weald Clay. The central Weald is therefore a hilly area, which reaches a maximum height of 208 metres at Crowborough Beacon, and is much dissected by rivers.

It was one of the clay members – the Wadhurst Clay – which yielded the ore for a flourishing iron industry in the central Weald. We have already referred to the Roman workings. Iron was mined again in the Middle Ages from shallow bell-pits whose sites are now overgrown; and it was smelted with the aid of charcoal produced from the local woodland. By the thirteenth century the district was rivalling the Forest of Dean in the supply of iron to London; and at its peak in the early seventeenth century it contained about half the furnaces of the whole country. Power was needed to drive the hammers and to work the bellows and to this end the valleys were dammed and water-wheels were constructed. The sites of 80 furnaces and 90 forges are known: they are widely scattered throughout the central Weald and extend westward on to the Weald Clay. The deciding factor was the existence of a suitable opportunity for water-power. The end of the Weald industry came after the discovery of the possibilities of coke for iron-smelting in 1730, but the last furnace (at Ashburnham) struggled on till about 1820. The many mill ponds and old mills are a reminder of the industry, and there are still roads and paths paved with blast-furnace slag.

The highest summits of Ashdown Forest are clothed in heath ('forest' in this connection means 'common'), while the lower slopes are wooded. The best farm-land is found in the well-watered valley floors. This is the home of the dark red Sussex cattle, claimed to be the oldest purely English breed in the country. For centuries these cattle were reared as draught animals, for ploughing and for conveying the heavy oak logs to the coast. The Sussex is now essentially a beef breed, which will thrive under poor conditions, and is virtually confined to south-east England, where there are more than 100 pedigree herds.

In recent years, however – and this is true of the rest of south-east England – milk-production has increased in importance, and

Sussex cattle are giving place to Shorthorns. Lambs from the nearby marshes are accepted for wintering, and fruit and hops are grown widely.

Romney Marsh

Romney Marsh, the largest area of alluvium in the south-east, now belies its name, for it has been throughly drained. Large tracts, however, are below high-tide level, and there are pumping stations at Appledore and Kenardington to raise the water into the Royal Military Canal. The latter, which now serves as a drain, was built as a defensive ditch when Napoleon threatened to invade this country.

Romney Marsh is reputed to be the most intensively stocked sheep pasture in the world. The Romney (or Kent) breed, which was developed here, is a hardy animal which alone can withstand the rigorous climate of the Marsh with very little attention. The best of the pastures will fatten 15 to 25 sheep to the hectare in summer without any supplementary feed. During the winter most of the lambs are sent into the uplands; but about a third of the animals remain behind throughout the winter, sheltered by only a few hurdles, and rarely receiving extra fodder. There are sheep sales at Ashford, Lyminge, and Maidstone.

Since the Second World War there has been an increase in arable farming in the Marsh, particularly by farmers with experience of the Lincolnshire Fens; and in the Burmarsh area (towards the north-east) one can see the mechanized cultivation and the fruit- and bulb-growing more characteristic of the Fens. Elsewhere beetroot, beans, carrots, and grass are grown for seed: indeed, contrary to the general belief, the typical Marsh farmer has only 50 per cent. of his land under permanent grass. But in the eleven 'marshland' parishes there are about 90,000 sheep.

Fruit and Hops

Kent possesses 28 per cent. of the total fruit area of England and Wales. This area includes one-third of the apple orchards (excluding cider orchards) and nearly one-third of the plum and damson orchards, 46 per cent. of the pear area (apart from perry pears), and more than 70 per cent. of the cherry orchards.

So remarkable a concentration of fruit-growing is not easily explained in terms of physical factors alone, though these are generally favourable. South-east England is one of the warmest parts of the country in summer, and is the sunniest in both summer and winter (the record is held by Eastbourne, with an average of about 1800 sunny hours a year); the Kent coast is also one of the

Plate 8.   A CHERRY ORCHARD AT TEYNHAM, KENT

In the production of fresh milk, vegetables, and fruit the English farmer can compete successfully with overseas producers. The picture illustrates a cherry orchard midway between Sittingbourne and Faversham, in the heart of the fruit belt of north Kent. The soils, derived from the brickearth and the Thanet Beds, are light, and warm up quickly in spring and summer. There is direct communication with London by rail and by the trunk road, A2. Sheep are grazed in the orchards in the early part of the year, but no animals are allowed in when the branches are heavy with fruit.

Photo John Topham Ltd.

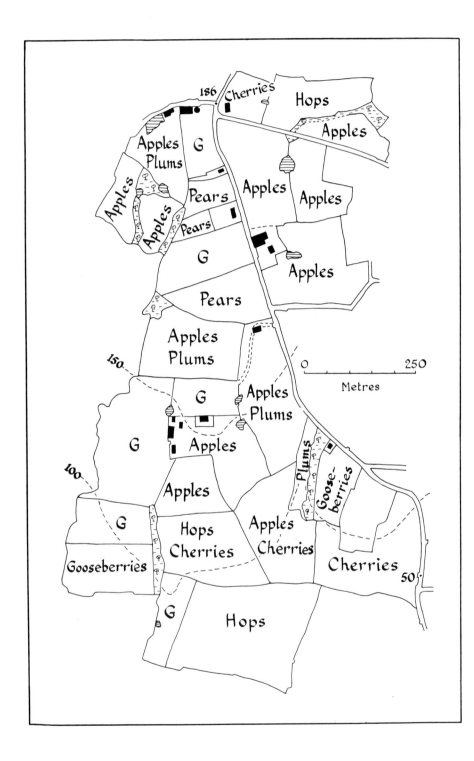

driest parts of the country, with less than 500 mm of rain. The proximity of the sea reduces to some extent the danger of frost, but this is still a risk when the blossom has formed, and high winds sometimes ruin a promising crop. Experience has led the grower to avoid the valley bottoms, where 'pools' of cold air are liable to collect on still nights.

In the main the orchards have been planted on the sandy and loamy soils: these include the brickearths, terrace gravels, and Thanet Sands of the estuarine belt between Sittingbourne and Faversham, the Lower Greensand soils of the Maidstone district, and the sandy soils of the central Weald (Fig. 91 and Plate 8). But in the Rochester area fruit-growing has extended on to the Clay-with-flints and even the London Clay, and it is clear that soil alone is not the controlling element.

Economic factors are probably as important as soil and climate. London provides not only the market but much of the labour: one farmer near Tenterden maintains hut accommodation for 50 families; the East Malling research station too is of fundamental importance, and since its establishment in 1913 it has succeeded in placing fruit-growing on a scientific footing.

The apple is by far the chief orchard fruit in Kent: dessert and cooking apples are grown in approximately equal quantities but the modern tendency is to increase the proportion of dessert varieties. Plums (with damsons) and cherries follow, and occupy roughly equal areas, though each amounts to only one-quarter the area of the apples. Fruit-growing is increasing, and the area planted in the 1950's was higher than ever before.

In contrast, the area under hops is declining. The reasons are complex: it is due in part to a higher yield per hectare, and in part to an increase in imported hops. The plant needs protection from strong winds, and hop gardens tend to occupy the valley bottoms. There are very many varieties of hops, which are suited to a wide range of soils. In particular each grower prefers to cultivate early, medium, and late varieties so as to economize on his labour supply. The chief hop areas lie to the south of Maidstone: they include Lower Greensand soils, and extend on to the Weald Clay and beyond into the High Weald.

Fig. 91.   A FRUIT FARM IN KENT

This farm of 84 hectares lies 2 km south of Tenterden in the south of Kent and not in the main fruit areas of north and mid-Kent. The soils are derived from the Wadhurst Clay and Ashdown Sand in the Hastings Beds. G stands for permanent grassland – usually grazed by sheep. The lined areas represent ponds. Heights are in feet. *By courtesy of the Association of Agriculture.*

The hop area is now less than half its extent 50 years ago, but is remaining steady. Kent is by far the leading producer in England and Wales, and accounts for 56 per cent. of the hop area of the country.

Industry and Towns

While south-east England is still predominantly rural in the interior, we find around the edges an almost continuous string of resorts; there is an important concentration of industry in the coastal area of north Kent; there are the packet stations of Dover, Folkestone, and Newhaven, and a small coalfield to the north-west of Dover.

The Coal Measures lie far below the Chalk downs between Canterbury and Dover, and 14 workable seams are known in them. Four collieries are working – at Chislet, Snowdown, Betteshanger, and Tilmanstone. The latter, with a shaft depth of 925 metres, is one of the deepest pits in the country. Unlike most others, the Kent coalfield has not given rise to an industrial area. From 1930 onward for a few years there was a surplus available for export, and a 12 km ropeway was constructed from Tilmanstone to Dover for that purpose. Today the whole of the output of $1\frac{1}{2}$ to 2 million tonnes annually is absorbed within the region, chiefly in power stations.

Two old-established industries of the lower Medway area consist of paper-making and the manufacture of cement; newer additions include mechanical and electrical engineering and oil-refining.

Paper-making dates back to the sixteenth century here, for the second mill to be built in the country (in 1588) was situated at Dartford: it seems that the purity of the water was one of the early considerations. Today paper-manufacturers control the quality of their process water, and the chief concern is the ease with which the fuel and raw materials can be imported. There are now ten or so mills in the Medway district, though some of these are quite small. Those at New Hythe (near Aylesford) and Sittingbourne, however, are outstanding.

The former (A. E. Reed's) is the largest mixed mill in Europe: it receives its pulp and coal by barge, transhipped at Rochester; but the small china clay coasters from Cornwall berth at the mill wharf on the river (Plate 9). The latter (Bowater's) contains the widest paper-making machine in the world, with a wire width of 813 cm, and the town of Sittingbourne is almost completely dependent on the two Bowater mills. They are supplied through the private port of Ridham Dock, which receives cargoes of logs and

Plate 9. THE MILLS OF THE REED PAPER GROUP AT
NEW HYTHE, NEAR AYLESFORD, ON THE RIVER
MEDWAY

*Paper-making requires bulky raw materials (woodpulp and china
clay), large quantities of coal for the powerhouse, and ample supplies
of water, both for process and cooling purposes. These requirements
are best satisfied on a navigable waterway, though the mills illustrated
receive most of their coal by rail.*

*The Reed mills include 15 paper-making machines, and are among
the largest in the world. The woodpulp is transhipped in Rochester
and arrives by barge (there are at least 14 barges in the picture); the
china clay arrives by small coaster direct from Cornwall. These
works employ 7000 people and are well placed to supply the London
market. The camera is pointing downstream.*

Photo by courtesy of the Reed Paper Group

pulp from Scandinavia and Canada, of coal from the north-east coast, and of china clay from Devon and Cornwall. There is an export trade, but much of the paper consists of newsprint for use in London.

Cement-manufacture has a clear physical basis, for this is one of the few districts where the chief raw material – limestone, in the form of chalk – approaches close to navigable water. Since 1851, when the first works was established at Frindsbury (north of Rochester) at least 21 separate undertakings are known to have been operating in the area. Today only five remain, but they are large, and together produce about one-fifth of the country's output. Four of them lie on the left bank of the Medway, between Snodland and Frindsbury (there is no railway on the right bank); the fifth is farther north, at Cliffe, where, as we have seen, an upfold brings the Chalk to the surface. Clay is supplied for these works from the Medway and Thames alluvium and from the Gault outcrop to the south; coal to heat the kilns comes by collier from the north-east coast or by rail from the Kent coalfield.

The engineering industries of Rochester may be traced back to the pool of skilled labour which was assembled in the district for work in the Royal Dockyard at Chatham. The seaplane and steam-roller works have long since departed, but their former premises are occupied by varied metal-working plants. Rochester is now noted as the home of electrical components for vehicles, and of 'Winget' concrete-mixing plant.

At the mouth of the estuary, on the Isle of Grain, is the Kent Oil Refinery, a relative newcomer to the district, established in 1953. The regional need was an addition to the supplies of petroleum products for the London area; locally a site was required fairly remote from built-up areas (on safety grounds), with a depth of water sufficient for the berthing of ocean tankers. These conditions were satisfied on the south side of the Isle of Grain, where a shel- tered channel, with 12 metres of water at all states of the tide, ap- proaches close to the shore. Today large tankers laden with crude oil from Kuwait arrive at the refinery, and smaller vessels distribute the refined products along the coast. Petroleum is by far the chief cargo handled on the Medway.

A whole string of resorts lines the coasts of south-east England, from Bognor Regis round the Sussex and Kent coasts as far as Herne Bay, taking in among smaller towns, Worthing, Brighton, Eastbourne, Hastings, Ramsgate, Margate. They are the product of only the last two hundred years, and their rapid growth waited until the coming of the railway, the motor-coach, and the family car.

Brighton (pop. 166,081) is the largest of these resorts today, and was the first to develop; indeed, it may fairly claim to be the pioneer of all seaside resorts. In 1750 a certain Dr Richard Russell of Lewes published a treatise on the use of sea-water in diseases of the glands: he recommended his patients to drink not spa water but sea-water. The idea found favour, and the Doctor found it worth while to move to Brighton, 10 km away. With the provision of stage coaches from London the number of visitors increased; and the Prince of Wales (later George IV) set the fashion when he paid his first visit in 1783. The following year he began to build what was to become his favourite palace – the Royal Pavilion – which still adds a whimsical air to the resort. The speed with which Brighton grew was unique for the period: the 600 houses which it contained in 1770 had multiplied twelvefold by 1831.

All the coast resorts depend for their existence on the nearness of London, and on the provision of speedy road and rail transport to and from the metropolis. The pre-eminence of Brighton among the towns of the south coast has been conceded by the establishment near there in 1961 of the first of the new universities. The general port for the large and growing population of this coast is Shoreham – the only commercial port between Southampton and Dover. Its activities are chiefly confined to the import of coal and petroleum.

In Newhaven, Folkestone, and Dover the south-east provides some of the best examples of packet stations in the British Isles. These are specialized ports for the handling of passengers, mails, and perishable and valuable cargoes across the narrow seas. They depend on the co-ordination of road and rail traffic with the arrival and departure of Channel boats. The harbours are artificial, and most of these ports would have disappeared were it not for their position between London on the one hand and the Continent on the other.

The cross-Channel traffic is not new: it can be traced back to Roman times; what is new is the extraordinary increase in the traffic in recent years. In 1860 the three ports were used by 215,000 people; by 1887 the number had more than doubled (486,000); by 1900 it had almost doubled again (871,000), and by 1933 it had reached more than a million (1,135,000). In 1956 Dover alone was used by 1,791,000 people; by 1969 the number had more than doubled, to reach 4,388,000, and there seems no limit to the growth of the traffic.

The port had its origin at the mouth of the small river Dour (Fig. 92). During the nineteenth century enclosed docks were

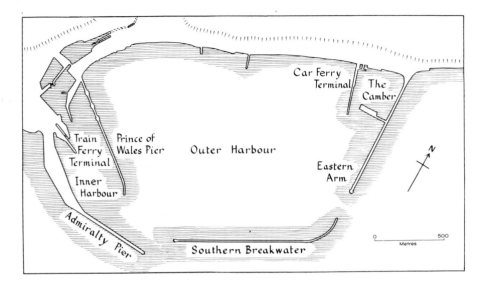

Fig. 92. THE PORT OF DOVER

The original harbour, selected by the Romans, was the mouth of the river Dour: here is the only gap in the rampart of chalk cliffs. The inner enclosed docks were built during the nineteenth century. The modern harbour was designed as a naval base, and is one of the largest in the world. The Camber, built as a submarine base, now forms the fishing harbour. During the 1930's some coal was shipped from the Eastern Arm; now there is no surplus for export. The passenger traffic is handled at the Admiralty and Prince of Wales Piers. Dover is by far our greatest passenger port. *By courtesy of the Dover Harbour Board.*

built; but the modern harbour, designed as a naval base, with 5 km of piers, was completed in the twentieth century. It now forms one of the largest artificial harbours in the world. Dover introduced a train ferry to Dunkirk in 1936; more recently, in 1953 Dover pioneered in the provision of car ferry facilities, which have proved increasingly popular; and the port now handles more than three times as many passengers as its nearest rival in the United Kingdom (Holyhead).

Newhaven is 35 km nearer to London than Dover, and has recently installed a car ferry: its opposite number on the Continent is Dieppe. Folkestone was developed in the days of railway rivalry as a competitor to Dover. Today it is associated particularly with the Boulogne route, but it also shares the Calais and Ostend traffic with Dover, and a unified control allows co-operation rather than competition.

The newest way (since 1968) to cross the Channel is by hovercraft, from Dover to Boulogne or from Ramsgate to Calais. Each 'flight' accommodates 254 passengers and 30 cars, and the crossing time is cut from about $1\frac{1}{2}$ hours to 35 minutes. A great advantage of the hovercraft is that its berthing requirements are minimal: the huge machine rides over the waves, up the sand and on to a concrete ramp and platform and there she sits!

The extraordinary increase in the cross-Channel traffic during the last decade has led to a revival of the project for a Channel tunnel. In 1964 the British and French Governments reached agreement in principle on the construction of a railway tunnel, and feasibility studies are currently in progress.

Throughout the development of south-east England we can detect the influence of the sea. Today that influence remains as powerful as ever.

FOR FURTHER READING

Books

A Fruit and Hop Farm in Kent (Association of Agriculture, 1952 onward).

CURWEN, E. C.: *The Archaeology of Sussex* (Methuen, 1937).

GALLOIS, R. W.: *The Wealden District*, British Regional Geology Handbooks (H.M.S.O., 1965).

GARRAD, G. H.: *A Survey of the Agriculture of Kent* (Newman Neame, 1954).

REES, HENRY: *British Ports and Shipping* (Harrap, 1958), Chapter 7.

WOOLDRIDGE, S. W., and GOLDRING, F.: *The Weald* (Collins, 1953).

WOOLDRIDGE, S. W., and LINTON, D. L.: *Structure, Surface and Drainage in South East England* (G. Philip, 1955).

Articles

GILBERT, E. W.: 'The Growth of Brighton', in *Geographical Journal* (September 1949).

LINTON, D. L.: 'The Sussex Rivers', in *Geography* (November 1956).

Maps

The 1-inch geological sheets 272 (Chatham) and 288 (Maidstone) illustrate the North Downs with their capping of Clay-with-Flints and include much of the orchard land. Sheet 318 (Brighton) is useful for a study of the bare Chalk of the South Downs: it includes examples of spring-line settlements and shows the effect of the longshore drift in deflecting the month of the Adur.

The region is covered by Bartholomew's $\frac{1}{2}$-inch sheets, Nos. 6, 9, and 10.

CHAPTER TWENTY-TWO

THE HAMPSHIRE BASIN
AND THE CHANNEL ISLANDS

IN THE HAMPSHIRE BASIN structure and drainage agree to produce a region with clear physical boundaries. Its limits are formed by Chalk scarps in an almost complete rim except in the south, where submergence has detached the Chalk of the Isle of Wight. So defined, the region includes the county of Hampshire (except for a narrow belt bordering Berkshire in the north), the southern half of Wiltshire, and most of Dorset. The Marlborough and Berkshire Downs we allocate to the Thames Basin.

Here is the largest expanse of the Chalk in Britain, together with one of the two districts of Tertiary strata. Without coal and iron, the region lacks heavy industry, and, apart from Southampton, is almost completely agricultural in character. It has close links with the sea: Portsmouth is a naval base; Bournemouth, Bognor Regis, Swanage, and Weymouth are coast resorts, and the regional capital, Southampton, is also a major port. The Channel Islands, physically closely linked with Normandy, have shipping connections with Weymouth and Southampton, and may be considered as outlying parts of the region.

Physical Basis

A distinctive feature of the Hampshire Basin is the extensive exposure and great breadth of the Chalk: it forms the subsoil over an area 100 km from east to west and 32 from north to south. The eastern half of this Chalk plateau forms the Hampshire Downs; the western section is Salisbury Plain. It is perhaps hardly necessary to observe that the term 'Plain' is a gross misnomer.

The Chalk was thrown in Tertiary times into three parallel folds which range east and west; hence the crenellated western edge of the Chalk of Salisbury Plain. The relief is 'inverted' – that is to say, the valleys represent denuded upfolds (where the strata have been stretched and weakened), while the intervening ridges represent the cores of downfolds (where the strata have been compressed and strengthened). From north to south the three upfolds are seen in the Vale of Pewsey, the Vale of Warminster, and the Vale of Wardour. In the south-west there is in addition a small elongated structural basin, rimmed by the North and South Dorset Downs and drained eastward by the river Frome.

The Chalk plateau has been deeply dissected by the Salisbury Avon and its tributaries, and by the Itchen and the Test. The larger streams have trenched below the water table so that they are permanently flowing; but the minor tributary valleys are shallower, and form the dry valleys which are typical of Chalk downlands. Within the plateau several erosion surfaces have been recognized; thus in north-east Hampshire Mr A. J. Stevens has distinguished a summit peneplain above 212 m, marine (wave-cut) platforms at 210 and 181 m, and a Chalk surface lately stripped of its Tertiary deposits at a lower level. These surfaces are important to the geographer in that the soil formed on each has its characteristic texture. The highest surface carries the most mature soil, for it has had the longest period in which to form: it is relatively deep, but acid and sticky in wet weather, and is therefore usually under grass. At lower levels the soils are lighter and more easily worked, and hence often cultivated. On the lowest surface the soil is 'immature', thin and calcareous, and traditionally has been utilized for arable and sheep farming as in the Heath and Wolds of Lincolnshire (p. 274). More recently the sheep have been removed and the land has been farmed in large estates with a high degree of mechanized cultivation.

The southern rim of the basin is formed by steeply dipping strata in the 'Isle' of Purbeck and the Isle of Wight. During the Alpine earth storm the pressure was from the south, so that the northern limbs of the upfolds are steep, while the southern limbs are gently inclined (*cf.* the Mendips, p. 180). The principle is well illustrated in the Isle of Wight: in the centre of the island an east-west ridge is formed by the Chalk dipping in places at 85° – almost vertically; yet in the south the strata are almost horizontal. Between the two outcrops the Chalk has been eroded to form a miniature 'weald' floored by the Lower Greensand, whose rapid crumbling along the coast has resulted in the formation of Sandown bay.

The centre of the Hampshire Basin is occupied by extensive spreads of the newer Tertiary strata, particularly the Bagshot and Barton Beds. Predominantly sandy in character, these have given rise to porous, leached soils which would not repay cultivation, and are left in forest. West of Southampton Water is the New Forest, and there are other tracts of woodland to the east and in the northern half of the Isle of Wight. The higher parts are capped by 'plateau gravels' which must have been laid down by streams of considerable volume. The soils which have developed on them are coarse and porous, and the land is left in heath. In the Ringwood portion of the New Forest there is a close correlation between the plateau gravels and the heath.

The coasts of the region bear the marks of submergence. Poole Harbour, Southampton Water, and the harbours of the Portsmouth district are evidently drowned valleys; and the geological strata exposed in the Isle of Wight match so closely that of the mainland that it is clear that both have a common history. Early in the Neolithic period the land is believed to have stood 30 metres higher than at present, so that the Isle of Wight was part of the mainland; it is likely that at that time all the Hampshire rivers joined to find a common outlet south-east of Selsey Bill.

Historical Geography
The chalklands were particularly attractive to early man. They provided clean, dry sites for settlement, and with the water table higher than at present, drinking-water would have been present in springs and shallow wells which are now dry. The extent of woodland which the Chalk originally carried has been debated; but movement through it must have been easier than through the damp oak forests of the clay lowlands. Flints were abundant, and provided early man with his tools; and locally there were large biocks of sandstone scattered about – the sarsens, or greywethers, believed to be remnants of a bed which formerly covered the Chalk. These huge stones were used in the construction of megalithic monuments such as Stonehenge and Avebury. Salisbury Plain, the focus of the Chalk ridges of England, was the centre of the pre-Roman cultures, and here their remains are most in evidence. The Bronze Age is represented by henge monuments and scores of round barrows; extensive areas of Celtic fields and a host of hill forts remain from the Iron Age.

In Roman times this was a closely settled region. Within 33 kilometres of Winchester are the known sites of about 40 villas. Winchester, Dorchester, and Chichester were tribal capitals; and Old Sarum was the focus of five roads (see Fig. 15, p. 62). This was clearly a productive region.

The Romans placed their towns in the valleys, but there appears to have been little systematic occupation and cultivation of the valleys until the Saxons arrived. Today the main valleys of the Chalk plateau have a dense rural population while the intervening ridges are uninhabited. Closely spaced villages border each stream; each occupies a patch of river gravel, and each is the focus of a parish which extends uphill as far as the ridgeway. The names of the villages betray their Saxon origin (Fig. 93).

Market towns have grown at the junctions of the valleys: Salisbury, at the focus of five valleys, is the best example; but the region lacks the close net of market towns which is to be seen in East Anglia. The higher parts of Salisbury Plain are of little agricultural value, and are used as military training grounds: here

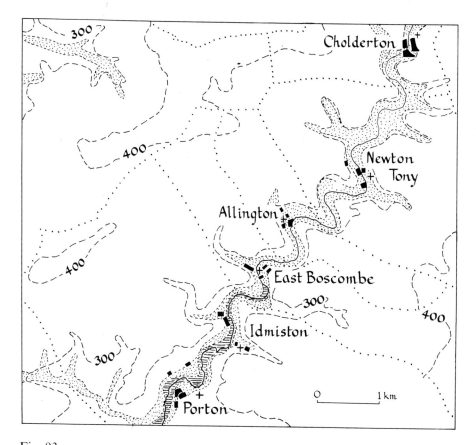

Fig. 93. VILLAGE SITES IN THE HAMPSHIRE CHALKLANDS

This is part of the gravel-strewn valley of the Bourne, a tributary of the Salisbury Avon. A string of villages occupies the gravels (shown by stippling). The stream is tiny and in dry weather ceases to flow. Since it forms no barrier, the parishes span the valley. River alluvium is indicated by horizontal shading; the Chalk is left unshaded. Heights are in feet. *Based on the Geological Survey 1-inch map.*

are large camps such as Larkhill, Bulford, and Tidworth, about 16 km north of Salisbury. The Tertiary beds too are of limited farming use, so that the towns of the region have grown in response to particular needs. Chichester (pop. 20,547), Winchester (pop. 31,041), Salisbury (pop. 35,271), and Dorchester (pop. 13,737) originated as Roman centres and have remained relatively small market towns. Portsmouth (pop. 196,973) owes its development mainly to the dockyard which was established by Henry VIII; Weymouth, Bognor, and Bournemouth are of more recent growth. It is worth while examining some of these more closely, together with the regional capital, Southampton.

Winchester is the lineal descendant of an Iron Age hill fort, situated on St Catherine's Hill, overlooking the river Itchen about 2 km south of the town. The Romans persuaded the Belgae to descend to the valley, and prepared for them a planned capital on a gravel terrace where a narrowing of the floodplain made it easy to bridge the river. The town was revived by the Saxons, and by A.D. 660 had superseded Dorchester as the royal capital and centre of Christianity for Wessex. As King Alfred's city, it can fairly claim to be the earliest capital of England. A walled town in the Middle Ages, it engaged in a considerable wool trade. Today Winchester is the county town and main market centre for the Hampshire chalklands; it has a famous public school and cathedral.

Salisbury, the centre for the western half of the Chalklands, occupies a remarkable nodal site at or near the confluence of five streams (the Nadder, Bourne, Wylye, Ebble, and Avon). The site selected by the Romans was on a hill 3 km north of the present town, and here developed a walled Norman town with its castle and cathedral. But it was cramped, windy, and almost waterless, and in 1220 Bishop le Poore abandoned the hill and occupied a newly planned town in the meadows by the side of the Avon. The cathedral raised by his masons, fashioned during the first flowering of English Gothic architecture, is one of the finest in the land, while the town retains in its centre even today one of the most pleasing examples of medieval town planning. It may be compared with the castle towns of the same period in north Wales (p. 107).

Portsmouth owes its rise to its dockyard. When the site was chosen the bulk of the population was in the south of England, the navy was recruited mainly in the south-east, and our traditional enemies were on the far side of the Channel. The harbour had great strategic value, for its bottleneck entrance was easily defended. The town has now expanded to occupy the whole of Portsea Island,

and has joined hands with the neighbouring resort of Southsea.

Weymouth is both a resort and a port. As a seaside resort it dates from the middle eighteenth century, and here in 1763 the bathing machine made its first appearance in England. The reputation of Weymouth was enhanced when towards the end of the century George III and the royal family paid several visits to the town. The port benefits from an unusually low tidal range; and since it is the nearest English port to the Channel Islands (it is 120 km from Guernsey) it has developed a flourishing trade in both goods and passengers. During the season about £4 millions of tomatoes and nearly £1 million of cut flowers are imported.

About 8 km to the south is the 'Isle' of Portland, which yields one of the most famous of English building stones. Portland stone, a pure white Jurassic limestone, has been used for many of the public buildings in London, including St Paul's Cathedral and the Wren churches. Today most of the quarries are exhausted.

Farming

There is a striking contrast between the rolling Chalk country, with its relatively high proportion of cultivation, and the largely unproductive Tertiary lowlands.

The chalklands themselves, however, exhibit considerable variety. A distinctive unit is Salisbury Plain – an open, rolling grassy downland, formerly providing hill pasture for sheep, but now uninhabited and given over to military purposes. Its eastern limit corresponds broadly with the county boundary between Wiltshire and Hampshire: beyond, the Chalk is partially covered by clay-with-flints, and here the open landscape gives way to small hedged fields, with patches of woodland on the superficial deposits.

Over the greater part of the chalkland arable and sheep farming is predominant. The soils tend to be thin and light: large fields and large farms are the rule, for in these conditions only extensive and highly mechanized farming is successful. On the lighter soils barley is the main crop; on the heavier, wheat. Roots form an essential part of the system, and sheep are folded on them. The pastures of the higher slopes are grazed by sheep, while those of the valley bottoms are grazed by cattle or cut for hay. Parts of these valley bottoms were in the past irrigated, and produced extremely rich crops of grass; but the artificial water channels have fallen into disrepair.

From the chalklands of the Hampshire Basin four of our breeds of sheep have originated: the Dorset and Wiltshire Horns and the Hampshire and Dorset Downs. Of these the Wiltshire Horn (now confined mainly to Buckinghamshire and Northamptonshire) is unique in that it produces little or no wool; but it matures early, and is valued in the production of prime lamb. The Hampshire Down is a short-woolled sheep; it too matures early, is a prolific breeder, and yields large quantities of high-quality meat. It has been one of our main export breeds.

The Tertiary lowlands are typified by the New Forest. The soils in general are sandy, but there are occasional exposures of clay, and frequently the hills are capped with gravels. The light soils are usually leached, and in places the development of hardpan impedes the drainage: these are areas of heath and sedge. The heavier soils support woodland, where in a state of nature the oak would be dominant: the pine, however, has been introduced, and adds variety to the scene. Cattle, pigs, and wild ponies and deer keep in check the gorse and heather and preserve the smooth 'lawns' of the New Forest. West of the Avon the physical conditions are similar, but since the land is not subject to Forest regulations much speculative building has taken place. The subsoil, indeed, is attractive for settlement, and the scenic charm helps to account for the recent growth on the outskirts of Bournemouth. The major towns (Bournemouth, Southampton, and Portsmouth) have stimulated farming in the region by providing an active demand for milk, fruit, and market-garden produce.

In the Hampshire basin there have been widespread changes since 1939. Much of the wartime increase in arable farming has become permanent, in both cash crops and fodder crops; in Hampshire this has occasioned a 15 to 20 per cent. decrease in the area of grassland. There has been a swing away from sheep to dairy farming, but stock-rearing in general has increased its relative importance. All the counties which share in the region registered a 60 to 70 per cent. decline in the numbers of sheep and at least a 50 per cent. increase in the numbers of young female cattle during the period 1939 to 1951. These are signs of a more intensive farming, itself linked with technical improvements in farm machinery and with an increased demand for fresh milk consequent upon rises in the standard of living.

Southampton (Fig. 94)

The rise of Southampton (pop. 214,826) to become one of the greatest passenger terminals in the world has been aided by distinct physical advantages. The land approaches from the direction of London are by way of the valleys of the Itchen and the Test; these aided rail connection with the capital, and modern Southampton

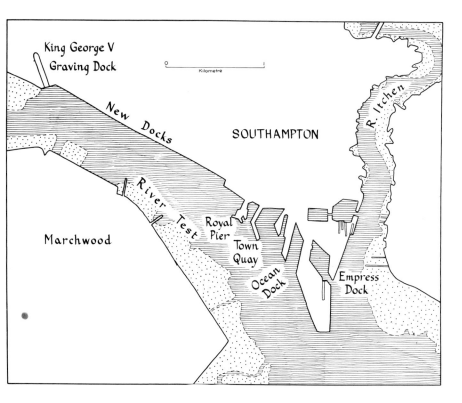

Fig. 94. THE PORT OF SOUTHAMPTON

The docks have been built on former mudflats, and reclamation has been progressive on both sides of the river Test. The 'New Docks' are now a most active part of the port. Extensive reclamation has taken place recently on the south side of the river where there is a generating station at Marchwood. The low tidal range has allowed the port to dispense with enclosed docks. The King George V dry dock is one of the largest in the world.

is essentially a railway port. Only $1\frac{1}{2}$ hours from London by express train, it functions as the passenger port for the capital.

The sea approaches are by way of the deep and sheltered Southampton Water: as a result of subsidence of the land (trimmed by modern dredging), a 10·7-metre channel is available at low water, spring tides. Most unusual of the physical advantages of the port are its tides. There is an exceptionally low tidal range – about 3·2 metres on the average, compared with 5·2 metres at London and 6·6 at Liverpool. On the rising tide there is a pause; and at high water there is an extended peak period (but hardly a 'double high tide'). This is followed by a rapid ebb (Fig. 95). Two hours of slack water at high tide provide a valuable aid in the berthing of the

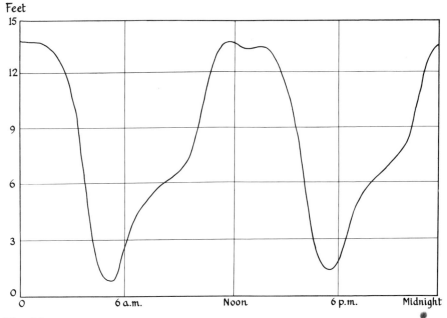

Feet

Fig. 95. TIDAL CURVES AT SOUTHAMPTON

Unusual features are: a relatively small range, a pause on the rising tide, a double maximum, and a rapid ebb. *By courtesy of the Southampton Harbour Board.*

largest liners, while the low tidal range makes it possible to dispense with lock gates. As in New York, all the major berths at Southampton are open.

Essentially Southampton is the port for the long-distance passenger traffic on the transatlantic, African, Australian, and Far Eastern routes. But since the passenger liners normally also carry some cargo, the port has a freight traffic of significance: it includes the handling of bananas from the West Indies (particularly appropriate to a railway port, since speed is essential) and the import of citrus fruits from South Africa. Ocean Dock, with its elaborate passenger terminal building, is one of the busiest in the port; the 'New Docks' share the transatlantic trade with Ocean Dock, and handle the South African traffic. At their extremity is the King George V Graving Dock, one of the largest dry docks in the world. In addition to its long-distance traffic the port has important short sea connections for passengers and goods with Le Havre and the Channel Islands, and takes part in the regular coastal traffic of Britain.

Centrally placed in southern England, and offering a large local demand for bunker fuel, Southampton has attracted important oil installations. Here, at Fawley, is the biggest refinery, not only in Britain but in the whole of the Commonwealth; and in its turn refining has led to the growth of petro-chemical industries. These include the first plant in the country for the manufacture of synthetic rubber.

The port functions of Southampton perhaps excite the imagination; but the city is also a shopping and commercial focus, and a university town.

The Channel Islands
Between 16 and 56 km west of Normandy and 80 to 160 km south of Weymouth are the Channel Islands – the only fragment of the old Duchy of Normandy to remain attached to the English Crown. The islands retain many of their own customs and their own coinage, judiciary, and legislature and many of the inhabitants continue to speak a Norman-French patois. Administratively they fall into two groups of 'bailiwicks' – Jersey on the one hand, and on the other, Guernsey, Alderney, Sark, Herm, and a few smaller islands. All are small: Jersey, the largest, covers about 120 square kilometres, and its area is less than a third of that of the Isle of Wight. But with a population of 72,532, Jersey has a density of over 600 per square kilometre – probably the highest of any rural area in the British Isles. These high densities apply to all the main islands; and in the summer the populations are swollen by about 300,000 visitors.

Well to the south of mainland Britain, and bathed in the waters of the North Atlantic Drift, the islands enjoy high average amounts of sunshine and exceptionally mild winters. Physically they form the summits of partially submerged Armorican ridges which extend westward from Normandy, and they have probably been separated from the mainland only in post-glacial times.

The islanders are traditionally hard-working and thrifty. From the sixteenth to the nineteenth centuries they engaged in the Newfoundland cod fisheries, or remained at home knitting stockings and 'jerseys'. Today the basic industries are tourism and agriculture. The latter might more accurately be termed horticulture, for the holdings are small, and rarely more than 10 hectares in extent.

Between Jersey and Guernsey there are remarkable differences in aspect which are reflected in the methods of production. In Jersey the land surface slopes from the summits of high granite cliffs in the north (at their maximum 140 metres high) to flat sandy bays in the south. This southerly aspect favours the open-air cultivation of early potatoes and tomatoes, which are grown in rotation.

In Guernsey, however, the land slopes in the reverse direction; there are cliffs in the south, reaching more than 90 metres, and a fairly regular slope down to bays in the north. Here much of the produce, including daffodils, gladioli, beans, radishes and grapes and about 40,000 tonnes of tomatoes annually, is grown in 400 hectares of greenhouses.

High yields in the islands generally are maintained by applications of seaweed as fertilizer, whose cutting is regulated by law. Both Jersey and Guernsey are famous for their pedigree herds of dairy cattle: their rather small stature is attributed to deficiencies of lime and phosphorus in the soils.

The produce of the islands is shipped mainly to Weymouth, Southampton, and Portsmouth, but small quantities go direct to London. The passenger traffic is handled at Weymouth, and at Jersey airport, which is one of the busiest in Britain. It would be idle to search unduly for comparisons between the Channel Islands and the Hampshire Basin; but they have suffered the same submergence, they share the same sea, and they have close economic ties.

FOR FURTHER READING

Books

CHATWIN, C. P.: *The Hampshire Basin and Adjoining Areas,* British Regional Geology Handbooks (H.M.S.O., 1948).

DURY, G. H.: *The Channel Islands,* in The Land of Britain, Ed. L. D. Stamp (Geographical Publications, 1950).

MONKHOUSE, F. J. (Ed.): A Survey of Southampton and its Region (British Association, 1964).

REES, HENRY: *British Ports and Shipping* (Harrap, 1958), Chapter 5.

Articles

CHEW, HILARY C.: 'Changes in Land Use and Stock over England and Wales, 1939 to 1951', in the *Geographical Journal* (December 1956).

STEVENS, A. J.: 'Surfaces, Soils and Land Use in North-East Hampshire', *Transactions and Papers, Institute of British Geographers* (1959).

Maps

Bartholomew's ½-inch sheets 4, 5, 7, and 8.

The Hampshire Basin is well covered by the 1-inch geological maps. The Chalklands are well illustrated by sheet 298 (Salisbury); there is a Special Sheet covering the Isle of Wight.

FLEURE, H. J.: *Guernsey,* British Landscape through Maps (Geographical Association, 1961).

CHAPTER TWENTY-THREE

THE THAMES BASIN AND LONDON

THE WORD 'BASIN' has two distinct meanings: the 'Thames basin' signifies the whole of the land drained by the river Thames and its tributaries; this includes the greater part of the London Basin, which comprises the land contained within a downfold of the Chalk, whose rim is represented by the North Downs and the Chiltern Hills. The remaining portion of the Thames basin consists of the Oxford Clay vale, and it has been customary to group this with the Midlands. But the Oxford region is linked to London by drainage, by water-supply, and by road and rail; and here we combine the two regions into a single chapter. The Thames basin possesses a wide range of solid geological deposits, but all are relatively young, and none are excessively hard; they are masked by extensive mantles of superficial deposits, including glacial and river gravels and clay-with-flints; and these have had profound effects on life and landscape.

Oxford and its Region

In the Oxford region the strata are tilted gently down to the south-east at an angle of a few degrees; they therefore outcrop in a series of narrow parallel bands ranging north-east and south-west, with the oldest in the north-west. Four formations combine to form the Oxford Clay vale: the Oxford Clay, the Corallian, and the Kimmeridge and Gault Clays. Between Oxford and Faringdon the Corallian consists of a resistant limestone which forms a north-west-facing scarp overlooking the Thames: these are the Oxford Heights. Elsewhere the Corallian forms a low-lying belt of sandy soils, distinguishable from the clays mainly by the ease with which they can be cultivated.

The three clay formations merge to form a broad vale whose soils are cold, wet, and stiff, and more suited to permanent pasture than arable farming, though with the addition of lime, potash, and phosphates, and with the aid of modern farm machinery, they can be made to grow arable crops. This is a wooded landscape, with small hedged fields and brick and tiled cottages; it extends westward to floor the wedge-shaped Vale of White Horse. Cultivation and settlements are attracted to the lighter soils where river gravels mask the damp clays.

From Palæolithic times onward the Oxford region, and particularly its river gravels, have proved attractive to man. Oxford itself is first mentioned in history in A.D. 912, and by the time of Athelstan (924–39) was issuing its own coins. The first bridge was in existence in 1004: it spanned the Cherwell at a narrowing of the alluvial flats between the gravel terraces. Within five years of the Conquest the Normans had erected a castle, and by the thirteenth century Oxford was a walled town with six gates. It corresponded precisely with the southern limits of the second terrace of the Thames in the angle between the mainstream and the Cherwell. To the east, south, and west it was protected by wide belts of marshland, and until the twentieth century the main direction of its expansion was northward.

The early growth of Oxford was linked with its position as a bridge town and river port at the head of commercial navigation of the Thames; in addition it commanded a gap through the Corallian ridge. Its university was established by 1200. In modern times its growth has been recent and rapid, and as in Coventry, this has been due largely to the establishment of the motor-car industry. In 1901 the city contained nearly 50,000 inhabitants. In 1912 Morris Motors built a factory at Cowley, on the outskirts of the city, and in 1926 they were joined by the Pressed Steel company, producing car bodies: largely as a result, the population of Oxford has grown to 108,564. Fortunately, the tranquillity of the college gardens and quadrangles which occupy so much of the central area remains undisturbed.

The clays are succeeded to the south-east by the Chalk of the Chiltern Hills: in its regularity the Chiltern scarp contrasts strongly with that of the Cotswolds – smooth and almost unbroken, it has virtually no outliers. Yet the Chalk must originally have covered a much wider area, for it reappears in Northern Ireland, forming a narrow band around the basalt plateau of Antrim, and exposing bold cliffs to the waves of the North Channel.

Along the foot of the Chilterns is a persistent bench or terrace, formed by the Upper Greensand and Lower Chalk. Here the soils are marly or clay loams; the level and well-drained land is largely under the plough or planted with fruit, and a regular row of villages has been attracted by spring-water, fertile soils, and easy communications. This, the most extensively cultivated belt in the Oxford region, is threaded by the prehistoric Icknield Way, and has been named the Icknield belt.

The first rise to the Chilterns is fairly gentle, and is formed by the Lower Chalk. At the base of the Middle Chalk is the hard Melbourne Rock, and this forms a bench half-way up the scarp. The slope then steepens again through the Middle Chalk, and its brow is formed by the Chalk Rock – a second hard band which marks the base of the Upper Chalk. The rest of the Upper Chalk is comparatively soft: it caps the ridge, and forms most of the surface of the dip slope. Eastward the Chalk dips gently and regularly; there are no major folds or faults.

As in the North Downs, the plateau surface of the Chilterns carries an extensive cover of clay-with-flints, which is missing from the sides and floors of the dry valleys. The deposit is water-retaining, and much of the surface is clothed in beech. Chalk downland is thus not typical of the Chilterns, and is in fact confined mainly to the scarp itself. The valley systems give special character to the Chilterns: deep and steep-sided, they branch out to reach almost every part of the plateau, and many have their beginnings almost at the crest of the scarp. Though they are now dry, their close resemblance to existing drainage systems implies that they have been cut by running water, perhaps when the water table was higher than at present, or perhaps during the Ice Age, when the frozen subsoil acted as an impermeable layer.

Some of the main valleys, however, have been cut right through the hills, and are sufficiently deep to penetrate the water table, so that they carry streams, such as the Bulbourne and Gade, south-east of Tring, and the Misbourne, south-east of Wendover. These valleys, which are so valuable as routeways between London and the Midlands, perhaps originated as overflow channels from a former lake, ponded back between the ice sheets and the Chilterns.

In the middle of the nineteenth century almost the whole of the available farm-land of the Chiltern plateau was under the plough and raised wheat, barley, and sheep. During the 1870's, however, competition from the newly exploited prairies of North America brought about a prolonged decline in the price of corn, and this was reflected in a change from arable farming to grassland.

On the outbreak of war in 1939 grants were payable to farmers who ploughed up their permanent pasture, and the Government had power to compel them to do so. There was an immediate rise in the arable area of the Chilterns and elsewhere, and the chalk-lands once again became almost completely arable. Even more remarkable were the increases which took place on the heavy soils of the Gault and Oxford Clays and the London Clay, where additions of up to 40 per cent. in the arable area took place between 1939 and 1944; this was made possible by the rapid advance of draining and mechanization.

The post-War period has witnessed again the reversion of arable to grass: the Chiltern farmer has turned from corn-growing to milk-production. In addition much land has been withdrawn for house-building, and a proportion of what remains is utilized for golf courses and country seats, or is farmed as a hobby.

The London Basin

Structurally the London Basin completes the fold whose southern portion is represented by the Wealden dome; and since the pressures came from the direction of the Alps, the southern limb of the downfold is steep and the northern limb more gentle. In consequence, the Chalk outcrop in the Chilterns is about 32 km wide, while that in the North Downs is only 8 km, and in places is far less.

Deep borings have shown that the Cretaceous rocks rest upon a floor of older rocks which range in age from Cambrian to Jurassic (Fig. 96). Directly underlying the Chalk is the Gault Clay, which effectively traps the water in the Chalk, so that below London is a reservoir of water which has been tapped for industrial purposes by numerous wells.

Above the Chalk are the Tertiary strata, whose lowest members (the Lower London Tertiaries) comprise sandy and gravelly deposits: these are well represented in the commons of Blackheath, on the south-eastern outskirts of the city. More characteristic is the London Clay, which forms the main mass of the Tertiary beds. A stiff, bluish clay, it underlies almost the whole of the region, and near London attains a thickness of 120 to 150 m. The soils derived from London Clay are sticky in wet weather but crack badly in dry weather, so that they are usually left under permanent grass. Owing to the heavy demand for milk from the metropolis, these districts are grazed by dairy cattle.

Over wide areas, however, the London Clay is masked by newer Tertiary strata, or by glacial drift, or river gravels or modern alluvium. The newer Tertiary rocks are represented mainly by the Bagshot series, a group of coarse sands and gravels, whose chief exposure is in the west of the Basin, though it appears in the centre and east in the heaths of Hampstead and the woodland of Epping Forest.

While the geological succession has been determined by the advance and retreat of the seas of Tertiary times, the present distribution of these strata on the surface is related to the Alpine

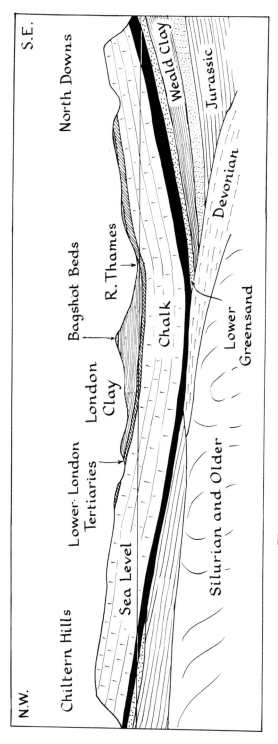

N.W.

S.E.

Chiltern Hills

North Downs

Lower London
Tertiaries

Bagshot Beds

R. Thames

London
Clay

Weald Clay

Sea Level

Chalk

Jurassic

Silurian and Older

Lower
Greensand

Devonian

Fig. 96.   GEOLOGICAL SECTION ACROSS THE LONDON BASIN

The black band represents the Gault and Upper Greensand; the unnamed band below the Weald Clay is the Hastings Beds. The
sections represents a distance of about 90 km. *After G. M. Davies.*

earth movements and subsequent erosion. Essentially the London Basin is a syncline which pitches eastward, and has there been invaded by the sea. The simple structure of the downfold, however, has been interrupted by ten or so minor ripples which intersect one another. We comment on only a few of these.

We have already seen (p. 305) that an upfold ranging east and west raises the Chalk to the surface to form the Isle of Thanet. Related perhaps to it is a parallel upfold farther west, which has been breached by the lower Thames. This is responsible for the exposure of Chalk on the north bank between Purfleet and Grays in Essex (see Fig. 103, p. 356) and on the south bank at Cliffe, in Kent; and in both places cement-manufacturers have taken advantage of the proximity of Chalk to navigable water.

At Windsor a dome brings the Chalk to the surface too, and the cliff which the Thames has cut into it offered a suitable crag for a castle. A syncline ranging from the neighbourhood of Harrow to Epping and beyond has strengthened and preserved the Bagshot Beds, so that strata which were formerly near the base of a downfold now remain to cap the hills of Hampstead and Epping. The unusually straight course of the lower Lea is related to the occurrence here of a monoclinal fold ranging north and south; and the river is in the process of migrating eastward in accordance with the dip of the strata.

The distribution of boulder clay in the London Basin suggests that the Quaternary ice sheet reached only the northern and north-eastern outskirts of what is now London, and that it sent narrow tongues of ice between and among the hill masses of south Essex and north-east Hertfordshire (Fig. 97). This southern limit of the boulder clay forms one of the most significant geographical boundaries of the region. South of it are the heavy and intractable soils derived from the London Clay, formerly thickly wooded and today left largely in permanent pasture; north of it are the 'sweeter' soils, more easily cultivated and less densely wooded in early times, derived from chalky boulder clay, and forming the southern fringe of the cornlands of East Anglia. Through Roman, early Saxon, and later periods there is clear evidence of a dense occupation and a close net of communications in the boulder clay areas, compared with the almost complete neglect of the driftless land.

In Pliocene times the ancestor of the Thames flowed well to the north of the axis of the London Basin, along the margins of the Chilterns, and its gravels lie 150 metres or more above the present level of the river. During later phases, as its terrace gravels indicate,

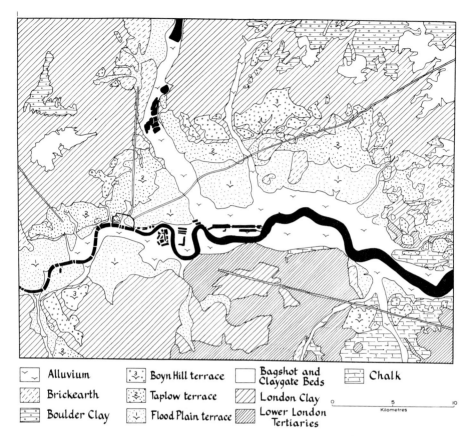

| | Alluvium | Boyn Hill terrace | Bagshot and Claygate Beds | Chalk |

Fig. 97. THE LONDON AREA: DRIFT GEOLOGY

On a floor of Tertiary rocks (mainly London Clay) are the flood-plains and three gravel terraces of the Thames and its tributaries. Boulder clay and brickearth are relics of the Ice Age. The extent of Roman London is indicated together with the lines of the known Roman roads. *Based on the Geological Survey 1-inch maps.*

the Thames has been migrating farther and farther southward, so that in its lower course the river is actually cutting into the Chalk of the North Downs.

Successive stages of uplift and standstill are recorded in the three gravel terraces of the Thames. In the London area and lower Thames these, together with the major portion of the modern alluvium, occur almost entirely north of the river. The oldest and highest is the Boyn Hill terrace; its scattered remnants lie well to the north of the river at about 45 metres above its surface. This is succeeded farther south by the Taplow terrace, at about 30 metres

O.D., on which London was founded, and in its turn the Taplow terrace gives way to the Flood Plain terrace, at about 15 metres. This southward migration of the course of the Thames has influenced the physical setting of London, since it has resulted in wide areas suitable for settlement on the north side of the river, where the gravels offered dry sites above the level of high tides. Early expansion was limited to the north bank; and in later centuries it was the north bank which offered the greatest expanses of alluvium for the siting of docks.

There is one other superficial deposit to describe – the brickearth. We have already referred to this in describing the fruit belt of Kent (p. 317). It is a buff-coloured loam, similar to the limon of the Paris Basin and the loess of north Germany, and it occurs in all three countries just beyond the limit of glaciation. It is fertile, retentive of moisture, and forms an excellent seed-bed; consequently it has been in great demand for market gardens. As its name implies, it has also been used on a large scale for brick-making. There are tracts of brickearth in Middlesex, along the Lea valley, and in south Essex. All these regions have played an important part in the supply of vegetables to London, but the spread of housing has seriously reduced their contribution during the last two generations.

London

The historical geography of London is too vast and complex a study to receive more than a brief mention here. It is clear, however, that the Romans were the first to build a town on the site, and that the area which they encircled with a wall – the present 'City' – has stood the test of time as an area eminently suitable for settlement.

Marching inland from their landing-points in Kent, the Roman legions found their northward progress barred by the alluvial flats of the Thames, then awash at high water. At Gravesend the flood-plain is 3 km wide, at Woolwich, 6 km. Here the Romans could not contemplate a crossing. But near the site of the city the flood-plain narrowed to a kilometre or so, and at once a crossing became feasible. Numerous coins and other small finds dredged from the river close to London Bridge indicate that here throughout the Roman period was the chief crossing-point of the Thames – almost certainly a bridge.

The south bank was marshy; but on the north bank a spread of Taplow gravels offered a firm, clean, and dry place for a town, with drinking-water from shallow wells and a navigable river at its gates. The shallow valley of a small stream, later known as the Wallbrook, divided the site into two low hills just over 15 metres high; farther west it was protected by a more considerable stream, later called the Holebourne, and its estuary, the Fleet (*cf.* Fig. 98).

The Roman city, covering 2·6 square km, was by far the largest in Britain, and its basilica or town hall was 150 metres long. The foundations of this immense structure lie below the present Royal Exchange, so that the centre of the modern capital corresponds with the site of its Roman counterpart.

Following the departure of the Roman legions (about A.D. 410) there is a gap of two centuries in the recorded history of London. But by the time of the Venerable Bede (673–735) London had once more emerged as 'the mart of many nations resorting to it by sea and land'.

Throughout the Middle Ages London occupied the same site and area as in Roman times; the medieval wall was built on the line of the Roman ramparts, but the earlier street plan was obliterated, and that of the 'City' is medieval. William Fitzstephen, writing some time before 1183, described the London of his day:

> On the East stands the Palatine Citadel [the Tower], exceeding great and strong, whose walls and bailey rise from very deep foundations, their mortar being mixed by the blood of beasts. On the west are two strongly fortified castles, while thence there runs continuously a great wall and high, with seven double gates and with towers along the North at intervals . . .

To the south flowed the Thames, 'a mighty river teeming with fish'. The Holebourne washed the walls on the west, and vessels anchored in its estuary. The names of the gates have survived as district names today. Through the middle of the town ran the Wallbrook, and owing to the blocking of its culvert below the wall there arose a wide marsh or moor to the north – hence 'Moorgate'.

The significance of the siting of London was already apparent. It was and still is the lowest bridge point of the Thames, attracting land traffic from both sides of the estuary. The building of a bridge (rebuilt in stone in 1209) restricted the passage upstream of seagoing vessels, so that London became, and remains, the effective head of ocean navigation, and hence a port. Its growth as a centre of roads, and later railways, was aided by the existence of convenient gaps in the Chiltern Hills and the North Downs, and the status of London as the nation's capital city has never been questioned. A reconstruction of Elizabethan London (Fig. 98a, p. 344) reflects the essential features of the medieval city.

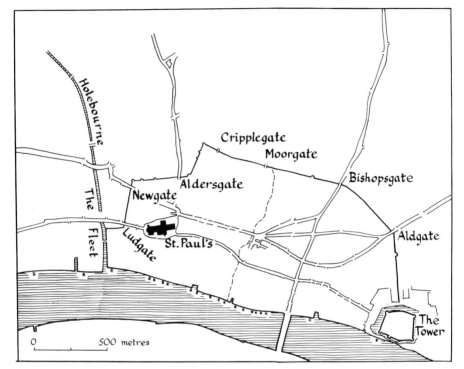

Fig. 98a. LONDON ABOUT 1600

The shape is that of the Roman town; the street plan and gates are medieval. The Thames was wider, and it was spanned by a single bridge. The large number of stairs leading down to the river reflect its extensive use as a highway. The presumed course of the Wallbrook is indicated by a broken line. *After E. Ekwall, 'Street Names of the City of London', Oxford, 1954.*

The Port

The beginnings of the modern port may be discerned in the trading expeditions of Elizabethan times. They brought in their wake, a great traffic with West Africa, the American colonies and West Indies, the Levant and India. In addition to riches, however, they brought a crippling congestion to the river, so that a House of Commons committee appointed at the close of the eighteenth century reported that the salvation of London could be achieved only by the construction of enclosed docks.

The dock-building era began vigorously in the nineteenth century with the construction of three groups of basins in five years (Fig. 99). The practice of particular docks specializing in distinctive cargoes (still a characteristic of London), was initiated by Parliament, which granted monopolies to the early dock-builders. Thus

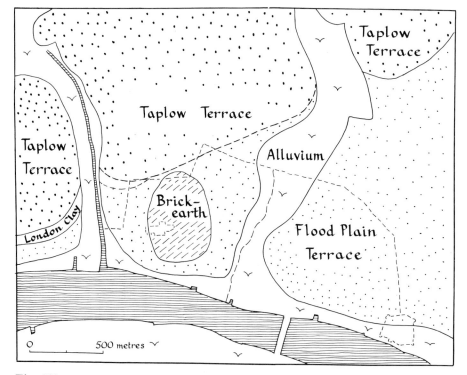

Fig. 98b. THE PHYSICAL BASIS OF EARLY LONDON

Just at the place where the flood-plain narrowed, firm ground (in the shape of gravel terraces) was present close to the north bank of the river. The City enclosed two hills and was protected to the south by the Thames and to the west by the Fleet. *Based on the Geological Survey 1-inch map.*

all vessels in the port arriving from or departing to the West Indies were required to use the West India Docks (opened in 1802); accordingly this group is still the headquarters in London for the sugar, hardwood, citrus fruit, and banana traffic.

The new docks proved adequate for 50 years. During that period the railway and the steamer proved their worth, and all the later docks were designed for steamships, and were linked automatically with the railways. For the first time docks were constructed on the extensive alluvial flats east of the Lea. The Royal Victoria Dock, opened in 1855, was followed by the Royal Albert in 1880, and by the King George V in 1921. These vast basins have the atmosphere of the Thames itself rather than a man-made excavation. Each is more than 1·5 km long; all are joined by deep cuttings so that they form in reality a single huge dock – the largest sheet of enclosed dock-water in the world, with 16 km of quays.

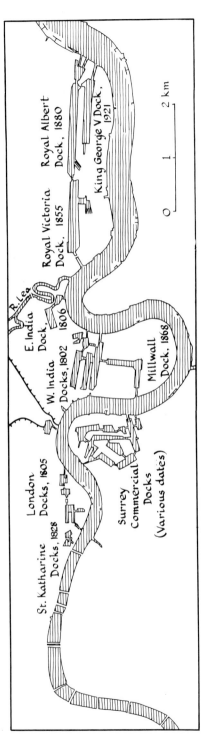

Fig. 99.   THE PORT OF LONDON : THE DOCKS

As Fig. 97 shows, London has an important physical asset in the extensive alluvial flats bordering the Thames. The most extensive alluvial areas are north of the river, and here are the major dock systems. The early docks were designed for sailing-ships; from the 1850's onward the docks were designed for steam and linked with the railways. Tilbury Docks are not shown here: they are about 16 km downstream from central London. With the increasing size of vessels, commerce is tending to move downstream. The London and St Katharine docks, the East India Dock and Surrey Commercial Docks are now closed. On the other hand, important extensions are taking place at Tilbury.

In 1848 the Millwall dock was built, within the loop of the Thames known as the Isle of Dogs. It specializes in grain.

Tilbury Docks, which date from 1886, have a special character. Since they are farthest downstream they can provide a greater depth of water, and so can accommodate larger vessels than any other group. The newest extension at Tilbury has a maximum depth of 12·85 metres of water (the *Queen Elizabeth II* has a draft of 9·9 metres).

While it is an economy to carry bulk cargoes as far inland as possible, passengers prefer to disembark early, for they can save several hours if they continue by rail. Tilbury is therefore the passenger port for London.

Some of the older basins are now obsolete: the London and St. Katharine Docks were closed in 1968 and the Surrey Commercial in 1970. In recompense, the Authority plans new docks lower downstream, probably for bulk carriers and container ships.

While the ocean giants berthed in the docks capture the imagination, the river itself remains a most important section of the port (Fig. 100). Here are discharged the whole of the coal and petroleum to enter London. Many industrial concerns, such as paper-mills and cement works, together with the public utilities (gasworks and power-stations) possess their own wharves or jetties; and in addition there is an extensive traffic in general cargoes handled by wharfing companies. In all, the tonnage handled in the river is actually twice as great as that handled in the docks.

The internal distribution of cargoes in the port is the responsibility of a large fleet of carriers. This comprises 300 tugs and 5630 lighters (barges), whose functions are many: they deliver cargoes to specialized warehouses, to industrial plants, to railway wharves, or to other vessels for transhipment.

On a typical day we should see upward of 100 vessels berthed in the river. Most of these lie below Tower Bridge, either at old-established river ports such as Greenwich and Purfleet or at industrial plants such as the Ford motor-works and the Beckton gasworks. But small craft and large colliers pass below the bridges of central London and reach Fulham and Wandsworth.

The colliers are known as 'flatties'. With squat superstructures and collapsible funnels and masts, they are specially designed to negotiate the bridges. They carry between 1700 and 2800 tonnes of coal on each journey. The largest have little room to spare when turning in the river, and must time their journeys carefully: if the tide were low they would touch the bottom; if it were high they would be unable to pass below the bridges. There are about

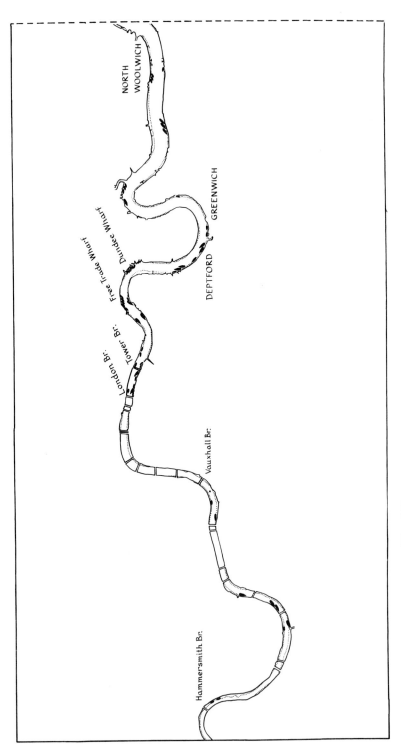

Fig. 100a. THE PORT OF LONDON : SHIPPING IN THE RIVER

Shipping in the river Thames, as reported in the *Journal of Commerce*, November 10th, 1955. Of the 114 vessels reported, 95 have been plotted. Six were in Regent's Canal Dock, and for the remaining 13 there was insufficient information.

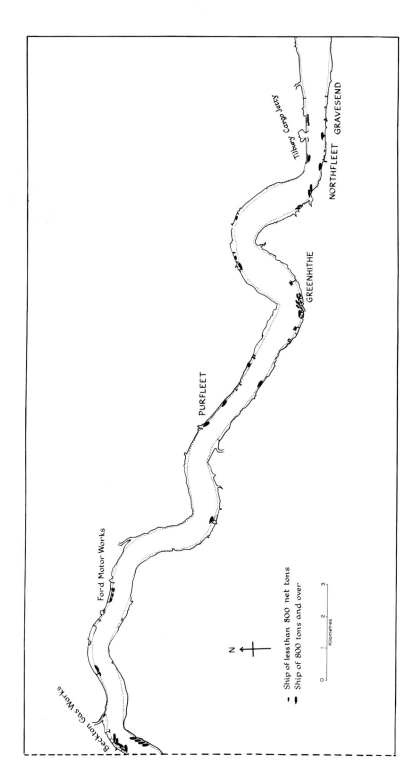

Fig. 100b. THE PORT OF LONDON: SHIPPING IN THE RIVER

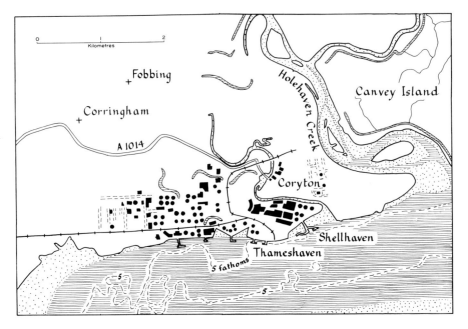

Fig. 101. THE LOWER THAMES: OIL INSTALLATIONS

A vital element in the choice of this area for the petroleum industry is the existence of deep water, as shown by the position of the submarine contour for 5 fathoms. It is remote from built-up areas, but within easy reach of the London market. There are refineries at Shellhaven and Coryton, storage facilities at Thameshaven, and a methane-gas storage plant on Canvey Island. *Based on the O.S. 1-inch map. Crown copyright reserved.*

4 dozen 'flatties', and 6 dozen other colliers; and together in 1969 they brought in 10·7 million tonnes of coal, most of it from the north-east coast. About two-thirds of the total is used by 19 Thames-side power-stations and 9 gasworks.

The oil-supplies for London are handled well below the docks, in the neighbourhood of Canvey Island, on the north side of the river, and at the Isle of Grain, on the south side. Here are three oil-refineries which together account for about a quarter of the nation's refining capacity; in addition there are large storage installations at Thameshaven (Fig. 101). The latter, with a capacity of 2 million tonnes, form the largest independent oil store in Europe.

Recent developments here include tankage on Canvey Island for Saharan natural gas (1963); the doubling in size of Coryton refinery (1967–69) and the opening of a new jetty at Coryton capable of receiving 300,000-ton tankers (1969).

Fig. 100 shows the vessels which were berthed in the river on one day in 1955. There are 115 of them, and most are below Tower

Bridge, but nine of them have passed through the bridges of central London. Of these, five are 'flatties', discharging coal at the Fulham and Wandsworth gasworks and at the Fulham and Battersea power-stations. The others are small craft from near Continental ports such as Rotterdam and Antwerp, and are carrying general cargoes to the up-river wharves; some of them have picked their way through as many as nineteen Thames bridges.

No vessels are berthed between Vauxhall and London Bridges, for here commerce gives way to administration, and for long stretches the river has been confined between embankments. But below London Bridge the wharves begin again, and in the next 7 kilometres there are two dozen vessels distributed among 120 different wharves, many of which are now disused. These wharves range widely in the facilities they can offer to shipping. Bellamy's Wharf, near the upper entrance of the Surrey Commercial Docks, offers 4·3 metres of water at low tide, and specializes in dried fruit, grain, and provisions. Here is the largest vessel in this stretch of the river, a ship of 4214 net tons from Basra, in Iraq, perhaps carrying a cargo of grain and dates. Other wharves provide only about 2·5 metres of water, and at many of them a vessel on the falling tide will settle down quietly on to the mud.

Below Deptford are several clusters of vessels. Four large colliers – one from Methil, in eastern Scotland, the others from the north-east coast – are discharging at the coal wharves at the entrance to the Royal Albert Dock; three others are bringing coal or loading coke at the Beckton gasworks, the largest in the world.

Five kilometres downstream on the same bank of the river are the Ford motor-works, with the largest privately owned wharf on the river. Here two small ships are loading cars and tractors for Cork and Antwerp. The eight vessels at Greenhithe, lower down on the opposite bank, are all from the well-known F. T. Everard fleet, whose headquarters and repair yard are here. The two ships at Northfleet are serving the local industries: a cargo of woodpulp for paper-making has arrived from Oslo, and a collier is discharging at the cement works. The largest vessel in the whole river, however, lies beyond the confines of our map: she is an ocean oil tanker, at Shellhaven, preparing to depart in ballast for Kuwait.

London is well in the lead among British ports. In 1969 London handled 26·3 per cent. of the total value of the foreign trade of the United Kingdom (including that handled by air). There followed Liverpool (14·0 per cent.), Hull (5·2), Harwich (4·2), Southampton (3·8), Felixstowe (2·8), and Manchester (2·4). To keep a proper perspective, however, it should be mentioned that Antwerp handles a greater foreign tonnage than London, while Rotterdam handles nearly three times as much.

The greatest single commodity by far in the foreign traffic of London is petroleum. In 1969 this commodity accounted for 64 per cent. of the foreign imports by weight, and 21 of the exports. The proportions would be even higher but for the fact that the traffic associated with the Kent refinery in the Isle of Grain is reckoned with the trade of the port of Rochester. The chief other foreign imports were grain (1·9 million tonnes), timber (1·3), paper (1·3), and sugar (1·0). On the export side were chemicals (603 thousand tonnes), vehicles (585), machinery (585), cement and other mineral products (401), and iron and steel products (247).

The trade of the port is still growing. The tonnage of vessels using it in 1963 formed a new record in its history (94·1 million net register tons), and this level has been in general maintained during the 1960's. These are healthy signs. By 1969 13 new berths had been completed at Tilbury, together with grain facilities and a freightliner terminal. Six of the new berths are designed for the container traffic.

Industry

London is not only the greatest port of the United Kingdom; it is also the greatest conurbation, the largest market, the chief reservoir of labour, and the greatest industrial area in the country.

In 1971 the Greater London Council area (p. 359) contained 7,379,014 people; if we include the outer metropolitan area, up to about 65 kilometres from Charing Cross, the figure rises to 12·7 million. The London region contains almost one-fifth of the employed persons of the United Kingdom. Since 1962 in the GLC area there has been an annual decline in employment of about 40,000; yet this has been accompanied by a substantial increase in office space. The figures suggest that Central London is retaining its attraction for finance and commerce while industry is migrating to the outskirts.

This 'drift to the south' is understandable, but it aggravates traffic and housing problems, and the Government is doing what it can to resist it. The problem has been attacked from three directions. Eight new towns have been built in the London region: these are Stevenage, Welwyn, Hatfield, and Hemel Hempstead, in Hertfordshire; Harlow and Basildon, in Essex; Bracknell, in Berkshire, and Crawley, in Sussex (Fig. 102). These are balanced communities, where residential building is matched by factories, and they are designed to receive 'overspill' from London. The

Fig. 102. NEW TOWNS IN THE LONDON REGION

Their population figures in 1971, with 1951 figures in parenthesis, were as follows: Basildon, 77,154 (24,661); Bracknell, 33,953 (5143); Crawley, 70,465 (10,707); Harlow, 57,791 (5825); Hatfield, 25,211 (9256); Hemel Hempstead, 69,966 (21,976); Stevenage, 66,975 (7311); Welwyn Garden City, 40,369 (18,804). In the Greater London Act of 1963 the County of Middlesex was abolished; its former boundary has been retained here to help the reader to locate the new towns. *After M. J. Wise*, 1956.

Board of Trade, by granting or withholding licences for the expansion of existing factories or the building of new ones, can control the direction of industrial development; and its post-war policy has been to encourage expansion in the 'Development Areas' such as south Wales and the north-east coast, and at the same time to discourage expansion in the London area. In so far as these measures are effective, Government policy must be accounted a factor in the location of industry.

The industries of London are many and varied. The capital has far more than its share of the servicing industries, such as banking and insurance, public administration, transport, and the distributive trades. London is strong in the manufacture of electrical apparatus, such as telephones, radio valves, electric lamps, and gramophones; in the manufacture of musical instruments and jewellery, in paper and printing, in dressmaking and tailoring, and in the manufacture of cine films. London is *weak* in the extractive industries, in the manufacture of textiles, in the motor-car industry, and in shipbuilding and marine engineering. For the most part we can say little concerning the localization of these industries: they have been attracted by the pool of skilled labour and by the market; they use relatively small quantities of raw material, and they are served by road transport.

In the localization of London's heavy industries physical factors play a more obvious part: these are concentrated in a zone along the lower Thames where the land is cheap, since it is unsuited alike to agriculture and residential development; and where water transport for the carriage of bulky commodities is available. Most plants have these advantages in common.

An important example is the Ford motor-works at Dagenham, established on a virgin marshland site on the north bank of the Thames about 18 kilometres east of central London. The Thames alluvium would not have provided sufficient support for the heavy equipment needed, and the floor of the works is a 13-ha platform of concrete, resting on 12,000 piles. This is the only fully integrated iron and steel works in the south of England, and it is served by the largest privately owned jetty in the river. Here on the same day you may see an ore-carrier from Sweden discharging its cargo by grab crane, and a freighter loading completed cars for export.

There are some undertakings, however, with special needs. Power-stations need huge quantities of cooling water – about 600 tonnes of water to each tonne of coal burnt – and can draw on the river. Both power-stations and gasworks must dispose of large quantities of ash, and for those with a riverside situation the sea may be the most convenient dumping ground.

Paper mills depend on navigable water for the receipt of their coal, wood-pulp, and china clay; they too need large quantities of cooling water for use in the power-house, but their process water is normally obtained from wells. Their location in the London area arises from the dominating influence of the capital in the market for newsprint, packaging material, and paper of all types. There are paper-mills at Purfleet, Erith, Dartford, Swanscombe, and Northfleet, and others in the Medway area (p. 318). The oil-refining industry of London we have already mentioned (p. 350).

A particular physical advantage of the lower Thames is the occurrence of the raw materials for cement-making. These consist of lime, clay, and water. The lime is dug in the form of chalk from vast quarries in the Purfleet district (Fig. 103) and at Swanscombe, while farther east are others at Cliffe and in the Medway valley. In some cases the clay is dug from pits in the London Clay; elsewhere Thames alluvium is used. The region supplies more than half of all the cement manufactured in the United Kingdom, and in the past has exported cement half-way round the world. Valparaiso Harbour was built with the aid of Thames cement, and New York's Broadway paved with it. In the coastwise export trade cement is second only to petroleum: it is shipped as far afield as Aberdeen, Inverness, Wick, the Shetlands, and the Outer Hebrides.

Zones

In most large cities particular functions are associated with specific districts. Nowhere are the results of this process more clearly illustrated than in London.

The square mile of the City is devoted to finance: here are the Bank of England, the head offices of other British and foreign banks, the Stock Exchange, and Lloyd's of London. It throbs with life during the week; but on Sunday it is deserted, for scarcely anyone lives there. To the east is the East End: it contains the docks, the clothing industry of Stepney, and the furniture industries of Hackney and Bethnal Green. To the west, in Fleet Street, is the Press; and beyond it the legal zone, represented by the Inns of Court and the High Court of Justice. Administration centres upon Whitehall, and is overlooked by the Houses of Parliament.

The West End includes the theatres, the fashionable shops and hotels, the foreign embassies and legations, Buckingham Palace and the three royal parks. Culture is concentrated mainly in South Kensington: here are the Victoria and Albert Museum and the Geological, Science, and Natural History museums, together with the Imperial College of Science and Technology, the Royal Albert Hall, and the Royal Academy of Music, and specialist organizations such as the Commonwealth Institute and the Royal Geographical Society. An outlier of the academic zone exists in

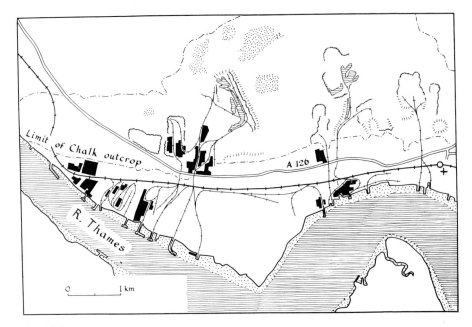

Fig. 103. CEMENT WORKS IN THE PURFLEET AREA

This district is about 23 km east of central London. An upfold brings the Chalk to the surface, and it has been quarried extensively for cement-making. In some of the exhausted quarries ponds have collected; in others, works have been located. Light railways link the quarries to the works and the works to the jetties for shipment. In this area is the Tunnel cement works – the largest in Britain. The inland stippled areas represent quarry waste; works are shown in black. The church and station in the east are those of Grays Thurrock. *Based on the O.S. 1-inch map. Crown copyright reserved.*

Bloomsbury, with the British Museum and the headquarters of the University of London, together with three of its colleges and many institutes. During the past twenty years the South Bank near Waterloo Bridge has been developed as a centre for music and the arts.

Water-supply and Food-supply

The inhabitants of Roman and medieval London obtained their water from the shallow wells which they dug in the terrace gravels. Such sources are quite inadequate as modern supplies; but fortunately there was water at deeper levels, contained in the porous Chalk and trapped by the underlying Gault Clay. It was discovered by accident in 1793, when the London Clay was pierced and water gushed out with some force. Other wells were dug, and the water from many of them overflowed on the surface – they were true artesian wells. Below London over a thousand wells have been sunk into the Chalk; there are 120 within a 400-metre radius of the Bank of England, and in the past they have supplied banks, breweries, laundries, dairies, and blocks of offices.

But continued pumping has so lowered the water table in the Chalk that yields have declined, and many wells have been abandoned. What is worse, the underground pressure has been so reduced that Thames water has been able to percolate into the Chalk, polluting some of the wells. Underground sources, which have never supplied more than about one-tenth of London's needs, are providing less and less. In an attempt to conserve the remaining resources the Government has imposed a licensing control over the boring of deep wells.

The whole of London's tap-water is supplied from the upper reaches of the Thames and the Lea, and is stored in large reservoirs at Staines and in the Lea valley. London uses about 1860 million litres *a day*, and two-thirds of this is supplied from the Thames. In addition the Thames yields about 727 million litres for the $3\frac{1}{2}$ million people in the catchment area above London. Recent investigations have been directed to the possibility of increasing the flow of the Thames headstreams, and the Thames Conservancy Board is of the opinion that by tapping underground water in such districts as the Cotswolds, Chilterns, and Berkshire Downs, an additional 910 million litres a day could be added to the Thames, thus ensuring sufficient water for London until well into the twenty-first century. Accordingly, the Board plans to sink 248 boreholes, at a cost of £8 millions. The first 9 were to be drilled during 1966–67 in the lower Lambourn valley, and the project is being reviewed in the light of this pilot scheme. In problems of water-supply at least, the Thames basin is essentially a single unit.

We have already touched on the subject of London's food-supply. Fresh milk is derived from dairy herds on the clays of the Oxford region, from the Chilterns, from the London Clay areas of south Essex and Hertfordshire, and from the Gault and Weald Clays of south-east England. Fruit for London is grown in Kent, East Anglia, and the Fens. Market-garden produce, formerly important on the brickearth of Middlesex, is now virtually extinct in that area, but continues to be of importance in the Lea valley.

Here, a century ago, the brickearths and terrace gravels were intensively cultivated for fruit and vegetables, for in addition to the fertile loamy soils, the region was well placed to supply Covent Garden market by road and rail. The distinctive activity of modern times in the Lea valley is the cultivation of fruit, flowers, and vegetables under glass. The outward growth of the built-up area

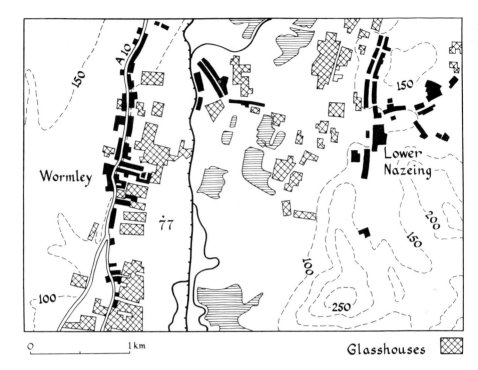

Fig. 104. GLASSHOUSES IN THE LEA VALLEY

The map illustrates a portion of the glasshouse area between Cheshunt and Hoddesdon, about 15 miles from central London. Market gardening began in the Lea valley at least 200 years ago, and was aided by brick-earth and gravel terrace soils. When the growers turned to glasshouse cultivation they utilized coal brought by the Lea Navigation (shown in the diagram). Today the soils are 'artificial' and the canal is little used; but the market is greater than ever. Buildings are shown in black; the horizontal ruling represents reservoirs. Heights are in feet. *Based on the O.S. 1-inch map. Crown copyright reserved.*

has resulted in the destruction of many glasshouses between Ponders End and Cheshunt, but expansion has taken place on the higher land to both the east and the west of the valley, where there is little danger of smoke pollution. With more than 400 hectares under glass, the Lea valley remains the country's leading district in this form of intensive production (Fig. 104). Tomatoes form the leading crop, about two-thirds of the area; in addition cucumbers, carnations, and roses are grown. The industry is well organized, and is served by a research station at Hoddesdon.

London's Prospects

We may conclude with a view of the new administration of London, as provided in the London Government Act, 1963: this came into effect on April 1st, 1965. Sweeping changes have been introduced

Fig. 105. GREATER LONDON: THE NEW LOCAL AUTHORITIES

The double line indicates the boundary of the former County of London and encloses the City and the twelve 'inner boroughs'. Beyond are the twenty 'outer boroughs'.

in the structure of London's political geography. While the City of London is preserved, both the counties of London and Middlesex have been abolished. So have the 28 Metropolitan Boroughs: these have been combined to form 12 inner London boroughs, and are joined by 20 outer London boroughs (reduced from about 60 former local authorities) to form the new Greater London (Fig. 105).

The grouping of authorities has led to problems in nomenclature, and new names have appeared on our maps. Stepney, Poplar, and Bethnal Green have combined to form the borough of Tower Hamlets; Hampstead, Holborn, and St Pancras formed Camden; Ilford, Wanstead and Woodford, and parts of Dagenham and Chigwell became Redbridge; East Ham, West Ham, and parts of Barking and Woolwich became Newham; Hornsey, Tottenham, and Wood Green became Haringey.

Many will regret the disappearance of the historic county of Middlesex; but the extension of the area of London government has long been overdue, and the reduction in the number of authorities within the area will no doubt effect valuable economics.

FOR FURTHER READING

Books

BIRD, JAMES: *The Geography of the Port of London* (Hutchinson, 1957).

CLAYTON, R. (Ed.): *The Geography of Greater London* (G. Philip, 1964).

—— *Guide to the London Excursions* (London School of Economics, 1964).

COPPOCK, J. T. and PRINCE, H. C. (Editors): *Greater London* (Faber, 1964).

HALL, P. G.: *The Industries of London since* 1861 (Hutchinson, 1962).

MARSHALL, M.: *Oxfordshire*, The Land of Britain, Part 56 (Geographical Publications, 1943).

MARTIN, A. F., and STEEL, R. W.: *The Oxford Region* (Oxford University Press, 1954).

MARTIN, J. E., *Greater London – An Industrial Geography* (Bell, 1966).

SHERLOCK, R. L.: *London and the Thames Basin*, British Regional Geology Handbooks (H.M.S.O., 1947).

WOOLDRIDGE, S. W.: *The Geographer as Scientist* (Nelson, 1956):
Chapter 10: The Physiographic Evolution of the London Basin.
Chapter 11: The Glacial Drifts of Essex and Hertfordshire and their bearing upon the Agricultural and Historical Geography of the Region.

WOOLDRIDGE, S. W., and HUTCHINGS, G. E.: *London's Countryside* (Methuen, 1957).

Articles and Pamphlets

BIRD, J.: 'The Industrial Development of Lower Thameside', in *Geography* (April 1952).

COPPOCK, J. T.: 'The Changing Arable in the Chilterns, 1875–1951', in *Geography* (November 1957).

—— *The Chilterns*, British Landscape through Maps (Geographical Association, 1962).

CRACKNELL, B. E.: 'The Petroleum Industry of the Lower Thames and Medway', in *Geography* (April 1952).

GRADY, A. D.: 'Changes in the Lea Valley Glasshouse Industry', in *Geography* (April 1959).

SCARGILL, D. I.: 'Metropolitan Influences in the Oxford Region', in *Geography* (April 1967).

WISE, M. J.: 'The Role of London in the Industrial Geography of Great Britain', in *Geography* (November 1956).

For Fitzstephen's account see Leaflets Nos. 93–94 (Historical Association, 1934).

Maps

Bartholomew's ½-inch sheets 14, 15, and 9 cover most of the region.

O.S. ½-inch special sheet, Greater London.

The region is well covered by the 1-inch geological maps. The site of the original foundation of London appears on sheet 256 (North London). The river terraces are well shown on sheet 257 (Romford). Sheet 272 (Chatham) covers the lower Medway; Oxford appears on sheet 236 (Witney).

PART 3
Economic Geography

CHAPTER TWENTY-FOUR

FUEL AND POWER

LIMITATIONS OF space require us to be highly selective in our discussion of the economic geography of the British Isles. Manufactures, farming, and fishing are all worthy of notice; but since these have already received attention in the regional chapters we limit the discussion in this and the following chapter to certain topics which have escaped treatment under the regions or which are more effectively studied on a national basis. They comprise the sources of energy – coal, petroleum, electricity, and nuclear power – and the means of transport – roads, canals, railways, coastal shipping, and air routes.

The Coal Industry

In relation to her size, the United Kingdom is extraordinarily rich in coal. Coal has been extracted since Roman times, and on a more systematic scale since the eighteenth century; yet in spite of all that has been removed, our reserves of workable coal are estimated to be sufficient to last for another 400 to 500 years at present rates of extraction.

Coal has played a vital part in the development of our manufactures: as we have seen (p. 240) it allowed industry to overcome the limitations imposed by water-power, and formed the basis of the Industrial Revolution, which originated in Britain but spread far beyond her shores. An essential stage in the process was the discovery by Abraham Darby in 1730 that when coal was baked in the absence of air it could be transformed into coke, and in this new form could be used to smelt iron ore. The coking process involved the release of coal gas, and perhaps as early as 1792 William Murdock succeeded in lighting his house with gas, and a new industry was born. The Watt steam-engine, which came into use in the 1770's, led to a great increase in the demand for coal; the canal system was evolved to transport coal; the first railway was designed to carry coal; and locomotives in their turn led to further increases in the demand for coal.

Two centuries of mining have left many scattered, shallow, and sometimes flooded workings. The modern trend is towards larger and deeper pits, many of which are situated in the concealed coalfields.

Coal output reached its peak in 1913, when as much as 292 million tonnes were produced. At this time the world's shipping was powered largely by British coal, and of the total 74 million tonnes were exported. In the 1950's output stood at about 200 million tonnes a year, but it has declined to only 133 million tonnes in 1970–71. Exports, too, have fallen dramatically, to as little as 3 million tonnes in the same year.

The virtual disappearance of the export trade is due to several factors. Much of the world's shipping (including the British navy) has adopted oil-burning engines. Overseas coalfields have been developed, and compete for the declining volume of traffic. More important is the expansion in demand from domestic power-stations, and industrial plants, so that little can be spared to meet overseas demands.

About 22 million tonnes of coal still travels along the coast but the shrinkage of the export traffic has left much redundant coal-handling plant and surplus capacity in general in our ports. The south Wales ports in particular were developed almost entirely to handle coal: in 1938 they shipped about 20 million tonnes, foreign and coastal; today they handle less than 3 million tonnes per annum. Expansion in oil and iron ore has to some extent offset the decline in coal, but the ports remain under-employed, and the Rochdale Committee in 1962 recommended the closing of Barry and of the Bute East and West docks of Cardiff.

Nevertheless, in 1970 a new coal terminal was opened at Immingham (Lincolnshire), to handle increasing shipments of Yorkshire coal. With an annual capacity of 6 million tonnes it ranks with the largest coal ports in Europe.

Not only does Britain raise a great volume of coal: she produces also a great variety. Coals can be arranged in order of 'rank', which corresponds broadly with differences in carbon content and heating capacity. Each rank has its ideal uses, though within broad limits some interchange is possible. At the head is anthracite: with a carbon content of about 90 per cent., it is hard, smokeless, burns with little flame, but has great heating value, and so is used for central-heating systems. It is mined in the western portion of the south Wales coalfield, which is one of the world's chief sources of anthracite.

Prime coking coals are confined mainly to south-west Durham and south Wales, and in both districts have led to the rise of important iron and steel industries. There follow, in order of rank, gas, steam, and house coals. The first is well represented in Northumberland and Durham, the York, Derby, and Nottinghamshire coalfield, and the south Lancashire coalfield. Steam coal is produced particularly in south Wales, and in the Tyne district. House coals are found in the Midland fields, and in Ayrshire and Fifeshire.

There has been a radical reorganization in the industry since nationalization took place in 1947. Many small, uneconomic mines have been closed; a few new, larger, and deeper pits have been opened. The changes have involved a great deal of hardship in the areas affected, but are inevitable if efficiency is to be increased.

Between 1956 and 1967 the number of working pits was reduced from 840 to 438 and by 1971 a further 80 had been closed. At the same time employment fell from 704,700 in 1956 to 409,700 in 1967 and to only 286,000 in 1971.

Mechanized coalcutting and loading has been greatly extended, from 2 per cent. of the output in 1947 to more than 90 per cent. in 1970–71. Power haulage has been introduced widely: in 1947 there were only 80 locomotives underground; now there are more than 1,200. As a result the average output per man-shift has practically doubled.

While the production of coal is still declining, technical improvements in its use have made the same quantity produce more energy. During the last 40 years or so generating stations have trebled their efficiency: in 1920 a tonne of coal yielded only 640 units of electricity; now the same quantity produces over 2000 units. But so rapid has been the expansion in the demand for power that the quantity of coal used in generating stations has doubled in the last 20 years.

The chief single use of coal in the United Kingdom is for the production of electricity: this now accounts for over half of the total mined. There follow in order, coke ovens (17 per cent.), industry (12 per cent.), and domestic uses (12 per cent.), Gasworks consume only 2 per cent. and the railways virtually none. About 57 per cent. of the coal is transported by rail, 20 per cent. by road, 11 per cent. by coastal shipping, and the remainder is used on the spot.

In the course of coking and gas-making valuable by-products are released. Each tonne of coal yields, in addition to 736 kg of coke and 6330 MJ of gas, 41 litres of tar, 14 litres of benzole, and 9·5 kg of sulphate of ammonia; and these in turn have a multiplicity of uses. The ammonium sulphate is used mainly in the preparation of fertilizers; from the tar are obtained pitch, fuel oil, lamp black, sheep dips, disinfectants, waterproofing materials, metal and wood preservatives, and creosote; from benzole are produced nylon and a host of chemicals used in the manufacture of plastics, photographic materials, drugs such as aspirin, dyes, saccharine, perfumes, food preservatives, metal and floor polishes, and paints and varnishes. The National Coal Board is the nation's largest producer of tar and benzole, and it still supplies 5 per cent. of the country's gas. In the course of mining large quantities of clay and shale suitable for brick-making are raised; and by virtue of the 58 brickworks which it operates, the Board is the second largest manufacturer of bricks in the country.

Thin seams of coal at shallow depth have often been riddled by earlier workings, but what remains can sometimes be recovered by open-cast methods. In 1970–71, 8·3 million tonnes were won in this way. The largest single working is at Westfield, Fifeshire (output, 1969–70: 1 million tonnes). The following table indicates the quantities of deep-mined coal contributed to the nation's output in the year ending March 1971, by the various coalfields.

Coalfield	Output in millions of tonnes
York, Derby and Nottingham	67·3
Northumberland and Durham	19·0
South Wales	11·7
Scotland	11·3
South Midlands	8·9
Staffordshire	8·3
South Lancashire, Cumberland and North Wales	6·1
Kent	1·0
Total output	133·3

The Gas Industry

The pre-War gas industry was fragmented. There were 1050 gas companies in the United Kingdom; most of them were small and isolated one from another, and all were located close to the market for which they were designed. A single large organization – the Gas Light and Coke Company – supplied London with gas, and accounted for 17 per cent. of the nation's output. This, together with nine other concerns, produced 42 per cent. of the total.

In 1949 the gas industry was nationalized, and reorganized on a regional basis. Twelve independent Gas Boards were established, ten for England and one each for Scotland and Wales. Far-reaching changes have since taken place in the industry. Over 700 small and uneconomic units have been closed, and their markets have been taken over by larger neighbouring works. Nearly 44,000 km of gas mains have been constructed towards the development of regional grids. The advent of natural gas has encouraged the construction for the first time of a widespread pipeline system, which is quickly extending into Scotland, Wales and the South-West (Fig. 107, p. 371). In the meantime there remain large tracts of the country which are served by only small and isolated works: the Highlands and Southern Uplands of Scotland, rural Wales, and much of East Anglia.

Unlike other public utilities, the gas industry buys much of its raw material from external sources. Coke ovens associated with the iron and steel industry are moderate contributors to gas-supplies. Three-fifths of the gas distributed by the Wales and the Northern Gas Boards is 'steel-works' gas, and half of the gas of the East Midland Board comes from a similar source.

In an attempt to combat the rising price of gas coal the industry is seeking other sources of gas. Various techniques have been evolved to use petroleum products as the raw material for gas-making, and works have been set up close to the refineries at Shellhaven, Fawley, and the Isle of Grain. In addition petroleum products are being piped from Fawley to the Southall plant of the North Thames Gas Board, and from the Coryton and Shellhaven refineries to the Romford, Beckton, Bromley, and East Greenwich gasworks. Accordingly, the proportion of oil-based gas is rising steadily: estimated at 27 per cent. of the total supply during 1963–64, it had reached 53 per cent. by 1968–69.

A more ambitious project, however, has been to import methane originating below the Sahara Desert. Two specially designed tankers were built in 1963 for the carriage of liquefied methane; they now run to and from the port of Arzew, in Algeria, and a new terminal on Canvey Island, on the Thames estuary. They carry the equivalent of 280 million therms annually – representing an increase of 5 per cent. in the nation's gas-supply. A main pipeline 320 kilometres long has been constructed from Canvey Island past London to Leeds; and 200 kilometres of branch pipes connect with Reading, Hitchin, Dunstable, Coventry, Birmingham, Sheffield and Manchester (Fig. 107, p. 371). But the real revolution in the gas industry stems from the discoveries of natural gas below the North Sea (p. 374). The following table illustrates the profound changes that have taken place in Britain's gas supplies in the space of only 5 years.

	1964–65 Million therms	1969–70 Million therms
Gas made		
Coal gas	1,462	427
Lurgi gas	75	33
Petroleum gas	406	1,747
Other gases	430	14
Gas bought		
Coke oven gas	447	330
Oil refinery gas	280	227
Sahara gas	287	272
North Sea gas	133	2,694
Total	3,520	5,744

Petroleum and Natural Gas

The United Kingdom plays a part in the world petroleum industry which is quite out of keeping with her small indigenous production. The country has a high consumption per head of oil; she manufactures oil-using equipment on a large scale in the form of cars, lorries, tractors, ships, diesel locomotives, and aeroplanes; she engages in oil-production overseas; she builds oil-tankers; she equips oilfields and oil-refineries; she transports oil on a large scale; and has one of the largest oil-refining industries in Europe.

Small quantities of indigenous oil have been produced in Britain since 1939 and an output of about 80,000 tonnes annually is achieved from wells in Nottinghamshire, Lancashire and Dorset (Fig. 107). Nearly a quarter of this total is raised from a single prolific well at Kimmeridge, which in 1970 produced 17,000 tonnes.

An output of 80,000 tonnes is insignificant when compared with the total requirements of the United Kingdom, which reached 136 million tonnes in 1969 (crude and refined); but the home industry has great value as a training ground for oil geologists, engineers, and drilling teams, in preparation for their work abroad. In addition, the information derived from borings has proved useful: our knowledge of concealed coalfields has been augmented, new deposits of potash have been discovered, and natural gas has been located. Musselburgh (east of Edinburgh) is supplied by natural gas from Dalkeith, Whitby (Yorks) from Eskdale.

Exciting finds below the North Sea, however, lead one to predict a tremendous surge in the production of indigenous oil during the next few years.

These were heralded by the discovery (in May, 1970) by the

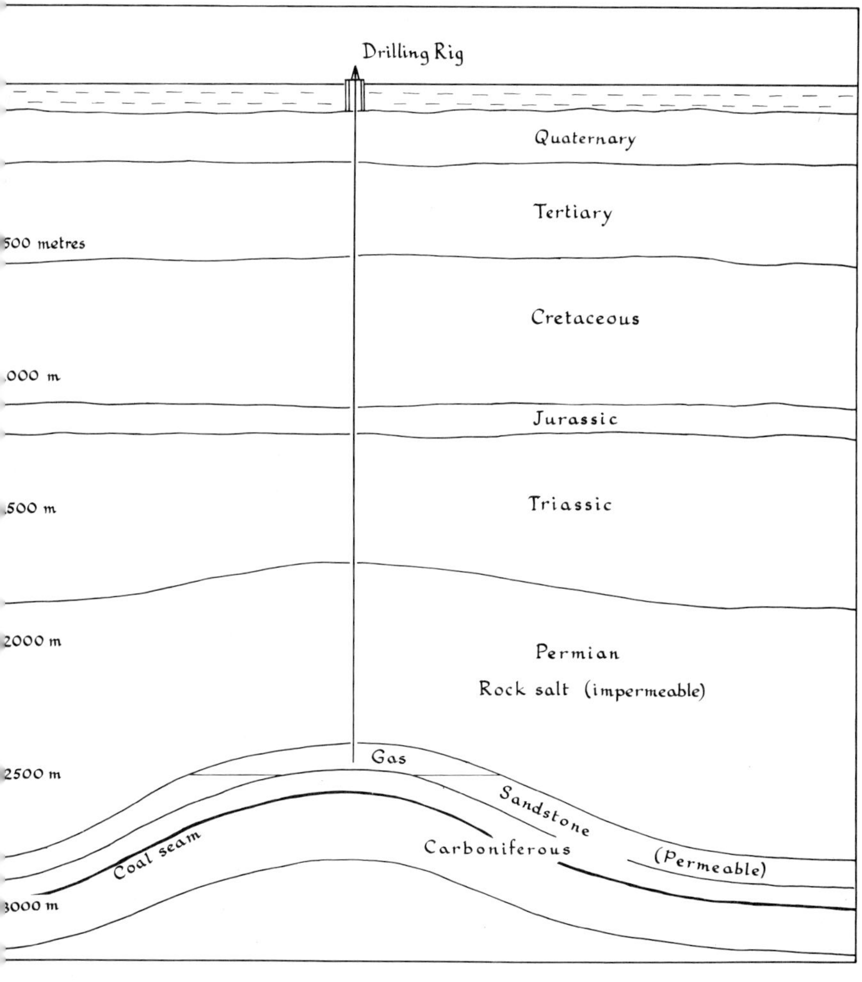
Drilling Rig
Quaternary
Tertiary
500 metres
Cretaceous
,000 m
Jurassic
,500 m
Triassic
2000 m
Permian
Rock salt (impermeable)
Gas
2500 m
Sandstone
Carbonniferous
(Permeable)
Coal seam
3000 m

g. 106. SECTION THROUGH A TYPICAL NORTH SEA GAS STRUCTURE
:tural gas is likely to be associated with favourable structures where coal seams underlie rock salt. e coal seam is the probable source of the gas; this migrates upwards if there is a suitable porous :k to contain it – here a Carboniferous sandstone. The rock salt above, being impermeable, prevents gas from escaping. *Modified, after T. Gaskell,* 1966.

American Phillips group, of the Ekofisk oilfield a short distance within the Norwegian sector of the North Sea. Four months later the same group, operating in the United Kingdom sector, drilled a successful oil well 180 miles east of Aberdeen. But the first major oil strike in the British sector was made by B.P. in October, 1970, 110 miles off Aberdeen. By October 1971 two further wells had delimited an important new oilfield, the Forties field, which is expected to have a capacity of up to 30 million tonnes annually, representing 20 per cent. of the current United Kingdom requirements of petroleum.

The discoveries are in water depths of 350 feet, and this, together with the severe winter weather, will make the recovery of the oil difficult and expensive; but there is little doubt that the industry will solve these problems, and that Britain will become less dependent on supplies from the Middle East.

British participation in the international oil industry dates from about a century ago, when the large amounts of capital needed were available in this country as a result of advances in industry and commerce. The early start has enabled United Kingdom companies, in association with Dutch interests, to become the second largest oil-producer after the United States, raising about one-third of the total output of the Middle East and the Caribbean, and one-third of all the oil entering into international trade.

As a seafaring nation the United Kingdom has established a large mercantile marine, which in 1970 stood at a record size. This has always included a high proportion of tanker tonnage.

The construction of tankers has provided a major part of the work in British shipyards, which in their turn have drawn on the resources of the steel and engineering industries and the many associated manufactures. In 1970 the British tanker fleet was the second largest in the world, and at 21·7 million tons d.w. it represented 14·3 per cent. of the world's tanker tonnage. As the size of tankers has increased, so has the value of their orders to the shipyards. In 1970 British shipbuilders launched two 250,000-ton tankers, and in 1971 there were on order eight others of this size: they represented a combined value of £100 million. The oil industry is clearly a mainstay of British ship-building. In addition the oil companies spend a sum of money almost equal to the cost of the oil-tankers on chemicals and specialized equipment for refining, drilling, and exploration.

The United Kingdom oil-refining industry is of rapid and recent growth (Fig. 107), as the following table indicates:

Total Throughput Capacity of United Kingdom Oil-refineries

Year	Millions of tonnes	Year	Millions of tonnes
1938	3·8	1965	72·2
1950	11·7	1970	112·5
1955	29·7	1975 (estimate)	135·5
1960	49·3		

Fig. 107.   THE UNITED KINGDOM: OIL AND NATURAL GAS

Britain produces small quantities of oil and gas from onshore sources: these are indicated by triangles. Far more significant are the deposits below the North Sea. North Sea gas was discovered and the main fields outlined from 1965 onwards; the North Sea oil discoveries were made in 1970 and 1971. The pipelines are those in commission or under construction by late 1971.

This rapid growth reflects the phenomenal increase in the demand for petroleum products during the last 30 years, consequent on the ever-growing use of the petrol engine in road, rail, and air transport, and in agriculture. So long as the demand for oil was relatively small, it was more economical to refine the crude petroleum on the oilfields themselves.

Owing to the large size of the ocean tankers, a deep-water site is essential for the establishment of an oil-refinery; in addition, it is an advantage to place the refinery close to the market it is intended to serve. A modern refinery is largely mechanized, but two or three hundred skilled workers are still required; yet a refinery must nevertheless be situated sufficiently far from the nearest built-up area to minimize the risk of fire or explosion. A large refinery plays an important part in the economy of its area, and oil normally dominates the volume of traffic in the port of which it forms part.

The first large-scale refinery in Britain was constructed in 1922 at Llandarcy, close to Swansea (the name was invented in honour of a director of the company). For long it was served by Queen's Dock, Swansea; but owing to the increased size of tankers it has been necessary to seek a deeper terminal, and a 96-kilometre pipe-line now connects Llandarcy with Milford Haven (p. 130).

In 1924 a refinery was built at Grangemouth, on the Firth of Forth; this too has been connected to a deep-water terminal, at Finnart on Loch Long, and is served by a 92-kilometre pipeline. The Finnart terminal, opened in 1959, was the first in the United Kingdom to accommodate 100,000-ton tankers. Both Llandarcy and Grangemouth have been greatly enlarged since they were built.

Southampton provides a ready market for bunker oil, and is excellently situated for the supply of installations in southern England; when the Esso company contemplated its first refinery in Britain this was the site selected. The refinery was opened in 1951, and has since been expanded; with a capacity of $16\frac{1}{2}$ million tonnes this is the largest, not only in Britain but in the entire Commonwealth. A group of related industries is growing in the area. In 1958 a plant for the production of butadiene was opened: this is the raw material for the manufacture of synthetic rubber, and is fed to a works near by – the first of its kind in the United Kingdom. In addition the Fawley (Southampton) refinery supplies gas to the Southern Gas Board and fuel to the Marchwood generating station. The future of this area is assured: a new oil-based gasworks has been built at Fawley, together with a vast oil-fired power-station.

Three major plants now serve London (Fig. 101, p. 350). The Shell company's installation at Shellhaven dates from 1916, but a new refinery was opened in 1950. On the south side of the estuary, on the Isle of Grain, British Petroleum opened their first refinery in the region in 1953, and this, the Kent refinery, has since more than doubled its original capacity. The Mobil refinery at Coryton began as a small plant in 1953, and has doubled its size since 1967 to reach its present annual capacity of 7 million tonnes. Our newest oil port is Milford Haven (p. 130) but in Bantry Bay, in the south-west of the Irish Republic, the Gulf Oil Corporation has built a great oil terminal to accommodate new monster tankers of 300,000 tons d.w. They need 22 metres of water to float, 1·6 km to turn, and up to 16 km in which to stop.

The table indicates the capacities of the United Kingdom refineries in excess of one million tonnes per annum, as at the end of 1970.

Refinery	Company	Millions of metric tonnes
Fawley (Southampton)	Esso	16·5
Stanlow (Manchester Ship Canal)	Shell	10·8
Kent (Rochester)	B.P.	10·0
Shellhaven (Thames)	Shell	10·0
Llandarcy (Swansea)	B.P.	8·0
Grangemouth	B.P.	7·0
Coryton (Thames)	Mobil	7·0
Killingholme (Lincolnshire)	Lindsey	7·0
Milford Haven	Esso	6·3
Milford Haven	Texaco	5·9
Teesport	Shell	5·5
Billingham-on-Tees	Phillips-Imperial	5·1
South Killingholme (Lincolnshire)	Conoco	4·5
Milford Haven	Gulf	4·0
Heysham	Shell	2·0
Belfast	B.P.	1·5
Total (including smaller unlisted refineries)		112.5

Oil is by far the most important single import by weight into Britain, accounting for about half the total tonnage. It represents eleven-twelfths of the total overseas tonnage imported into Southampton, half that of London and Manchester, and more than one-third that of Liverpool.

A new industry has developed in the shape of petro-chemicals; these reach the consumer in such varied products as plastics, synthetic rubber, detergents and nitrogenous fertilizers. Between 1958 and 1968 the sales of British petro-chemicals doubled and the industry expanded twice as quickly as the average of all manufactures.

Interest in the possibility of North Sea gas was first aroused in 1959, when a well in the Groningen province of the Netherlands reached strata enormously rich in natural gas: it had struck the second largest known gas field in the world.

A Geneva Convention ratified in 1964 defined the rights of the bordering states over the Continental Shelf, and the way was now open for prospecting. During 1964 23 companies gained concessions in 88,000 sq km of the British section, and huge drilling rigs were built in British shipyards or towed from overseas. In September 1965 the British Petroleum Company, 65 km east of Cleethorpes, struck gas at about 3000 metres, and this was followed by further strikes by Shell-Esso (April 1966) and the Gas Council-Amoco and Phillips groups (May). An eventual daily output of 112 million cubic metres is now envisaged from the North Sea gasfields – four times the present consumption. The B.P. wells are linked to Easington, just north of the Humber, and the gas is being fed into the existing methane pipeline south-west of Sheffield. Gas from the fields to the south is brought ashore at Bacton in Norfolk, 15 km south-east of Cromer. Figure 107 indicates the extent of the known gas fields and the pipeline system by late 1971.

Electricity

In the majority of generating stations in this country the thrust is exerted by steam raised from the burning of coal. The pattern of the distribution of these power-stations is related to three main requirements: a near-by market, cheap coal, and a source of cooling water.

The distribution of power-stations broadly reflects the pattern of population density, but there are certain significant departures. Central Scotland draws much of its power from the hydro-electric stations of the Highlands, so that the capacity of its generating stations is smaller than one might expect. Colliery districts, although they use large quantities of electricity, generate much of it independently of the public service. The Sheffield region is a more important consumer than its population alone might suggest, for its steel industry is based largely on electrical heating. This close relation between the distribution of generating stations and the market arises because it is expensive to transmit peak loads over long distances – more expensive than the cost of carrying coal by sea, but cheaper than carrying it by rail over more than about 65 km.

In the absence of navigable water, the cost of stockpiling the coal asserts itself. Power-plants are now so large that they must draw their fuel from a wide area; a centre of communications is therefore more convenient than an actual colliery site.

Most power-stations make use of direct cooling, and require vast quantities of water for this purpose. A station of 300 MW needs about 55 million litres an hour for direct cooling, so that a riverside site is indicated. The concentration of power-stations along the lower Thames is thus related to supplies of cooling water as well as water-borne coal. The Trent is ideal for the provision of cooling water: it is calculated that below Burton the Trent could support a 400 MW generating station every 16 km. Since this river flows close to the largest coalfield in Britain, and through a densely peopled region, it offers an ideal combination of circumstances, and it is here that the greatest advances have been made in the building of power-stations.

If there is insufficient water available for direct cooling recourse may be had to cooling towers, but this involves greater expense. The water requirements of a station of 400 MW would then be reduced to about 1,820,000 litres.

Before the First World War power-stations served limited and isolated areas, and if there were a breakdown or an exceptional demand in one area it could not draw on the resources of a neighbour. The system was wasteful, as it involved the existence of much unused capacity, provided against such contingencies.

Later expansion was regulated by an Act of 1926, which established a national transmission system ('the Grid'), at 132 kV (132,000 volts). The country was divided into eight regions, and the aim was to provide in each of them sufficient generating plant, which, when linked together, would meet the demand. The eight regions were joined by transmission lines, but were regarded as independent units, and little interchange of energy in fact took place.

During the Second World War changes in the geographical demands for electricity were so rapid that it became necessary to operate the grid as a single unit. Post-war needs rose so sharply that the former independent units could no longer remain self-sufficient. It became clear that there would need to be a transfer of power from the West Riding, the east Midlands, and north-east coast – all rich in coal – to London and southern England, and to Merseyside and the north-west; and in order to avoid a multiplicity of circuits it was decided to establish a 'super-grid' with transmission at 275 kV.

As existing in 1967, this consists of a ring of transmission lines linking the Midlands by way of the Trent to the West Riding, across the Pennines to the Mersey, and back to the Midlands. A second ring encloses the London region, joining power-stations at

Tilbury and Elstree to Iver and Weybridge, and returning to cross the Thames from Northfleet to West Thurrock (Fig. 108). The two rings are joined by two parallel lines; there are connections north-ward to Tyneside and through Carlisle to Scotland, while further links serve the West Country and south Wales.

From Northfleet, in Kent, a line runs to Canterbury and Lydd; from here a cross-Channel cable, completed in 1961, links with the French transmission system. Peak demands as between England and France occur at different times, so that a substantial saving in total capacity is made possible to both countries.

For a generation the demand for electricity in the United Kingdom has increased at about 7 per cent. annually, approxi-mately doubling every ten years. Since 1951 the rate has been even higher – about 8½ per cent. annually. Sales in 1950 amounted to 41,490 million units; sales in 1969–70 had risen to 168,230 million units. Agriculture has shown the greatest expansion in demand, for during the period the nation's farms increased their consumption of electricity fivefold. In 1950 only 36 per cent. of the farms were connected to the public supply: the corresponding figure by 1963 was 89 per cent.

The modern trend is to close down small, uneconomic units and to build larger and larger plants; accordingly the number of power-stations has been reduced from 290 in 1951 to 193 in 1970. The increase in size has been spectacular. In 1951 the largest generating stations were of 250 MW capacity (a megawatt is a million watts); in 1965 the largest power-station in operation (at High Marnham on the Trent, about 16 km west of Lincoln) had a capacity of 1000 MW. Larger installations followed. By 1967 19 new power-stations were being built (excluding nuclear plants). Among them were five very large plants, each of 2000 MW capacity: they com-prised Aberthaw B (Glamorgan), Eggborough (Selby, Yorks), Fiddlers Ferry (Lancs), Fawley (Southampton) and West Pennar (Pembroke). The last two are oil-fired. By 1970 three of these were complete, and the projected power station at Drax (Yorks) was laid out for a possible ultimate capacity of 4000 MW. The age of giant power-stations has begun. The latest advance has been the adoption of an even higher voltage for trunk transmission lines constructed since 1965: these will all eventually transmit at 400 kV. There will thus be a further economy in the number of new lines needed to cope with the expanding transmission system. In sum, the Central Electricity Generating Board remains the greatest single industrial builder in Britain and the custodian of the largest generating system under unified control in the world.

Fig. 108. ENGLAND AND WALES: ELECTRIC POWER- STATIONS AND MAJOR TRANSMISSION LINES

The supergrid transmission lines indicated were operating in 1967, and the nuclear power-stations are those in operation and under construction. For completeness the Blaenau Ffestiniog hydro-electric station (close to Trawsfynydd) has been included with the coal-fired stations. *By courtesy of the Central Electricity Generating Board.*

Nuclear Power

The siting of nuclear power-stations is controlled by factors which differ from those concerned in the location of conventional power-stations. The source of fuel supplies is of little account, for a 500 MW nuclear power-station requires only half a tonne of uranium a day, compared with the 5000 tonnes of coal used by a conventional power-station of the same capacity. Nuclear power-stations can therefore be placed in close relation to the market, providing that other site factors can be satisfied: these are the proximity of cooling water, remoteness from built-up areas, and convenience for linking with the super-grid.

We have seen that in southern England and Merseyside the quantity of coal available does not meet the demands for electricity. These are the regions which would benefit most from the establishment of nuclear power-stations, and here indeed are located 8 of the 9 at present envisaged. Three are in the West Country, 3 in the English Channel area, and 2 in north-west Wales.

The need for cooling water is an important locational factor, for nuclear stations require almost twice as much water as directly cooled coal-fired stations. All but one of the nine nuclear stations are on the sea-coast or on the shore of an estuary, where an unlimited supply of water is available. The remaining one, at Trawsfynydd, in north-west Wales, is situated on a large reservoir which was constructed to supply the hydro-electric station at Maentwrog. Though the catchment area is small, this is a district of heavy rainfall. As in coal-fired stations, the water is not 'consumed', but is returned to the source, though at a higher temperature.

Nearness to the super-grid is important owing to the high cost of constructing the 275 kV transmission line. At £25,000 a mile, a station 40 miles from the grid would involve an additional expenditure of £1,000,000. So far as distance from built-up areas is concerned, the Government has indicated that while the design of these power-stations is inherently safe, they will nevertheless not be sited close to large towns. The minimum requirement appears to be at least 8 km from towns of more than 10,000 inhabitants.

Capital costs are heavy – $2\frac{1}{2}$ to 3 times as great as those associated with conventional power-stations; and this fact, coupled with high interest rates, means that the electricity so produced is initially expensive. But with the increasing size of nuclear power stations the cost is falling: the electricity from Wylfa Head is only half as expensive as that from Berkeley. The latest nuclear-power stations are expected to be fully competitive with coal-fired stations.

The construction of a nuclear-power station brings a wave of activity into the region. The transport of the heavy equipment involves the reconstruction of miles of roads, and may involve the revival of decayed ports. The labour force required for building runs into two or three thousand, most of whom are needed for five or six years; the permanent employment, however, is much smaller, and amounts to 300 to 400 men.

The following table summarizes the capacities and dates of the 14 power-stations which are constructed or under construction in Britain. It will be seen that in four cases there are two nuclear power stations on the same site: this is an obvious economy once the improvements in access have been made and connection to the super-grid effected. In 1970 10 per cent. of our total energy was provided by nuclear power; and at present the United Kingdom leads the world in the production of atomic energy.

Station	Approximate construction period	Capacity MW			
Berkeley, Glos.	1957–62		275		
Bradwell, Essex	1957–62		300		
Hinkley Point, Somerset	1957–72	A	500	B	1250
Trawsfynydd, North Wales	1959–64		500		
Dungeness, Kent	1960–70	A	555	B	1200
Sizewell, Suffolk	1961–?	A	580	B	2500
Oldbury-on-Severn, Glos.	1962–66		600		
Wylfa Head, Anglesey	1962–71		1180		
Hunterston, Ayrshire	1964–72	A	320	B	1250
Hartlepool	1968–74		1320		

Hydro-electricity

The energy available from falling water is directly proportional to the volume of the water and the vertical distance through which it falls. Hydro-electricity may therefore be developed successfully where the head of water is relatively small, provided that a large volume is available; this is effected in the Shannon scheme (p. 96), where the power canal, leading to Ardnacrusha, has the appearance of a great river. More usually in the British Isles a smaller volume is available, but it is possible to use a greater vertical distance. This is generally true of north Wales and the Scottish Highlands.

Apart from volume and vertical distance, there are several other conditions which must be met for the successful development of hydro-electricity. A heavy rainfall well distributed throughout the year is desirable; there should be little interruption by freezing; an

impermeable bed-rock is important, for it produces a high proportion of runoff, and allows the construction of naturally watertight
reservoirs; finally, there needs to be a near-by market for the
power so produced.

Most of these conditions are satisfied in the Scottish Highlands,
where more than half the area is over 370 metres high, and there are
many natural reservoirs in the form of ribbon lakes. But there is
no large and immediate market, and about 20 per cent. of the
power produced is used in the Lowlands.

Over 50 hydro-electric stations are operating in Scotland (Fig,
41, p. 145), and every major river contributes to the supply of
power. The installations range in capacity from 130 MW at Sloy
to ·54 MW at Gisla, in Lewis, and from a head of 415 metres at
Finlarig to a mere 5·5 metres at Morar. There are concentrations in
the Inverness district and in the upper Tay basin, but stations are
scattered also along the west coast, and are found in the larger
islands of the Inner and Outer Hebrides.

The production of hydro-electricity in Scotland has grown at a
faster rate than that of thermo-electricity in the rest of Britain.
Since 1950 generating capacity has quintupled from 284·7 MW to
reach 1452 MW in 1970–71, and the number of consumers has
almost doubled from 244,000 to 473,343. The expansion continues.
During 1970–71 the new aluminium plant at Invergordon was
connected to the grid and 10,020 new consumers were served. By
the end of March 1971, 97 per cent. of all the potential consumers
in the region were connected to the public electricity system.

This is operated as a public service, and not solely as a profit-
making organization; and many of the new connections were made
in remote rural areas which could never receive the benefits of
electricity were economy the only consideration.

The main recent advances have been made in the development
of pumped storage schemes:

Station	Completion Date	Capacity MW
Cruachan	1966	400
Foyers	1974	300
Loch Lomond	(under survey)	

In north Wales there are three hydro-electric plants. The
smallest and earliest is at the foot of Snowdon in Cwm Dyli, and
has a capacity of 5½ MW. The Maentwrog plant (Fig. 31, p. 117)
has a capacity of 24 MW; the Dolgarrog installation in the Conway
valley draws its water from a group of lakes, and the catchment area

has been greatly extended by the construction of tunnels and aqueducts; its capacity is about 28 MW (Fig. 30, p. 116).

Far larger is the installation at Ffestiniog, opened in 1963: this embraces a pumped storage scheme, by which water is used to generate power during peak periods, and pumped back to the reservoir at off periods.

In the nation as a whole hydro-electricity forms only a small proportion of the power resources – little more than 3 per cent. – but in the north of Scotland it has played a vital part in transforming social and economic life.

FOR FURTHER READING

Books
MANNERS, G.: *The Geography of Power* (Hutchinson, 1964).
Annual Report and Accounts, Electricity Council.
Annual Report and Accounts, National Coal Board.
Annual Report and Accounts, North of Scotland Hydro-electricity Board.

Articles
Gas – A Special Report, *The Times*, October 5th, 1970.
Gas Industry – A Special Report, *The Times*, October 6th, 1969.
GASKELL, T.: 'Source of the North Sea Gas', in *Geographical Magazine* (December 1966).
HOYLE, B. S.: 'The Production and Refining of Indigenous Oil in Britain', in *Geography* (November 1961).
Institute of Petroleum, *Memoranda*.
MANNERS, G.: 'Recent Changes in the British Gas Industry' (*Transactions and Papers, Institute of British Geographers*, 1959).
—— '1970s Power Game', in *Geographical Magazine* (March 1970).
MORGAN, M.: 'Natural Gas and Britain', in *Geographical Magazine* (January 1967).
MOUNFIELD, P. R.: 'The Location of Nuclear Power Stations in the United Kingdom', in *Geography* (April 1961).
—— 'Nuclear Power in the United Kingdom: A New Phase', in *Geography* (July 1967).
'North Sea Gas – A Special Survey', *The Times*, October 4th, 1967.
RAWSTRON, E. M.: 'The Distribution and Location of Steam-driven Power Stations in Great Britain', in *Geography* (November 1951).
—— 'Changes in the Geography of Electricity Production in Great Britain', in *Geography* (April 1955).

CHAPTER TWENTY-FIVE

TRANSPORT AND POPULATION

THE MOVEMENT of people and goods is an essential part of our economic life, and forms of transport have geographical as well as technical aspects. In this final chapter we examine the major characteristics of transport by road, canal, railway, coastal shipping, and air, and conclude by a brief study of recent changes in the distribution of population.

Roads

The courses of several prehistoric trackways are known, but they have had little influence on the siting of modern roads. It was the Romans who first planned and established a road system in Great Britain, and many of their routes have been incorporated into the modern network. It is instructive to compare the Ordnance Survey map of Roman Britain with that published on the same scale in the style of the International 1:1,000,000 map, which indicates the main roads.

In Roman times nine roads focused on London. The lines of some of these have been lost, but others remain in use after nearly 2000 years. The A2 from Dover through Canterbury to London stands on its Roman line; so does the road from London to Norwich by way of Colchester. For most of its route the Roman Ermine Street from London (Shoreditch Church) to Lincoln and beyond has given rise to modern roads (A10, A14, A15); and Watling Street, from London (Marble Arch) through Towcester and Atherstone to Wroxeter (near Shrewsbury) is represented by the modern A5.

The Fosse Way, planned as a temporary frontier for the Roman Empire, later became a civil highway, and has left its mark on the road system. It runs in an almost straight line for 320 km linking Exeter with Lincoln, and its route shows a thorough understanding of the local physical geography. In places it is now neglected and overgrown, but modern roads follow its line from Leicester to Lincoln and from Cirencester to High Cross.

The coastal road through south Wales follows essentially a Roman line; so does that from Dolgellau to the north-east, through the Bala-Towyn trough (p. 104). In the north, the road from York northward along the flank of the Pennines, and westward through Brough and Penrith to Carlisle, originated with the Romans. Northwich is linked with Manchester, Chester, and Lancaster by Roman routes.

In the Southern Uplands of Scotland, the road from Glasgow to Carlisle by way of the Annan and Clyde is mainly of Roman origin. Roman routes can be recognized in many other stretches of modern highway, such as the Lichfield to Derby road, the Droitwich to Stratford-on-Avon road, and the Alcester to Birmingham road.

The planning and building of new roads has been extremely rare in the past; but from the late seventeenth century onward many stretches of existing road were improved by turnpiking. In the mid-eighteenth century General Wade constructed new roads for military purposes in the Scottish Highlands. In the early nineteenth century Thomas Telford was busy in the same region: in addition to constructing the Caledonian Canal he was responsible for the building of 1500 km of roads, and among many bridges, that spanning the Tay at Dunkeld, at the entrance of the Highlands, on the main road between Perth and Inverness (A9). He was later commissioned to improve the most important road across the Southern Uplands – that between Carlisle and Glasgow – which, as we have seen, had been pioneered by the Romans. Perhaps Telford's greatest claim to fame, however, rests on his construction of the Holyhead road, from Shrewsbury, through the difficult mountain country of north Wales, and across the Conway river and the Menai Strait by two magnificent suspension bridges.

The first half of the twentieth century witnessed the advent of the motor-car and the rapid expansion of motor traffic, entailing crippling congestion at key points of a road system designed for horse traffic. Road improvements were confined mainly to the provision of roundabouts and bypasses; but in the 1950's came the beginning of a more fundamental approach to the problem in the shape of the motorway, specially designed for fast traffic.

The motorway system is like a ladder arranged from north to south with three rungs running east and west (Fig. 109). The provinces are served equally with the capital. The eastern side of the ladder runs from London to Leeds, and its first section, a stretch of 110 km from London to Crick, was opened in 1959 as the M1 (Plate 10). By 1970 the M1 was complete from London to Leeds, and had sent off a spur to the north-east (the M18) to link with the Doncaster bypass.

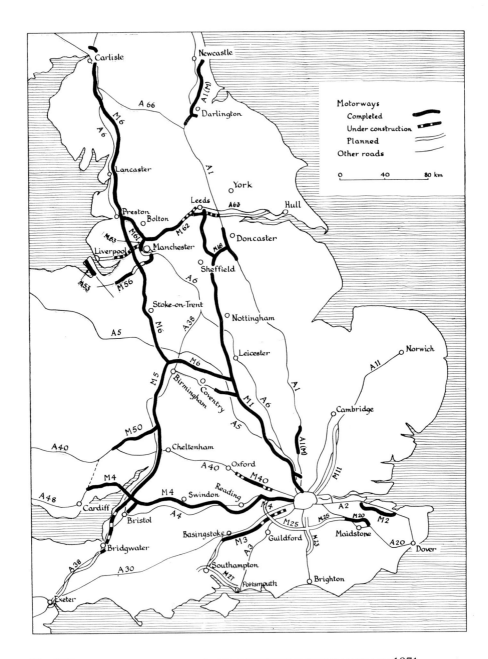

Fig. 109. ENGLAND AND WALES: THE MOTORWAY SYSTEM IN LATE 1971

Essentially it comprises a ladder with three rungs. In addition in Scotland there are relatively short stretches of motorway focusing on Glasgow and Edinburgh, and in Northern Ireland, on Belfast.

The western side of the ladder will be from Exeter to Carlisle, bypassing Birmingham, Stoke-on-Trent, Manchester, Preston and Lancaster. By the end of 1971 this was complete from Carlisle to Avonmouth, and construction was well advanced southward to Bridgwater in Somerset (Fig. 109). From Strensham, just north of Tewkesbury, a spur extends westward off the M5 to Ross-on-Wye (M50).

The southern rung of the ladder is the M4. It runs from London westward to south Wales by way of the Severn Bridge which has been built close to the former Aust Ferry. The new bridge has greatly relieved the considerable congestion in Gloucester. This 224-km motorway links London with Reading, Swindon, Bristol, and Newport. It connects with the M5 just north of Bristol.

The central rung of the ladder (M6) is 56 km long and was ready for opening in 1972: it leaves the M1 at Catthorpe (north of Rugby), skirts the north of Coventry and Birmingham, and connects with the M5 at Rayhall (near Walsall). The northern rung is to run from a point on the M1 south of Leeds to the M61 north of Manchester. This is the Lancashire-Yorkshire motorway (M62) which by the mid-seventies will stretch from Liverpool to Hull.

Other short stretches of motorway serve special local needs. The north-east coast has the Durham motorway linking Darlington with Newcastle, and with a spur to the Tyne tunnel east of Newcastle. In the south-east there have been improvements along the two parallel routes between London and Dover. These are the Medway Towns motorway (M2) and the Mid-Kent motorway (M20). Within the same district is the Dartford to Purfleet tunnel. Opened in 1963 after seven years of building, it provides a much-needed road link between Essex and Kent east of the built-up area of London.

Three other schemes, all of motorway proportions, represent local but important improvements on the A1 – the trunk route east of the Pennines from London towards Edinburgh. They are the Stevenage bypass, its continuation, the Baldock bypass, and the Doncaster bypass. Farther north on the same route is the Durham motorway, which we have already mentioned.

Finally, new motorways are planned to link London with Cambridge (M11), Oxford (M40), Basingstoke (M3) – part of which is now open – and Crawley (M23); and a new orbital motorway will run south of London (M25).

In sum, the motorway project makes an impressive contribution towards the solution of the problems set by the post-war expansion in road transport.

Plate 10.
'SPAGHETTI JUNCTION'

The photograph illustrates the Worsley Braided Interchange ('Spaghetti Junction') which has transformed Manchester into a hub of the motorway system. In the picture are the M62 from Leeds to Manchester (top right to bottom left), the M61 to Preston (top left) and the East Lancashire Road, A580, from Manchester to Liverpool (bottom right to centre left). The camera faces north. Photo by courtesy of A. Monk and Company, Ltd.

Canals and River Navigation

To view the canals and navigable rivers in proper perspective one should remember that when they were built roads were unsurfaced and the railway had not yet arrived. Rivers were improved and canals were dug largely for the carriage of coal, and the inland waterways played a vital part in distributing fuel in the early stages of the Industrial Revolution. In south Wales the canals carried coal from the upper valleys to the ports; in south Lancashire they followed the river valleys and focused on Manchester; in the West Riding they led to Leeds and Bradford; in the Black Country they formed a complex network. At a later stage the regional waterway systems became linked together: canals were constructed across the Pennines, and the Birmingham network was joined to the Humber, the Mersey, the Severn, and the Thames.

Today roads and railways have almost eclipsed the inland waterways, which now carry less than 1 per cent. of the freight traffic of the United Kingdom. Nevertheless, locally the waterways are important in the economic life of their regions. In this section we take no account of the Thames, which forms part of the port of London, or the Manchester Ship Canal, which is essentially the Port of Manchester.

The lower Medway carries an important traffic, amounting to over two million tonnes annually. It consists of coal and wood-pulp, which are transferred to barges below Rochester Bridge and distributed to the paper-mills farther upstream. Coastal craft laden with china clay from Cornwall, however, discharge direct at the mills. The river Lea, which joins the Thames just above the Royal Docks, carries a similarly heavy traffic as far upstream as Enfield: it includes coal for local gasworks and timber for the furniture and woodworking industries of east London.

Connecting both with the Lea and with the Thames at Brentford is the Grand Union Canal, which runs north-westward to Birmingham: it carries coal and general merchandise to the extent of 250,000 to 500,000 tonnes annually, the journey from London to Birmingham taking 3–4 days. The Black Country canals form the only network still in use, and carry between ½ million and 1 million tonnes annually; but the long-distance links with the Humber, Mersey, and Trent are now insignificant.

Below Worcester the Severn is in use, mainly for the carriage of oil; and the traffic becomes greater in volume between Gloucester and Sharpness, where a canal avoids the meanders and shallows of the lower Severn. Consisting of oil and general cargoes, it amounts to over ½ million tonnes a year.

In Lancastria the canals of the Manchester region are in use no longer, with the exception of the Bridgewater Canal and the Weaver Navigation whose traffic amounts to over ½ million tonnes. The only trans-Pennine canal still in use is the Leeds and Liverpool canal; its summit section carries less than 25,000 tonnes annually; nevertheless, coal from the West Riding arrives in south Lancashire by this route to supplement local supplies.

Far heavier is the traffic on the Aire and Calder Navigation, downstream from Leeds and Wakefield to Goole. It amounts to more than 2 million tonnes annually, and consists mainly of coal, shipped in ingeniously contrived amphibious containers, and transhipped at Goole into colliers with the aid of specially designed hoists.

The Don carries more than ½ million tonnes downstream from Sheffield (mainly coal), and the Trent handles a similar quantity below Newark; but the Fenland rivers and the Yorkshire Ouse now carry little cargo. Scotland has been provided with three canals (the Caledonian, the Forth and Clyde, and the Crinan Canals) but they handle hardly any commercial traffic.

Railways

We may perhaps introduce the British railway system by noticing the routes of some of the more famous of the various 'named trains'.

Scotland is linked with London by both the east- and west-coast routes. The *Flying Scotsman* continues a tradition begun in 1862, and runs from London (King's Cross) to Edinburgh by way of Peterborough, Doncaster, York, Newcastle, and Berwick. Its counterpart on the west is the *Royal Scot*, which proceeds from London (Euston), through Rugby, Stafford, and Crewe, Preston, Lancaster, Shap Fell, and Carlisle to Glasgow. The *Irish Mail* has been running since 1848: it links London (Euston) with Holyhead, by way of Crewe, Chester, and the north Wales coast, crosses the Menai Strait by means of the tubular bridge constructed by Robert Stephenson in 1850, and connects with the steamers to and from Dun Laoghaire.

The *Cornish Riviera Express* has been running since 1904. Now diesel-hauled, it travels to Penzance by Reading, Exeter, and Plymouth. Bristol is served separately by the *Bristolian*. The *Brighton Belle*, which ran between London and the south coast for nearly 40 years, terminated in April 1972. Eastward from London

(Liverpool Street) is the *Hook Continental*, which reaches Harwich, to connect with the packet steamers to and from the Hook of Holland. South-eastward runs the *Golden Arrow* from London (Victoria) to Folkestone, linking with the Channel steamers to and from Boulogne.

Just as the railway spelt the decline of the canal era, so the locomotive in its turn has had to face severe competition from the bus, coach, and private car. For short hauls and country services there is little doubt that the bus is more appropriate than the locomotive; and it is likely that many a branch line would never have been constructed had the alternative method of transport been available earlier.

The Beeching proposals of 1963 were based on the astonishing facts that half of all the mileage open to freight traffic carried only 5 per cent. of the total freight; and half the passenger network carried only 4 per cent. of all the passenger traffic. Surveys of the railway traffic were published for the first time in 1962. They showed concentrations of goods traffic in the north-east coast area, in the York, Derby, and Nottinghamshire coalfield, in south Wales, and in Lanarkshire. Most of the freight was handled in a triangle whose vertices are at Hull, Liverpool, and London; but the rural areas handled very little.

The passenger survey revealed a heavy concentration of traffic on London, in a region extending as far east as Southend, as far west as Reading, and as far south as Brighton. In addition there was a considerable passenger traffic between all the large cities.

The proposals of the Beeching Report were drastic. In the words of *The Times* (March 28th, 1963), they heralded 'the end of the passenger railway network in this country as so many millions of travellers have known it for the greater part of this century.' It was proposed to close 2128 stations (one-third of the total); to close one-third of the route-mileage; to withdraw passenger services completely from about 8000 km of track, and stopping trains on many other routes. North Devon and Cornwall would be left with one passenger line; there would be only one route through central Wales, and no trains north of Inverness.

Later in 1963 proposals were announced for the elimination of a number of inessential long-distance routes. It was pointed out that in several cases the passenger has a choice of two or more parallel routes, and that this was an uneconomic legacy of the days of competing companies. It is proposed to close one of the routes from London to the West Country, the Rugby and Leicester route to Sheffield, the Leamington route to Birmingham, two of the trans-

Pennine routes, and the Eden valley route from Leeds to Scotland. But these surgical operations should not be allowed to mask the major improvements which have been taking place since 1955.

Steam locomotives have now all been withdrawn, and their place taken by diesel and electric locomotives. The initial outlay on a diesel is greater than that of a steam locomotive, but its running costs are lower, its life is longer, and it is capable of greater speeds. It is also cleaner.

On trunk routes, on country services, and in shunting, the transition was rapid. Between 1961 and 1966 the number of steam locomotives fell from 11,691 to 1689, while the number of diesels rose from 3179 to 4962. At the same time electrification was in progress, bringing the promise of even greater economies. This, however, involves a major reconstruction of the track. Nevertheless, by 1970 about 3200 km of route had been electrified, including the services from London to the Kent and Essex coasts, Southampton and Bournemouth; from London via Rugby, Birmingham, Stafford and Crewe to Liverpool and Manchester; and routes in the Glasgow region and Scottish Highlands. It is proposed to electrify the line from London to Leeds and York, and in 1970 it was decided to electrify the route from Crewe to Glasgow. The use of rail containers is expanding, and in 1968 British Railways reconstructed the Harwich quays to improve the links with their container vessels.

Modernization has greatly speeded the main line services. For example, the 640-km journey from London to Glasgow in 1965 took $7\frac{1}{2}$ hours. In September 1970, the introduction of double-headed diesel trains reduced the time to under 6 hours. By 1975 electrification of the service will have reduced the time to 5 hours. Such improvements in timing are tending to attract passengers away from the competing air services.

As a result, a reduced but more efficient railway system will provide faster, heavier, and cleaner passenger trains and larger and faster freight wagons, with an increased number of freight express services. The new railway system will be enabled to pay its way, and to play an appropriate part in the transport services of the country.

Coastal Shipping

A bird's eye view of British coastal shipping on a given day would comprise about 400 vessels distributed around our shores, with many others in port. Two cargoes dominate the coastal traffic – coal and oil – and each amounts to about 20 million tonnes carried annually.

The coal trade is restricted to a few well-defined routes, of which the most prominent is from the ports of the north-east coast to London. From Blyth in the north to the Tees in the south a stream of colliers sets sail for the Thames each day: they berth at the cement-works, the paper-mills, the merchants' wharves, the gas-works and the power-stations. This is the busiest section of our coastal traffic, and its mainstay is coal. In all, about 55 ships each day ply the stretch between the Tees and the Thames, and a further 10 join the throng from the Humber. The east coast stands in sharp contrast with the west coast, along most of which there are only five vessels a day.

A second stream of colliers supplies Belfast and Dublin across the Irish Sea from the Clyde and the Mersey. But colliers are seen on many other routes: coal moves from the Tyne and the Humber to east-coast ports such as Ipswich and Aberdeen, and southward to Shoreham, Southampton, and the Channel Islands. The ports of the south-west, such as Falmouth, Plymouth, and Exeter, are served mainly from south Wales, which carries on also a brisk coal traffic with Bristol. The coastwise coal trade has behind it centuries of tradition; but it is declining slowly with the location of power-stations nearer the coalfields, and with the increasing use of alternative sources of energy. It is nevertheless clear that the large modern collier will for long remain an essential ingredient in the pattern of coastwise trade.

The oil traffic consists of the movement of refined products from the refineries to bulk storage plants. There are large oil installations at Avonmouth (Bristol), Hamble (Southampton), Saltend (Hull), and Dingle (Liverpool), while the largest in Europe, with a storage capacity of 2,000,000 tonnes, is at Thameshaven (London). Among smaller installations are those at Bridgwater, Portslade, Workington, Tyneside, Leith, Dundee, Inverness, Limerick, and Londonderry. All are linked regularly to the oil-refineries by the 80 or so vessels which comprise the coastal oil-tanker fleet, and where larger quantities need to be moved ocean tankers assist their smaller cousins.

Coal and oil between them account for nearly three-quarters of all the nation's coastal traffic. The remaining 25 per cent. or so includes many varied cargoes. A regular movement of live animals eastward across the Irish Sea matches the westward traffic in coal, but is carried in different vessels. Cattle, sheep, and pigs are shipped in comparable numbers. More than a dozen specialized vessels handle this traffic, mainly from Dublin and Belfast to Birkenhead and Glasgow, and they are aided by other general-purpose vessels, designed to carry in addition passengers and cargo. In all about 40 vessels are needed to carry on the busy services across the Irish Sea.

A row of small but active ports in south Devon and Cornwall engages in the coastal trade. Par, Charlestown, and Fowey, as well as Plymouth, ship china clay from St Austell Moor and Bodmin Moor and feed paper-mills scattered the length of our coasts: regular shipments are made to the Thames and Medway, to Leith and Aberdeen, to Preston and the Mersey. Falmouth and neighbouring smaller ports are outlets for granite quarries and ship road-making stone along the coast to south-coast ports and as far as Ipswich, in stoneless East Anglia. In north Wales Penmaenmawr and Llandulas perform a similar function for the north-west, and ship 'granite' and limestone respectively to Liverpool, Manchester, Glasgow, and Belfast.

Cement is carried northward from the Thames and Medway to most east-coast ports – to Blyth, Leith, Aberdeen, and Inverness, and reaches even the Outer Hebrides and the Orkneys and Shetlands. From the same district scrap metal is moved to Tees-side steelworks, while southward in the season come seed oats and seed potatoes from the ports of eastern Scotland to those of eastern England, and as far as the Bristol Channel.

In addition to the individual commodities we have mentioned, there is an extensive trade in general cargoes around our shores. Every port of consequence in Britain is joined to its neighbours by scheduled sailings (usually weekly) which are operated by the Coast Lines group. Their vessels are to be found not only in the major ports such as London, for they join the Hebrides, the Orkneys and Shetlands, and the Channel Islands to mainland Britain, and sail regularly around the intricate coast of northern Scotland. Over many fields of traffic coastal shipping competes successfully with road and rail transport; and by joining the outlying parts of Britain to the mainland it performs a service which no other form of transport can undertake.

Air Transport

There are over 20 licensed airports in Scotland, 5 in Northern Ireland, 2 in Wales, and over 100 in England. About 33 of them, however, handle the bulk of the passenger and freight traffic of the United Kingdom.

Of these London is by far the chief. In 1970 it handled 15·6 million passengers, representing nearly two-thirds of all the United Kingdom passenger traffic, and a six-fold expansion since 1954.

Rather more than half of these people are travelling to or from the Continent; about 16 per cent. of them are moving to or from other parts of the United Kingdom; and about 11 per cent. are on their way to or from the United States. Smaller proportions are travelling to and from the Irish Republic and Africa. The freight traffic handled at London Airport during 1970 amounted to about 340,000 tonnes.

No other airport approaches the scale of the passenger traffic at London; but Luton, Manchester, and Glasgow each handle nearly 2,000,000 passengers annually, most of whom are travelling to or from other parts of the United Kingdom. Jersey and Belfast each deal with over a million people, Birmingham and Edinburgh with nearly 700,000.

In the next rank are Southend, Liverpool, Guernsey, the Isle of Man, Newcastle, and Prestwick (Ayrshire), each of which handles about 300,000 to 400,000 passengers. Of these, Liverpool has important Irish connections, Prestwick engages in the transatlantic traffic, and Southend concentrates on the Continent. The remainder deal mainly in domestic traffic.

Among the smaller airports of Britain are those which provide valuable links with the outlying island groups. Land's End airport handles traffic with the Scillies. In Scotland the main airports of Wick, Inverness, Aberdeen, Glasgow, and Edinburgh connect with the Shetlands (Sumburgh), the Orkneys (Kirkwall), and the Hebrides (Stornoway, Benbecula, Barra, Tiree, and Islay).

Population

We have examined some of the changes which have taken place in the various modes of transport. Not only have they improved the transport of goods from producer to consumer: they have given a new mobility to the population, which is reflected in the speed with which changes in its distribution have taken place.

In England and Wales this new mobility is well illustrated by the growth of the coast resorts, which cater for the annual migration to the sea of a large proportion of the population. It is difficult to believe that two centuries ago there were no seaside resorts. Yet until the nineteenth century many people were reluctant to live by the sea through the fear of pirates or of foreign invasion. A few enterprising folk, however, had discovered the joys of sea bathing in the early eighteenth century. We first hear of this diversion at Scarborough about 1730, and a little later it had spread to Brighton and Weymouth. At Weymouth in 1763 the residents were startled to see Ralph Allen of Bath immersing himself in the sea with the aid of a 'bathing-machine' which he had invented. As we have seen (p. 321), the habit of sea bathing was endorsed by Dr Russell of Lewes, who published his treatise in 1750; and the seal on the growing fashion was set by royalty. Towards the end of the century Weymouth became fashionable when George III paid a series of visits to the town, together with the royal family. In a similar way, Southend sprang into favour after a visit in 1804 from Queen Caroline and Princess Charlotte.

While most resorts originated as fishing-villages, occasionally one developed on a virgin site. Such was Southport, which was founded in 1792. In that year an enterprising innkeeper of Churchtown, 2 km from the Lancashire coast, built a bathing house on the shore. Six years later he had an inn built for himself, and at a banquet the place was christened 'Southport'. By 1850 Southport had become the supreme resort of Lancashire, and only later was it surpassed by Blackpool.

As each improvement in transport took place, so the resorts became larger. Stage-coaches were replaced by the railways, and these were supplemented by motor-coaches, and, more recently, by the family car. The latest phase of the holiday fashion is seen in the establishment of 'camps' and caravan sites along our coasts. Usually temporary, they are rarely marked on maps; but they are very obvious elements in the human geography of the district.

So a whole industry has developed, seasonal yet flourishing. For long it was confined to beaches within easy reach by road and rail of a large centre of population: thus Manchester folk flocked to the coast of north Wales; Torquay, however, managed to compete with the more accessible centres on account of its railway links. In the last few years Ireland has increased her share of the holiday traffic, partly as a result of the growing popularity of air travel.

The most remarkable feature of the population distribution in Ireland, however, is its high density in rural areas. Ireland contrasts with Great Britain in that it lacks large concentrations of population engaged in manufacture: the nearest approaches to this are found in the Dublin, Belfast, and Cork districts.

South of a line joining Dundalk Bay and Galway Bay most of the land carries 30 to 60 persons to the square kilometre; north of it the density rises to between 60 and 120 per square kilometre. In the west there are large tracts of bog in the counties of Donegal, Mayo, Galway, Clare, Limerick, Kerry, and Cork. These are uninhabited; but in the neighbouring coastal districts the density rises to between 120 and 190 per square kilometre. As we have seen

(p. 89), these are districts where farmer-fishers supplement the produce of their tiny holdings with a harvest from the sea. In western Mayo there are places with 190 to 250, and in north-west Donegal with over 250 persons per square kilometre.

All these are remote rural areas, with small farms and little development of town life. They have lost population in the past through emigration – mainly to·Great Britain – and a serious decline continues. Between 1956 and 1961 Leitrim lost 9 per cent. of her population; Monaghan lost 9·6; Cavan, 8·3; and Mayo, Roscommon, Longford, and Donegal all experienced losses of about 7 per cent. Only in the Dublin area was there an actual increase of population during the period. The basic difficulty is a lack of material resources sufficient to support a population which approaches suburban densities. Some degree of redistribution appears inevitable, for these districts are far from markets, and far from the highways of commerce.

Similar problems are seen in parts of Northern Ireland, where there have been serious declines in Fermanagh and in the Sperrin districts west of Lough Neagh. But there have been increases around Londonderry and Belfast, and in the latter district a conurbation appears to be developing, to embrace Lisburn, Larne, and Newtownards. On balance, during the inter-censal period 1951–61 Northern Ireland made a slight gain in population of 52,206 and a gain of 100,145 between 1961 and 1971.

Like Ireland, Wales has had a long tradition of emigration. Welsh folk move to London and to other centres of light industries; they move to the coasts of England, where the men can maintain links with seafaring and the women can keep boarding-houses. Many enter the teaching profession; in addition, there has been a downhill migration of farmers into the better lands of the Welsh border, in Cheshire, Shropshire, Herefordshire, and Gloucestershire. Central Wales has declined in population; but on balance Wales gained 42,000 people (1951–61) and a further 80,000 (1961–71), mainly in northern and southern coastal districts.

During 1951–61 Scotland increased her population by 82,000 and by 48,000 between 1961 and 1971, mainly in the outskirts of Edinburgh and Glasgow. But the most startling change has been in England, with an increase between 1951 and 1971 of 4,710,000, and a remarkable redistribution.

In the north people have moved from rural to industrial areas (particularly to Tees-side and Tyneside); but at the same time 250,000 people have moved south. In the Birmingham conurbation people have moved from the centre to the outskirts, and the surrounding counties increased their populations by 7 to 9 per cent. during the inter-censal period.

In the metropolitan district there has been a similar tendency. Greater London (as defined on the census of 1951) actually declined by 2·1 per cent.; but as a result of 'overspill' all the home counties increased their populations; and during the process eight new towns were built (Fig. 102, p. 353). Between 1951 and 1971 many counties expanded their population between 25 and 50 per cent., and Berkshire, Buckinghamshire, Essex, Hertfordshire, and West Sussex increased by well over that figure. During the decade 1961–71 Greater London decreased in population by nearly 8 per cent., but the outer metropolitan area increased by nearly 19 per cent.

We have described the changes; but we must leave the reader to ponder their causes and implications for the years ahead.

FOR FURTHER READING

Books

REES, HENRY: *British Ports and Shipping* (Harrap, 1958), Chapter 14.
Report of the Committee of Inquiry into the Major Ports of Great Britain (H.M.S.O., 1962).

Articles

APPLETON, J. H.: 'Some Geographical Aspects of the Modernization of British Railways', in *Geography* (November 1967).
British Railways Yearbook
CARTER, H.: 'Population Changes in Wales, 1931–1951', in *Geography* (April 1956).
COUSENS, S. H.: 'Population Changes in the Irish Republic, 1956–1961', in *Geography* (November 1962).
LAWTON, RICHARD: 'Putting People in their Place', in *Geographical Magazine* (September 1969).
TANNER, M. F.: 'Population Changes in England and Wales, 1951–1961', in *Geography* (November 1961).
THOMAS, J. GARETH: 'Distribution of Welsh-born Population of England and Wales', in *Geography* (November 1957).
VAUGHAN, T. D.: 'Population Changes in Northern Ireland', in *Geography* (July 1960).

Maps

O.S. Map of Roman Britain, third edition, 1956.
    Atlas of Britain (1963): Airports; 1951–1961 Population; Coastwise Cargo Shipping and Inland Waterways (Clarendon Press, Oxford).

Index